Date	Description	Debit	Credit	Balance
5-7			20	21,777.77
5-10	Interest pcir		2.64	29,922.41
5-10	Unemp Ins.		288	30,210.41
5-11			20	30,190.41
5-12			20	30,170.41
5-14		1385.00		31,555.41
5-17	Unemp Ins.	288.00		31,843.41
5-24	Unemp Ins.	288.00		32,131.41
5-29			60.00	32,071.41
6-1	Unemp Ins.	288.00		32,359.41
6-1			1500.00	30,855.41
6-1			20.8	30,839.41

The Principal

Third Edition

The Principal

Creative Leadership for Effective Schools

Gerald C. Ubben
University of Tennessee, Knoxville

Larry W. Hughes
University of Houston

Allyn and Bacon
Boston • London • Toronto • Sydney • Tokyo • Singapore

Senior Editor: Ray Short
Editorial Assistant: Christine Svitila
Marketing Manager: Kris Farnsworth
Production Administrator: Annette Joseph
Production Coordinator: Holly Crawford
Editorial-Production Service: Lynda Griffiths, TKM Productions
Composition Buyer: Linda Cox
Cover Administrator: Suzanne Harbison

Copyright © 1997, 1992, 1987 by Allyn & Bacon
A Viacom Company
Needham Heights, Mass. 02194

Portions of this book previously appeared in *The Elementary Principal's Handbook: A Guide to Effective Action* by Larry W. Hughes and Gerald C. Ubben. © 1994 by Allyn and Bacon.

Library of Congress Cataloging-in-Publication Data

Ubben, Gerald C.
    The principal : creative leadership for effective schools / Gerald
C. Ubben, Larry W. Hughes. -- 3rd ed.
        p.   cm.
    Includes bibliographical references and index.
    ISBN 0-205-19865-1
    1. School principals--United States.   2. School management and
organization--United States.   3. School supervision--United States.
4. School personnel management--United States.   I. Hughes, Larry
W.   II. Title.
LB2805.U2   1996
373.12'012'0973--dc20   95-53714
                                                                CIP

Printed in the United States of America

10 9 8 7 6 5 4 3 2 1   01 00 99 98 97 96

Credit: Page 37 adapted and reprinted from *Leadership and Decision-Making,* by Victor H. Vroom and Philip W. Yetton, by permission of the University of Pittsburgh Press. © 1973 by University of Pittsburgh Press.

Contents

PART II   *School Program Design and Delivery*

Preface

Increasingly, the emphasis is on leadership at the school site. Such was always vital to the development of the high-performance learning community. One wonders why anyone would have thought differently. Did anyone think differently? Probably not; it's just that leadership is being thought of more broadly these days. Leadership cannot be thought of as manifest only in the acts of a single person. We never believed it could, and this was implicit in the approach taken in our earlier books. But we're becoming more explicit, and this third edition will reflect that.

We continue to define the principalship as a series of necessary functions that need to be carried out rather than as the acts of a single person. But make no mistake—it *is* a single person who arranges the organizational conditions within which these functions are carried out to productive ends and it *is* a single person who encourages and develops leadership in others on the staff.

That person is the principal. When the role is filled by a person with the requisite attributes and management skills, great things will happen. When it is not, about the best that can be expected is a pleasant status quo and the worst is a place where learner needs go unattended. We spend much of our professional lives in and about schools. We have seen good schools and bad schools. There may be some bad schools out there with good principals and good staffs who are living lives of quiet desperation, but we have never encountered a good school that had a bad principal.

This third edition of *The Principal: Creative Leadership for Effective Schools* stresses both the leadership and the management aspects of the principalship. There is a disposition in some quarters to diminish the managerial side of the operation of the high-performance school and the high-performing principal. To this, we simply say, "Nonsense," and write to that point in the first chapter.

Our purpose in writing a book about the principalship remains the same as it was over 10 years ago when the first edition was published. We were discontented, as were our students, with texts that seemed to be either completely theoretically based or how-to-do-it manuals. Our students found the former, when well written, to be interesting but often irrelevant to their work lives. The latter they found to be too highly prescriptive and too little conceptual, and of equally limited use in their professional work.

So, we continue to try to put between two covers a proper balance so that aspiring and practicing administrators may find both intellectual challenge and cause to reflect on what, with effort and analysis, "might be." It is our hope that administrators also will find the sort of practical knowledge about how the alligators might be kept at bay while the swamp is being drained.

This book is no different in approach than our others, but readers and professors will find some substantive changes. We devote more attention to the practicalities of making better use of staff on site in decision making, in program analysis and curriculum reform, and in improved instructional delivery systems. Moreover, each chapter concludes with a series of suggested activities to provide expanded opportunities for practitioners, students, and professors to reflect on the concepts presented in the chapter. We also include 22 case studies from the world of practice. We didn't make these cases up; we found them in the schools with which we work.

We continue to hope that readers will find this book to be useful now and on the job. Let us know.

G. C. U.
L. W. H.

The Principal

Chapter 1

The Good Principal

A Creative Blend of
Substance and Style

*Corporations and governmental agencies everywhere have
executives who imagine that their place on the organizational
chart has given them a body of followers. And, of course, it
has not. They have been given subordinates. Whether the
subordinates become followers depends on whether the
executives act like leaders. —JOHN GARDNER[1]*

The Gardner statement lends a proper perspective to an examination of the role of the
principal today. At no other time has the expected behavior of the principal been so
intensely focused on aspects of leadership. To be sure, good principals have always
operated in a maner designed to encourage followership, but there are increasing
expectations that *all* principals demonstrate the characteristics of leaders. These expectations issue from such disparate sources as parents and other community members,
boards of education, and especially teachers and other school staff members.

Persons of Homeric proportions are not required, however; few of such exist in any
given era. What is required is intelligent, well-trained, and humane individuals who
have the necessary human, conceptual, and technical skills to lead groups of professionals and clients into rich educational adventures. When the job of the principal is
done well, great things happen. When the job is not done well, when the school is inadequately led and managed, young people are materially hindered in achieving their
potentials.

This chapter focuses on the leadership and management skills required for excellence in the school environment. Although leadership must not (*cannot*) be considered
the sole province of the designated executive head, without an effective leader as principal, one cannot expect leadership to emerge adequately from staff or students. Ini-

tially, we will consider the role of the principal as leader and manager—the two are inseparable. Although one might be a good manager of the status quo and not be a leader, it is inconceivable that a good leader would not also be a good manager.[2]

We begin the discussion with an overview of the new expectations for principals, as manifested in the work of the National Policy Board for Educational Administration (NPBEA), and proceed to an analysis of the concepts *leading* and *managing*. Examined in the chapter, as well, will be certain historical underpinnings—how we got to where we are—and relevant leadership and organizational theories—a discussion of leadership and management in context. The chapter concludes with a look at what it takes to achieve a high-performance school.

The National Policy Board for Educational Administration

In 1992, NPBEA[3] completed its study of the knowledge and skill bases required for effective principals.[4] The NPBEA distinguished between the academic knowledge base about which major universities were mostly concerned (the study of school administration *qua* administration) and the professional knowledge base about which educators were concerned (applications to practice). "The principalship, like any professional knowledge base, does not represent simply a body of subject content. It consists of knowledge and skills organized in a useful way, preferably into *work-relevant patterns that make expert knowledge functional* (emphasis added)."[5] The study uncovered 21 knowledge and skill bases arrayed under four domains: functional, programmatic, interpersonal, and contextual. The study and the ensuing platform has been responsible for important changes that have occurred, are occurring, and will continue to occur in the reform of administrator preparation programs. Let us turn now to some important knowledge base issues.

Leading and Managing

> *Conceptually separating management and leadership helps to show that these terms really are interrelated. While* leadership *may describe dynamic efforts, such as translating into action a vision for the organization, creating change, and developing new policies,* management *emphasizes a supportive status quo to provide people stability and balance in the workplace so they can work in relative comfort.*[6]

As this quote from Achilles and colleagues shows, it is faulty reasoning to think of leading and managing as dichotomous terms. Both are necessary and are complementary. In this section, we separate the concepts only to demonstrate the essence of each, not to diminish their interrelatedness.

Leadership

> *As often as any important business has to be done in the monastery, let the abbot call together the whole community and himself set forth the matter. And, having*

heard the counsel of the brethren, let him take counsel with himself and then do what he shall judge to be most expedient.[7]

Historical Perspective

It is useful to consider the plethora of research about leadership and management in work organizations that has been conducted in the near past and in both the private and public sectors. This research base has much implication to the practice of school administration and specifically to the principal.

It is difficult to decide where to start with a historical overview. Machiavelli's speculative work, *The Prince*, could be one entry point. But then why not go back further to A.D. 529, as we did with the quotation that opens this section and the Benedictine Rule that guided abbots in their practice of leadership in monasteries? Or to Moses and his legions of 10, or, in a giant historical leap forward, why should we not at least synthesize Barnard's *Functions of the Executive* and his concept of efficiency and effectiveness.[8] And what about the others, including Taylor, Follet and Mayo, Roethlisberger, and the grand contributions they made. These should all be studied—but not here. For our purposes, we will begin in the 1950s in this overview and beg the reader's indulgence.

The Ohio State Leadership Studies.   An array of leadership studies was conducted at The Ohio State University in the early 1950s. Persons in various kinds of organizations were asked to describe their leaders. Two major behavior categories ultimately were uncovered and these were labeled *consideration* and *initiating structure.*[9]

Consideration was defined as the degree to which a leader acts in a warm supporting way and shows concern for subordinates. Being approachable, accepting of suggestions, looking out for the welfare of subordinates, consulting with subordinates before making decisions, and other similar qualities comprise this category.

Initiating structure was defined as the degree to which leaders define and structure their own roles and the roles of subordinates toward the attainment of the organization's formal goals. Examples of specific behaviors in this category include criticizing unsatisfactory work, letting subordinates know what is expected of them, maintaining definite standards of performance, offering new approaches to problems, and other similar qualities.

The Michigan Studies.   Additional leadership studies were conducted at the University of Michigan, also in the 1950s, largely under the direction of Rensis Likert and the Institute of Social Research.[10,11] Behavioral comparisons of ineffective and effective managers revealed that effective managers had a task orientation that generally focused on such administrative functions as planning, coordinating, and facilitating work. This did not occur at the expense of good interpersonal relations, however. Effective managers were more likely to treat subordinates considerately and to allow some degree of autonomy in deciding how to conduct their work and at what pace. Importantly though, effective managers set high performance goals for subordinates and used group methods of supervision. Also discovered was that high morale (defined as the total satisfaction a worker gets from a work situation) does *not* necessarily result in high productivity. However, the kind of managerial practice that results in high productivity also tends to result in high morale.[12] High morale may describe what Blake and Mouton (to follow) call a 1,9 management style orientation characterized by great concern for people but with no evident thrust toward productivity.

Blake and Mouton.   Conceptually related to, but independent from, both The Ohio State leadership studies and the Michigan leadership studies is the work of Robert Blake and Jane Mouton. Their concept resulted in the Managerial Grid©. The Grid is based on two dimensions (attitudes) about the workplace: *concern for people* and *concern for production*. Concern for people closely parallels the concept of *consideration* and concern for production parallels *initiating structure*.

The concept is useful for analyzing what managerial attitudes might get in the way of the best job getting done. Is there balance? Is one or the other of the dimensions being emphasized to the exclusion or near exclusion of the other? Is neither emphasized enough? The answers to these questions permit the development of managerial training programs that are skill focused and developmental, so that a managerial deficiency that will deter the effectiveness of the organization can be, if not totally corrected, at least positively addressed.[13]

From Traditional Leadership Theory to Contingency Theory

As supportive of effective schools research findings as are the leadership studies at Ohio State and Michigan and the research applications of Blake and Mouton, none of these take into account the difference in situations demanding leadership nor the expectations and normative behavior of subordinates and superordinates. The dominant trend in leadership theory over the past several years has been toward the development of a situational or "contingency" theory of leadership. Fiedler's work is basic to this trend.[14]

Fiedler's Contingency Model.   The reason it is difficult to describe the ideal leader may be best clarified by the seminal work of Fred Fiedler. His model suggests that there is a situational nature to effective leader behavior. It helps explain why some studies have shown that a highly directive, task-oriented leadership style promoted effective work group performance, while other studies have revealed that a nondirective, "human relations" orientation worked best, and still others found some sort of balance resulted in high performance.[15]

From a large number of studies, Fiedler concluded that the interaction of three factors will determine leader effectiveness:

1. *Leader-Member Relations*. This refers to the leader's feeling of being accepted by subordinates. A leader's authority depends at least partly on the acceptance of the group to be led. A person who is respected by and inspires loyalty in the work group needs few of the vestments of rank to get the group to perform the task at hand in a willing and competent manner.

2. *Task Structure*. This is the degree to which the subordinate's tasks are routine and precisely defined as opposed to being relatively unstructured and loosely defined. (On

a continuum of "tight" to "loose," one could posit that teaching would tend to be on the loose end.)

3. *Power Position.* This refers to the power inherent in the leadership position and includes the means available to the leader from those at higher administrative levels and authority. This is the extent to which the leader possesses reward, coercive, and legitimate power. The ability to hire, discipline, transfer, provide salary increases, and other less direct rewards and punishments affect the power position.

In measuring the style of the leader, Fiedler returned to the product of The Ohio State University studies. He used two styles as his points of measurement: task oriented (initiating structure) and relationship oriented (consideration). Fiedler's research indicated that the behavior of effective leaders varies according to the nature of three contingency variables: leader-group relations, the degree of structure in the task, and the position power of the leader.

Fiedler hypothesized that the nature of group productivity resulted from a match between leader orientation (task or relationship orientation) and the favorableness of the particular work situation (a mix of personal traits, group beliefs, and situational variables). He concluded that one could not simply speak of effective and ineffective leadership practices, but only of effective and ineffective practices in one situation or another.[16]

Although his methodologies and conclusions have been criticized by some, a great contribution of Fiedler's work is his questioning that there is one best way to lead. Fiedler has established the usefulness of the contingency approach to the study of leadership. He provided an expanded way of thinking about the need for varying leader behavior and introduced the notion that successful leaders will manifest more *or* less in the way of relationship- and task-oriented behavior given certain situations and certain kind of work groups. However, the theory really doesn't have very much to say about how a leader ought to go about successfully managing a work group. A contingency concept advanced by Hersey and Blanchard does examine the specific behavior that is most likely to result in successful problem solving and group productivity.[17]

Hersey and Blanchard and Situational Leadership. Four distinct leadership styles are posited by Hersey and Blanchard: telling, selling, participating, and delegating. Each is viewed as an appropriate style depending on the particulars in the situation. The key variable in the situation is what Hersey and Blanchard call the "maturity" of the work group, which is defined as the readiness to tackle the task facing the group. (Readiness might include attitude as well as ability.)

Groups that are highly mature respond best to delegation; immature groups respond to a high degree of direction (telling). As the group grows in maturity, the leader is most effective next by selling the group, then, as greater maturity occurs, by engaging in practices that call for group participation. Hersey and Blanchard's guiding principle is that as subordinates acquire greater experience, ability, and commitment to the tasks that confront them, better productivity will be attained through greater sharing of decision making. This concept seems reasonable and is consistent with other theories, in that power sharing through delegation and participation should result in greater productivity in groups that have demonstrated mature attitudes and high skills.

The Hersey-Blanchard model suffers from an inadequate research base. Neither the model itself nor any of its components has been validated. Perhaps the best-researched contingency model has been that of House's Path-Goal theory of leadership.[18]

Path-Goal Theory of Leadership.   This theory was expounded by R. J. House in 1971 and refined and extended by a number of others in subsequent years in an effort to explain how a leader's behavior makes a difference in the motivation and the satisfaction of his or her subordinates. House wrote, "The motivational function of the leader consists of increasing personal payoffs to subordinates for work-goal attainment, and making the path to those payoffs easier to travel by clarifying it, reducing roadblocks and pitfalls, and increasing the opportunities for personal satisfaction en route."[19]

The effect of leader behavior on satisfaction and motivation to work toward organizationally productive ends depends on the situation. Characteristics of subordinates, such as ability and personality, and characteristics of the organizational environment, such as type of task and importance of the work, are the key determinates. Situational variables also determine the kind of leadership behavior preferred by the work group.

House identified four categories of leader behavior.[20] *Supportive leadership* is leadership that includes giving consideration to the needs of subordinates, displaying concern for their welfare, and creating a friendly climate in the work unit. *Directive leadership* lets subordinates know what they are expected to do, gives specific guidance, asks subordinates to follow rules and procedures, formulates schedules, and coordinates the work. *Participative leadership* is consultative and takes subordinates' opinions and suggestions into account when making decisions. *Achievement-oriented leadership* sets challenging goals, seeks performance improvements, emphasizes excellence in performance, and shows confidence that subordinates will attain high standards. It is more than interesting to note how closely this combination of categories relates to certain correlates of leadership in effective schools: climate, clear expectations, emphasis on excellence, and decision-making practices.

Leader behavior has an impact on subordinate performance in several ways. In situations where there is role ambiguity and/or task ambiguity, directive leadership that clarifies the roles and tasks will increase motivation and performance because it will increase the expectancy of subordinates that their efforts will lead to higher performance.

In situations where the tasks to be accomplished are tedious, boring, or stressful, supportive leadership behaviors are most likely to increase satisfaction and performance. By being considerate, offering kind words and moral and physical support, and trying to minimize the negative aspects of the work that needs to get done, the leader makes the situation more tolerable.

Achievement-oriented leadership results in subordinates who have more confidence in their ability to attain high goals, and thus increases the likelihood that there will be a serious and sustained effort. House described two conditions that make participative leadership appropriate: (1) when subordinates are assigned a challenging task that is also ambiguous and (2) in other tasks when subordinates have a high need for independence or are "antiauthoritarian" in their personalities.

Contingency theory rests on a rich research base, and not a little of that research came from studies that undergird noncontingency theory. Systematic inquiries continue to uncover even more about the complexities of leadership. The important thing is that students and practitioners of school administration are provided with great insights about leadership variables that will determine the effectiveness of schools.

Implications of Contingency Theory to Site-Based School Management.   Contingency theory certainly has much implication to the degree to which one could expect the successful implementation of site-based school management to occur, not to say the degree to which the issues of teacher and client empowerment are to be addressed. Expectations of the work group, "maturity" of the work group, positional power, other conditions in the environment, and personality variables and skill of the ascribed leader make predictions about organizational effectiveness complex, indeed. And the "beat goes on." Much is known and enough is known to influence the direction of thinking and training but not enough to stop studying the phenomenon.[21]

Transformational Leadership and Transactional Leadership.   Leadership and management are not dichotomous terms; the same can be said for *transformational leadership* and *transactional leadership*, although the former could be seen as an extension of the latter. Good management creates a necessary state of orderliness and certitude to aspects of the school organization but not to the exclusion of a necessary state of turmoil as new goals and processes are established and as the school family addresses new challenges and struggles to create an even more productive future.

This begins to describe the difference between transformational leadership and transactional leadership. Transactional leadership is solely status-quo oriented and assumes a highly stable environment. The notion of transformational leadership is much different. Such a leader builds on the status quo, to be sure, but goes well beyond it.

Norris has written, "*Transactional leadership* is a 'bargain basement' approach, offering to followers specified external rewards and privileges in exchange for the completion of duties and responsibilities outlined by the organization."[22] The "transactions" involve relationships between both the school and the larger organization and between the principal (leader) and his or her staff. Leaders get things done by making tasks clear and providing rewards (favors, pats on the back, good evaluations, awards, released time, etc.) to staff members who perform appropriately and well—that is, those who behave congruently with organizational expectations.

The transformational leader is much more than this. A different mental set characterizes such leaders. Transformational leaders use their knowledge and skills and their perceptions of changes that are needed to work both inside and outside the organization to map new directions, to secure new resources and refocus existing resources, and to respond to the realities of a very unstable present and, at times, an unforeseeable future. To such leaders, change is inevitable—the challenge is to make the most of it in increasingly more productive ways.[23]

The qualities of *vision* and *political acumen* have been pondered frequently as these seem to relate to effective leadership behavior. The following section focuses on what has been pondered, and puzzled about, and seen. We turn now to the issue of vision.

Vision

It is vision that seems to distinguish leaders from those who are simply good managers. *Vision* is "the capacity to create and communicate a view of the desired state of affairs that induces commitment among those working in the organization."[24]

Create, *communicate*, and *commitment* are the key words. Organizational study after study, whether that organization was in the public sector or the private sector, a school or a business, reveals that leaders have vision. Bennis[25] found that the key ingredient among executives of highly successful organizations was "compelling vision." Others, both before and after the Bennis inquiry, have found much the same thing. Norris,[26] for example, called it "creative leadership" and wrote,

> *Leadership is creative to the extent that the leader:*
> * *has a wide knowledge of educational theory and principles*
> * *possesses the ability to analyze current situations in light of what should be*
> * *can identify problems*
> * *can conceptualize new avenues for change.*

She continued, "Creative leadership requires that the leader make full use of the analytical as well as the intuitive mind." Visionary leaders ask such questions as: Who are the human beings that inhabit the school setting? What are the needs of these individuals? What unique problems face them as they seek to bring meaning to their lives?[27] And, we add, What is it going to take to get the answers to these questions?

Vision, then, is asking questions about what might be, standing for something, making certain others know what that "thing" is, and determining appropriate courses of action for getting to expressed goals. Unfortunately, vision is an uncommon quality.

Savvy and Political Acumen, Creative Insubordination, and Risk Taking

Good principals know how to get things done; they know both how to work in the system and how to work the system. Sometimes this means getting things done in an irregular manner.

Cuban used the word *political* to represent the means of getting done what needs to be done in an unpredictable, uncertain world.[28] These are situations where principals use both formal and informal influences to persuade, deflect, and use any resources at hand—students, teachers, parents, other school system administrators—to build support for a desirable outcome or to overcome opposition to such an outcome.

It is difficult to express this ability in words. We are not at all sure it can be taught, or if it can, how it can be taught. It seems, to use Norris's terminology, to be "intuitive." It is simply there—a *je ne sais quoi*, an indescribable something. It is knowing when to break the rules—when to short circuit the system. Prescribing when to do this is impossible. Good leaders seem to know when it is more important to risk having to "beg forgiveness" than to "ask permission." Some have called this *discretionary disobedience*; we label it *creative insubordination*. Whatever it is called, the behavior does seem to be common among good leaders.

Management

It is without question that productive schools require a high degree of consistency and not a little certitude as manifest in well-understood policies to guide the daily operation. This is true of all organizations. Organizational members expect that routine matters will be dealt with in fair and expeditious ways. Many aspects of the school must remain in a stable state so that the other aspects can change in an unchaotic way. "In this sense the status quo keeps the organization on an even keel so that members understand what is required and how they need to behave to help achieve organizational goals."[29] Good management, then, is both positive and necessary.

Much of what is known about the skills constitute that good management practices is a result of developments in assessment center technology. Research dating from 1954 to identify skills necessary for success as a first-line supervisor at American Telegraph and Telephone Company[30] to the more recent and continuing research and development efforts of such professional organizations as the National Association of Secondary School Principals (NASSP)[31] and the National Association of Elementary School Principals (NAESP) have uncovered discrete skills, the presence of which determine effectiveness. NASSP's research reveals six abilities that are important to successful school administration:[32]

- The ability to plan and organize work
- The ability to work with and lead others
- The ability to analyze problems and make decisions
- The ability to communicate orally and in writing
- The ability to perceive the needs and concerns of others
- The ability to perform under pressure

These are the result of extensive and intensive job and task analyses of what it is that principals have to do and be good at in order to manage the enterprise effectively.

In their analysis, DeMont and Hughes discovered marked similarities between the skills identified for private and public sector middle managers. They concluded that even with the similarities in labels and definitions among the several systems, there would be differences in the relative need to use the skill. Also, there would be differences in the level of acceptable performance between different kinds of organizations and depending on the hierarchical level at which the person was performing.[33, 34]

Many school systems across the nation are employing assessment centers as a means to identify who should become a principal in the district; other systems are using the process for targeted professional development purposes.[35] At present, South Carolina, Missouri, and Kentucky employ the NASSP assessment center process as an administrator certification requirement.

Functional Aspects of the Job
Schools vary in size and complexity. Similarly, the role of the principal will vary from place to place, as a result of organizational and community expectations. Nevertheless, the *functions* that must be managed by the principal are similar irrespective of where the position is located or how many students there are.

Five functional aspects comprise the principalship. Four of these take place inside the school; the other occurs in interaction with the outside world. The "inside" functions include staffing and instructional improvement, curriculum development, student services, and resource procurement and building utilization, including budgeting and maintenance. The "outside" function is public relations.

It is important to distinguish between the *principal* as a person and the *principalship* as a collection of important tasks and responsibilities that must be carried out in order for the goals of the school to be efficiently achieved. It is, in a phrase, essential to distinguish between "managing" and "doing." Careful delegation, matching the skills and interests of staff members with functional aspects, and providing for a coordinated effort are elements of good management.

The dimensions of leadership and management cut across these five functions. Leadership is the way principals *use themselves* to create a school climate characterized by student productivity, staff productivity, and creative thought. Think of good management as the systematic application of an array of skills to provide for an orderly and efficient school environment. Figure 1–1 depicts the relationship of the five functions and the two dimensions.

The Organizational Setting

Leadership and management do not occur without context. Effectively managing and leading any organization requires daily interaction with a large number of groups and the wide variety of individuals comprising these groups. Teachers, parents, children, administrators, classified personnel, merchants, and a host of other "outsiders" and "insiders" all become important reference points. Moreover, persons within these groups, although often sharing common goals, rarely behave similarly or see the same things similarly. People have varying perceptions of the nature of schooling and their own role in the schooling process. They are influenced and motivated in different ways and by different means.

FIGURE 1–1   The Five Functions and Two Dimensions of the Principalship
Source: Larry W. Hughes and Gerald C. Ubben, *The Elementary Principal's Handbook: A Guide to Effective Action*, 4th ed. Boston: Allyn and Bacon, 1994, p. 5. Used with permission.

To get maximum results, it is helpful to think of the school as a social system. Social systems theory provides a sound basis for understanding the behavior of people in organizations. The implications of social systems theory to the principal are many. It explains why even well-conceived plans sometimes do not turn out well. It explains why different motivational strategies must be employed for individual staff members. And it helps explain why much attention needs to be directed to the informal interactions of people in the organization.

Social Systems Theory

The work of Jacob Getzels and Egon Guba is fundamental to the application of social systems theory to schools.[36] Essentially, Getzels and Guba posited two dimensions to the organization: the nomothetic (institutional) dimension and the idiographic (personal) dimension. It is the interaction of these two dimensions that results in the observed behavior of individuals in the organization. The principal's responsibility is to serve as the agent for productive interaction. Figure 1–2 is a depiction of social systems theory.

If the principal is to be able to understand the nature of the observed behavior and thus have the opportunity to predict and control it, the elements of the theory and the interrelationships need definition. *Institution* simply refers to the fact that all organizations have certain necessary functions that must be carried out, no matter what. The necessary function of the school is to provide an articulated program of studies and require all eligible children to participate in this program.

Roles are the official positions and offices that have been established to carry out the functions of the organization. The behaviors that are to comprise a role are called *role expectations*. Every role has certain normative responsibilities and these will differ by role. The role expectations for a learning resource specialist, an assistant principal, and a first-grade teacher are very different. Job descriptions are an attempt to differentiate the official organizational expectations of each role incumbent.

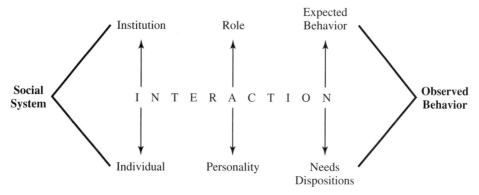

FIGURE 1–2   Depiction of a Social Systems Theory
Source: Larry W. Hughes and Gerald C. Ubben, *The Elementary Principal's Handbook: A Guide to Effective Action,* 4th ed. Boston: Allyn and Bacon, 1994, p. 22. Used with permission.

Thus, at least some general understandings and predictable behavior exist. It is not easy, however, because roles are occupied with real people who stamp each role with their own individuality. So, the principal must consider the idiographic or personal aspects of social behavior. These, too, require definition and, as the model in Figure 1–2 indicates, these aspects may be analyzed in parallel fashion to the nomothetic dimension.

Personality in the context of the social systems model may be defined as the "dynamic organization within an individual of those 'needs-dispositions' that govern his unique reactions to the environment."[37] In other words, every one of us is a complex of previous experiences that have provided us with differing orientations to life, to organizations, and to other people. These affect our sense of what is pleasurable, important, and real. Personality is to needs disposition as role is to role expectation.

In order for the principal to understand (and reasonably predict) the behavior of a teacher or other staff members, it is essential that the principal know both the role expectation of the particular job and the needs disposition of the individual. In the productive organization, much attention is directed to helping all workers understand what the organizational expectations are.

The challenge to the principal is to try to address both individual and organizational needs to achieve as much congruence as possible. The greater the congruence, the more satisfied and productive the worker and the more effective the organization.

The Organizational Iceberg

A different way of thinking about organizational behavior is to picture an iceberg with the visible part of the iceberg representing the formal or institutional dimension of the organization. This is the public part of the organization and is manifest in the stated goals and objectives, the organization chart, the job descriptions—all of those things that are official.

Not readily apparent is that part of the organization that lies below the surface—the personal or informal dimension. Manifest in this dimension are the perceptions of organization members about the organization, the differing influence and power patterns that exist irrespective of formal title, the informal reward and sanctioning systems, feelings of trust and confidence, and incipient individual or group paranoia. The below-the-surface organization greatly affects the degree to which the above-the-surface organization is really as it appears and the degree to which the organization reaches its stated and legitimate goals. The "iceberg" is depicted in Figure 1–3.

Understanding Organizations through Metaphors

Another way of examining what organizations are like and how they can be understood is provided by Gareth Morgan.[38] *Mapping organizations* might most easily be accomplished, wrote Morgan, by using metaphors to describe them. Metaphors provide an insightful and useful way of understanding the differences among the common practices, beliefs, attitudes, and policies that are the public *and* the private dimensions of an organization. According to Morgan, eight principal metaphors describe organizations:

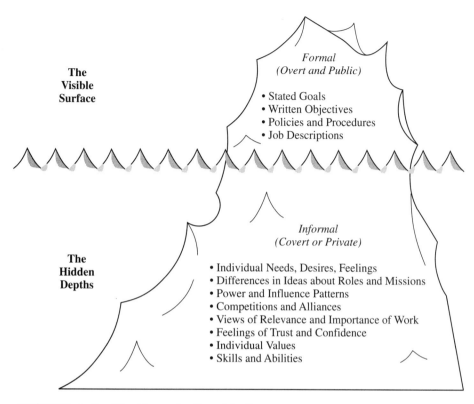

FIGURE 1–3 The Organizational Iceberg

Source: Larry W. Hughes and Gerald C. Ubben, *The Elementary Principal's Handbook: A Guide to Effective Action,* 4th ed. Boston: Allyn and Bacon, 1994, p. 24. Used with permission.

Organizations as machines derives from the principles of scientific management.

Organizations as organisms describes organizations as having a life cycle and composed of needs, wants, and special interests. An appreciation of the dynamic aspects of organizations as these interact with their environment is suggested.

Organizations as brains places great emphasis on the rational aspects of organizations yet also implies flexibility, problem-solving ability, and creative action.

Organizations as cultures implies that organizations can be best understood by examining the underlying core values that seem to determine behavior and action.

Organizations as political systems intimates that organizations might be best understood by observing the power and authority patterns that exist—examining the nature of special interests and how certain agendas are revealed.

Organizations as psychic prisons contemplates organizations as systems that create their own sense of reality irrespective of the larger societal reality. The word *parochial* comes to mind, but to Morgan it is more than this. Members may feel trapped and lose a sense of what the larger reality is and thus never explore alternatives that others outside the organization readily see and implement.

Organizations as emblems of flux and transformation indicates that organizations are in a constant field of forces militating for change and adaptation. Organizations are viewed as part of a continuous evolutionary process responsite to the larger societal environment.

Organizations as instruments of domination implies that the best way to understand organizations is to see them as elitist structures where in a few individuals (the "elites") promote their own selfish interests at the expense of and through manipulation of others.

Thus, Morgan provides eight lenses through which one may study, analyze, and predict behavior of organizations. The seventh metaphor—organizations as emblems of flux and transformation—seems more consistent with the leadership principles posited in this chapter. Yet, each of the metaphors provides a way for the leader to examine existing conditions and perhaps suggest strategies for overcoming resistance to change and counterproductive behavior.

High-Performance Organizations

A current guiding phrase to describe leadership in the high-performing organization is *total quality management*. The phrase comes from the work of W. Edwards Deming, who was credited with rebuilding the Japanese economy after World War II. Only in the past few years has he become a prophet in his own land. His "14 points" have much relevance to the development of the high-performance school and the leadership behavior characteristic therein. Figure 1–4 is a recapitulation of the essence of the management system proposed by Deming and applied here by us to the school organization.

Fundamental to the theory is a clear and well-understood sense of purpose at all levels of the organization, teamwork and empowerment of all workers, and a prevailing drive to serve the customer. The customer is anyone inside or outside the organization to whom members of the organization provide services and products. The

FIGURE 1–4   The High-Performance School

Total Quality Management: Deming's Fourteen
Essentials Applied to the School Organization

Point 1: *Create a constancy of purpose for improvement of products and services.* This means that the focus must be on helping students reach their maximum potential by providing a basis for students and teachers to work together continuously to improve.

Point 2: *Adopt a new philosophy.* Continuous improvement will occur through greater empowerment of teacher-student teams. Instructional decisions and decisions regarding scoping and sequencing of learning events are to be joint efforts involving all the stakeholders.

Point 3: *Cease dependence on mass inspection to achieve quality.* Using test scores as the primary way to assess student achievement and progress is wasteful and frequently unreliable. The end of a unit or a term is too late to assess student process. Tests

FIGURE 1–4   *Continued*

Point 4:
should be diagnostic and help to prescribe new learning events rather than as summative evidence of the achievement of short-term goals. Too, students must be taught to assess their own work and progress.

Point 4: *Stop awarding business on the basis of price tag alone.* Use high-quality instructional materials—the best available. Free or cheap materials are too often that way because they do not serve learners well.

Point 5: *Improve constantly the system of production and service.* The litany of the school organization should be "why are we doing what we are doing?" (a goals question) "What are we doing?" (an examination of the way we are trying to do "it") and "Can it be done a better way?" (an evaluation question). All in the organization need to be empowered to both ask and answer these questions.

Point 6: *Institute training on the job.* In-house programs for both new and old staff members should characterize the work environment. Educators must show students and community what being a good learner is all about. Skills improvement for all in the school organization should be the goal and mechanisms to insure this must be in place.

Point 7: *Institute leadership.* Leadership acts should be encouraged irrespective of title or position. Leadership consists of working with all members of the school organization and the community as coach and mentor. Leading is helping others achieve worthwhile goals.

Point 8: *Drive out fear.* Fear is counterproductive. In a free society and in a productive school no one is motivated by fear. Positive institutional changes result from shared responsibilities, shared power, and shared rewards.

Point 9: *Break down barriers between departments [and grade levels].* Synergy is required, not just collective energy. Competition between departments dissipates energy that should be directed toward common ends. Create cross department and multilevel teams devoted to quality. Implement link-pin task forces to break down role and status barriers.

Point 10: *Eliminate slogans, exhortations, and targets.* Educators, students. community members may collectively arrive at slogans and symbols that harness energy and cause them to pursue common goals and celebrate success, but these will develop out of their working together. Externally imposed sloganeering is hollow, however, and to little result.

Point 11: *Eliminate numerical quotas.* It is not possible to summarize all of the ways a person can grow and learn in the barest symbol of languages—a number or a letter. So, stop trying to do this. When a grade or a score becomes the basic symbol of success, short-term gains replace lone-term learning and development.

Point 12: *Remove barriers to pride of workmanship.* Humans generally want to do good work, and when they do, feel pride in it. They should be helped to do so. Self-fulfillment is a strong motivator. Realistic and cooperatively established goals result in satisfaction and pride.

Point 13: *Institute a vigorous program of education and self-improvement.* Educators and students require continuous learning programs. Self-renewal must be goal oriented, systematic and regular, and the effective organization provides the mechanisms for this to take place within the workplace.

Point 14: *Put everybody in the [organization] to work to accomplish the transformation.* Teachers, administrators, staff, students and community are stakeholders and should contribute to the realization of the new philosophy. Top-level commitment and community commitment are required. Teachers and students cannot do it alone. Nor can an administrator.

customers of the third-grade teacher are, for example, students, parents, community, and the fourth-grade teacher for whom the third-grade teacher is preparing students.

Total quality management is an integrated strategic system to achievement satisfaction, which involves all administrators, teachers, and other staff members to improve the school's services and products continuously. *Quality* means providing clients with services that meet their expectations and needs, *the first time and every time*. We will return to the concept of total quality management consistently throughout the remainder of this book.

Summary

In this chapter we have focused on three subjects: leadership, management and the environment within which these occur. A rich research and theory base from which to examine factors of leadership may make a difference between success and failure as a school principal. Contingency theory seems to offer the most promise for understanding what it takes to be successful.

The effective administration of a school requires good management skills as well. The research undergirding the development of assessment center technology offers good insight about how successful principals go about addressing the five functions of the principalship.

Leading and managing occur within a work environment, and there is much to be known about the nature of the work environment. Social systems theory provides a useful perspective. But the effective school environment is also a professional environment characterized by a high degree of individual and unit autonomy. The high-performance school provides such an environment.

Activity

1. Review Case Study 1 at the end of this book. Apply the concepts expressed in this chapter. What relevance do the notions of Achilles and colleagues have with regard to managing and leading? What relevance has social systems theory? Which, if any, of Morgan's metaphors might describe the organization in the case?

Endnotes

1. John Gardner, *On Leadership* (New York: Free Press, 1990), p. 3.
2. Some theorists have argued that many great leaders have not had very high marks for their management skills and will often cite such people as Winston Churchill, Golda Meir, and Martin Luther King as examples. Perhaps this is true, but someone in their cadres did, and there was a clear recognition that things had to be managed well or the great ideas and personal thoughts would have gone for naught. Managing is *not* doing, anyway. It is arranging conditions so that things get done—and leaders do that.
3. The NPBEA is sponsored and supported by the Association of Colleges for Teacher Education, Association of School Business Officials, Council of Chief State School Officers, National Association of Secondary School Principals, National Association of Elementary School Principals, American Association of School Administrators, Association for Supervision and Curriculum Development, National School

Boards Association, National Council of Professors of Educational Administration, and University Council for Educational Administration.

4. Scott E. Thompson, ed. *Principals for our Changing Schools: The Knowledge and Skill Base* (Fairfax, VA: National Policy Board for Educational Administration, 1993).

5. Ibid., p. xi.

6. Charles M. Achilles, John L. Keedy, and Reginald M. High, "The Political World of the Principal," in *The Principal as Leader*, ed. Larry W. Hughes (New York: Macmillan, 1994), p. 32.

7. St. Benedict, *The Rule of St. Benedict*, trans. Abbot J. McCann (Westminster, MD: Newman Press, 1952). Originally promulgated in A.D. 529 by St. Benedict.

8. Chester I. Barnard, *The Functions of the Executive* (Cambridge, MA: Harvard University Press, 1938).

9. Andrew W. Halpin and B. J. Winer, "A Factorial Study of the Leader Behavior Descriptions," in *Leader Behavior in Description and Measurement*, ed. R. M. Stogdill and A. E. Coons (Columbus, OH: Bureau of Business Research, The Ohio State University, 1957).

10. Rensis Likert, *New Patterns of Management* (New York: McGraw-Hill, 1961).

11. Rensis Likert, *The Human Organization: Its Management and Value* (New York: McGraw-Hill, 1967).

12. Rensis Likert, *Motivation: The Core of Management* (New York: American Management Association, Personnel Series #155, 1953). For a highly specific application of Likert to school administration, see Thomas Sergiovanni and R. J. Starratt, *Emerging Patterns of Supervision: Human Perspectives*, 3rd ed. (New York: McGraw-Hill, 1988).

13. Robert R. Blake and Jane S. Mouton, *The Managerial Grid III: The Key to Leadership Excellence* (Houston: Gulf Publishing, 1985). See also Blake and Mouton, *The Managerial Grid* (Houston: Gulf Publishing, 1964); and Blake and Mouton, *Corporate Excellence Through Grid Organization Development* (Houston: Gulf Publishing, 1968).

14. Fred E. Fiedler, *A Theory of Leadership Effectiveness* (New York: McGraw-Hill, 1967).

15. Fred E. Fiedler, *Leadership* (New York: General Learning Press, University Program Module Series, 1971). Readers interested in pursuing this further may find the work of Hersey and Blanchard helpful: Paul Hersey and Kenneth H. Blanchard, *Management of Organizational Behavior*, 3rd ed. (New York: McGraw-Hill, 1977).

16. Fred E. Fiedler, *Leadership* (New York: General Learning Press, 1971). See also F. E. Fiedler and M. M. Chemers, *Leadership and Effective Management* (Glencoe, IL: Scott, Foresman, 1974).

17. Paul Hersey and Kenneth Blanchard, *Management of Organizational Behavior: Utilizing Human Resources*, 4th ed. (Englewood Cliffs, NJ: Prentice-Hall, 1982).

18. Robert J. House, "A Path-Goal Theory of Leader Effectiveness," *Administrative Science Quarterly 16* (1971): 321–338.

19. Ibid., p. 324.

20. R. J. House and T. R. Mitchell, "Path-Goal Theory of Leadership," *Contemporary Business 3* (Fall 1974): 81–91.

21. *Site-base management* and *empowerment* have become almost fad words—poorly defined and often misunderstood. Insights about the problems confronting the leader concerning these issues can be found in the following references: Larry W. Hughes, "School-Based Management, Decentralization, and Citizen Control—A Perspective," *Journal of School Leadership* 3, no. 1 (January 1993): 40–44; V. I. Karant, "Supervision in the Age of Teacher Empowerment," *Educational Leadership* 46, no. 8 (August 1989): 27–29; C. R. Harrison et al., "Site-Based Management: The Realities of Implementation," *Educational Leadership* 46, no. 8 (August 1989): 27–29; G. I. Maeroff, "A Blueprint for Empowering Teachers," *Phi Delta Kappan* 69, no. 7 (July 1988): 481–491.

22. Cynthia Norris, "Cultivating Creative Cultures," in *The Principal as Leader*, ed. Larry W. Hughes (New York: Macmillan, 1994), pp. 69–70.

23. For an elaboration of these two views of leadership, see James MacGregor Burns, *Leadership* (New York: Harper and Row, 1978).

24. Thomas J. Sergiovanni, *The Principalship: A Reflective Practice Perspective* (Boston: Allyn & Bacon, 1987), p. 57.

25. Warren Bennis, "Transformation Power and Leadership," in *Leadership and Organizational*

Culture, ed. T. J. Sergiovanni and J. E. Corbally (Champaign-Urbana, IL: University of Illinois Press, 1984).

26. Cynthia Norris, "Developing Visionary Leaders for Tomorrow's Schools," *NASSP Bulletin* 74 (May 1990): 6–10.

27. Ibid.

28. Larry Cuban, "Principaling: Images and Roles," *Peabody Journal of Education* 63, no. 1(1986): 107–19.

29. Achilles et al., "Political World."

30. Douglas W. Bray et al., *Formative Years in Business: A Long-Term AT&T Study of Managerial Lives* (New York: Wiley-Interscience, 1974). See also Douglas W. Bray and D. L. Grant, "The Assessment Center in the Measurement of Potential for Business Management," *Psychological Monographs* 80 (1966).

31. NASSP has available a variety of descriptive materials and research reports, including validation studies. Write to NASSP, 1904 Association Drive, Reston, VA 22091. The NASSP process is designed for the K–12 spectrum; the skills identified are generic and applicable for elementary as well as secondary school principals.

32. In the NASSP system there are actually 12 discrete skills and attributes: problem analysis, judgment, organizational ability, decisiveness, leadership, sensitivity, stress tolerance, oral and written communication, personal motivation, educational values, and range of interests. What is described here are the more general categories of skills.

33. Roger A. DeMont and Larry W. Hughes, "Assessment Center Technology: Implications for Administrator Training Programs," *Planning and Changing* 15, no. 4 (Winter 1984): 219–25.

34. Larry W. Hughes, Larry W. Hillman, and Roger A. DeMont, "New Wave School Managers and the Application of Assessment Center Technology," *Record in Educational Administration and Supervision* 6, no. 2 (Spring 1986): 13–15.

35. See, for example, Larry W. Hughes, Mary E. Murphy, and Martha Wong, "This Administrator Assessment Center Aims for Excellence," *The Executive Educator* 8, no. 3 (March 1986): 21–22+.

36. Jacob W. Getzels and Egon G. Guba, "Social Behavior and the Administrative Process." *School Review* 65 (Winter 1957): 423–441.

37. Ibid.

38. Gareth Morgan, *Images of Organizations* (Newbury Park, CA: Sage, 1986).

Selected Readings

Achilles, Charles M. "A Vision of Better Schools," in *Instructional Leadership: Concepts, Issues and Controversies*, ed. William Greenfield. Boston: Allyn and Bacon, 1987.

Bass, Bernard M., and Bruce J. Avolio, Eds. *Improving Organizational-Effectiveness through Transformational Leadership*. Thousand Oaks, CA: Sage, 1993.

Burns, James MacGregor. *Leadership*. New York: Harper and Row, 1978.

Cusick, Philip A. *The Educational System: Its Nature and Logic*. New York: McGraw-Hill, 1992.

Deming, W. E. *The New Economics for Industry, Government, Education*, Cambridge, MA: Massachusetts Institute of Technology, 1993.

Gardner, John W. *On Leadership*. New York: Free Press, 1990.

Hughes, Larry W. *The Principal as Leader*. New York: Macmillan, 1994.

Keedy, John L. "Creative Insubordination: Autonomy for School Improvement by Successful High School Principals." *The High School Journal* 76, no. 1 (September 1992): 17–23.

Morgan, Gareth. *Images of Organization*. Newbury Park, CA: Sage, 1986.

Murphy, Joseph, and Karen Seashore-Louis. *Reshaping the Principalship: Insights from Transformational Efforts*. Thousand Oaks, CA: Corwin Press, 1994.

Thompson, Scott E., ed. *Principals for Our Changing Schools: The Knowlege and Skill Base*. Fairfax, VA: National Policy Board for Educational Administration, 1993.

Walton, M. *Deming Management at Work*. New York: Putnam, 1987.

C h a p t e r 2

Instructional Leadership

> *The principal needs to anticipate and eliminate potential stumbling blocks and create a climate conducive for students' and teachers' learning.... The principal needs to nurture opportunities for the staff to learn the skills for collaboration.*
> —*PAULA A. CORDEIRO*[1]

In the first chapter, the focus was on the principal as a leader in general. In this chapter, the focus narrows to the principal as an *instructional* leader. This is not to imply that other leadership acts are unimportant, but rather to emphasize the centrality of instruction to the main business of the schools—student growth and development.

Demonstrating high energy, setting standards of excellence, establishing goals, being a positive example, creating a motivating work environment, all within a context of collaboration, so that a high-performance learning community exists—these are manifest in instructional leadership above all else. That is the subject of this chapter. As a prologue, let us first turn to an examination of what describes a high-performance organization.

Characteristics of the High-Performance Organization

The phrase *high-performance organization* has now come into common usage. We first discovered it in an unfortunately obscure work by Marshall.[2] He described five conditions as characteristic of schools that could be labeled high performing:

- A supportive outcome-based learning environment in which high standards of education, social development, and health are achieved by all learners
- An outcome-based environment in which the system of instructional decision making and delivery responds to each learner's needs, interests, abilities, talents, styles of learning, and styles of living
- An outcome-based environment in which curriculum assessment and human resources development are mutually reinforcing

- An outcome-based environment in which the resources for learning are planned, focused, and managed by teams of educators with input from parents and other citizens
- An outcome-based environment in which communication and community involvement are an integral part of the human resource and economic development of the community

Sergiovanni, writing to this same point,[3] observed that a high-performance school and the principal therein deemphasizes "top down hierarchies and detailed scripts that tell people what to do." Rather, "one gets control by connecting people to outcomes rather than rules.... The key to effective leadership is to connect workers tightly to ends, but only loosely to means."[4]

Senge has offered a perspective and a structure for the improvement of the instructional processes.[5] His thesis is fundamental to principals who wish to lead their schools to new heights of performance. He described the skills needed to build what he labels "learning organizations." In such an organization, the leader's responsibility is to provide opportunities for the staff to engage in "generative" learning. As organizational members learn, their capabilities and perceptions expand. In a similar vein, Cordeiro pointed out, "An organization that generates learning is able to grow and develop in an infinite number of ways. Most organizations are adaptive but not also generative. Schools have become proficient at adapting [others'] models."[6]

Others' models or another school's problem solution may not in any way appropriately address problems and challenges confronting one's own school. Adaptation may simply result in frustration and in a local problem not solved. In the learning organization, people ask *why* a condition is the way it is and devise ways to address the "whys." The focus is on the problem, not on the symptoms. For example, in the learning school organization, when staff members are confronted with a high student failure rate, they do not leap to a solution such as having before and after school remediation programs. Instead, they examine the factors that may be contributing to the lack of student achievement and devise new structures to address those factors.

A Model for Instructional Leadership

Effective instructional leadership requires a complex set of relationships between principals and their beliefs and the surrounding environment of the school. The principal's values and previous experiences, as well as the expectations of the community and the institution in which the principal finds the school, all must be taken into account.

Initially, upon first assuming the position, the principal should consider the community's expectations and the institutional context (organizational framework in which the school is positioned) as fixed entities. However, over the course of several years, these areas can come under the influence of a strong instructional leader and be modified to enhance the instruction program of the school.

The principal's instructional leadership behavior should have a much more immediate influence on the internal structure of the school. A school's internal structure includes its instructional practices, organizational structure, climate, and culture. It is in the design, development, implementation, and interaction of these internal structures that the principal has opportunity for maximum influence on student outcomes.

The model can be divided into four sets of forces that influence student outcomes. The outer circle consists of the external structures: expectations, values, and beliefs that influence a principal's behaviors. The second circle shows the leadership behaviors and forces exhibited by the principal. The third ring identifies the internal structures created within the school by the principal and staff, with the final target being the student outcomes—the focal point of the school. These outcomes influence future expectations, values, and beliefs of the institution, community, and principal.

External Structures

Values and Beliefs of the Principal

What a principal values and believes should be passed on to all children are the things that become the principal's contribution to the school. Most often, when asked, "What do you think is most important for children to learn?," the principal will have a particular area of interest high on the priority list that he or she is most willing to talk about. Most principals will emphasize basic skills as being important. But beyond the basic skills emphasis, the list can become very diverse. For example, one principal indicated that conservation and ecology were important to him and thus to his school. The mounted stuffed animals around the school and the nature trail being developed behind the school were symbols of his interests. Another prinicipal serving in an impoverished area, was particularly concerned that children know how to function successfully within our culture. "We have to get the welfare kids off of the welfare cycle," the principal said. A principal from a rural area believed exposure to the fine arts was important for children, so he brought artists, paintings, and performing groups into the school regularly—things that rural children sometimes are not exposed to. He also saw that every child had at least one field trip a year to an outside cultural activity—a play, a museum, or a musical activity.

A principal's beliefs about the ability of all children to learn is extremely important. In most of the research about high-performing schools, principals have a strong belief in and commitment to the ability of all children to learn regardless of race, social conditions, or gender. These beliefs are extremely important because staff members will become attuned to what they believe the principal considers important. This contributes strongly to the establishment of a school culture characterized by high expectations for all.

Community Influences and Expectations

The local community also exerts great pressure on a principal's behavior. Principals of inner-city schools find a high percentage of their time being spent on student behavioral problems that are a direct outgrowth of community and domestic problems at home. High unemployment and high crime rates, poverty, and hunger directly affect the school and expectations for the school. The principal of the highly affluent suburban school is heavily influenced by community demands and expectations of high achievement. National Merit Scholarships, high SAT scores, entrance into the Ivy League colleges, and the athletic stature of the school all become pressures on the principal.

The demands and expectations for a school can change, however. Academic demands for a school can be expressed by a call for high test scores. Some communities will even demand academic excellence that goes beyond mere competence to call for the development in children of attributes such as arts appreciation, curiosity, creativity interpersonal competence, problem-solving skills, critical thinking skills, strong work ethics, and communication skills.

Communities also influence a principal's behavior by their willingness to directly contribute resources to the school in the form of funds and services. If large amounts of money must be raised outside of regular revenue channels by such means as school-based fund-raising activities by children or volunteers, the funds often will be directed to particular interest areas. Parents and community volunteers contributing their time directly to various projects in the school program can be another major influence.

Good instructional leaders are able to harness the interests of the community, taking advantages of its strengths while at the same time focusing on its needs. Over time, an effective instructional leader will even mold the community's expectations for the school, changing satisfaction with mediocrity or special interests to expectations for excellence in the entire program.

Institutional Influences

Every school is influenced by the organization of which it is a unit. A local school is one part of an intricate network of units nested together into districts, regions, and states. The autonomy of the local school varies greatly from school district to school district and, interestingly, even within districts. While all schools have mandates relative to federal, state, and local programs, some principals are much more effective than others in tailoring these programs to meet the needs of their local schools. For example, in one school district, the principal complained about the effort of the central office to impose a districtwide curriculum on his school, citing how the district was presently highly decentralized, allowing the judgment of the local staff to prevail in curriculum matters. He went on to complain how imposing a districtwide curriculum would reduce his role to simply that of a curriculum manager instead of a leader. Another principal in the district, however, saw the same set of circumstances as an opportunity to bring together additional resources to meet the problems of her school. She got most of her teachers onto the curriculum committees and volunteered her school as a pilot for the project. She also commented that her school's enthusiastic participation in some projects gave her increased power to say no to other influences when necessary.

Institutional influences on the local school also are found in the availability of both materials and human resources. School principals often find their time consumed with raising money for this project or that, detracting from their major role as instructional leaders. Efforts to obtain grants that relate directly to the good of the school can often be legitimate, but funding activities through candy sales and bazaars are generally misdirected efforts and consume valuable time.

The quality of the faculty and staff of a school represents another major institutional constraint or influence. Most often, upon assuming a principalship, principals inherit a staff from their predecessors. Efforts to influence the staff may initially be limited to organizational and staff-development activities. Yet, positively influencing the quality of the staff through the selection process may be the most important long term action of the principal. In fact, some research suggests that principals are effective because they have a staff that allows them to behave as they do. The level of authority given to a principal in employing staff becomes a major factor over time in the principal's ability to influence the development of the staff.

Principal's Instructional Leadership Behaviors

An effective principal must exercise a series of specific instructional leadership behaviors. Sergiovanni listed five leadership forces or behaviors available to a principal: technical, human, educational, symbolic, and cultural.[7]

Earlier writers organized administrative skills into three skill areas—technical, human, and conceptual.[8] Sergiovanni expanded the third area, conceptual skills, into a series of behavioral forces described as educational, symbolic, and cultural. The five forces are:

Technical

Technical forces include being a good manager and applying good planning, organizing, coordinating, and controlling techniques to ensure optimum effectiveness of the organization. This includes such things as efficient office management practices, good scheduling techniques, and appropriate use of goals and objectives. Technical behaviors are basically the things that would ensure good, efficient management (about which we wrote in the first chapter).

Human Forces

These behaviors emphasize human relations skills, implementing good motivational techniques, and building good morale within the organization. The appropriate use of participatory management is an integral part of this behavior. These skills become major contributors to the climate of the school.

Educational Forces

These behaviors focus on the conceptual knowledge of education. Skills include the ability to diagnose educational problems, carry out the functions of clinical supervision, evaluate educational programs, help develop curriculum, implement staff-developement activities, and develop good individual educational programs for individual children.

Symbolic Forces

These behaviors demonstrate to others those things that the leader believes important and of value to the organization. It involves *purposing*—"that continuous stream of actions by an organization's formal leadership which has the effect of inducing clarity, consensus, and commitment regarding the organization's basic purposes."[9]

Symbolic actions also can be expressed by principals modeling behavior they wish to emphasize. When a principal teaches a reading class, for instance, the importance of that activity is being emphasized by example. The key is the signal sent out by the principal regarding what is considered important.

Cultural Forces

The cultural leader functions as the "high priest" of the school. In this role, the leader seeks to strengthen the values and beliefs that make the school unique. The leader attempts to build traditions of the school around those things most highly valued. This is done by sharing with others what the school most values; by orientation of new members of the group—students, staff, and parents—to the values and beliefs of the organization; by telling stories of past glories to reinforce these traditions; or simply by explaining the standard operating procedure that is expected to be used. The cultural leader also publically rewards those who reflect the desired culture and are its most ardent followers.

The cultural force of leadership bonds students, parents, and teachers together as true believers in the school. It takes on almost a religious fervor and a special sense of personal worth and importance grow out of membership in the organization. The cultural life of a school is "constructed" by someone, hopefully the instructional leaders of the school, and reflects a proper set of values, beliefs, and traditions that provide the foundation for school excellence. It is possible to have a strong or weak culture as measured by the amount of influence it has on participants.

Goal Setting

Well-understood, well-advertised goals for schools and classrooms are absolutely essential. School climate, consistency in decision making, and accountability for what happens in the instructional delivery system—three very different aspects of schools that aspire to high performance—result from the nature of the goals that are established and *the nature of the goal-setting process*. Stated simply, "The glue that holds together the myriad actions and decisions of highly effective principals... [are] the goals that they and their staff have developed for the school and a sense of what their schools need to look like and to do in order to accomplish those goals."[10]

High-performing organizations are characterized by committed, energetic people who sit down together, examine problems confronting their organization, and figure out ways to overcome these problems. Tanner called this "breaking the bonds of isolation" and creating a "climate of professional inquiry."[11] The principal's job is to facilitate this exchange. The questions to be answered are:

- Why are we doing what we are doing? (a goals question)
- What are we doing? How are we going about achieving our goals? (a process question)
- Can it be done a better way? (an evaluation question)

Involving Others in Goal Setting and Action Planning

Principals engage staff, students, and community in goal setting and problem solving because all are stakeholders and each, to one degree or another, has a contribution to make and responsibilities to assume for why things are as they are. Four assumptions guide the principal:

1. People at the working level tend to know the problems best.
2. The face-to-face work group is the best unit for diagnostic and change.
3. People will work hard to achieve objectives and goals they have helped develop.
4. Initiative and creativity are widely distributed in the population.

These assumptions undergird the high-performance organization.

It is axiomatic that any effective organization must have a clear sense of direction. Once developed, the goals need to be explicated by specific objectives and the accomplishment of these objectives must be manifest in instructional activities in the classroom.

High Expectations, Praise, and Hoopla: The Motivating Work Environment

High standards of accomplishment are characteristic of productive schools. Research about productive educational settings has shown that invariably present was a leader who had high expectations, advertised these expectations, facilitated efforts to achieve the expectations, and monitored progress. This has been so, whether the leader was a teacher in a single classroom working with children or a principal with a staff to manage.

High expectations result in high performance. Even where excellence is not obtained, the result is far higher than what might ever have been predicted. Moreover, staff and principal have a benchmark from which to move to the next higher level, and a diagnostic basis to determine how to get there.

Hoopla

Effective organizations celebrate success! Good leaders use every device at their disposal to call attention to excellent work and great accomplishments (so do good teachers). Recognition lunches, awards banquets, T-shirts emblazoned with "We're Number 1," gold stars, trophies. public announcements, acknowledged favors and special privileges, "Teacher of the Week," "Student of the Day," "Custodian of the Month," school-created important sounding titles, whatever and whenever—when such devices are well intended and well merited, they enhance school productivity. In writing about such activities in highly successful private sector organizations. Peters and Waterman called this "unabashed hoopla and people respond to it."

> *When we first looked at this phenomenon, we thought large doses of hoopla and celebration might be limited to companies like Tupperware, where the president*

and his senior managers are said to participate for thirty days a year in Jubilees, aimed at feting the success of their top 15,000 salespersons and managers. But we found hoopla going on in high tech companies as well....And at Caterpillar we were told of an event to introduce new equipment where huge pieces of earth-moving machinery were dressed in costume.

...The people orientation also has its tough side. The excellent companies are measurement-happy and performance oriented, but this toughness is born of mutually high expectations and peer review rather than emanating from table-pounding managers and complicated control systems.[12]

Summary

The focus of this chapter has been on the principal as an instructional leader in a high-performance school. We have stressed, however, that leadership in instructional and curricular endeavors is not the sole province of the principal. Indeed, high performance can occur only as leadership is encouraged to emerge from the stakeholders—staff, students, and community. Setting high standards and exemplifying these is an essential leadership act of the principal, nonetheless. It is the principal who is in the position to facilitate staff development, orchestrate time, and schedule factors so that teachers have opportunities to work together to solve instructional and curricular problems.

Activities

1. Review the elements of the high-performing school. Apply each of the five elements to your own school and indicate by example the decree to which your school addresses these elements. What strategies would you, as principal, engage in to overcome any deficiencies?

2. Review Case Studies 2, 3, and 5. For any, or all, analyze the problem presented and, applying the concepts development in this chapter, set forth a strategy for overcoming the problem. You do not have to solve the problem, but you must accept it as *your* problem and, based on reasonable (and stated) assumptions and the data provided, provide a framework wherein you expect the problem would be mitigated, if not solved.

Endnotes

1. Paula A. Cordeiro, "The Principal's Role in Curricular Leadership and Program Development," in *The Principal as Leader*, ed. Larry W. Hughes (New York: Macmillan, 1994), p. 176.

2. R. Marshall, *Restructuring the American Work Place: Implications for the Public Sector* (Eugene, OR: Labor Education Research Center, University of Oregon, 1992). (LERC Monograph Series)

3. Thomas J. Sergiovanni, "The Roots of School Leadership," *Principal* 74, no. 2 (November 1994): 6–9.

4. *Ibid.*, p. 7.

5. Peter Senge, *The Fifth Discipline* (New York, Doubleday, 1990).

6. Cordeiro, "The Principal's Role," pp. 162–163.

7. Thomas J. Sergiovanni, "Leadership and Excellence in Schools," *Educational Leadership* 41 (February 1984): 4–13.

8. The original work was that of Katz describing the technical, human, and conceptual skills of a manager. Robert L. Katz, "Skills of an Effective Administrator," *Harvard Business Review* 33, no. 1 (1955): 33–42.

9. Peter B. Vail, "The Purposing of High Performing Systems," in *Leadership and Organizational Cultures*, ed. Thomas Sergiovanni and John E. Corbally (Urbana-Champaign, IL: University of Illinois Press, 1984).

10. Kenneth Leithwood, "The Principal's Role in Teacher Development," in *Changing School Culture through Staff Development: 1990 Yearbook of the Association for Supervision and Currilculum Development.* ed. Bruce Joyce (Alexandria, VA: ASCD, 1990), pp. 71–90.

11. Laurel N. Tanner, "The Practical Affairs of Improving Teaching," in *The Principal as Leader,* ed. Larry W. Hughes (New York: Macmillan), pp. 190, 194.

12. Thomas J. Peters and Robert H. Waterman, *In Search of Excellence* (New York: Harper and Row, 1982), p. 240.

Selected Readings

Blase, Joseph, and Peggy C. Kirby. *Bringing Out the Best in Teachers: What Effective Principals Do.* Newbury Park, CA: Corwin Press, 1991.

Daresh, John C., and Marcia A. Playko. *Supervision as a Proactive Process: Concepts and Cases.* Prospect Heights, IL: Waveland Press, 1995.

Griffin, Gary A. "Leadership for Curriculum Improvement: The School Administrator's Role," in *Critical Issues in Curriculum: The 87th Yearbook of the National Society for the Study of Education,* ed. Laurel Tanner (Part I, pp. 244–266). Chicago: University of Chicago Press, 1988.

Hoy, Wayne K., C. John Tarter, and Robert B. Kottkamp, *Open Schools/Healthy Schools.* Newbury Park, CA: Sage, 1991.

Hughes, Larry W. *The Principal as Leader.* New York: Macmillan, 1994.

Leithwood, Kenneth A. "The Principal's Role in Teacher Development," *Changing School Culture through Staff Development: 1990 Yearbook of the Association for Supervision and Curriculum Development,* ed. Bruce Joyce (pp. 71–90). Alexandria, VA: ASCD, 1990.

Senge, Peter. *The Fifth Discipline.* New York: Doubleday, 1990.

Sergiovanni, Thomas J. "The Roots of School Leadership." *Principal* 74, no. 2 (November 1994): 6–9.

Chapter *3*

Decision Processing and Decision Making

Not all the problems that arise around here require a GII decision process or even a CII or CI, only the important ones—the ones that have to do with children's learning and staff development and a few that don't but which the staff cares a lot about…. I just try not to shoot myself in the foot in those latter instances. Principals need to communicate the how and why of decision making, with the goal of encouraging high level decision making processes in others. —HERB KARPICKE[1]

GII? CII? or CI? This chapter will focus on both rational and heuristic decision-making situations and examine ways to organize to solve continuing school-based problems. We will discuss, as well, the "garbage-can" model for decision making. Decision processing is distinguished from decision making. Decision processing is the way one goes about arriving at the maximum feasible decision—the decision that will work. This chapter is about both decision processing and decision making, with a decided emphasis on the former.

Don't Just Stand There, Do Something: The Garbage-Can Model

Seldom is it good practice to begin with a bad example but we're going to violate that principle to try to make a point in favor of rational problem analysis and decision making. We use as our "bad example" an examination of the garbage-can model of decision making. The garbage can model inverts the problem-solving process from a focus on finding solutions to problems to a focus on identifying a problem for which the principal or the work group has a solution. What we have in the garbage can are solutions in search of a problem. Hoy and Tartar wrote, "The garbage-can model explains why solutions are proposed to problems that do not exist, why choices are made that do not solve problems, why problems persist in spite of solutions, and why so few problems are solved."[2]

Now, it is true that not everything in and about the organization proceeds on a rational basis at all times. In the first chapter, we wrote about the informal dimension of organizations and the mighty impact this dimension has on the direction organizations take. Moreover, principals have their own notions and preferences of what it is they would like to see solved or what solutions they would like to try out, whether there is a real problem or not. Principals have hunches about what might be getting in the way of the school being more effective. Good, we say; principals ought to be thinking about such things.

However, locking in on a hunch or presenting a solution to a nonexistent problem simply because one is intrigued by the solution takes one to the garbage can. The garbage can contains unfocused solutions and activities, pet ideas and political exigencies, as well as time limitations, budget constraints, and inadequate information. "Don't just stand there, do something" often becomes the driving force. Activity replaces productivity.[3]

Even if nonrational behavior, or even apparently irrational behavior, can be explained by the garbage-can model, better ways are at the disposal of the principal who wants the school to be a high-performing organization. The way to stay out of the garbage can is through systematic problem analysis and avoidance of solutions that do not really address what is getting in the way of the school becoming maximally productive.

The school did not become what it is overnight and it won't become better overnight and it won't become better *ever* unless problems are correctly identified, issues defined, and solutions generated that focus on what it is that is getting in the way. Rational processes are required. This in no way diminishes the effectiveness of intuitive leaps nor does it diminish the importance of "hypothesis testing." It simply suggests that until the problem is thoroughly analyzed, intuition is restricted and bad hypotheses are stated. (We devote much attention in Chapter 6 to the manner in which problems can be analyzed and solutions generated that take the work group to resolution or at least to problem mitigation. Force-field analysis is one of the ways discussed.)

Decision Making as Problem Solving

Increasingly, final decision making on a wide array of operational issues is being done at the school site. The decentralization of decision making has greatly increased the responsibility of prinicpals and staffs in the school building.

The remainder of this chapter is organized into four parts. Here, decision making as a problem-solving process is discussed. A rational problem-solving model is presented. Next, the chapter will describe two kinds of decision settings: routine (or structured) and multialternative (or unstructured). Then, how to select an appropriate decision process becomes the focus of the chapter. Three interrelated conceptualizations of decision processing are discussed. The chapter concludes with an examination of the work group—departments, grade levels, or entire school faculties—as problem-solving units. The concepts of enlightened suzerainty and site-based management and such mechanisms as quality circles are discussed.

A problem exists when there is a state of uncertainty caused by either an unwelcome event or by the need to choose a course of action to achieve certain predetermined goals. Thus, something is a problem when there is a difference between what is currently occurring (the real situation) and what would desirably be happening (ideal situation).

Viewing decision making as problem solving has the advantage of delaying an act or judgment until there is a reasonable basis for that act or judgment. Moreover, not all problems are worthy of responses. Some problems, on just a little reflection, will be solved only at the price of creating a larger problem; other problems are not important and are best ignored; still other problems belong to someone else and should be redirected to the appropriate person. The first decision that needs to be made is about the nature and severity of the problem.

Figure 3–1 depicts a rational problem-solving/decision-making model. Whether the problem is complex, such as how to respond to a school pressure group, or relatively simple, such as what to do with a sick student, the intellectual process is the same.

How to deal with a sick student may not take very much time, but assuming that the student is really ill and that it is the principal's problem, clearly the rest of the process makes sense. In the analysis of the problem, one considers the legal ramifications and school district policy. This provides a framework. Alternative solutions might include sending the student back to class but requiring no participation in class activities; sending the student to the health room until school is over; sending the student home; calling an ambulance and removing the student to a hospital; as well as other possible alternatives.

Each of these alternatives can be quickly evaluated in light of the severity of the problem, the feasibility of the solution, the age of the person, the time of day, and anticipated consequences of any particular action. It may make a difference, too, whether or not there is a responsible adult present in the home.

Once a judgment is made about the best alternative and it is implemented, the results should be evaluated. Did it work? Was the principal or the school, and especially the student, better off or worse off? (At the very least, one ought to be better off after a decision than before.) If not, why not? Thus, a basis for nonrepetitive error is established.

How long should such a process take? In the instance of the sick student, probably no more than five minutes, less for an experienced principal who knows the policies and the students. A relatively quick diagnosis and a phone call or two will do it. In the instance of a citizens' group upset about a curricular issue or upset about grade placement policy, the process may require more study and time, but the steps are the same and the purpose is the same—to reach a sound judgment in a timely manner that will result in a solution that is in the best interests of all concerned.

Decision Settings

Problems occur in a variety of forms; they differ in content, in the process by which the problem is addressed, and in the kind of impact made on the organization and the people in the organization. When should one make a straightforward unilateral decision? When should one involve groups in the agonizing process of consensus?

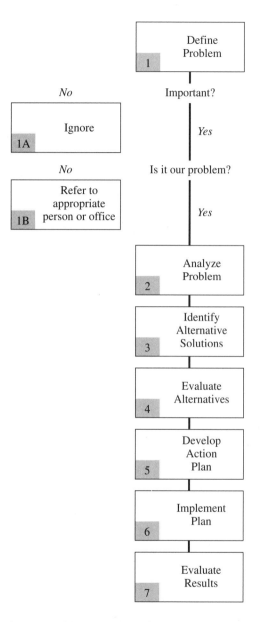

FIGURE 3–1 Rational Decision Making: Steps in Systematic Problem Solving

The answer is not difficult to see in the extreme. If the situation is a fire in the basement, an order is issued to clear the building; one does not call a committee together to achieve consensus on which fire exits to use. (However, it would not be inappropriate to involve affected groups or individuals in advance in the development of policies and procedures for how to cope with such emergencies.) It is more useful to think about decision settings than about specific decisions. Problems may fall into two general decision settings: structured settings (routine, recurring issues) and multialternative, unstructured, or innovative settings.

Structured Decision Settings

Many things that happen in the school organization are recurring in nature. The basis for an orderly, goal-oriented school is an array of proven, reliable, productive activities that are instituted, monitored, and terminated by an appropriate set of habituated decisions.

The range of responses to any given issue may be clearly limited by law, policy, and/or custom as well as by time constraints and the maturity of the group affected by the decisions. The principal can expect certain kinds of problems to recur frequently and regularly, given a particular environment or set of circumstances. Routine response mechanisms to these are expected by members of the staff so that they can go about their work with a minimum of disruption. To the maximum degree possible, the decisions and decision processes that respond to recurring activities should be routinized.

Need for Written Policies

Arranging conditions in the school so that recurring problems are resolved with a minimum of disruption and false starts can be readily achieved. A school building policy and rules and regulations manual developed with the assistance of staff and students is called for.

Such a manual should contain statements of basic responsibilities of teachers, counselors, administrators, and classified personnel in each of five functional aspects of the school: pupil personnel services, staffing and staff relations, building management and financial operations, public relations, and curriculum and instructional development. The roles and responsibilities of various personnel with respect to matters pertaining to the functional aspects are carefully delineated, lines of communication are spelled out and common procedural questions are answered. Importantly, too, the document should also spell out student responsibilities—the rules and regulations every student is expected to live by.

In such a document, the delegation of specific management tasks to designated people will ensure a necessary degree of stability because it clarifies the "who is to do what" question and because it permits the principal to manage by exception rather than by direct participation in all decisions.

The Importance of Routine Decision Processes

In a well-managed school, routine day-to-day activities are carried on without the constant involvement of the principal. The primary responsibility of the principal is not the routine operation of the building but rather the creation of organizational conditions whereby school operations may be readily modified to meet changing demands and opportunities.

Thus, structured or routine decision making, while encompassing problem situations running from the highly important to the mundane, is best formalized to the extent that relatively little stress on individuals or the organization occurs as decisions are promulgated and implemented. Such is often not the case in those settings wherein a variety of responses are available (*multialternative*) nor in those settings where no acceptable alternatives are apparent (*unstructured or innovative*).

Multialternative, Unstructured, and Innovative Settings

Even though many of the decisions that need to be made in and about the school are structured and only a limited number of options are available, frequently there are issues for which a wide array of alternative actions is available, and the principal may be confronted with a seemingly endless number of possibilities. Many of these alternatives may appear nearly equal in value *or* there may be an inadequate information base from which to determine the efficacy of the alternatives.

Unanticipated problems, unique situations, and fast-changing conditions are characteristics of organizational life. Decisions in such situations often require "leaps into the unknown"—creative problem resolution that by its very nature produces both individual and organizational stress. In these decision settings, one needs to move from rational decision making to creative decision making. The principal and/or the decision-making group changes from primarily left-brain use to right-brain use.

It is not a once-and-for-all change, however. Generating creative responses to unstructured problems requires some structuring and a return to rational processes when the alternatives are ultimately weighed and an action plan is developed. The generation of alternatives and creative responses requires the combination of some rational processes, frequent abrupt changes to creative processes, and then a return to the rational process. Problem definition, for example, is a rational process, and goal setting or mission statements require rational processes. On the other hand, the development of alternative solutions is an intensely creative process.

It is not an either/or proposition. Groups or individuals do not have to be either creative or rational. Problem-solving groups, or individuals, make use of both orientations and must do so to be effective. Creative processes in the work organization need a structure or framework to be useful. Totally nongoal-oriented "think tanks" are a luxury most organizations cannot afford on an ongoing basis. Organizational creativity is goal oriented.

Techniques for Unstructured, Innovative Decision Making

Several techniques can be used to address problems of an unstructured nature. Three of these—brainstorming, structured absent group, and nominal group—are generally descriptive of the possibilities.

Brainstorming.   Brainstorming has as its only purpose the generation of ideas, no matter how impractical the ideas may seem at first consideration. Whereas the usual kinds of meetings or conferences tend to be noncreative, a brainstorming group devotes itself *solely to creative thinking*. To function properly, the group remains, during the period of the brainstorm, completely divorced from the mundane world. The role of the group leader is one of facilitator rather than gatekeeper.

The best method is to record ideas on a flip chart. Using flip charts keeps the ideas visible and thus stimulates other ideas. Moreover, when the session ends, the paper can be given to a secretary for duplication and subsequent circulation to group members.

At some point following the brainstorming session, the group reconvenes for the purpose of judging and modifying the ideas. This session is one of analysis. The purpose is to select those ideas that singly or in combination with other ideas seem to provide a creative solution to the problem.

From the analysis session, the group decides on the four or five solutions that offer a basis for the systematic resolution of the problem. At this point, a group may engage in any number of systematic planning approaches and work the solutions into an implementation phase.

A criticism of the brainstorming technique is that the results may be affected by peer pressure (or hierarchical pressure if it is a vertically organized group). Also, unless the leader is especially well skilled, a few outspoken members may dominate and thus reduce the number of contributions from other members. To avoid this, many leaders turn to either the structured absent group or to the nominal group technique.

Structured Absent Group. This technique does not require a group to convene. Individuals are asked to participate in a simulation activity in which each is presented a case study describing an organizational issue. Included is a modest amount of descriptive data. The organization may be fictitious, but the issue is real. Individuals are asked to respond to three items:

1. Given the issue, what do you think is the problem? What might be some subproblems?
2. What might be two or three actions of a short-term nature that could be expected to reduce the intensity of the problem?
3. Suggest at least two actions or processes that might ultimately resolve the problem.

The responding individuals submit their suggestions to the person charged with ultimately working on the problem. (A variation on this is to have the individuals actually meet as a problem-solving group to share their solutions and arrive at an action plan. This latter is similar to the nominal group technique described next.)

Nominal Group Technique. As in brainstorming, a small group convenes to focus on an organizational problem. However, the use of this technique requires that although members of the group work on an identified problem in the presence of each other, they do so without immediate interaction.

Once the problem is explained by the convenor, group members are given a few minutes, individually, to write as many alternative solutions to the problem as possible. After the time has elapsed, a presentation of alternatives occurs. Participants give one alternative solution at a time, which is posted on flip chart paper. This continues in round-robin fashion until all alternatives are posted. No discussion of alternatives takes place until all of the alternatives have been recorded.

The value of the process is that divergence is encouraged because alternatives are developed privately. A disadvantage, of course, is that unlike brainstorming, there is no way for one individual's idea to spark another individual. However, a "creative tension" occurs because participants are aware that others are working on the same problem and they also know that everyone's product will be displayed.

Decision Processing

An array of problem-solving processes is at the disposal of the school administrator, ranging from a unilateral "This is what must be done" telling process to engaging work groups in consensus decision making. The effective principal uses a range of techniques and processes to arrive at the maximum feasible decision.

The Maier Model

Maier and Verser have discussed the need for decision makers to consider two discrete elements: the requirement that a decision be one that is of high quality and that the decision be one that carries with it the likelihood that subordinates will accept it.

Decision quality refers to objective decisions in the problem-solving process that have to do with achieving organizational goals and maintaining control, aside from any consideration of subordinate motivation. Is the decision technically sound? Is it based on the best information available? A high-quality decision occurs when the best available alternative is selected. (Unfortunately, it is often only through retrospective analysis that one knows whether or not this was so.)

Decision acceptance refers to the degree of commitment required of subordinates to implement the decision. Acceptance is crucial when the administrator is dependent on subordinates to implement a decision. Although it is not possible to know unerringly when to involve others in a decision-making process, who those others should be, or what the nature of their involvement should be, there is always a need to consider the feelings, attitudes, and skills of those who will be charged with implementing the decision. Any decision that will require behavioral change will probably require work-group commitment. The nature of work-group involvement will depend in great part on the complexity of the problem to be solved, the degree to which those affected by the decision will be required to behave differently in order for the decision to be properly implemented, and the degree to which subordinates will accept a unilateral decision.

The Q/A Interaction

Using the two factors of technical expertise (quality of decision required) and need for group acceptance (hearty compliance and/or behavior change required) as prime determinants, a quadrant model can be developed to help determine the answer to the involvement question. Figure 3–2 displays such a model.

That quadrant in which both the quality of the decision and the need for work-group commitment is high (Q∗A, the upper right quadrant) presents the greatest challenge to the leader. Into this quadrant fall those decisions that require much in the way of technical expertise and knowledge in order for a good decision to be reached. But it also describes a situation wherein no matter how technically superior the solution may be, in order for that solution to be put into effect much work-group acceptance will be necessary. That is, the decision must fall within the work group's "zone of hearty compliance." Without consideration of the needs and opinions of the group, compliance may be questionable. This may be so for several reasons: because an apparent solution is contrary to present practice or present attitudes; because it requires work-group

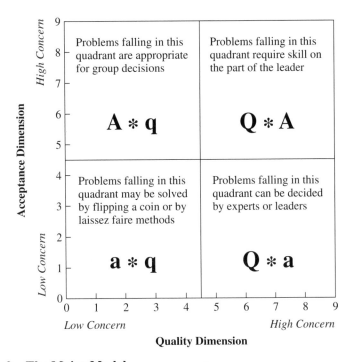

FIGURE 3–2   The Maier Model

Source: Maier, R. F. and Gertrude C. Verser, *Psychology in Industrial Organizations,* Fifth Edition. Copyright © 1982 by Houghton Mifflin Company. Used with permission.

members to perform in ways that are initially more difficult or for which they have not been trained; because of the simple lack of agreement about the efficacy of the decision; or for any number of other reasons including threat, fear, distrust of administrators, or anger. If any of the previous conditions can be presumed, then something beyond a simple unilateral decision process probably will be required.

What kinds of issues might fall within this quadrant? Any curricular change certainly would, as would budget development. Changes in school policies affecting large numbers of students and school constitutional questions would also seem to fit here. Operating in this quadrant will require good human relations skills as well as technical competence in the subject under review.

The upper left quadrant (A*q) depicts those situations where group feelings may be intense, but great technical expertise is not required because the subject is not a complex one. Any number of resolution schemes are available; the appropriate one must be that which is fair and sensitive to the needs and desires of the work group. Assignment of unpaid extracurricular duties, balanced work schedules for routine duties, and school calendar development, among myriad other decision situations, might fall into this category. Among appropriate ways to handle problems in this quadrant would be the formation of advisory committees, delegation of decision making to standing or ad hoc bodies, or informal consultation with leaders of the groups affected.

The Q*a quadrant contains those kinds of decisions that affect the quality of the organization in a technical sense but do not have a great impact on the human side of the enterprise. Equipment selection, design of conflict-free schedules, and the design of a management information system, among other examples, might fall into this quadrant.

In the remaining quadrant (a*q), neither great technical competence nor sensitive human relations is a critical consideration. What is needed is a concrete act to resolve a simple problem. Time is the only critical element. A decision has to be made in a timely fashion, so that people in the organization can go about their work in an orderly, efficient and knowledgeable manner.

The Maier model is a good analytical tool. It emphasizes that selection of the best decision process will result from an analysis of the nature of the problem and the nature of the work group.

Vroom and Yetton,[5] as well as Vroom and Jago,[6] extended these concepts and provided a basis for choosing the decision process most likely to result in the maximum feasible decision. Effective leadership, as manifested in good decision making, depends on understanding the conditions of a problem situation, assessing correctly how much participation or "power sharing" is required to be successful, and establishing the form that that participation should take.[7]

The Vroom-Yetton Decision-Process Model

Vroom and Yetton have placed five available decision processes on a continuum from no subordinate influence to maximum subordinate influence:

> *The AI Procedure.* The leader solves the problem alone using whatever information is available at the time. (The available information is considered to be sufficient.)

> *The AII Procedure.* The leader obtains the necessary information from subordinates who may or may not be told about the problem or why the information is requested. The subordinates' role in this procedure is simply that of providing data, not in developing or evaluating alternatives.

> *The CI Procedure.* The leader shares the problem with one or more subordinates *individually*, asking for ideas, suggestions, and alternatives, but does *not* bring, the relevant subordinates together to do this. The leader then makes the decision which may or may not take into account the ideas of the subordinates.

> *The CII Procedure.* The leader calls the appropriate subordinates together and shares the problem with the group, soliciting ideas, suggestions, and alternatives. Then the leader makes the decision which may or may not take into account the ideas of the subordinates.

> *The GII Procedure.* The leader shares the problem with subordinates as a group. The group as a whole generates and evaluates alternatives, with the ascribed leader's role that of peer. The process is consensus decision making. The leader serves as chair or convenor of the meeting but does not attempt to exert "official" influence in the direction of any specific decision. The leader is willing to agree to and implement any solution which has the support of the group.[8]

The Vroom-Yetton process offers much more guidance to the leader in selecting an appropriate decision procedure than the Maier model. Both AI and GII may appear at first to be the "riskiest" of the procedures, but neither is any more or less risky than the others, and when used appropriately each will provide the best route to the maximum feasible decision. How does one choose among the processes?

The relative utility of the five procedures depends on several aspects of the situation within which the problem exists. It depends, as well, on leader judgments about the nature of these aspects:

1. A clear definition of the problem (i.e, what is it that is not what is desired?).
2. The amount of information possessed by the leader and subordinates or, if the information is not currently possessed, whether or not it is known where to find the needed information. This is the degree to which the problem is "structured." An unstructured problem would be one for which inadequate information is available and it is uncertain where to find the needed information.
3. Whether or not it is likely that subordinates will accept a unilateral decision from the leader.
4. Whether or not it is likely that subordinates will cooperate—with the leader or with each other—in trying to collectively reach a good decision (i.e., one that would be in the best interests of the organization).
5. The amount and intensity of disagreement the leader perceives exists among subordinates about preferred alternatives.

Vroom and Jago: The "New" Model

Continuing research has led to refinements and enhancements in the original Vroom-Yetton model. The conceptual framework and the basic assumptions remain unchanged, however. An important enhancement is that the model has been extended to include considerations about the extent to which a given problem solution is either *time driven* or one in which good opportunity for work-group development exists; that is, it is *development driven*. (*Note:* The model handles either problem situations involving a work group and superordinate or individual subordinate/superordinate problems. Our discussion here focuses only on group situations.)

Time-Driven Considerations
The available time to resolve an issue may impinge greatly on the degree to which members of a work group can be involved in problem solving and the form that this involvement takes. CII and GII decision procedures require an investment of time considerably greater than the other procedures. Is the problem important enough—that is, is group commitment necessary and is a high-quality decision required—to justify the expenditure of the labor hours that will be required?

Even if the quality of the decision is not crucial (i.e., there are a number of alternatives, any one of which would adequately resolve the issue), but acceptance is critical and not likely to result from a unilateral decision, then an investment of time will be worth the trouble.

Judicious use of time is an important consideration, however. CII and GII decision processes do use up both the time and the energy of subordinates and peers. A four-hour group meeting between the principal and an advisory group of eight others consumes 36 labor-hours of work time. What other important activities had to be delayed or not done because of the meeting?

Development-Driven Considerations

Much may be gained from broad participation in decision making by a school staff and school community. Such involvement encourages idea sharing, trust, high performance standards, and work group effectiveness. It also capitalizes on the abilities of the informal leaders on the staff.

However, skills in decision making need to be nurtured and work groups need to be helped to improve these skills. Consider a school or a department with many new personnel or a school suddenly functioning under a mandate for site-based management and similarly a mandated teacher and/or community advisory council. If group members have heretofore been relatively uninvolved and unfamiliar with decision making in an organizational context, there is work to be done by the principal.

Thus, the principal might employ a CII or a GII process on less intense problems with a new group as a way to provide a basis for group members to learn to work together. Later in this chapter there is a discussion about how to set an appropriate framework for group decision making.

The Decision Tree

Help in selecting the most likely process to lead to the maximum feasible decision is available in the form of a decision tree. Eight questions to be answered yes or no comprise the branches of the tree. These questions are addressed *only* after the problem to be solved has been satisfactorily defined.

1. How important is the technical quality of this decision?
2. How important is subordinate commitment to the decision?
3. Does the leader have sufficient information to make a high-quality decision?
4. Is the problem well structured?[9]
5. If the leader were to make the decision alone, is it reasonably certain that subordinates would be committed to the decision?
6. Do subordinates share the organizational goals to be attained in solving this problem?
7. Is conflict among subordinates over preferred solutions likely?
8. Do subordinates have sufficient information to make a high-quality decision?

Figures 3–3 and 3–4 depict the decision tree. Figure 3–3 would be used in instances where the principal considered group development the driving factor; Figure 3–4 would be used where time was the primary concern.

QR Quality Requirement: How important is the technical quality of this decision?

CR Commitment Requirement: How important is subordinate commitment to the decision?

LI   Leader's Information: Do you have sufficient information to make a high-quality decision?

ST Problem Structure: Is the problem well structured?

CP Commitment Probability: If you were to make the decision by yourself, is it reasonably certain that
                                your subordinate(s) would be committed to the decision?

GC Goal Congruence: Do subordinates share the organizational goals to be attained in
                                solving this problem?

CC Subordinate Conflict: Is conflict among subordinates over preferred solutions likely?

SI   Subordinate Information: Do subordinates have sufficient information to make a high-quality decision?

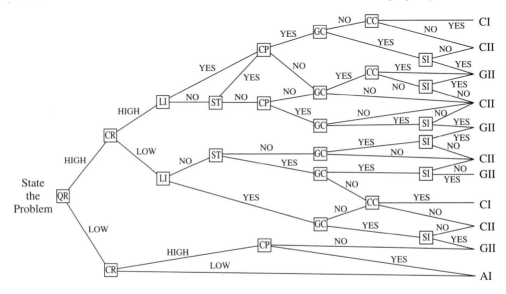

**FIGURE 3–3   Vroom-Jago Development-Driven Decision Tree:
Group Problems**

Source: Reprinted from *The New Leadership: Managing Participation in Organizations* by Victor H.
Vroom and Arthur G. Jago, 1988, Englewood Cliffs, NJ.: Prentice-Hall. Copyright 1987 by V. H. Vroom
and A. G. Jago. Used with permission of the authors.

Implications of Decision-Processing Models

Using such tools as the Maier model or the Vroom-Jago decision tree for problem analysis does not remove the need for sensitive judgment. Indeed, the effective use of these
models requires the highest order of judgment. The administrator is after the maximum
feasible decision—the decision that offers promise of long-term problem resolution or
problem mitigation *and* the one that those most affected will work to carry out. The
processes described here are designed to take the administrator to this sort of decision.

QR	Quality Requirement:	How important is the technical quality of this decision?
CR	Commitment Requirement:	How important is subordinate commitment to the decision?
LI	Leader's Information:	Do you have sufficient information to make a high-quality decision?
ST	Problem Structure:	Is the problem well structured?
CP	Commitment Probability:	If you were to make the decision by yourself, is it reasonably certain that your subordinate(s) would be committed to the decision?
GC	Goal Congruence:	Do subordinates share the organizational goals to be attained in solving this problem?
CC	Subordinate Conflict:	Is conflict among subordinates over preferred solutions likely?
SI	Subordinate Information:	Do subordinates have sufficient information to make a high-quality decision?

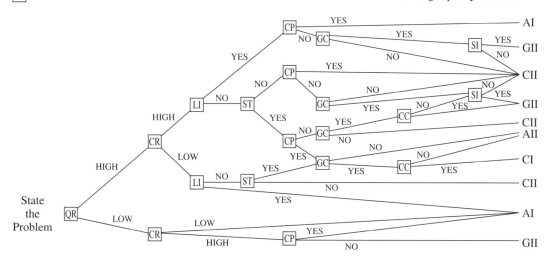

FIGURE 3–4   Vroom-Jago Time-Driven Decision Tree: Group Problems

Source: Reprinted from *The New Leadership: Managing Participation in Organizations* by Victor H. Vroom and Arthur G. Jago, 1988, Englewood Cliffs, NJ.: Prentice-Hall. Copyright 1987 by V. H. Vroom and A. G. Jago. Used with permission of the authors.

What one has, with the rational decision processes just presented, is a basis for reducing the risks and analyzing the strengths and weaknesses of relative positions. The decision tree, the Maier model, and any of a number of other rational processes are tools for the manager to use to arrive at a maximum feasible decision. The models are not a substitute for thinking; they are to stimulate thinking to provide the basis for sound judgments.

Your Turn

You are the principal of a 1,200-pupil junior high school and are confronted with the situation stated below. Analyze the situation. At the conclusion of the case, you will apply the Vroom-Jago tree.

Case Study

The school houses grades 6 through 9. There is need to review the social studies series currently in use. Because your own teaching field is social studies, you have more than a casual interest in and knowledge about the situation. You also have a strong opinion that the current series does not adequately depict the contributions made by minorities.

The social studies department seems split on the issue, containing two teachers who do not want to use any text at all; several teachers who are very satisfied with the current text; and three or four others who favor at least two other series. (Board of education policy requires one adopted text series but does permit supplemental works when it can be shown that there is good reason to do so.)

The chairperson of the department is undecided on the matter and requests that you "do something." A review of staff evaluations reveals that one of the teachers who wants no text at all is among the top rated in the school. She is unhappy with the more conservative posture of many other colleagues and has indicated that unless a more positive stand on the multicultural nature of society is taken by the department, she will go elsewhere A *cause célèbre* looms.

Your task is to decide what decision process will lead you to the maximum feasible decision by applying the Vroom-Jago model.

Using the Decision Tree

To use the Vroom-Jago tree, first clearly state what you believe to be the problem. Then assume you are development driven and, using Figure 3–3, begin at the left side of the model with question "QR." If your response to this question is "high," then you proceed to question "CR," and so on.

For each answer, take a moment to justify your response. Proceed through the decision tree until a terminal is reached. The terminal will indicate the maximum feasible decision procedure.

Authors' Analysis of the Case

Using the tree, the maximum feasible process appears to us to be CII. At issue is the selection of the social science series, and this is what we see as the problem to be solved. So stating, the tree is entered and question QR receives a "high." (There is clearly a quality requirement; the issue is a high priority and there are "unequal" solutions.)

The next question asks about the importance of subordinate commitment to the decision. We believe there is a need for "high" commitment. Little commitment would seem to mean the text would not be used or would be misused. We are now at the leader information question and our answer to that is that the leader (us) does not have enough information. Nor do we believe the problem is "structured"—the answer to this particular issue would not seem to be "programmable." We are now at "CP." Do we think that subordinates will commit to a unilateral decision made by us? Perhaps; you'd really have to be there to know, but given the nature of the problem and the presumed intensity of feelings, our answer is "no." And how about "goal congruence"? It wouldn't seem that you could count on this given the information about the range of beliefs on the staff, so we said "no" and the terminal we are taken to is CII. Had the response to the goal congruence question been "yes," we would have had to address the conflict question. Depending on the answer to that—and a "yes" there would seem the likely response—we could have ended up at GII.

In either instance—and good judgment must be present for good decision processing—you are taken to the process that will most likely achieve the best result.

The Work Group as a Problem-Solving Unit

The school executive is looking for the best solutions to problems—routine and non-routine. Such solutions will not occur in an organization of interacting humans unless processes are employed that make appropriate use of the collective intelligence of these humans. Thus, effective principals deliberately and frequently engage their staff in problem-solving activities.

Productive relationships develop as a result of engaging in important activities together. It is then possible for the strengths and weaknesses of fellow members to be known, revealing who can be counted on for what kinds of expertise. Knowing where certain kinds of expertise exist permits the principal to create effective teams to focus on troubling schoolwide issues, existent or anticipated. Thus, effort spent to help a work group develop problem-solving skills will pay rich dividends.

Setting Realistic Decision-Making Limits

Irrespective of the maturity of the staff, few problem-solving groups can be permitted to operate completely unfettered. Real-world constraints must always be contended with. Any group charged with helping to resolve an issue needs to know the "rules of the game" if the expectation is a decision that can be implemented. The following considerations provide a solid basis for maximum effective use of problem-solving groups:

1. Decide if the task force is to be advisory in nature. That is, is it a CII or is it a GII? Are decisions to be suggestions only, or is the group to be charged with coming up with final decisions?
2. Cooperatively set a realistic time line. This would include further data collection periods, preparation of final reports, generation of new program alternatives, and the anticipated implementation date, among other milestones.
3. Establish a tentative budget for the project phases. Possible line items include released time costs, materials costs, transportation, and meals.
4. Review any districtwide policies or state laws that might impinge on the nature of any resolution scheme. For example, is there a systemwide or statewide adopted basal reading series that must be "lived with" no matter what? Does the state provide for experimental programs?
5. Establish the "essential conditions" that any decision must fit in order to be acceptable.
6. Set up regular interaction sessions about progress and findings.

Levels of Decision Making and Participation

Who should be involved in decision processing? Who makes the final decision? Does participatory management mean committees for everything? How will anything get done? Good decisions require good information and a willingness on the part of those affected to implement the decision. But that does not translate to mean the same approach to every problem-solving activity, nor does it mean the executive never takes action without some kind of agonizing consensus session.

The persons to be involved in decision processing *and the nature of that involvement* of necessity will differ, depending on the issue to be resolved, if the product is to be the maximim feasible decision. The work of Robert Lancto provides much help in the consideration of who needs to be involved in what and to what end.[10]

Lancto proposed five levels of participation in decision making in the school and submitted that the kinds of decisions to be made vary by level. Sometimes the participation is at the advisory level; sometimes it will result in final decisions. In shared decision making, the staff works with the principal in two ways: (1) giving advice before the principal makes certain decisions and (2) making decisions in predetermined domains. Figure 3–5 illustrates the decision levels and provides examples of the kinds of decisions to be made at the several levels.

The model is useful because it clearly sets forth varying degrees of participation in school-based decision making. It helps avoid misunderstandings about roles, responsibilities, and authority to act.

Site-Based Management: Enlightened Suzerainty

Historically, suzerainty meant that there was one nation that controlled another nation in international affairs but otherwise permitted domestic sovereignty. The term was originally used to describe a feudal lord to whom fealty was due because the lord provided protection and sustenance in time of need. In matters domestic and in the usual course of events, the local unit (family or town) operated in an independent manner; in relations with the outside world (foreign affairs), the lord would prevail.

If the negative feudal connotations are removed, one has an appropriate conceptual model for the organization of schools and school systems. Suzerainty does provide local autonomy. Individual school units (buildings, departments, and teachers) should be imbued with autonomy when it comes to operating within the local sphere.

Finn maded a similar point in his discussion of the need for "strategic independence."[11] He argued that school effectiveness reforms should allow for a considerable degree of autonomy at the school building level. The basis for this contention lies in the belief that the school is a unique, complex unit with its own culture, norms, and relationships. An already effective school may have achieved its stature through innovative, unorthodox strategies and structures that the imposition of stringent standards and policies from the central office might destroy.

The prescription, therefore, is strategic independence, but not total freedom from control from the central office. What this means is that system policymakers should continue to be expected to set standards for student achievement and other desired out-

FIGURE 3–5   School-Based Decision-Making Levels

Levels of Participation

1. Decisions made by individual teachers
2. Decisions made collectively by teachers (may also involve students and parents in an advisory role)
3. Decisions made collectively by teachers, principals, and other auxillary administrators (parent and student participation where appropriate)
4. Decisions made by administrators, department heads, and building supervisors after consultation with staff (schoolwide advisory councils are often a good mechanism for this)
5. Decisions made solely by the principal or other designated administrator

Typical Kinds of Decisions to Be Made at Each Level

Level 1: Classroom teaching strategies; enrichment; remediation

Level 2: Selection of instructional materials and texts; use of time and allocation of resources within a grade level or department—including staffing patterns

Level 3: Curriculum decisions involving more than one group or instructional unit; scheduling; scoping and sequencing across subjects and grade levels; sequential texts, materials, and other instructional protocols involving two or more instructional, support, or administrative units; any other decisional matters affecting more than one unit

Level 4: Schoolwide scheduling; budget recommendations to the central office; balancing resources/resolving conflicts; appraisal and evaluation strategies; development of school effectiveness reports to district offices and state agencies

Level 5: Legal issues such as teacher remands; official recommendations to superintendent on the reemployment of staff and tenure; final decisions on the general use of the building and other physical facilities; allocation of resources for the school plant in general; selection and assignment of support staff

---

comes for the school system as a whole, but they should avoid specifying the means by which these ends are to be achieved in any particular school.

Complex school systems can neither be organized as confederations nor should they be organized as highly centralized bureaucracies. Thus, our preference is for enlightened suzerainty. Individual school units need to be free to grapple independently with and solve problems indigenous to the unit. However, some problems are best dealt with at levels above the individual school unit, or are problems that are shared with a number of other schools. Such problems require a different kind of problem-solving mechanism and less local autonomy.

There are any number of ways to engage others in problem-solving activities. Simply being asked for an opinion is a degree of involvement. More formalized mechanisms may be appropriate, however, to be employed for specific purposes. Of particular interest to the principal may be quality circles, which are important because these are "local" problem-solving groups.

Quality Circles

Some problems are better addressed and solved at the operational level, without interference from a superordinate structure. In such instances, the superordinate structure serves as a support unit providing such resources as might be needed and performing in an oversight role only.

The argument in favor of quality circles is that autonomy is placed appropriately, permitting maximum latitude in decision making at the lowest possible operating level. The quality circle is an action group. It resolves problems rather than simply identifies them.

A quality circle is a small group of workers with similar responsibilities who voluntarily meet for an hour or so each week to discuss their problems, investigate causes, recommend solutions, and take corrective action. It is organized horizontally rather than vertically. No structural changes are required in the organization; it fits into any existing structure. There may be a systemwide steering committee to facilitate communication between quality circles. Other distinguishing features are:

1. Quality circles consist primarily of a regular work group (e.g., department, grade level, or cross-level group of teachers, librarians, counselors, etc.).
2. They are voluntary.
3. They meet regularly once a week.
4. They solve problems rather than simply identify problems for the principal or others to solve.

Such a group needs the principal's support, of course. Support may take the form of providing a meeting place and a ready ear. The principal may or may not be a member of the quality circle, but someone who is part of the school's administrative team is a member. The role of the administrator is that of convenor and facilitator. Having an administrative representative who may also serve as group leader is helpful because it ensures upward communication.

Staying Out of the Garbage Can

We began this chapter with an examination of the garbage-can model and an admonishment to stay out of there. To be sure, certain political realities and certain other extra- and intraorganizational forces must be contended with, but these too can best be attended to by more rational decision-making approaches. Political exigencies, budget realities, limitations of time, and insufficient information can be—and must be—factored into rational decision processes. But the garbage can contains unrelated collections of unfocused thoughts and conditions. Stay out of the garbage can. How? Figure 3–6 offers hope. It is a flowchart designed to remove clutter from decision processing and decision making. It takes into account the social and political realities of the milieu within which the school operates.

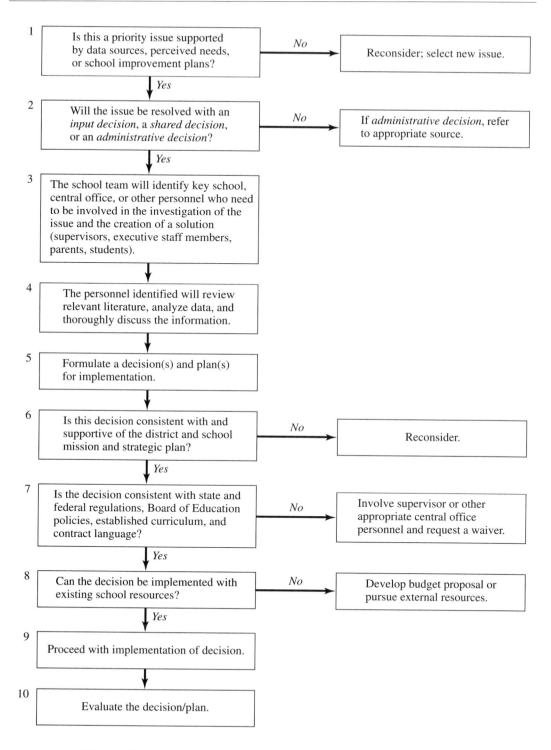

FIGURE 3–6   Decision-Making Flowchart

Summary

The essential executive act is decision making. Decision making is problem solving—or it ought to be. But decisions are not made very well in a vacuum. Moreover, there are few decisions that are made in the organization that do not affect the lives of others and require others to behave differently tomorrow than they did today.

Thus, the final act—the decision—must be subject to an intellectual process. The first step is to discover what the problem is. Subsequent steps (the decision-making process) may require creative approaches and the wisdom of others in the work group.

Much research about decision processing has been conducted over the years. One of the most useful applications of this research has been the Vroom-Jago model. In this approach, various conditions existing in a problem situation are subjected to analysis and the decision maker is led to a decision process that is most likely to result in a maximum feasible decision.

It is important that decisions be made and problems solved at the appropriate level. Staff at the building levels, operating under the concept of enlightened suzerainty, can be expected to develop good solutions to troubling issues.

Activities

1. Reflect on some happenings in and about your own school setting. Can you identify any situation, problem, or issue where the decision making could best be described as having relied on the garbage-can model? Describe this situation, problem, or issue. Describe alternative processes that might have worked better.

2. Review Case Studies 2 and 5. Apply the Maier model, then apply the Vroom-Jago model. Use both the "development-driven" and the "time-driven" trees. Pay particular attention to your statement of the problem. Discuss your approach with a small group of your colleagues. Try to achieve consensus on both the nature of the problem and the maximum feasible decision process.

Endnotes

1. Dr. Herb Karpicke, Principal, High School for the Performing and Visual Arts, Houston Independent School District, Houston, Texas, February 9, 1995.

2. Wayne K. Hoy and C. John Tartar, *Administrators Solving the Problems of Practice* (Boston: Allyn and Bacon, 1994), p. 61.

3. A good discussion of the garbage-can model can be found in the work of James G. March and Johan D. Olsen, *Ambiguity and Choice in Organizations,* 2nd ed. (New York: Oxford University Press, 1980).

4. Norman R. F. Maier and Gertrude C. Verser, *Psychology in Industrial Organizations,* 5th ed. (Boston: Houghton Mifflin, 1982), p. 173.

5. Victor H. Vroom and Philip W. Yetton, *Leadership and Decision Making* (Pittsburgh: University of Pittsburgh Press, 1973).

6. Victor H. Vroom and Arthur G. Jago, *The New Leadership: Managing Participation in Organizations* (Englewood Cliffs, NJ: Prentice-Hall, 1988).

7. Maier's work and the work of Vroom and Yetton and Vroom and Jago are based on earlier con-

cepts advanced by Simon. Simon's "Zone of Acceptance" model was based on two questions: "Is the issue relevant to others in this organization?" and "Do others in the organization have the expertise to deal with the issue?" If the answer to both of these questions was no, then whatever decision was made was likely to fall within the subordinates' zone of acceptance. Thus, little or no involvement in the decisional process would seem necessary. If the answer to both questions was yes, then Simon wrote there was a need to engage others in an examination of alternatives or, at least, in the collection of additional information. Herbert A. Simon, *Administrative Behavior* (New York: Macmillan, 1947).

8. These five procedures are reprinted from *Leadership and Decision-Making,* by Victor H. Vroom and Philip W. Yetton, by permission of the University of Pittsburgh Press. © 1973 by University of Pittsburgh Press.

9. A "structured" problem is one in which the decision maker knows three components of the problem: the current state (what "is"), the desired state ("outcome"), and the mechanisms needed to get from one state to the other. The problem, in effect, is programmable; creative solutions are not needed. The more structured a problem is, the less likely great participation in its solution will be required.

10. Robert M. Lancto, "An Inquiry: Shared Decision-Making," *The Journal of SAANYS* 18, no. 3 (Winter 1987–88): 13–17.

11. Chester E. Finn, "Toward Strategic Independence: Nine Commandments for Enhancing School Effectiveness," *Phi Delta Kappan* 64, no. 8 (April 1984): 519–524.

Selected Readings

Hallinger, Philip, and Don Richardson. "Models of Shared Leadership: Evolving Structures and Relationships." *The Urban Review* 20, no. 4 (December 1986): 229–245.

Hoy, Wayne K., and C. John Tartar. *Administrators Solving the Problems of Practice* (Boston: Allyn and Bacon, 1994).

Hughes, Larry W., and Gerald C. Ubben. *The Elementary Principal's Handbook: Guide to Effective Action,* 4th ed. (Boston: Allyn and Bacon, 1994).

Kamlesh, Mathur, and Daniel Solow. *Management Science: The Art of Decision Making* (Englewood Cliffs, NJ: Prentice Hall, 1994).

Keith, Sherry, and Robert H. Girling. *Education, Management, and Participation* (Boston: Allyn and Bacon, 1991).

March, James G., and Johan D. Olsen. *Ambiguity and Choice in Organizations,* 2nd ed. (New York: Oxford University Press, 1980).

Vroom, Victor H., and Arthur G. Jago. *The New Leadership: Managing Participation in Organizations* (Englewood Cliffs, NJ: Prentice Hall, 1988).

Chapter *4*

The School and the Community

"You gotta know the territory."
—THE MUSIC MAN

There they were: salesmen—old-time "drummers"—being jostled along, on board a train, moving from town to town, purveying their various wares. How best to sell the product? No matter what the product, went the refrain to the song in progress, "You gotta know the territory!" And that means understanding the customer. The customer is as important as the product.

We don't want to carry the analogy too far but there is much to be learned from the refrain to the opening number in the often revived *The Music Man*. And, for the educator interested in developing a good public relations program, the "territory" to be known is complex, indeed.

The entire school territory (community) is involved in the process of education. A high-performing school requires broad-based community support, and support will come from communities that are well informed and well engaged in the educative processes that go on in the school. This does not happen automatically.

Communication between parents and other citizens, businesses, health and social-care agencies, several levels of government, teachers, administrators, and students is essential and is the glue that binds the learning community together. Establishing good communication processes is an essential task of the principal. It is not easy. Communities are diverse, attitudes vary, and formal and informal forces vie for attention and make demands on the school that are often contradictory and at cross-purposes. The territory is complex and so must be the school-community public relations program.

Schools do not exist apart from the society to be served. They get their support from the "outside" world, and those who make policy and those who permit policy to be made reside in the outside world. Inevitably and inexorably, individuals and groups attempt to establish policies and procedures in the school that are consistent with—indeed generative and supportive of—their values, beliefs, and ideals.

These are days of individual school-based autonomy and in some places a mandated use of such decisional mechanisms as citizen and teacher advisory councils organized at the school level. The principal's role as a community relations expert has expanded and pressures have mounted for more effective ways to communicate with the "publics" comprising the school commutiny. These pressures are visited on teachers as well.

To perform this role even adequately well requires both knowledge about the makeup of the school community and about how best to communicate with community members. It is increasingly apparent that the strongest support base for the school is "grass roots" in nature, but there are seemingly infinite varieties of grass to be found in the lawns of many school communities. Moreover, it isn't only parents who feel they have a vested interest in schooling practices.

Also, one need not be a graduate sociologist to be aware of the impact such phenomena as technocracy, urbanization, and the increasing complexity of social relationships have had on the nature of interaction between school and community. The increasing esostericism of professional educational practices, a concomitant of these changes, has widened the gap between school and community. The dissolution of the small, closely knit communities of years past has made schools and the people in the area unsure of the other. The same situation obtains in the medical and legal professions as well as other welfare delivery agencies that attempt to address the varied and complex needs of people who live in a community. The term *community* has been corrupted to simply mean groups of people living in close proximity and served by many of the same social and governmental agencies.

Described in the first part of the chapter are differing orientations that individuals and groups of individuals—organized and unorganized—may have about the schools serving their communities. Also examined is the nature of certain influence patterns and the effect these may have on the operation of the schools. In the second part of the chapter, the focus is on ways to communicate more effectively with the publics that constitute the community.

The School in the Complex Community: The Impact of the Gesselschaft Society

Our society is characterized by multiethnicity and cultural pluralism, and this age is characterized generally by criticism and skepticism about public agencies and the efficiency with which these agencies dispatch services. Thus, the particular need for the development of better mechanisms to provide for effective communication between the school and the community is glaringly apparent.

There is ideological unity in a "real" community. A *real community* is a community that reflects well-understood belief structures and mores, is relatively independent from other communities, has a common bonding, and is made up of individuals who manifest a personal sense of identity with the community that is eternal and true for all other members. This type of community is described as *sacred* in orientation and carries the label *gemeinschaft*. It doesn't describe very many places in the western world today.

What does describe life in most western world communities today is the term *gesselschaft*. In the gesselschaft community, people are unified largely by civil units rather than by kinship ties. There is a great division of labor and proliferation of organizations, each with special membership and interests. Formal social controls are set by law and enforced by various civil agencies. In such communities there is a basic anonymity and people may live *in* the community without being *of* the community. This is the *secular* community, and in this community there may be much conflict.

Few things that have to do with human society can be unerringly assigned. When one thinks of gemeinschaft and gesselschaft, it's more conceptually sound to place these terms at opposite ends of a continuum and think of communities as appearing on various points in between. Where a community lies on the sacred-secular continuum influences the nature of decision-making practices in that community.

One problem in the largely gesselschaft society in which we live, with its evident cultural pluralism, is that various individuals and groups may reflect widely differing points of view and hold diverse perceptions of what the institutions serving their particular location ought to look like and ought to be doing. The politics of confrontation and conflict within which the school and other social institutions are often caught up is simply a manifestation of this.

The school is the closest community agency to residents, in both a literal and figurative sense. In geographic proximity, the school is "just around the corner" and often becomes the first line of communication with the area served. It is closer than the mayor's office; in most cases it is even closer than the fire station. And, the school affects mightily the community's most prized possessions—its children and its pocketbook. It should not be surprising then that the schools are frequently the subject of perusal and subsequent criticism, and if sometimes the result of the perusal is more visceral than cerebral, then administrators need to be nonroutine in their response patterns.

Informal Community Forces

Influence and power are distributed unevenly throughout communities. Moreover, informal power must be distinguished from formal power. Formal power is manifest in the elected and appointed governmental offices of the community—the mayor, city council, police chief, superintendent, and board of education, for example. *Informal power* refers to the ability of various individuals or groups to get certain things done in the community in a way that is satisfying to the individual or group. It may refer to individuals who are at or near the top of their respective social or occupational hierarchies. It may also refer to groups that are composed of, or individuals who represent, members of various special-interest groups, and who, on any given issue, mobilize substantial portions of the population to respond in a particular way.

The ability to influence is dependent on the presence of two elements: substantial resources and commitment *Substantial resources* does not necessarily mean control of large sums of dollars: it may simply mean the control of large groups of people. People are a resource. Most of the early civil rights successes were characterized by displays of latent power and were conducted without huge sums of money, relatively speaking.

Commitment refers to a singular belief in the basic rightness of whatever it is that is being proposed (i.e., the group "hangs together" no matter what), and when coupled with control of some resources, a formidable force is present.

Neighborhood Influence Systems

As communities have become more and more complex and sources have become diffused, neighborhood influence systems have become increasingly important. Such influence systems often reflect racial, ethnic, religious, or economic homogeneity.

Neighborhood influence systems may be especially important in the principal's sphere of interaction. We noted earlier that the individual school building remains, in most places, the closest community agency, certainly in terms of geographic proximity. Thus, it is handy, if nothing else, to members of the immediate neighborhood who have opinions to express. However, school personnel, and especially the principal, are also in an excellent position to feel the pulse of the surrounding area, and to interact directly with that group.

Individual schools need to develop effective mechanisms to receive information from, and to dispense information to, neighborhood leadership. Research suggests that an individual community member's decision to support or not support any particular community issue is more often than not based on the influence of friends and neighbors rather than on the presence of any outside objective data. It would seem, therefore, that the school principal should become familiar with the leadership structure of the neighborhood the individual school may serve.

Every social group has a leadership structure that, with diligence, can be identified. Such a structure represents the best thinking of the social group. This rich resource can be capitalized on.

There is a leadership structure in any community or neighborhood, except the most anomic. This structure may be readily identified, often through reputational means by surveying the "store-front" churches as well as the well-known churches, the local welfare agencies, the better *and* less well known social clubs, and the membership of union locals, among any number of other somewhat formal sources. If a community is characterized by heterogeneity in racial, ethnic, or social makeup, more than the usual effort will be required because well-known organizations may not reflect this heterogeneity. Further, a neighborhood leadership structure may not be composed of, or contain very many, people who are also parents of children attending the schools.

Old mechanisms will not suffice for the principal interested in developing effective school-community relations programs based on mutual trust and a willingness to examine issues of mutual concern. Traditional community groups often do not have a membership composed of anything approximating the real nature of the community or the neighborhood served by the schools, and there may exist a leadership structure that has not yet been recognized but that has important things to say about schools. An examination of the membership of local, formal parent-teacher organization and a comparison of certain characteristics of these people with general demographic characteristics of the student body of the school may reveal that certain groups of people are missing. If different kinds of people are missing, one can be sure that many key neighborhood influentials are not being reached by school messages.

Community Groups

The most intense memberships are held in groups that can be classified as *blut und bod*. These are groups with kinship and territorial bonds rooted in certain ethnic, racial, or historical ties.

> *A common language, a common dietary, a common neighborhood, common experience with outsiders, a common history, make people feel more comfortable with one another, more at ease. They understand one another, they read one another; they get one another's messages. They feel they can count on one another for support. They constitute an in group; everyone else is an out group.*
>
> The bonds that hold people together also separate them from others; *invisible lines are drawn to protect the boundaries between them and outsiders (emphasis added).*[1]

Moreover, people in the community are also often members of an array of different formal and informal groups that may impinge on the schools. They are members of clubs and associations, some *blut und bod* in nature, characterized by such self-help groups as, for example, the American Indian Movement, the League of United Latin American Citizens, the NAACP, or the National Organization of Women. People belong, as well, to unions and professional associations, to political parties, and to neighborhood improvement leagues. All of these organizations demand loyalty from their members and may from time to time oppose certain school system procedures, policies, and practices. Membership in what at times may be adversary groups can be the source of much community-school conflict. In addition, the rapid change in many school attendance areas may intensify the problem of communication and school responsiveness.

Pressure Groups

No discussion of community influence systems would be complete without some attention to the nature of pressure groups. Pressure groups can be distinguished from the usual community decision-making systems because of the relatively short-lived nature of their activities and their tendency to form and re-form around issues or causes. Often, a group will form because of a specific decision made by the school leadership which is perceived to have an impact on the certain group's life space or belief system.

Pressure groups should not be dismissed lightly. They are a source of great disruption in many communities and sometimes a source of productive change. It is difficult to put the term *pressure group* in a non inflammatory context. Immediately, thoughts of book burnings, witch hunts, placard-carrying demonstrators, and impassioned pleas from the pulpit or the podium come to mind. One may also imagine school boards and superintendents hastily capitulating to the onslaught of such charges that the schools are "godless"; that the English department is assigning lascivious literature: and that sex education is corrupting our youth; among a host of similar kinds of charges, emotion-ridden in context and within which rational behavior often is nearly impossible.

But a pressure group may also be composed of parents arguing persuasively for the return of an art program. It may be a collection of citizens raising important issues of equity or insisting on balanced reporting in textbooks about the contributions of minorities. It may be a group raising questions about district employment practices or the lack of bilingual programs; or insisting that a district or school provide wheelchair access to a building. Most of the legislation and court orders ensuring or extending rights at local, state, and national levels have occurred because, early on, a small group of concerned citizens organized to call attention to an undesirable situation.

It is clearly the right of citizens to protest when they feel that the school is failing to accomplish the right thing. The wise school administrator looks at community opinion as an invaluable source of information.

Conflict may not be inevitable, but it is frequent in any society. Conflict is also not necessarily disruptive or negative. Often, it is out of conflict that greater understanding results, provided the situation is characterized by openness, a willingness to compromise, and well-understood and agreed-upon procedures for resolution.

Negotiating with Pressure Groups

From time to time, all school administrators will be confronted with requests from organized groups of people who represent a particular point of view about a school-related issue. Frequently, such pressure groups begin their inquiries at the school level in the principal's office. The issues may run the gamut, from complaints about teachers, textbooks, or specific courses of study to alleged institutional racism and demands for more equitable staffing or pupil assignment decisions. These are often legitimate concerns, but legitimate or not, they must always be dealt with sensitively and sensibly.

The following guidelines may help a besieged principal:

1. *Identifying.* An early identification should be made of the group that is in opposition to, or is likely to be in opposition to, certain school programs. Who are they? More importantly, who are the leaders?

2. *Discussing.* Can the leaders be talked with? Once the opposing group and the leader(s) of that group have been identified, it is appropriate to engage in a closed-door session to explore the elements of the issue. The administrator may gain a more definitive notion of just what it is that is troubling the group. This meeting or series of meetings may result in ways, if the cause is legitimate, for the school to help the group achieve its goals. It may require great insight to find out what the real issue is because stated "reasons" for opposition to this or that school issue are often at variance with the real causative factors. (At this point, it is also important to apprise the central office of the potential hostile situation and to seek counsel.)

3. *Analyzing.* Following the informal meetings, it is important to reach a decision. Some important points must be considered at this time, including the question of how strong the opposition really is. Do they have a good chance to "beat" the school in its present position? Most importantly, do they have a solid point on which to differ with the school? It is at this time that the decision must be made about whether the issue will be fought on the basis of the initial position of both sides or whether some accord is possible.

In all situations, it is important to determine what the real goal is and what results or gains can be expected from the achievement of that goal. In other words, is the school's position or is the school administrator's position tenable? If so, evidence must be present to substantiate why it is tenable. Many school administrators have ended up in hot water because of a refusal to negotiate or compromise or because of an unwillingness to give up irrelevant points of contention.

4. *Negotiating.* Is there room for compromise? The political system under which a democracy operates functions on compromise. Politics is the delicate art of compromise. Desirable changes can be achieved without compromising principles and without loss of integrity.

Of course, compromising may not be necessary. Perhaps simply sitting down with members of the pressure group and explaining the school's position and the facts may dissuade the group from further action. However, administrators who have engaged in community conflict situations over the years would suggest that compromise and negotiation is the more likely process. The pressure group's motives may be highly complex. Its needs and goals are every bit as important to its membership as are the needs and goals of the particular administrator or school system in question.

In any effort to influence or achieve compromise, timing is important. One really can't wait until an organized campaign is under way to effect compromises or modify points of view. The time to influence a pressure group is before the particular group has launched its initial fusillade and before school personnel are totally and publicly committed to a position. Common sense suggests that it is increasingly difficult to change someone or some group when there will be much loss of face, real or imagined, by doing so.

5. *Marshaling Resources.* Seek help from other community members. Assuming that all efforts to negotiate with the opposition are unsuccessful, what does the administrator try next? The first step is to find out who is on the school's side, or who it appears ought to be on the school's side. Some community analysis can be conducted even at this stage and may prove fruitful. Who besides the school really stands to lose? Principals should not forget about other less-organized neighborhood groups of people who, though they seemingly may have a low potential for power, might have a high potential for unity on the particular issue and who could be called on for counsel and other help.

Evaluating the Legitimacy of the Critic

Members of the community have the right to legitimately question and criticize the schools, although defining the word *legitimate* in this context is difficult. One of the best benchmarks for judging legitimacy is to observe the behavior exhibited by the particular group. Is the group willing to meet with appropriate educational system personnel out of the harsh glare of TV lights or without benefit of newspaper rhetoric? Is the group willing to consider other sides of the issue? Is criticism mostly characterized by reason and rationality, or does it seem mostly emotional in nature? Will the critics accept demonstrable facts? If these conditions are not met then one may question the "legitimacy" of the critic and prepare for battle.

Implications for the School Principal

School leaders need to identify the influential people and groups in the community or neighborhood. Power structures and influence systems vary from community to community and neighborhood to neighborhood. There is an indeterminacy and amorphousness about power structures and influence systems. The degree to which various leaders in a community are able to agree on a direction formal schooling ought to take, and the degree to which they are able to accept certain principles and guidelines, will determine in great part the extent of reform, modification, and growth of the educational institution in the community.

The Need for Well-Developed Policies

If conflict can be expected on educational issues, if ideological unity is not characteristic of very many complex communities, and if criticism can be expected as a part of the normal life of the administrator of any public institution, what can be done to modify the divisive effects of such actions and instead capitalize on the rich diversity of views and opinions to improve the schools? Foremost is to provide a broad set of policies, both at the school district level as well as at the school building level, that establish a framework within which diverging views can be heard in a regular and systematic manner. Such a framework provides, in effect, procedural due process whereby dissident factions in a community can formally register their concerns.

Figure 4–1 is a sample form that some districts provide to those individuals who are objecting to the use of certain educational material. Such a complaint form could be adapted to other issues and, if used judiciously, provide a vehicle for citizens to make their views known in a rational and systematic way.

Working with Review Boards

Individual principals would be wise to establish some kind of review body on whom the principal could rely for advice, counsel, and the development of criteria for judging potentially controversial instructional materials. The importance of involving an array of appropriate personnel in the development of policies to anticipate problems is important because it provides the basis for information sharing and good decision making. Principals cannot be expected to know everything. No principal should expect to be able to respond instantaneously to a critic. The advice and counsel of the school staff, as well as the community, and the development of broadly based policies and policy review boards are needed to provide for effective decision making and intelligent responses to questions that may issue from the community.

Working with Other Community Agencies

Many community agencies and organizations in addition to schools have—or could have—an impact on the quality of children's lives. The school principal is in an uncommonly good position to coordinate the efforts of these agencies.

It often happens that the principal serves in that role anyway because the elementary school is most often the closest social agency available to patrons. And, patrons

FIGURE 4–1 Citizen's Request for Reconsideration of Educational Medium

Title of medium _____

   Type of medium: (circle)

     Book   Film   Filmstrip   Recording _____
                                               (other)

   Author/artist/composer/other _____

   Publisher/producer (if known) _____

Request initiated by _____   Phone_____

Address _____

Complainant represents_____

_____   Self

_____   (Name of organization) _____

_____   (Identify other group) _____

  1. After having read/viewed/listened to the item in question, to what do you object, and why? (Please be specific; cite pages, frame, other)

      _____

  2. What do you believe is the theme of this item? _____

      _____

  3. What do you feel might be the result of students reading/viewing/listening to this item?

      _____

  4. For what age group would you recommend this item?_____

      _____

  5. Other comments _____

      _____

      _____

   _____   _____

       Date   Signature of Complainant

look to their schools for all sorts of help that has to do with their families' well-being. The "closeness" of the school is for many as much a matter of psychological proximity as it is a physical proximity. Many community members look to the school for help in matters neither of the school's doing nor jurisdiction simply because they know of no other place to turn.

The sad fact is that in our complex society the important and varied welfare delivery agencies often operate in a most uncoordinated way. Principals frequently find themselves dealing with court orders, child protective services, police departments, city and state health and human services departments, and businesses and industries in an effort to help just one particular child or family. Sometimes these agencies even conflict with each other in their efforts and in their policies.

We are not aware of any administrator training programs that specifically prepare principals for this "add-on" role. But it is there, and while it may not be a part of the job description, effective principals recognize the importance of developing good contacts with these outside agencies and providing referral and follow-up services to their patrons who may be in need.

Developing close relationships with the police department, for example, to assist in such programs as Drug Abuse Resistance Education (DARE), where police officers work in the schools, only makes good sense. Becoming personally connected with child protective services directors and counselors among other welfare delivery agencies will pay rich dividends. Business partnerships such as "adopt-a-school" can provide enriched educational offerings as well as create an intimate involvement of the private sector in community service and an important support base.

Formal Community Forces

Agencies at all three levels of government exert influence and control over the formal education system, often in direct prescriptive and regulatory ways. Even though locally managed and substantially supported by locally assessed taxes, as established by the law, public school districts are really state institutions; school boards of education members are state officers. In practice, of course, the support and control of the public school systems in this nation are vested in federal, state, intermediate, and local governments. A kind of partnership thus exists, although the nature and role of the partners vary among the states.

In the federal system of the U.S. government education is a function of the separate states. Of course, no state may provide for a school system that violates the constitutional rights of citizens.[2] The U.S. Constitution itself is strangely quiet about education. The state receives its authority to operate and control public education within its boundaries through the enactment of the Tenth Amendment to the U.S. Constitution.[3] Thus, the education system is established under powers reserved to the states, and the manner in which the system is maintained is a plenary responsibility of the state. Private and parochial schools also operate under the aegis of the states.

All of the state constitutions specifically provide for public school systems. The legal basis on which the schools are conducted and maintained may be found in state constitutional and statutory law and in the body of common law as it is established by judicial decisions. Opinions written by state attorneys general also affect the operation of the schools until such time as these might be set aside by statute or by the judiciary.

Several trends in school district organization that are in response to societal change have become evident in the last several years. The establishment of educational cooperatives wherein several independent school districts combine to share specified services while remaining functionally independent is one such development. In this type of arrangement usually undertaken by several smaller school districts, the local district remains relatively independent while enjoying some of the benefits of a larger school unit.

Other trends include the development of school district units by region rather than by county civil division and the decentralization of larger urban districts into smaller administrative units to encourage better communication with, and more responsiveness to, the immediate community being served. The establishment of *magnet schools* has also been a phenomenon. Magnet school operation creates especially complex community-school relations problems because of a widely dispersed school population.

A current trend of some importance is the formal establishment of school advisory councils, sometimes composed of teachers and community members, sometimes composed of only one or the other. Where not mandated by law, these are often created by district school boards acting in response to community demand. This organizational framework is an aspect of the school-based management movement.

The Local Board of Education

The policymaking body of a school district is the board of education. The board of education is a corporate and political body and has the power expressly and implicitly given to it by statute. In many communities, members of the board of education are elected by the people in the communities that they serve; others have appointed boards of education. The method of the selection of members for the lay governing boards of private and parochial schools varies widely.

Irrespective of the method by which members are selected, the duties of the school board are both legislative and quasi-judicial. The local school board has great latitude in daily operation of the schools, subject always, of course, to constitutional and statutory limitations.

The size of boards varies considerably both within states as well as between the various states. Although uncommon, some local school boards have as many as 17 members. Legal requirements for school board membership are minimal, usually including no more than such prerequisites as being a registered voter in the district, being nominated for the office, and being elected. Age requirements are common, and certain people often may not serve on a board of education if they hold some other governmental position that would be deemed to be a conflict of interest.

State Education Agencies

Within the limitations of a particular state constitution, the state's legislature has wide power to determine the purposes and the procedures for the subordinate levels of the education hierarchy. Usually, however, the laws issuing from the state legislature deal with general powers and purposes, leaving specific implementation to a state education agency and various intermediate and local school systems. The state education agency, or state department of education, itself is a creature of the legislature and is imbued with certain discretionary powers.

There are a vast number of other state agencies that have some influence on various aspects of the school systems in a state. In order to carry out various legislative and constitutional provisions about education, any number of other boards of control exist, including controlling boards for higher education, vocational education, tenure, retirement and similar activities. These are all in addition to a state board of education, which exists to determine policies that are then implemented by the state education agency. There are a variety of agencies concerned with budgeting, accounting, building standards, health, school lunches, library services, civil defense, and myriad other activities in which the schools, along with many other of the public welfare delivery systems, engage. In short, although the local school system is often viewed as an autonomous unit, it is subject to the controls and impingements from an array of other legally established community and state agencies.

All states have a chief state school officer who may be known as commissioner of education, state superintendent of schools, or, a similar title. The number, term, and method of selection of State Board of Education membership varies. Similarly, the method by which the state superintendent is selected varies.

Federal Influences on Education

Even though the U.S. Constitution is silent about a public education system, it is clear to even a casual observer that the role of the federal government has developed from one of "silence" to active shared responsibility, with not a little control. The general welfare clause of the U.S. Constitution is most often cited as the constitutional provision that permits federal aid to public education. Federal programs tend to be categorical—that is, for an identified special purpose rather than generalized aid.

Categorical aid and specialized programs result in considerable federal influence and, inescapably, restrictions. Few would quarrel with the intent behind PL94-142, the Education for All Handicapped Children Act, or with the legislation that resulted in the Occupational Safely and Health Act (OSHA),[4] for example. But the implementation of both of these pieces of legislation has not been without some administrative frustration. At times, positive legislative intent gets caught up in a maze of rules that seem to inhibit rather than facilitate. Nevertheless, the school administrator's task is to make it work the way it was intended to work.

The federal interest has also resulted in the use of the schools as a tool for major social reform. This can best be exemplified by the 1954 Supreme Court decision in *Brown* v. *Board of Education of Topeka* in which the Supreme Court determined that "separate but equal" state provisions and *de jure* segregated educational systems in the United States were unconstitutional. The federal interest is pervasive, and while it rises or declines in emphasis—depending on the philosophic stance of the executive and legislative branches of government—it nevertheless impinges greatly on the direction that local systems take.

In sum, then, the governance of education reflects the structural characteristics of the federal system of government. Each level of the government has its own areas of responsibility and autonomy. All of the levels interface, however, and there is both mutual obligation and dependence. Congress authorized many educational programs for those purposes that have been deemed to be especially important to the national interest. The U.S. Constitution itself grants to the states the responsibility for providing for public education; in turn, the states have delegated many of their powers to the local school district, while at the same time maintaining a vast number of regulatory controls over various aspects of the school operation, particularly in fiscal and program matters.

The previous sections have established a contextual base. It is to the subject of the relationship of the publics to their specific schools that we now turn. In the final part of this chapter, the focus is on school public relations practices and techniques. The subject is how principals can build a solid citizen support base and communicate effectively with school patrons.

Promising Public Relations Techniques: Dealing with the Formal and Informal Forces

No one is in a better position to have a positive impact on the relationship between the school system and the community than the principal and the building staff. No single school district person is in a position to interact in person with greater numbers of community members than the principal. A district may spend huge sums of money on slick publications and a well-functioning, centrally located community relations office headed by a public information officer, but it is the principal who can be more influential on a day-to-day basis with individual school patrons. Even in this mass media environment it is still the face-to-face encounter that provides the best basis for understanding and is the most influential in molding public opinion.

The greatest opportunity to influence and persuade, and to hear and feel the community pulse, occurs in the more intimate and often face-to-face settings likely to occur at the building level. Nevertheless, although this portion of the chapter will focus on public relations at the building level, some attention will be given to districtwide public relations activities as well.

School-community communication endeavors may take several forms, any one of which has limitations. A high-quality, school-community relations program will make use of a variety of media, and an alert principal will tailor the particular message to be conveyed to the appropriate medium.

Getting the Message Out: One-Way Public Relations Techniques

There are numerous ways to broadcast a message from the school. Cooperative endeavors involving the print and electronic media, building or system-developed newsletters and brochures, and even the routinely sent report card can all be put to effective use. These are, however, one-way devices; there is little or no way to know if the messages was either received or understood.

Print and Electronic Media

Few communities are not served by at least a weekly newspaper, and no community is outside the reach of radio and television. These mass media are commonly used to impart information about the various agencies serving the community.

Newspapers vary from weekly or biweekly advertisers, with perhaps a few columns reporting highly localized activities, to urban dailies with several editions. Depending on the kind of newspaper, a principal's role will vary from writing news releases that will be published mostly word for word to meeting with news reporters who will recast the stories in their own words.

In any case, the development of good relations with the working press is essential. Reporters or editors will ask principals for information about developing stories or news items more often than for stories containing general information about what's going on in the schools.

The news media have their problems, too. Newspapers and television stations are businesses, with advertising to sell, bills to pay, and subscribers to satisfy. Some people are surprised to learn that 30 percent or less of newspaper space is devoted to stories and 70 percent or more to advertising. This percentage affects the amount of school news that will get printed. Moreover, news editors deal with many other agencies and pressure groups, each championing various causes or matters for the "public good," so there is competition for available space.

Also, it is a frequent complaint of reporters that schools tend to engage only in "gold-star" story writing. The charge is that many school administrators are only too eager to publicize praiseworthy news items but will back away from or become upset about legitimate adverse criticism. An adverse story *is* legitimate news, and when such a story breaks, the school official and the newspaper both have a job to do. Covering up a weakness or refusing to respond to a legitimate inquiry about a potentially embarrassing situation can only lead to bad press relations and a widening credibility gap.

Techniques for Dealing with the Mass Media

News releases need to be developed in a way that conforms to the requirements of the different media. Releases for radio and television must be shorter, more repetitious, and in a style that is more conversational than that used for newspapers.

Relationships with representatives of the various media, as well as district policy, will determine whether the person releasing the news concentrates on writing and distributing releases or on furnishing suggestions and information to journalists who in turn write their own material. In urban settings with large dailies and "live eye" television, reporters generally write their own stories but do need to be advised about promising sources, fast-breaking news, upcoming events, and policy changes. They also need to be provided with good "backgrounding."

In small towns and cities and in suburban and rural districts, local news will generally be disseminated by an array of daily, biweekly, and weekly newspapers, ranging from mini-versions of the large city dailies to four-page advertisers. In many of these places, a school official will frequently write an entire story with little assistance from an editor. The stories should be accurate, short, and written in an attention-getting fashion.

Articles and stories about scheduled events should be prepared well in advance, with photographs of speakers or others involved in the program provided to the news media *before* the event occurs. Often, as a matter of policy, newspapers will not print information about a past event. Follow-up reports should be prepared for the media as soon as possible after an event The school principal should know the various media deadlines. Missing a deadline will mean the story may never get printed.

Increasingly, even small school systems are employing public information officers to facilitate and coordinate the flow of information from school to community. The duties vary, and in some school systems the job may be only part time. Even where the job is full time and the public relations program well developed, for most of the public and the mass media, it is still the principal who will be sought as the prime source of fast-breaking news, and in time of crisis. Figure 4–2 contains eight practices to facilitate a good working relationship with representatives of the media.

District Policy Considerations

The latitude a principal has with the press will depend in great part on the press policy of the school district. News media personnel, however, are most sensitive to what they perceive to be censorship and normally respond negatively to the suggestion that every story or every interview must be cleared with the central office. A policy that requires all school personnel to refer reporters and editors to the central office rather than answer questions, or that sends the news media to the central office for all information will damage press relations, if rigidly enforced. Obviously, fast-breaking news items of a potentially explosive nature will require discretion on the part of the school principal.

The public information program needs continual evaluation. It really isn't very valuable to send out large numbers of news releases if few are used, and submitting too much material in an indiscriminate way may result in few stories being published. The lesson is clear: The news media are most impressed by articles that contain only timely and worthwhile information. These will stand the best chance of getting reported.

School News Items File

There are many missed opportunities to get the school before the public in a positive way. The typical school is a beehive of activity, much of which would be of interest to one segment or another of the public. The difficulty is that many schools have no cen-

FIGURE 4–2   Working with the Media

- Give reporters story ideas and information but remember it is editors and news directors who decide what should be covered.

- Be aware of when reporters' deadlines fall and balance the time of releases so that morning and afternoon papers get an equal share.

- Articles about scheduled events need to be prepared well in advance and any photographs submitted at the same time.

- Releases for radio and television usually must be shorter, more repetitive, and in a more conversational style than those for the print medium.

- Avoid provoking reporters with "no comment" types of statements. Help reporters write potentially adverse stories by giving complete information and backgrounding.

- Anticipate the reporter's needs and have any background information written ahead of time for distribution. (Don't trust that a "general beat" reporter knows very much about schooling.)

- Avoid jargon and "in-house" language; it may not be understood especially by a "general beat" reporter.

- Invite newspersons—reporters and their editors—to the school for lunch and periodic tours without trying to sell them on a story at the time. Get them acquainted with the school scene.

tral place where ongoing activities are recorded. Thus, when a reporter calls or an editor requests a story, media needs often cannot be adequately met.

An especially effective practice is the use of a School News Item File, depicted in Figure 4–3. Many activities in the school are probably newsworthy, but without encouragement and facilitation, they will otherwise go unreported. Each staff member should have a supply of the news item forms to jot down those projects that might be especially interesting, and on a regular basis these forms should be sent to the principal's office. The principal can then file the reports in a folder labeled according to the kind of project, and a news reporter can simply review the files, selecting any particular items to follow up. This helps both the reporter, whose responsibility it is to find news, and the principal, whose responsibility it is to provide news but not necessarily to write the story.

Newsletters and Bulletins

Frequently, the principal and the school staff will attempt to communicate with the home and outside agencies through newsletters and bulletins. These can be useful if employed judiciously and if well done. But a bad message is conveyed when a newsletter arrives home crumpled in the pocket of a student, hard to read, and containing out-of-date information. If newsletters and bulletins are to be employed, the format should be simple, the information conveyed should be written concisely, it should be free of educational jargon, and the method of getting these messages home should be

Type of News Item:

_____ Curriculum Project
_____ Activities of Staff
_____ School Awards
_____ Student Activities (field trips, special recognition, etc.)
_____ New or Interesting Instructional Techniques
_____ Continuing Difficult Problems
_____ Other

Title of Project or Item:

Description of Project or Item:

Persons Involved: (how many, and who—names, addresses, titles, etc.)

Dollars Involved and Sources of These Dollars:

Who to Contact for Further Information:

It's news to somebody. Report It!

FIGURE 4–3   School News Item File

via the mail. Newsletters sent home with children often do little but contribute to a neighborhood litter problem. If the newsletter is not produced with care and printed in an attractive manner, it is simply not worth the bother. Care should also be taken to recognize the multilingual nature of many communities.

It is so easy to prepare newsletters and bulletins that appear professional in makeup. There are a number of desktop publishing programs available that are not difficult to learn and will result in an eminently attractive product—complete with graphics. Irrespective of the computer system that is being used in the school, good desktop publishing programs are plentiful.

Report Cards

Report cards are often overlooked as public relations mechanisms, but they are the single-most regular way in which schools desseminate information to the home. Both teachers and parents like them to be uncomplicated. Yet consideration of all of the ways in which a student is growing, developing, and learning defies summing up progress with a single letter grade. Thus, the development of an appropriate reporting procedure will require careful study by the staff and include the use of a faculty-layperson committee to develop a report form that is easy to understand but also contains important kinds of information relative to the student's progress.

If the purpose of a parent reporting system is to develop an effective communication link and if the parents highly values written reports, then the school should use some form of written report card. A written report of grades alone is not adequate, however, and a more personal communication link, such as additional comments written by the teacher on the report card or a parent-teacher conference, should be added.

To effectively report a child's progress, a report card should provide three kinds of information. First, it should estimate the child's overall ability compared to other children the same age. This can be done through standardized tests or the teacher's judgment of the child's ability based on diagnosis and observations. Second, the report card should indicate the child's individual progress. During the elementary and middle grades, this should be based on estimated ability and a measure of the child's achievement in the classroom since the last marking period. This statement is not a comparison to other children but the teacher's estimate of whether the child is achieving as much as possible. The sample report card uses A, B, C, D, F. Finally, the report card describes the child's conduct in school. Conduct maybe rated with a check mark to indicate satisfactory behavior or with a code that indicates outstanding citizenship, satisfactory behavior, or unsatisfactory behavior.

It is much more meaningful to parents if an appropriate one- or two-sentence comment is written by a subject grade to provide parents with more detail regarding the progress of their children. Everyone knows that most teachers don't have the time to manually write a comment by each grade. They will generally do this only for extreme cases. However, with computer-generated report cards, it is possible for the computer to have on file a "comment bank" of commonly used appropriate teacher statements from which teachers may select a statement for each child. A list of 100 or so statements that the teachers themselves created would probably cover most contingencies. All the teacher needs to do is record the appropriate code number under the teacher comment section, and the computer then inserts that statement on the report card.

FIGURE 4–4   The Fog Index

> 1. Find the average number of words per sentence in your written message.
> 2. Count the number of words having three or more syllables.
> 3. Add the two factors above and multiply by 0.4. This will give you the Fog Index. It corresponds roughly to the number of years of schooling a person would require to read the passage with ease and understanding.

The Fog Index

Writing well requires careful consideration of who it is that will be receiving the message. We've called attention to the need to consider the multilingual nature of many school communities, but effectively conveying information in writing requires more than using the native language of the intended receiver; it requires using that language meaningfully. That dictates straightforward sentences, unencumbered nouns and verbs, and common language. Simplicity, lack of clutter, and avoidance of jargon and pedagogical phraseology are required. And this can be done without talking down to people. Newspapers accomplish it daily. To test your messages for ease of understanding, subject them to the Fog Index depicted in Figure 4–4. The messages should not rely on someone having a high school education to understand them. The nearer the messages come to a sixth or seventh-grade level, the better.

    (*Note*: The previous paragraph, when analyzed using the Fog Index, reveals a 13th-grade level. What "did us in" was a few sentences that exceeded 13 words in length. Are we bothered by this? Not much. This is a graduate-school textbook. However, this note rates 5.6. Do you think it "talks down" to you?)

Getting the Message Out and Back:
Two-Way Public Relations Techniques

Information dissemination is not synonymous with *communication*. Because of the failure to make this distinction, many public relations efforts fail. The final part of this chapter is a discussion and description of proven communication techniques.

The Message Was Sent—What Happened?

The *co* in communication means a closed loop. That is, communication means that the message was not only sent *but* that it was received and responded to in a way that indicates it was understood. There are five important questions to ask when examining the quality of information devices:

1. If the message was received, was it read [heard]?
2. If it was read [heard], was it understood?
3. If it was understood, was it understood in the right spirit?

4. If it was understood in the right spirit, will it be acted on in a positive way?
5. How do you know?

An array of communication techniques and structures is available. The remainder of this chapter is a discussion of promising approaches.

Community Advisory Councils

The trend to greater autonomy at the school building level has brought with it increasing use by principals of community advisory councils. In some states, legislation establishing greater school unit autonomy and the concomitant greater principal accountability has also mandated that there be community advisory councils. Parents, teachers, and sometimes students are included in such councils.

Issues often arise about what is *policy advising* and what is *policy making*. Clearly, the reason for having advisory councils is so that there is a formally established way for community and faculty representatives to share information with the principal and suggest alternative approaches to the solution of problems of schooling. In the best of worlds, this provides the principal with additional expertise and useful insights that will result in maximum feasible decisions. Our point is that "advising" is not the same as "decisioning" although it would seem to be a foolish principal who found himself or herself always operating contrary to the advice of the council.

Membership on the Advisory Council
State law or local district policy may prescribe the nature of membership of the council and/or how members are to be selected. Lacking this, it would seem fundamental that members, whether elected or appointed by the principal, should represent a cross-section of the local community.

Achieving Maximum Output from an Advisory Council
Lack of clarity and understanding about the role of council members and about the difference between helping to make policy and policy implementation can become a source of conflict. People work best when they know what the expectations and limitations are. To establish a framework to guide advisory council activities, the school principal should:

1. Establish the essential conditions that any solution, action plan, or policy must meet if it is to be acceptable. That is, are there financial, legal, or district policy considerations that must be taken into account? Are there things that are known to not be in the best interests of learners? Are there things that, in good conscience, the principal would not carry out?
2. Help the group establish a specific time line and a set date for task completion.
3. Indicate what resources are available to the group.
4. Specify what specific outcomes are desired.
5. Establish the limits of the group's authority in the issue at hand. That is, is the principal asking for a final decision, for some alternative decisions, or simply for some advice?

Focus Groups

Research bureaus, professional associations, and advertising agencies, among other organizations, have used focus groups for years to define issues, anticipate problems, explore reactions to potential problems, develop alternative scenarios, and plan leaps into the future. A focus group is an example of a *non probability sampling* technique. The technique employs directional rather than quantitative data and can be used to great effectiveness as both a school public relations technique and a creative problem-solving technique. Focus groups, however, are not decision-making bodies nor are they even advisory bodies. They are groups of community members whose opinions about an issue the principal wants to learn. The purpose is both problem sensing and problem solving, but the problem "sensor" and the problem "solver" is not the focus group. The focus group is to provide feelings, attitudes, and information.

Focus groups are composed of a small number of people—8 to 10 is the recommended number—each group representing a segment of the school-community population. The purpose of meeting with focus groups is to gain an assessment of how people feel about a school-related issue or problem—or anticipated problem. Typically, the meetings last no more than an hour and no more than four questions are asked of the group. A moderator takes notes on the discussion, noting the key concepts, levels of intensity, and new information. Verbatim comments are recorded to the degree possible, absent editing. It is not important that the group meet in the school, and in any given instance, it might be better if it did not. Union halls, church basements, or apartment complex hospitality rooms might be a more convenient and comfortable choice for meetings.

Business and Other Community Partnerships

Many benefits are to be gained from well-organized business/industry/education partnerships. Such benefits include:

- Getting important people engaged in the important work of educating children. For example, in one of the author's cities, the executives of a leading business have developed a training program in ethics and give their top staff released time to work with children in this program; a local psychiatric hospital offers free counseling services to its "adopted school"; a leading manufacturer of computers releases its personnel to work with teachers and students in more effective use of computer technology (and not just in the use of the manufacturer's own computers, either); another business sends school principals to its executive training program; still another employs science teachers in its research and development department during summers and at other times; still others offer in-service programs as well as tutorial services; another provides work opportunities for students who need financial help to stay in school; and the list could go on.
- Helping community leaders better understand the complexities of educating a child and helping them develop an appreciation for the problems and pleasures of teaching.

- Capitalizing on the technical expertise that is available in the community and using that expertise for staff updating as well as for program analysis and student tutoring.

To be maximally effective and to avoid costly misunderstandings, cooperative programs must be well coordinated. Although the principal doesn't need to be the one who manages the program, he or she is responsible for making sure that the program is well coordinated. Figure 4–5 provides guidance for the development of productive school-business partnerships.

Key Communicators

Many principals capitalize on their knowledge of the community influence structure and develop a list of "key communicators." These are the persons to be contacted when there is a need to disseminate information about the school quickly. Key communicators are influential people in the immediate community who have an identified interest in the school. These people are influential because they interact with large numbers of other people and are trusted. A loose organization of such individuals is easily formed. From time to time, the group might meet with the principal and other professionals in the building to discuss what is going on at the school that would be of general community interest. After an initial meeting, the key communicators are kept informed about such things as school budgets, new curricula, teacher turnover, and new construction. The group, as individuals and in collective feedback sessions, keeps the principal informed about "rumblings and rumors" in the community.

This group is simply a collection of important people. As always, care should be taken to see that all dimensions of the school community are tapped. The notion of

FIGURE 4–5   Guidelines for Productive School-Business Partnerships

1. Be certain that the program that is implemented is objective and balanced, and that the goals of the business and the school are compatible. Just because it's "free" doesn't mean it is in the best interests of the students and staff of the school.
2. Focus only on that part of the curriculum about which the business partner has an interest or understands. The key word is *focus*. Businesses can't solve all of the problems of the school, and may have difficulty staying interested in problems that are too broadly based.
3. Don't overlook staff development as a school need. Materials and equipment for the school is good. Instructional assistance is good. Dollars for special projects are good. But so are expertise, materials, and money earmarked for projects that expand the abilities of teachers and administrators. These have a multiplier effect.
4. Appoint a school-based coordinator. More good ideas have been bungled by poor management and bad communication than for any other reason. If it is worth doing, is worth appointing a person with good management and public relations skills to oversee.
5. Give the business partners credit for their efforts. Give praise to your partner at every opportunity and do this publicly and often.

using key communicators capitalizes on communications research which continues to indicate that individual members of a community get most of the information from which attitudes and beliefs are formed in a word-of-mouth fashion—even in this mass media age.

Principal-Organized Interaction Sessions

In effective schools, principals often have regular "tell-it-to-the-principal" interaction sessions. Concerned about establishing and maintaining good relationships with students and parents, principals have initiated two kinds of sessions. One is a student-principal program conducted regularly in the principal's office or over lunch in a more secluded part of the school cafeteria. Attendance is limited to 8 or 10 students. It is important that a representative sample of the students participates. In these open-forum sessions, students express interests and discuss grievances they have, making suggestions about the general improvement of the school.

The same sorts of session can be scheduled for parents and other community members. Patrons are invited to the meeting, with the secretary taking reservations for a dozen or so patrons. Special invitations are necessary to ensure representativeness.

The rules for the meeting are that "anything goes," except personal complaints about individual teachers. (These latter issues must be reserved for private individual sessions.) Two or three hours will provide an opportunity for an informal exchange of ideas. For the principal, it's an excellent sensing mechanism to find out what patrons are concerned about and to get some notion of impending problem situations. For the patrons, it's a good opportunity to learn about the operation of the school and to raise questions about the educational practices.

One of the difficulties in engendering community support is the inadequacy of the information exchange between the school and the home. Organized, yet informal, parent-principal forums help. Complex ideas are difficult to express in the usual one-way bulletins or news stories that frequently serve as major sources of information for parents and other community members. Complex ideas are best tested in a face-to-face setting.

Parent-Teacher Conferences

Planned parent-teacher conferences can be an important element in a school-community relations program. Thought must be given about such things as working parents, one-parent households, a parent's occupation that would preclude attendance at parent-teacher conferences scheduled during the normal school day, the language spoken, and transportation difficulties, among other factors, influencing the success of the endeavor. These and other constraints can be overcome with diligent work on the part of school personnel.

Parent-Teacher Organizations

Historically, a PTA or PTO has served as the main, and sometimes only, organized school outreach program. Principals should use whatever devices are available to facilitate a two-way flow of information, but in the case of parent-teacher organizations, the effectiveness has varied markedly throughout the country.

Nothing good automatically happens just because an organization is labeled in such a way as to suggest a formal relationship with the school. Parent-teacher organizations can provide a useful avenue for interaction between school and community if the meetings are organized to provide an opportunity for both formal and informal interaction and if the organization is given important tasks to perform. The key would seem to be *active involvement in tasks*. Parent organizations, just like other community organizations, are competing for the time of their members. Whether a parent or a teacher elects to spend Thursday evening at a PTO meeting will depend on whether that time is viewed as productively occupied.

A good parent-teacher organization will spend less time meeting formally and more time in subgroups considering important tasks to be performed around the school and the community. Organizing business-industry-education days for the career development program in the school, developing after-school programs for children and adults in the community, recruiting and training paraprofessionals, and working on curriculum review teams are the kinds of activities in which an effective parent-school organization engages.

One common problem that inhibits the usefulness of a parent-teacher organization as a communication device is the unevenness of the membership makeup. Even though the school may serve a heterogeneous population, the active membership is often composed almost entirely of those from only one thread in the societal fabric. Thus, the principal should examine the membership rolls of the parent organization carefully. If these organizations are to be used as effective communication devices and the school community is heterogeneous, a membership that reflects the school community at large becomes most important. If not, then it is likely that important opinions are not being heard and the organization is not serving to promote an information exchange with the broader community.

In those schools that are "magnets" and that draw a substantial number of students from widely dispersed areas, a traditional parent-teacher organization may be difficult to maintain, even with the most intense efforts. Under such a circumstance, energy might be directed more efficiently to other involvement techniques.

Community Surveys

An often overlooked technique is the use of surveys. Surveying community attitudes and opinions can be effective, especially as a school district enters an evaluation phase in an effort to establish or review educational goals, objectives, and priorities. Such a survey can lead to numerous community committees and a revitalization of community involvement in educational policymaking.

Educational surveys may be conducted in a variety of ways. Mailed questionnaires to a random sample of the population living in a particular school attendance area is the most common. A better technique to employ, if the time and person power are available, is to conduct house-to-house interviews using a structured interview technique, calling on a random sample of the population, making sure that all parts of the community are included in the sample. Telephone surveys may also provide a reasonable alternative.

When done right, however, surveys are expensive to conduct. Often, too, the number of responses is disappointingly small—so small or so unrepresentative that the results are unreliable. However, finding out periodically and regularly what community members think is very important. Demographics change—often rapidly, public opinion is fluid, and -good information is essential to good administrative decision making. At the very least, the principal does not want to be blindsided. A crisis rarely occurs without some early indications, unrest, and dissatisfaction. "Be prepared" is a good motto.

Summary

Schools are a part of the greater social system of the community. People in the community have a right not only to be informed about school happenings but also to be engaged in these happenings. If school principals do not use available means to interact with members of the community, the school will become static and unresponsive to changing community and societal needs.

Principals need to analyze their existing public relations activities in light of the community being served. Are there both one- and two-way programs? Is membership and attendance at parent-teacher organizations, "booster groups," or other school organizations representative of the school population? Are there focus groups and advisory committees? Are there partnerships with other agencies?

The skilled principal will analyze the existing public relations program and the community that is to be served. Modifications in the public relations program should be based on that analysis.

Activities

1. Discover and list the kinds of public relations activities in which your school is currently engaged. Do one or two activities seem to be the basis? Are any of these activities "two-way" in nature?

2. Collect some demographic data about the community your school serves and the makeup of the student population. Racial and ethnic data for both the community and the student population will provide a starting point, but go beyond this. Check census tract data. Do a drive-about of the attendance area. Note housing types, dwelling areas, kinds of neighborhoods, and commercial centers both by location and type.

   Examine the rolls of important school groups—advisory councils, PTA/PTO, booster clubs, and so on. To what degree does the active membership in the groups you have identified reflect the nature of the community population and the student population?

   Find a map of the attendance area. Color code the location of the people who are active members of the identified groups. Does this reveal anything that might suggest public relations problems that need to be addressed? Does it suggest that a greater array of techniques needs to be engaged in? What new efforts seem to be suggested?

3. Analyze Case Studies 6, 11, 20, and 22. What approach will you take in these community relations situations? What concepts presented in this chapter might assist you in your analysis?

Endnotes

1. Jesse Bernard, *American Community Behavior* (New York: Holt, Rinehart and Winston, 1965), p. 358. The ideological unity of *blut und bod* groups makes such groups at once powerful forces on any given issue about which they care.
2. See Chapter 5 for a discussion of this issue.
3. "The powers not delegated to the United States by the Constitution, nor prohibited by it to the States, are reserved to the States respectively, or to the people."
4. As with most such social legislation, these two acts came about as a result of much concerted action on the part of informal sectors of society that exerted much pressure for federal action.

Selected Readings

Bagin, Donald, Donald Gallagher, and Leslie Kindred. *The School and Community Relations*, 5th ed. (Englewood Cliffs, NJ: Prentice-Hall, 1994).

Crowson, Robert L. *School-Community Relations, Under Reform* (Berkeley, CA: McCutchan, 1991).

Davis, Donald. "Schools Reaching Out." *Phi Delta Kappan* 72, no. 5 (January 1991): 376–380.

Kowalski, Theodore J. *Public Relations in Educational Organizations* (Columbus, OH: Merrill, 1996).

Owen, Helen. "Is Your School Family-Friendly?" *Principal* 72, no. 2 (November 1992): 5–8.

Saranson, Seymour B. *Parental Involvement and the Political Principle* (San Francisco: Jossey-Bass, 1995).

Wayson, William W., Charles M. Achilles, G. S. Pinnell, M. N. Litz, and Luvern Cunningham. *Handbook for Developing Confidence in Schools* (Bloomington, IN: Phi Delta Kappa Foundation, 1988).

Wilson, C. D., and D. Bailey. "Organizational Correlates of Citizen Participation Effectiveness," *Urban Education* 25, no. 2 (January 1990): 175–194.

Legal Rights and Responsibilities of Students and Staff

The administrator at the building level must be prepared to effectively lead the instructional program while administering a plethora of policies, regulations, state statutes, and federal law.
—*RICHARD D. STRAHAN*[1]

Students, parents, community members, and professional and nonprofessional staff may not always be right but they always have rights. They also have responsibilities. This chapter is about those rights and responsibilities and about the legal framework within which principals must operate to provide at once the lawful and humane school environment.

We do not intend to try to replace with a single chapter the need for aspiring and practicing school administrators to take coursework in school law. But we do intend to establish certain legal bases for the school operation and to examine legal issues with which the principal will most likely have to contend.

Schools have not been unaffected by the seemingly exponential expansion of lawsuits and threats of lawsuits. It is, as one urban principal sighed, "a very litigious world I live in." This statement was uttered just before he left for a court hearing on a teacher dismissal case. Earlier in the year, he had been involved as a named party in a suit alleging that certain practices at his school were in violation of the First Amendment. In both instances, the school's position was upheld but the amount of time required to see the issues through to the end was exhausting. Could either of these events have been avoided? In the particular instances, probably not. But, because the principal knew the laws governing both issues, he was able to operate in a manner that withstood court inquiry.

This chapter, composed of four sections, begins with an analysis of the legal foundation of schools in the United States. Subsequent sections focus on the specific rights and responsibilities of staff and students. Attention is directed to issues of educational equity, including the rights of the disabled, due process, concerns of religious groups, and other matters of tort liability.

Legal Bases for Schools: A Federal, State, and Local Perspective

Historically, schools are creatures of the states, but in practice, the support and control of schools has been a partnership between local, state, and federal governments. Even private and parochial schools and school systems do not exist as autonomous entities, because these too must meet certain state curriculum and teacher certification standards. Too, certain federal regulations impinge when these schools accept available federal funds.

The legal framework within which school systems operate is manifest in the acts passed by federal, state, and local legislative bodies, court decisions, constitutional law, and rules and regulations enacted by regulatory and administrative bodies such as the state departments of education or other governmental departments. A further source of legal guidelines is the opinions of various attorneys general that stand until tested in a court of law or modified by subsequent legislative acts. An extralegal impingement also exists: community sanctions, attitudes, and belief structures that modify, often very directly, the development and implementation of local policies. Within this framework, local administrators have latitude in the development of policies, rules, regulations, and procedures.

Limitations on local authority depend also on prevailing court philosophy in any state. In some states, the prevailing philosophy is that boards of education may adopt any reasonable policy not specifically prohibited by statute. In other states, courts insist that there be specific statutory permission before a particular policy can be adopted. Generally speaking, courts have tended to uphold the rule of reason—that boards of education may adopt any reasonable policy within the law. Courts in all states do insist on strict adherence to laws concerning management of public funds, however. School boards and administrators must find clear statutory authority for the expenditure of funds derived from public revenues.

It is at the school building level that the policies of the school board and the laws governing education are most often implemented. It is also at the school building level that most of the litigation involving the school system begins.

Most of the individual rights enjoyed in this country derive from the Constitution of the United States and are largely located in the first 10 amendments of the Constitution (the Bill of Rights) and in some subsequent amendments, notably the Fourteenth Amendment. Those amendments of special relevance to the operation of schools are:

Amendment One deals with freedom of religion and expression and rights to peaceful assembly and petition. It grants the rights of all citizens to assemble peacefully and to petition the government for redress of grievances. Amendment One has often been cited in civil rights cases involving students.

Amendment Four focuses on the rights of persons and states that the people and property shall be protected against "unreasonable searches and seizures," meaning that appropriate warrants must precede such police action. The educational implications here affect the confidentiality of records, interrogation of pupils, and the proceedings of juvenile court.

Amendment Five guarantees the due process of law. It says that certain rights to life, liberty, and property are inviolate, and that people cannot be deprived of them without due process of law.

Amendment Six provides for judicial procedure and guarantees a speedy public trial, an impartial jury, information about the nature of the charge, confrontation by witnesses against the party, the right of the accused to obtain witnesses in his or her own behalf, and the right to have counsel.

Amendment Eight prohibits cruel and unusual punishment and excessive bail. The educational implications are clear, especially with regard to the question of corporal punishment although undue mental anguish has also been cited as a "cruel and unusual" punishment.

Amendment Nine guarantees the "rights of the people" and states that the enumeration in the Constitution of certain rights shall not be construed to deny or discourage other rights retained by the people. This simply means that even if the Constitution is silent, it does not imply that other rights are not enjoyed.

Amendment Ten indicates that the powers that are not delegated to the United States by the Constitution nor prohibited by it to the states are reserved to the states respectively or to the people.

After the Civil War, the Fourteenth Amendment, the "States' Bill of Rights," was adopted. It states that "no state shall make a law which abridges the rights of citizens in the United States nor deny anyone the equal protection of the law." It states further that all persons, whether born or naturalized in the United States and subject to the jurisdiction thereof, are citizens of the United States and of the state wherein they reside. Thus, each state must guarantee the same rights to its citizens that are guaranteed by the U.S. Constitution. It is important to call attention to the phrase "all persons." The amendment does not say all adults; it says all persons, and that includes children.

The courts have made it clear that constitutional protections apply to students both in and out of school. Freedom of expression and other basic rights, if not always clearly defined in the schools, are well established in the law. As the Supreme Court pointed out in *Tinker* v. *Des Moines School District*, "Students do not surrender their rights at the school house door."[2] Courts require specified procedures to safeguard those rights against the abuse of institutional authority. The matter of procedural due process, which will be discussed more completely later in this chapter, guarantees certain rights by the fair application of rules and regulations.

Nevertheless, even though students do have rights at school, these are balanced against the rights and responsibilities of administrators and teachers to maintain order and provide a good learning climate. The courts have been particularly careful to ensure that the school has the ability to effectively carry out the educational mission.

Application of the Laws

Of course, some rules of law are not universally accepted. Different courts often hand down conflicting decisions in seemingly similar cases, even within the same state. Too, the opinions of attorneys general will vary over the years and between states. At the federal level, a change in the party controlling the executive branch will often affect the rigor and vigor with which an attorney general or the Justice Department interprets and enforces the law.

Legislative acts at both state and federal levels vary from term to term as this or that current concern becomes law, or is countermanded by superseding law, or reaches a "sunset" provision. Also, the interpretation and the application of laws sometimes change over the years.

For these reasons, it is important for the principal to continually keep abreast of new developments on the legal front. This chapter will help, but the legal framework is constantly evolving. Subscribing to a legal update service provided by many of the professional associations, as well as attention to the day-to-day occurrences in one's community and state, is good advice for any educator.

Issues of Equity

Increasing attention has been placed on the need to assure that all persons have equal access to the fruits of education, irrespective of their gender, race, ethnicity, or any disabling condition. A host of laws, often federally generated, have been promulgated and much litigation has occurred in the effort to ensure equity. Of special relevance to the school principal are the laws, court decisions, and educational guidelines with respect to sex discrimination, desegregation, provision of the least restrictive educational environment for students with disabilities, and employment opportunities for people with disabilities who are otherwise qualified.

Gender Discrimination

The issue of gender discrimination has arisen in both academic matters and cocurricular matters. More frequently in recent years, issues of gender discrimination have been located in the cocurricular realm.

In academic matters, gender discrimination has been found to occur most often in class assignments and admission to programs or schools. Gender has been determined to be an illegal criterion for assignment and admission. It has been held also to be a violation of the equal protection clause of the Fourteenth Amendment to use higher admission standards for females than for males for admission to an academic school. The circuit court, in *Berkleman* v. *San Francisco Unified School District*,[3] said that merit is the only sound basis for admission, not such "unsupported" needs suggested by the school district officials' position that "an equal number of male and female students is an essential element in a good high school education."[4]

Nevertheless, the "separate but equal" concept with regard to schools for boys and girls is still viable where a school district (or any educational unit) can show that genuinely equal educational opportunities are provided students in these schools, when these schools are compared to all other schools or units in the system.[5] The burden of proof is on the school system, however.

In some schools, too, females have been excluded from certain specialized vocational and prevocational courses. This practice has been challenged, and in most such cases, women were admitted to the courses before the cases came to trial. Clearly, even though there is little in the way of case law, such exclusion practices are contrary to the current thrust of the law. Unless the school administrator or the school board can show some rational basis for excluding one gender or the other from a course or program, there should be no policy that would differentiate the enrollment. It is doubtful that such a basis could be developed; few human activities are physiologically determined.

Most of the recent litigation focusing on gender discrimination has had to do with participation in cocurricular activities, specifically participation in athletic competition. Title IX of the Education Amendments of 1972 (PL 92-318) is a bulwark against gender discrimination in the cocurricular realm. Title IX established, among other things, that organized athletic programs in the public schools must be accessible irrespective of the gender of the aspirant.

There are two situations in which claims have arisen. The first is the failure of a school district to fund and provide a team for a specific sport for its female students, and then, while not providing a team, also prohibiting females from participating on the team it does have. The issue in these cases is not whether a female has a constitutional right to participate in a particular sport but whether the state, having provided an athletic program, can deny an opportunity to participate to members of one gender. The asserted protective purpose in maintaining separate teams is frequently stated this way: Girls cannot compete effectively with boys in sports because of the inherent physical differences between the sexes; thus, it is argued frequently, separate teams are reasonable and indeed even necessary. Several courts have accepted this conclusion but have held that they could not sanction a failure to provide a separate athletic program for girls.[6]

Separate but equal athletic programs are also statutory law in section 86.41 of Title IX(B), "Administration of Athletics." But, there is a provision that states if a school district does not fund and offer separate athletic programs, it must allow members of the excluded sex to try out for the team it does have, unless the "sport involved is a contact sport."

Some courts have determined that even in cases of contact sports, a school must allow a girl to participate if there is no girls' team. For a school to maintain different teams for boys and girls, the reason for the disparity in treatment must be "substantially related" to the achievement of an important government objective; however, "overbroad and archaic" generalizations about differences in the genders are not acceptable.[7]

When a school attempts to use safety as a rationale for forbidding coeducational teams, the school must show that there is a sufficient relationship between the announced goal of safety and a rule that would automatically exclude one gender.[8] Accordingly, girls must be given the opportunity to demonstrate that the presumption they are more prone to be injured is invalid. "They must be given the opportunity to compete with boys in interscholastic contact sports if they are physically qualified."[9]

Elementary and Secondary Education Act (Reauthorization)

The reauthorization of ESEA contains some new wrinkles, most of which focus on expanding educational equity. Title I (formerly Chapter 1) has been redesigned to address the National Education Goals in a more specific manner. Addressed is the belief that all students can achieve high standards of excellence and that local districts should have greater flexibility in designing programs to increase achievement.

The funding formula for Title I has been revised to target more dollars to schools with the highest concentration of poverty. Equally important is the new provision that permits schools to use Title I money to upgrade the entire school's educational program. Title I money may be combined with other resources, as well. Under the provisions, by 1996–1997, a school may develop a program to include the entire school *if* 50 percent or more of its students come from low-income families.

Among other provisions are grants for projects designed to focus on the unique problems of urban and rural schools with high-poverty populations. The projects must focus on ways to close the achievement gap between disadvantaged students and students in more affluent areas.

Providing for the Disabled: "The Inclusion Revolution"

Public schools historically have been involved in the education of youngsters who are disabled, but in the last several years, such activities have taken on a more precise and legally defined basis. Legislation culminating with the Education of All Handicapped Children Act of 1975 (PL 94-142) has mandated the provision of the "least restrictive learning environment" for children who are disabled. Public Law 94-142 provides for ready access to appropriate public education for these children between the ages of 3 and 21 and mandates the integration of these children into settings that formerly may have been limited to nondisabled children. The term *mainstreaming* has been applied to this practice.

PL 94-142 is buttressed by other federal laws: PL 94-143, the earlier PL 93-112, and more recently, the Individuals with Disabilities Education Act (1990), which have established certain rights to education and fair treatment for children with disabilities.[10] These rights include:

- Right to a free appropriate education at public expense, without regard to severity of disability
- Right to service in the least-restrictive setting when the disability requires service in something other than the normal school setting
- Right to prior notice before any decision is made to change services given to a child
- Right of parents to give consent before their child is evaluated, placed in a special program, or changed in placement
- Right to full due process, including representation by legal counsel, right to confront and cross-examine school personnel, right to a verbatim transcript, right to appeal, and right to be heard by an impartial hearing officer (not a school employee)

- Right to assignment without discrimination on the basis of sex, race, or culture
- Right to program placement without discrimination on the basis of sex, race, or culture, and to placement in a facility that is comparable to that offered to nondisabled clients of the system
- Right to be served in accordance with an individual program plan that states annual goals, measurable intermediate steps, the names of persons who will provide services and their qualifications, a timetable for beginning each step in the service and its anticipated duration, a schedule for evaluating the success of the program, and the right to be transferred if the program is failing
- Right to be protected from harm through the use of unregulated experimental approaches, untrained staff, inclusion in a program with others who are physically assaultive, freedom from unreasonable corporal punishment, and freedom from work assignments without compensation
- Right to see all records and to contest them in a hearing, with the right to place in the record information that the client feels presents a balanced picture

Thus, "separate but equal" as a concept appropriate to the education of children with disabilities has been found to be generally unacceptable.

The passage of PL 94-142 was the culmination of many years of litigation and legislation to protect the civil rights of children who are disabled. The legislative act ensures specified substantive and procedural provisions for such children, as well as an escalating funding formula to ensure a free and appropriate public education for all students who are disabled.

Of specific importance to school principals is that the law insists on:

1. A zero reject policy
2. Specific due process procedures
3. Nondiscriminatory testing
4. A written and promulgated individual educational plan for every child who is disabled (to be developed jointly with parents and reviewed at least annually)
5. Provisions for a least-restrictive environment

The act's "stay-put" provision directs that a child who is disabled "shall remain in his or her then current educational placement" pending completion of any review proceedings, unless the parents and state and local educational agencies otherwise agree.

The stay-put provision prohibits school authorities from unilaterally excluding children with disabilities from the classroom for dangerous or disruptive conduct growing out of their disabilities *during the pendency of review proceedings*. The act is unequivocal in its requirement that the "child *shall* remain in the current educational placement."

Doe and Smith, students who were emotionally disturbed, were suspended indefinitely for violent and disruptive conduct, pending the completion of expulsion proceedings by the school. In *Honig* v. *Doe and Smith*,[11] it was held that the implementing regulations under the act allow the use of normal, nonplacement-changing procedures, including *temporary* suspensions for up to 10 school days for students posing an immediate threat to others' safety, and allows for interim placements where parents and school officials are able to agree. Further, the act authorizes schools to file a suit for "appropriate" injunctive relief where such an agreement cannot be reached. In such suit, there is a presumption in favor of the child's current placement, but school officials can rebut only by showing that maintaining the current placement is substantially likely to result in injury to the student or to others.

The Individualized Education Program

For each child there must be developed a formal individualized educational plan (IEP). The IEP is developed by a team, including the appropriate professional educators (diagnosticians, teachers, psychologists, and principals, for example) and the child's parents. Parents must give consent before a child with disabilities may be placed in a program. The IEP must contain:

- The child's current level of performance
- A statement of goals and objectives
- The nature of the educational services to be provided
- The place(s) and time(s) the services will be provided
- The person(s) who will be working with the child

The litmus test is whether the IEP is "reasonably calculated" to enable the child to advance from grade to grade.[12] Moreover, removing a child who has a disability to a disciplinary setting may be a change in placement and thus requires that the school comply with the act's procedures.[13] If the school cannot meet the needs of the child in the 180-day school year, the act requires a program longer than the normal year.[14]

The Supreme Court has held that schools may be required to reimburse parents for expenditures incurred in private school placement if the court ultimately determines that the private school placement is proper and that the school district's proposed IEP is not proper under the act.[15]

Individuals with Disabilities Education Act (IDEA)

Passed by Congress in 1990, this is the so-called inclusion act. It requires that the educational placement of each child who has a disability is to be determined at least annually, that the plan is based on the child's individualized education program (IEP), and that the child is educated as close as possible to his or her home. Unless the IEP requires some other arrangement, the child is to be educated in the school that would have been attended had there been no disability. In selecting the least-restrictive environment, consideration is to be given to any potential harmful effect on the child or on the quality of services needed.

Simply put, these regulations require the school to make a substantial effort to find an inclusive solution for the child. Federal courts have held that this act requires that children with very severe disabilities must be included in the regular classroom they would otherwise attend if not disabled (even when they cannot meet the academic expectations of the class) *if* there is a potential social benefit, *if* the class would stimulate the child's linguistic development, or *if* the other students could provide appropriate role models for the student.[16]

Parents are increasingly aware of these rights and have shown a willingness to go to the courts to force school districts to include their child in "regular" classes even when the child who is disabled may not be able to keep up with the standard work of the class. The burden for showing both the parent and the court how exclusion is in the best interests of the child rests on the school.

Aside from the legal implications of IDEA and PL 94-142, the implications of these acts with regard to teacher training and in-service development are immense. Inclusion is clearly a way of reconceptualizing the method by which special services are delivered to children with disabilities. Rather than sending the child to a special class full time or to a school in the district that houses only special classes, the new model requires that the special education services be brought to the child.

Employment Issues

School administrators have the responsibility to practice fair employment policies and provide equal opportunity for job aspirants. Increasingly, in these days of greater authority for employment decisions to be made at the school site level, there is a need for the principal and the school staff to be aware of the federal and state laws and court decisions that regulate decision making about personnel selection and termination.

At the federal level, the Equal Employment Opportunity Commission (EEOC) is specifically charged with the enforcement of Title VII of the Civil Rights Act of 1964 (race, color, religion, sex, and national origin); the Equal Pay Act of 1963; the Age Discrimination in Employment Act of 1967; the Rehabilitation Act of 1973; the Americans with Disabilities Act of 1990; and the Federal Civil Rights Act of 1991. The EEOC actively follows up complaints to obtain full compensation and benefits for employees who have been discriminated against in an unlawful manner.

Frels[17] points out:

Site-based management gives the principal and others who share decision making a greater say in who joins the school as teachers or in other staff positions. The rationale for school-based staff selection is based on the premise that the principal should not be held responsible for what teachers do when the principal has little or no voice in the selection of staff... [But] With the right of the principal and others at the campus level to make more staffing decisions comes greater legal risks that discrimination in hiring will occur.

Frels[18] also identifies five important steps that should be taken to lessen the legal exposure of principals in personnel matters:

1. *Non-discrimination criteria for selection must be mandated.*
2. *Those who are involved in staff selection should receive adequate training.*
3. *Pools of qualified candidates can be screened centrally, with ultimate selection at the campus level.*
4. *The termination process should afford the necessary due process and have enough* systemwide uniformity *to guard against claims of unequal treatment individually and on a class basis [emphasis supplied].*

5. Some centralized authority should retain oversight and control of the employment and termination process to ensure non-discriminatory treatment.

Americans with Disabilities Act (ADA)

This 1990 piece of federal legislation specifically protects the employment rights of the disabled. The law is sweeping in its protection for such persons in employment and in state and local government services. Organizations in both the public and private sectors come under the act, whether or not the particular entity receives any federal funds. Students and employees are covered and certain accommodations are required. Generally speaking, the following guidelines apply to employment practices:

1. All positions are open to qualified applicants with disabilities.
2. Position openings must be posted in places that can be reached by people who are disabled.
3. Applicants may not be asked if they have a disability or how it was caused. Only those questions that have to do with the ability to perform essential job functions should be asked.
4. Medical information on an employee's disabilities must be kept in separate file.
5. Employers must accommodate employees who are disabled unless the changes would impose an "undue hardship."
6. Readers, interpreters, and attendants should be provided unless that would be a "hardship."
7. Preemployment testing cannot discriminate against persons with sight, hearing, or speaking limitations.

The implications of the act to the school administration seem clear. Essential job skills will need to be even more carefully established and demonstratively related to the tasks that need to be performed before an otherwise qualified person with disabilities is denied employment because of a presumed inability to carry out job responsibilities. The burden for showing this will rest with the school district and the school administrator.

First Amendment Rights of Students

The school's power to control students is not broad enough in scope to proscribe protected speech. In the *Tinker* case[19] three students wore black armbands to publicize their objections to the Vietnam conflict. The Supreme Court held that wearing the armbands was protected because it was closely related to protected political speech. Political speech must be encouraged and protected because open speech is the basis of our national strength and of the "independence and vigor" of Americans. First Amendment rights, when allowed "in light of the special characteristics of the school environment, are available to teachers and students." Where there is no proof that the student has interfered with the school's work or the rights of other students, the school may not limit free expression merely because they fear a disturbance. The Constitution requires the risk of dispute to foster the democratic system.

Student Publications

Since scholastic newspapers fall within the ambit of the First Amendment's prohibition on censorship, a court would require a strong showing on the part of the school to uphold any censorship. The school would have to show that publication of the forbidden articles would materially and substantially interfere with the requirements of discipline in the operation of the school. Students are *not* free to publish without supervision, however, and administrative review has been held to be appropriate. In *Nicholson*, for example, the court held:

> *Writers on high school newspapers do not have an unfettered constitutional right to be free from pre-publication review. The special characteristics of the high school environment particularly one involving students in a journalism class that produces a school newspaper, call for supervision and review by faculty and administration. The administrative review of a small number of sensitive articles for accuracy rather than for possible censorship or official imprimatur does not implicate First Amendment rights.[20]*

This same court also held that the school possessed a substantial educational interest in teaching young student writers journalistic skills that stressed the tenets of accuracy and fairness.

A more recent case involving the First Amendment rights of students decided by the Supreme Court is *Hazelwood School District* v. *Kuh1meier*.[21] Former high school students who had been staff members on the school newspaper filed suit in federal district court, alleging that their rights had been violated by the deletion of two pages from an edition of the paper. Included in the deletion were two articles. One of the articles described school students' experiences with pregnancy; the other discussed the impact of divorce on students at the school. The newspaper was written and edited by a journalism class and the class was a part of the regular school curriculum.

Pursuant to the school's practice, the teacher in charge of the class had submitted page proofs to the principal, who subsequently objected to the pregnancy story. He objected because, even though no names were used, he believed that the pregnant students might be identified from the text and because he believed that the references to sexual activity and birth control were inappropriate for some of the younger students.

He objected to the article about divorce because the page proofs he had been furnished identified by name (deleted by the teacher in the final version) a student who complained of her father's conduct The principal indicated he thought the parent should have been given an opportunity to respond to the remarks or to consent to their publication. Believing that there was insufficient time to make the changes if the paper was to be issued before the end of the school year, he directed that the pages be removed even though other unobjectionable articles were included on the same pages.

The Court held that the First Amendment rights of the students had not been violated; that such rights were not automatically coextensive with the rights of adults in other settings, and must be applied in light of the special characteristics of the school environment. In the opinion of the Court, the school need not tolerate student speech that is inconsistent with its basic educational mission even though the government could not censor similar speech outside of the school.

School newspapers cannot be characterized as a forum for public expression. School facilities may be deemed to be public forums only if school authorities by policy or by practice have opened the facilities for any indiscriminate use by the general public, or by some segment of the public, such as student organizations. Otherwise, no public forum has been created and reasonable restrictions may be imposed on the speech of students, teachers, and other members of the school community. The school, in this case, was found not to have deviated from its own restrictive policies.

School Library Books

To what extent do school boards (and, by implication, administrators) have discretionary authority to remove books and materials from a school library? Courts have held that although a school board has broad discretion in adding books to a school library, it may not remove books simply because it dislikes the ideas contained in those books. The school may not remove books in order to "prescribe what shall be orthodox in politics, nationalism, religion or other matters of opinion.[22] The question of whether the removal of the books is an unconstitutional abridgment of a student's First Amendment rights is decided on an analysis of the board's intention. The board may not remove books in order to prevent access to ideas that it disapproves of or when those ideas fall under the protection of the First Amendment. The circumstances that permit exception to this principle are narrow. However, it would be permissible to remove books that were "pervasively vulgar" or educationally unsuitable.

These latter issues require definition, of course. The wise principal will work with the staff to develop criteria to determine "educational suitability." Help is available from the National Council for the Teaching of English and from the American Library Association. Whatever the court meant by "pervasively vulgar" in unknown—such phrases lack definition and are useless to the school administrator.

Required Reading Material

In *Grove* v. *Mead School District No. 354*,[23] a student and her parents argued that the use of a particular book that was a part of the English curriculum violated the First Amendment's prohibition of state establishment of religion. The court held that the factors that must be considered were whether there was a heavy burden on the individual's exercise of religion; if there was a compelling state interest justifying that burden; and if there could be some accommodation that would not impede the school's objective. The court decided that the burden on the student's exercise of religion was minimal because she was allowed to read an alternative book and avoid the classroom discussions of the other book.

This accommodation was made in order to allow the school to continue to provide a well-rounded public education; to do otherwise would have critically impeded the school's function. When there is no coercion used with the student, and the school is pursuing a valid end of public education, such an accommodation does not violate the student's right of free exercise of religion. A more extensive discussion of this issue is presented in a later section of this chapter.

Searching Students

A particularly difficult legal issue is that of conducting searches of students and their property. Freedom from unreasonable searches and seizure of property is a Fourth Amendment right. The Fourth Amendment's prohibition of unreasonable searches and seizures applies to searches conducted by public school officials. In carrying out searches and other disciplinary functions pursuant to school policies, administrators act as representatives of the state, not merely as surrogates for the parents, and they cannot claim the parents' immunity from the strictures of the Fourth Amendment.

Although school officials may search students or their possessions when it is "reasonable" to do so, the court has not given specific examples of what is reasonable. Whether a search is reasonable depends on the factual context of the search. The search of a child's person or property is a violation of the expectation of privacy of the student; however, this expectation of privacy is balanced against the interest of teachers and administrators in maintaining discipline and security.

These principles lead to the following test of the legality of a search: Is the search reasonable under all of the circumstances of the search? More specifically, is the search justified at its inception, and is the search related in scope to the circumstances that justify the interference in the first place?

Under ordinary circumstances, a search by a school official will be justified at its inception when there are reasonable grounds for suspecting that the search will show that the student has violated or is violating either the law or the rules of the school. The severity of the violation is a factor, however. One shouldn't search a student for minor infractions.

Religion in the Schools

As noted earlier, the First Amendment to the Constitution states "Congress shall make no law respecting an *establishment* of religion, or prohibiting the *free exercise* thereof (emphasis added)." The federal and state courts have held in many cases that every governmental body (including school districts) must remain neutral with respect to religion. Schools are prohibited from taking any kind of action that tends to either "establish" or support religious beliefs, *or* tends to prevent the "free exercise" of religion. The courts mean that public school personnel may not require, lead, or encourage the study or discussion of scripture or any other religious activities during the school day or in connection with school-sponsored extracurricular activities.

May students study about religion when it is directly related to curricular offerings? Generally, yes. For example, a history teacher developing a lesson about the early settlement of what became the United States could certainly examine the centrality of religious beliefs to the migration of the Pilgrims to this continent and the degree to which those beliefs affected their lives. Also, for example, it would seem impossible not to discuss the Spanish Inquisition or the effect of the spread of Islam on the development of the Mediterranean region, including parts of southern Europe, if a class was engaged in a study of western civilization. And, how could one introduce such plays as *The Crucible* without examining the basis for the Salem witch trials?

Religious Clubs

If the school has an "open forums" policy, and the formation of after-school clubs of a noncurricular nature that meet on school grounds is permitted, then such nonschool-related clubs as chess clubs, science fiction clubs, and bible study groups are permitted. But this is permitted only to the extent that the groups are student sponsored and not school sponsored and are not held during school hours.[24]

Students may also distribute religious tracts on school grounds *if* other groups are permitted to distribute materials about their organizations. If a school regularly permits students to distribute noncurriculum, nonreligious materials in the hallways, then it must allow students to distribute religious materials. Our advice is to not permit any noncurriculum materials to be distributed by students. Note, too, though, that all of this applies to students. School personnel are *not* permitted the same liberties.

Objectional Materials

What about objections of this or that religious group to instructional materials being used or to certain ceremonies such as Halloween parties (don't forget those Halloween demons and satanic creatures!) In an elementary school in Wheaton, Illinois, a new supplementary reading program for K–5 students was introduced after a curriculum review committee screened the series for educational suitability and quality. The series included the work of Dr. Seuss, C. S. Lewis, Ray Bradbury, Maurice Sedak, A. A. Milne, and other noted authors. Some parents filed suit and alleged that the series fostered a religious belief in the existence of supernatural beings including "wizards, sorcerers, [and] giants." They further alleged that the material "indoctrinates children in values directly opposed to their Christian beliefs by teaching tricks, despair, deceit, parental disrespect and…denigration of Christian symbols of holidays."

Ultimately the courts held that the burden on the parents was, "at most, minimal"; they were free to provide religious instruction on their own, and "the use of the series did not compel their children to affirm or deny any religious doctrine." The teaching of reading and creativity was viewed by the court as a fundamental and compelling governmental interest, and the court noted that the tolerance of religious diversity is among the appropriate values for public schooling.[25]

The selection and use of instructional materials should always be subjected to careful review by teachers. Moreover, good educational practice requires that the development of new curriculum be subjected to such criteria as suitability and quality, and that the formation of curriculum review committees only makes good sense in any case. Although prudence and sensitivity are always important, principals and teachers should not be intimidated by parent's religious beliefs. Efforts to "cleanse" the curriculum by this or that religious group in accordance with any particular religious orthodoxy may be very harmful—indeed, it may be at extreme cross-purposes to the very reason that we have schools. This does not mean that a discerning excusal policy may not be advisable, but it does mean that wholesale elimination of educational materials in the face of parental complaint is a dereliction of duty and contrary to good educational practice.

Now to Halloween and other such celebrations: The schools have also been accorded latitude here in the instance of parental objection on religious grounds. In

Florida, some parents objected to Halloween celebrations as satanic celebrations that inculcated a belief in witches. The court held that "witches, cauldrons, and brooms in the context of school Halloween celebrations appear to be nothing more than a mere 'shadow,' if that, in the realm of establishment clause jurisprudence."[26]

Due Process

The general issue addressed by due process considerations is that of the constitutional rights of personnel and students balanced against the duty of the school board to control and protect the school system and protect the rights of students to obtain an education.

Substantive Due Process

Substantive due process is concerned with the basic legality of a legislative enactment. School policies, rules, and regulations must stand the test of substantive due process. A person punished or denied the right to behave in some way by an existing law, rule, or regulation when that law, rule, or regulation is itself contrary to certain constitutional guarantees has legal recourse to set aside the punishment or denial and make the rule invalid. Moreover, substantive due process requires that there must be sufficient evidence or documentation of violation to warrant action by school officials or sufficient reason to believe that, if the rule is not invoked, current or subsequent acts by the parties involved will result in disruption of the educational process. The burden of proof rests with the school officials, not the transgressor.

Tinker is often cited in reference to presumed disruptions.[27] Rules are invoked because the school principal says, in effect, "If this rule is not enforced and obeyed, the process of education in the school will be impeded." In *Tinker*, two important legal principles of a substantive nature were applied by the Supreme Court in holding for the students: There was no disruption; therefore, the presumption of the rule was false and students had the constitutional right to defy the rule. The wearing of the armbands was analogous to free speech (a First Amendment guarantee) and the students had the right to express themselves.

The two rules of thumb that must be applied are: Will the behavior cause substantial disorder to the education process or normal operation of the school? and Will the behavior be an invasion of the rights of others? The burden of proof rests on the principal. Courts are critical of administrative action predicated on presumption. The collection of sufficient evidence to show reason for administrative action is essential.

Guidelines to Ensure Substantive Due Process

School policies, rules, and regulations, as well as the administrative actions enforcing them, should be subjected to the following guidelines:

1. *Legality.* Is there a basis in state and federal constitutional and legislative law for the policy, rule, or regulation? Are the constitutional rights of those for whom it was written protected?

2. *Sufficient Specificity*. Are the conditions under which the policy, rule, or regulation will be invoked detailed? Are the terms and phraseology used definitive? Vague and unclear statements are sufficient to cause the courts to abrogate.

3. *Reason and Sensibleness*. Does the rule or regulation really enhance the educational climate; that is, is it really necessary? Is there sufficient reason to believe that without the rule, the rights of others will be unprotected or the school will be disrupted? A rule maybe declared unreasonable in and of itself or in its particular application.

4. *Adequate Dissemination*. Has information about the rule been distributed in such a way that persons affected can be expected to know about it, know what it means, and know what the penalties are?

5. *Appropriate Penalties*. Are the punishments appropriate to the nature of the infraction? Severe penalties for minor transgressions must be avoided.[28]

Procedural Due Process

Procedural due process is an orderly, established process for arriving at an impartial and just settlement of a conflict between parties. It entails fair warning and fair hearing.

Fair Warning

Fair warning simply means that a person must be aware of the rules to follow, or behavior that must be exhibited, and the potential penalties for violation. The age of the person and the length of experience must be taken into consideration as well. Moreover, there must be a correlation between the penalty and the rule that has been broken.

Fair Hearing

A fair hearing is composed of the following specific aspects:

The individual must be given a written statement of the charges and the nature of evidence. This is often called a "Bill of Particulars." Clarity is very important. The accused, and, in the instance of pupils, the accused's parents, must comprehend the contents of the written statement. The background and educational level of the individuals involved and the complexity of the statement should be taken into account. A personally delivered statement to the parents would provide an opportunity for clarifying charges and would be appropriate at times. The precise nature of the charges and the evidence must be incorporated in the statement. Vague rules and imprecise charges have resulted in the reversal of more school board and administrative decisions than any other defect.[29]

The individual must be informed of certain procedural rights. Having rights but being kept unaware of them is the same as not having rights. Individuals must be provided information specifying the appeal and defense processes available. Information such as to whom the appeal should be made, the time limit under which the appeal can be advanced, and other elements of procedural due process is necessary.

Adequate time must be provided to prepare a defense. In serious issues, ordinarily a minimum of 5 days should be provided for an individual to prepare a defense; 10 days almost certainly will sustain a court inquiry.[30]

There must be an opportunity for a formal hearing.[31] Five components comprise a proper formal hearing:

- The case must be presented to an impartial hearer. The school official bringing the charge may not also serve as hearer.
- The individual must have the opportunity to present evidence.
- The individual has the right to know and confront whoever brought the charges and to question that person or those persons.
- The individual has the right to produce witnesses and to cross-examine witnesses. The individual must have the opportunity to disprove the accusations of a hostile witness and include testimony of those who can explain the defendant's side of the issue.
- The individual has the right to counsel. This does not necessarily mean an attorney, but there is no reason why it could not be. It may be simply a friend, parent, or citizen on whose advice the defendant wishes to rely.

Common Tort Liability Settings

A tort is an act *or an omitted act*, including breach of contract that results in damage, injury, or loss to the injured person(s), who then may seek relief by legal action. Torts may be intentional, may result from negligence, or may be caused by carelessness. School employees are liable for their failure to carry out prescribed duties or the failure to carry out these duties correctly. Individual staff members are expected to behave in a reasonable manner in the discharge of their duties, avoiding acts that are capricious, arbitrary, or negligent.

Tort liability suits usually require adequate evidence of the following:

- A prescribed or implicit duty on the part of the defendant for the care of the plaintiff
- An error of commission or omission by the defendant
- Damage, loss, or injury sustained by the plaintiff
- Indication of a cause-and-effect relationship between the error and the circumstance at issue
- Absence of contributory or offsetting comparative negligence on the part of the plaintiff [32]

The best defense against law suits is precaution. Principals and teachers cannot be expected to be prescient but they should anticipate possible dangers. The discussion that follows will examine common liability settings and describe certain aspects of the legal environment.

Pupil Injuries

A school is not usually a hazardous place, but children frequently do sustain injuries in and about the school. Most of these injuries are accidental and minor, the result of normal behavior. Nevertheless, teachers and administrators do have a responsibility to provide reasonable and prudent protection for their charges, and they are legally liable in tort for injuries arising from their negligence.[33]

The main test of negligence is "foreseeability." That is, the behavior of an individual would be called negligent if an ordinarily prudent person would have foreseen that certain actions, or a failure to act, would lead injury to another. The principles of sovereign immunity or statutory immunity may protect educators in some instances. However, the scope of that immunity varies from state to state.

The principal is responsible for taking all steps to promote the well-being of the children within the school and to guard the welfare of the staff. Therefore, to both staff and students, the principal has a particular duty to plan and supervise in a manner that will minimize the possibility of injury. At the very least, this involves providing information to staff members about their legal responsibilities and developing a set of rules and regulations that, if carefully followed, will result in protection for students.

Schools should be especially cautious in instances where it is "foreseeable" that student injury might result. Certain parts of the school environment present particular problems.

Physical Education, Field Trips, and Other Extracurricular Programs

Field trips, other extracurricular programs, and physical education are inherently more hazardous than the regular academic program. Greater supervision is required to avoid liability as a result of negligence. Carefully developed and well-understood written rules and regulations for the governance of these activities are important.[34] Adequate regulations cover such categories as pupil conduct while a participant or spectator, medical examinations for participants, medical care for sick and injured participants, transportation to and from the activity, duties of teachers and other supervisors, and notification and approval in advance by a parent or guardian.[35]

Laboratories and Shops

These two instructional areas present more hazards than any other in the school. Even general science classes frequently engage in experiments within the classroom, often involving chemicals as well as common electric- or gas-powered laboratory equipment. Moreover, good educational practice in teaching science involves such outside classroom events as off-campus field trips and on-campus outdoor activities.

Similarly, greater emphasis on career education and career exploration means that more and more middle and elementary schools are developing prevocational shops with at least rudimentary power equipment as well as common hand tools. In addition, classes such as cooking and sewing continue in popularity and require power- and hand-operated equipment.

Constant and immediate supervision is expected of teachers functioning in these instructional spaces. Teachers must adequately instruct students in the care and use of equipment they will be operating. If there is evidence that a student has been permitted to use a particular tool, or perform an experiment before being trained and told the consequences of improper usage, negligence will be difficult to disprove. Greater care is expected of teachers supervising students who are exposed to dangerous equipment.

Even a brief teacher absence from a room where a class in engaged in hazardous activities is very risky.[36]

Playgrounds

Where supervision is regular, planned, reasonable, and proper, a negligence charge in case of pupil injury on the playground is not likely to be sustained. Consideration should be given to the kind of playground equipment in use, the size of the playground, and the number and age of the pupils to be supervised.

The courts generally appreciate the fact that a teacher is unable to keep every child within view and out of hazard at all times. Nevertheless, negligent supervision is often held to be the proximate cause of injury. If, for example, a teacher permits a child to leave a supervised group and the child is injured in a known, existing hazardous condition, then the teacher may be liable. If a teacher assigned to playground duty leaves a post for no good cause and a child is injured in a known or foreseeable dangerous condition, there may be tort liability because of negligence. Also, although teachers would not be expected to repair playground equipment, permitting pupils to use equipment known to be faulty, or beyond the maturity level of the child, could result in a claim of negligence.

The principal has three major responsibilities. First proper rules of behavior, consistent with good safety practices, must be developed and implemented. Second, adequate adult supervision on the playground should always be provided when children are present. Third, the principal must arrange for frequent and regular inspection of the playground and playground equipment and a reporting system about any hazardous conditions. Staff and students must be apprised of these, and action should be taken to have the conditions corrected.

The Classroom

Teachers are normally in charge in the classroom and thus are most frequently held responsible for the safety of the children there. However, the principal has some responsibilities that, if not met, may result in a charge of negligent behavior. The primary responsibility of the principal with regard to classroom activities is to ensure that there is a teacher or a responsible adult present at all times. The principal should always be aware of a teacher's absence from the classroom. Failure to have a plan to provide for pupil supervision when a teacher becomes ill or is tardy to class could cause the principal to be charged with negligence if an injury resulted while the students were unsupervised. A common practice is to have a check-in sheet for teachers in the morning so that the principal can know immediately of any unanticipated absence or tardiness of personnel who have responsibility for the supervision of students.

Generally speaking, however, the temporary short-term absence from the classroom by a teacher would not, in and of itself, be considered a negligent act of general supervision. If, for example, a student misbehaves and in so doing injures another student during a teacher's brief absence from the room, a court would not ordinarily find negligence, because the teacher's absence was not the proximate cause of the accident. However, in all cases, the age, maturity, and intelligence of the student will bear on the question of teacher negligence in such absences. The best rule is not to leave students unattended.

Regulating Student Conduct

In even the best-run schools, students misbehave. Principals and teachers may prescribe reasonable controls against the misconduct of children. Many kinds of disciplinary action are available to school administrators and teachers when pupils violate school policies and rules. These include such minor punishments as short-term removal from the classroom, withholding certain privileges, detention after school, isolation from the rest of the class, being sent to the principal's office, and so on. The courts have generally upheld the right of school administrators and teachers to impose such minor punishment. Other forms of disciplinary action, however, such as suspension and expulsion from school[37] or the use of corporal punishment, are more often tested in the courts, and school administrators and teachers must take great care in the prescription of these punishments. Figure 5–1 depicts a basic information form to document disciplinary action.

In any case, the question of both substantive and procedural due process is extremely important.[38] The reasonableness and legality of the rule or regulation violated must be examined with care, and the legal issue of whether the student has a right to a prior hearing is important. Clearly, administrators should take care in imposing minor as well as major punishments to ensure that pupils or personnel are treated fairly and are not victimized by capricious or arbitrary action.

Corporal Punishment
Corporal punishment is disciplinary action by the application of physical force. As a means of modifying behavior, it is probably the oldest disciplinary tool. It also is one of the least efficacious. Acts of corporal punishment are probably the cause of more court cases than anything else.[39] However, under *in loco parentis*, the courts continue to uphold the right of teachers and principals to use "reasonable" force to ensure proper conduct or to correct improper conduct.[40]

In the *Baker* case,[41] the court held that corporal punishment may never be used unless the student was informed beforehand that specific misbehavior could occasion its use. The court also said that corporal punishment should never be employed as a first line of punishment. Another official also must be present and be told of the wrongful act before the student, to give the student an opportunity to protest spontaneously. A written explanation must then be sent to the parent, stating the reasons for the punishment.

Important guidelines must be followed if the use of corporal punishment is to be adjudicated as prudent and reasonable. Corporal punishment is generally held to be prudent providing:

* The state law and the local policy permit it.
* The punishment takes into consideration the age, size, gender, and health of the student and is not excessive.
* There is no malice; the punishment is given for corrective purposes only and is not immoderate.

FIGURE 5–1   Report of Disciplinary Action: Robert Craig Junior High School

---

Date:_____

Student's Name:_____   Homeroom:_____   Grade:_____

Time:_____

Person Reporting:_____

Title of Person Reporting:_____

Nature of Offense:

Student's Account:

Action Taken:

I have had a chance to tell my side._____
                                        (Student Signature)

Date of Hearing:_____   Person Conducting Hearing:_____

Time:_____   Other Person(s) Present: _____

Infraction: State Law:_____   School Policy:_____

Board of Education Policy: _____

Central Office Policy: _____

Teacher Rule:_____ Common Sense: _____

- The student understands why punishment is required.
- An appropriate instrument is used.

Sometimes courts consider other attendant circumstances such as whether there was permanent injury suffered as a result of the punishment.

To ensure the fairest treatment possible for the student, it is important for the principal and the teacher to establish reasonable rules and to make sure that the punishment for breaking these rules is suitable. It is also important to reasonably administer the rules and apply them equally to all students. It is possible to administer a reasonable rule so improperly that it becomes unreasonable. Any vindictiveness or viciousness in administering corporal punishment must be avoided. If the teacher or the principal knows that he or she is uncontrollably angry, then it is not time to punish the child corporally—or in any other way.

Suspension/Expulsion

Suspension is a dismissal from the school for a specific, but relatively short, length of time. *Expulsion* means permanent or long-term dismissal from school and, in most states, can be accomplished only by the board of education; permanent exclusion from school is outside the authority of the school administrator.

Attendance at a public school is generally viewed as a right rather than a privilege, but the enjoyment of this right is conditioned by the student's willingness to comply with reasonable regulations and requirements of the school. Violations of these may be punished by suspension or, in extreme cases, by permanent exclusion. Under a suspension, a student is usually required to meet some set of conditions established by the administrator before being readmitted.

The dividing line between a short- and a long-term exclusion from school is not clearly defined, but as a result of *Goss* v. *Lopez* has probably been established as 10 days.[42] In *Goss*, the court clearly established the right of school administrators to suspend students to maintain order in the school system. However, in this case, the court did find that school officials had violated the student's constitutional right to procedural due process. Nine students were temporarily suspended from school *without a hearing* and thus were held to be denied due process. The school board had contended that due process was not applicable to suspensions because there was not a "constitutional right" to public education. The court disagreed with this, saying:

> *Although Ohio may not be constitutionally obligated to establish and maintain the public school system, it has nevertheless done so and has required its children to attend. Those young people do not "shed their constitutional rights at the school house door...." The authority possessed by the State to prescribe and enforce standards of conduct in its schools, although concededly very broad, must be exercised consistently with the constitutional safeguards.[43]*

Second, the school board had argued that even if public education was a right that was protected by due process, in this instance the due process clause should not apply because the suspensions were limited to 10 days and this was neither a severe nor a grievous infringement on the students' right to an education. The court disagreed here also and faced the question of what kind of process is due in the instance of short-term student suspensions. The court held that only rudimentary process was required to balance student interests against the educator's need to take quick disciplinary action. The court said:

> *The student [must] be given a written notice of the charges against him, if he denies them, an explanation of the evidence the authorities have and an opportunity to present his side of the story.... There need be no delay between the time "notice" is given and the time of the hearing. In the great majority of cases the disciplinarian may informally discuss the alleged misconduct with the student minutes after it has occurred. We hold only that, in being given an opportunity to explain his version of the facts at this discussion, the student first be told what he is accused of doing and what the basis of the accusation is.[44]*

This is important because it implies that while due process provisions must always be present, even in less than major punishment, the nature of the punishment and the infraction will determine the degree to which one must engage in elaborate vestments of due process. In minor infractions it would be necessary only to provide rudimentary forms of hearing. Even here, however, the important lesson is that the child to be punished must in all instances be treated fairly and that there must be clear indication of the absence of capricious action. Expulsions are a different matter. In the case of an expulsion, it would seem clear that all of the vestments of due process be clearly applied.

Opposition to the use of suspensions and expulsions as punishment for misconduct is growing. More often, schools are developing a disciplinary procedure called *in-school suspension* as a means of avoiding the disruption and negative effects cited above. The in-school suspension usually involves taking the student out of the regular classroom for a period of time and placing the student in another learning situation within the school building, either in an independent learning situation with supervision or in a designated special class. When this procedure is coupled with counseling by the principal, the guidance counselor, or some other clinician to diagnose and treat the problem, it is a sound practice.

Detention

It is well established that principals and teachers do have the authority to temporarily detain students from participating in extracurricular activities and even to keep children after school as a punishment, providing, of course, that the student has a way of getting home. As in other punishments, the detention must be reasonable. False imprisonment may be claimed if the principal or a teacher either wrongfully detains a student or detains a student for an unreasonable amount of time as a punishment. In this, as in all other punishments, the main test is one of fairness. If school officials act fairly and in good faith in dealing with students, their actions will probably be upheld by the courts.

Privacy and Confidentiality of Student Records

The question of the confidentiality and accuracy of student records is important, and since the passage of Public Law 93-380, Family Educational Rights and Privacy Act of 1974 (FERPA), the issue has been legally clarified. This act states that students and parents are permitted to inspect and review records and must be given a copy of any part or all of the educational record on request. It also requires that in any dispute concerning the contents of a student's educational record, due process must be provided. Where a record is found to be inaccurate, the inaccuracies must be expunged.

The act essentially requires that the schools and other agencies permit an individual to determine what relevant records are maintained in the system of records; to gain access to relevant records in such a system of records; to have copies made; and to correct or amend any relevant record.

Further, the records about an individual may not be disclosed to outsiders except by the consent of the individual in question. The consent must be in writing and must be *specific* in stating to whom the record may be disclosed, which records may be disclosed, and, where applicable, the time frame during which the records may be disclosed.

In some instances, disclosures may be made without the consent of the pupil or the pupil's parents. Information may be disclosed within the school to teachers or guidance counselors who have a "need to know"; where there is a court order; where there is required disclosure under the Freedom of Information Act; and for routine usage such as the publication of names of students who made an honor roll or information for a directory such as class lists or sports brochures, which might include such information as the student's name, address, gender, or birthplace. Even in this latter instance, however, it would be best to get prior permission through some sort of routine process. The district may be held liable for a common law tort for the disclosure of private facts about a student without consent if the disclosure results in any unwarranted publicity.[45]

Guidelines to assist principals in developing fair policies about student records include:

1. Develop procedures to ensure that parents and students know what kind of information is contained in school records at a given time and are informed of their rights concerning control over the process of information collection and recording.

2. Encourage mature students and their parents to inspect the records. The rights of parents to do this are now well established, but most parents are unaware of these rights. Increased communication and greater trust on the part of the parents will be a major benefit and such a policy might provide a substantially more accurate record.

3. Develop systematic procedures to obtain explicit and informed parental or pupil consent before information contained in school records is released to outside parties, regardless of the reasons for such release or the characteristic of the third party. Most schools will, on occasion, give out information to law enforcement or other agencies without obtaining consent from the student or the parents. Aside from the possible legal implications of a violation of privacy, this practice can have no other effect than that of discouraging a trustful relationship among the parent, the child, and the school.

Summary

The constitutional roots, case law, and legislative bases on which the interactive relationships of students, teachers, parents, and principals legally occur has been the subject of this chapter. A working knowledge about the legal principles, important court decisions, and current law is essential. Understanding the laws governing the operation of schools is important—not just in order to stay out of court but also, and perhaps more importantly, to provide the kind of orderly, productive, and humane school basic to the continuation of a democratic society.

Activity

1. Case Studies 7, 13, 16, 18, and 22 contain problems that have legal as well as instructional, curricular, and public relations implications. Review these cases with the concepts presented in this chapter in mind. What questions of law seem to arise? How would you go about addressing these questions? What additional information, if any, do you need? Where would you get this information? Considering just the information you have from this chapter, the

case, and your own experience, what solutions do you suggest?

Endnotes

1. Richard D. Strahan, "Building Leadership and Legal Strategies," *The Principal as Leader*, ed. Larry W. Hughes (New York: Macmillan, 1994), p. 291.

2. *Tinker* v. *Des Moines Independent Community School System*, 393 U.S. 503, 89 S.Ct. 733 (1969).

3. 501 F.2d 1264 (9th Cir. 1974). See also *Bray* v. *Lee*, 337 F. Supp. 034 (D. Mass 1972).

4. Ibid. at 1269.

5. *Vorcheimer* v. *School District of Philadelphia*, 532 F.2d 880 (3d Cir. 1976).

6. For example, *Brenden* v. *Independent School District*, 343 F. Supp. 1224 (D. Minn. 1972), aff'd. 477 F.2d 1292 (10th Cir. 1973); *Herver* v. *Meiklejon*, 430 F. Supp. 164 (D. Col. 1977).

7. See *Clark* v. *Arizona Interscholastic Association*, 695 F.2d 1129 (9th Cir. 1982).

8. *Force by Force* v. *Pierce City School District*, 570 F. Supp. 1020 (W.D. Mo. 1983).

9. *Yellow Springs Exempted Village School District Board of Education* v. *Ohio School Athletic Association*, 433 F. Supp. 753 (S.D. Ohio 1978).

10. PL 94-143 is entitled "Developmentally Disabled Assistance and Bill of Rights Act"; PL 93-112 is "Rehabilitation Act" and was enacted in 1973.

11. 484 U.S. 305; 108 S.Ct. 592; 98 L.Ed.2d 686 (1988).

12. See *Board of Education of Hendrick Hudson Central School District* v. *Rowley*, 458 U.S. 176 (1982).

13. See *Adams Central School District* v. *Deist*, 334 N.W.2d 775 (Neb. 1983).

14. See *Board of Education for the City of Savannah* v. *Georgia Association of Retired Citizens*, 52 U.S.L.W. 3932 (June 26,1984).

15. *School Committee of the Town of Burlington, Mass.* v. *Mass. Dept of Education*, 53 U.S.L.W. 4509 (April 30,1985).

16. For example, in *Board of Education, Sacramento* v. *Holland* (786 F.Supp. 874 [ED Cal. 1992]), the court ordered the school district to place a child with an IQ of 44 in a regular second-grade class and rejected the district's complaints about expenses as exaggerated. In *Oberti* v. *Board of Education of the Borough of Clementon School District*, (789 F.Supp. 1322 [D.N.J. 1992]), the court rejected the claim of the school district that a child would be so disruptive as to significantly impair the education of the other children.

17. Kelly Frels, "Legal Aspects of Site-Based Management," *School Law in Review*, 1992 (Washington, DC: National School Boards Association, 1992), p. 5.

18. Ibid.

19. *Tinker*, loc. cit.

20. *Nicholson* v. *Board of Education, Torrance County Unified School District*, 682 F.2d 858 (9th Cir. 1982).

21. 108 S.Ct. 562 (1988).

22. *Board of Education, Island Trees Union Free School District No. 26* v. *Pico*, U.S. 853 (457 1982).

23. 735 F.2d 1528 (9th Cir. 1985).

24. *Lamb's Chapel* v. *Center Moriches Union Free School District*, 124 L. Ed. 2d 352 (June 7, 1993). See also *Westside Community School Board* v. *Mergens* (496 U.S. 226 [1990]) for a definition of a *noncurriculum-related school group*. In the latter judgment, such a group was defined broadly to be any student group that does not directly relate to the body of courses offered by the school. If a school permits student groups such as a scuba diving club, a political club, and so on, to meet at school facilities during noninstructional time (before or after the school day), it must also permit a *student-organized* religious group to meet. The only way a school could deny access to a group that wished to advance the teachings of Mohammed or Karl Marx or Jesus or Confucius would be an open forum or public forum policy. The only way it can deny access is to convince a judge that the group advocates the violent overthrow of the

government or that the group's presence will lead to violence, damage to property, injury to persons, and the like.

25. *Fleischfresser* v. *Directors of Sch. Dist.* 200, 15 F. 3d 680 (7th Cir. 1994). See also *Mozert* v. *Hawkins County Pub.* Sch. 827 F. 2d 1058 (6th Cir. 1987), *cert denied* 108 S.Ct. 1029 (1988).

26. *Guyer* v. *School Bd.*, 634 So.2d 806 (Fla. Dist. Ct. App. 1994).

27. Tinker, op. cit. See also *Burnside* v. *Byars*, 363 F. 2d 744 (5th Cir. 1966).

28. Procedures and punishments must be tailored to fit the offender and the offense. See, for example, *Rhyne* v. *Childs*, 359 F. Supp. 1085 (1973), affd, 507 F.2d 675 (5th Cir. 1975).

29. Full disclosure requires an explanation of the evidence the school officials have against the student. See *Goss* v. *Lopez*, 419 U.S. 565; *Board of Curators of the University* v. *Horowitz*, 435 U.S. 78 (1978); *Keough* v. *Tate County Board of Education,* 748 F. 2d 1077 (5th Cir. 1984), for example.

30. Although procedural due process is required by the U.S. Constitution, the courts have a different fact pattern in each case. There is no set formula for what is sufficient procedural due process. Too, the various district and circuit courts have given slightly different variations of the test for what is adequate.

31. It is important to remember that while this process appears to take on the vestments of a court of law, it is *not* a court of law. It is simply a procedure for fair and impartial treatment. After the process is complete, the individual still has the right to take the issue to civil court if he or she feels the issue was decided wrongly or the punishment too severe.

32. Contributory negligence is determined by whether or not the party who was injured exercised the degree of caution others of the same age, sex, maturation level, and experience would have exercised under the same conditions. Comparative negligence requires that the plaintiff be charged with proportional liability for his or her acts that contribute to the injury when the plaintiff is old enough to be held accountable for those actions.

Obviously, more supervision is expected of those in charge of young children. Personnel in elementary schools are less likely to be able to claim contributory negligence than those who supervise older students. Nevertheless, whatever the age, a student who disregards or acts in direct defiance of an admonishment of a supervising adult would probably be found guilty of contributory negligence if the refusal to follow directions resulted in the injury.

33. Of course, not all injuries to students are actionable; some are simply unavoidable, the result of pure accident. Only those injuries resulting from negligence provide an actionable basis.

34. For example, the failure to provide safety equipment when playing sports is negligence (*Berman* v. *Philadelphia Board of Education*, 310 Pa. Super. 153; 456A.2d 545, Pa. Super. Ct. 1983) or the failure to give proper instructions in the way to perform physical ability tests (*Ehlinger* v. *Board of Education of New Hartford Central School District*, 96 AD 2d 708; 465 N.Y.S. 2d 378, N.Y. App. Div. 1983).

35. However, advance approval by a parent or guardian for a child to go on a field trip does not foreclose the right to sue if the child is injured.

36. Greater than usual care is required. For example, in a New York case where student employees dropped chemicals from a laboratory window and those chemicals were later retrieved by a young child who was injured by them, the failure to either keep the chemicals under lock and key or to supervise the student employees was held to be negligence. *Kush by Marszalek* v. *City of Buffalo*, 59 N.Y. 2d 26; 449 N.E. 2d 725; 462 N.Y.S. 2d 26 (1983).

37. *Suspension* is generally defined as dismissal from school for a specific, although relatively short-term, period of time. The term is two or three days and often the maximum of a week. Usually, the principal of the school has the right to suspend. *Expulsion* is defined to mean permanent dismissal and normally is an action that legally can be taken only by a school board.

38. In the instance of suspension, one of the most limiting cases was that of *Mills* v. *Board of Education*, 348 F.Supp.866(1972), in which the court ordered that there must be a hearing prior to a suspension invoked for any period of over two days. In *Goss* v. *Lopez*, 95 S.Ct. 729 (1975), the Supreme Court ruled basically that school officials must accord students and school employees their constitutional right of due pro-

cess even in routine disciplinary actions. *Goss* held that a junior high school student suspended for as much as a single day is entitled to due process. In *Wood* v. *Strickland*, 95 S.Ct. 992 (1975), the Supreme Court ruled that school board members and school officials can be held personally liable for pecuniary damages when students are denied constitutional rights, even by accidental omission.

39. If a teacher or a principal uses excessive force or causes untoward injury he or she may be held liable for battery. There is often confusion about the terms *assault* and *battery*. Battery is the actual unlawful inflicting of physical violence on another. Assault is a threat to commit battery. There can be assault without battery.

40. The Supreme Court has affirmed the right of school personnel to use corporal punishment as long as there is no state law or local policy to the contrary. A lower court ruling upheld that corporal punishment may be administered provided that only "reasonable force" is used and provided that students knew beforehand that certain behaviors could result in physical punishment. *Ingraham* v. *Wright* 430 U.S. 651 (1977), and *Baker* v. *Owen*, 385 F. Supp. 294 (1975).

41. *Baker,* op. cit.
42. *Goss* v. *Lopez,* 95 S.Ct. 729 (1975).
43. Ibid., 736.
44. Ibid., 740.
45. *Klipa* v. *Board of Education of Anne Arundel County*, 54 Md. App. 644, 460 A 2d 601 (Md. App. 1983).

Selected Readings

Alexander, Kern, and M. David Alexander. *American Public School Law*, 3rd ed. (St. Paul: West, 1992).

Hughes, Larry W. (Ed.). *The Principal as Leader* (New York: Macmillan, 1994). See especially Chapter 11.

Rogers, Joy. "The Inclusion Revolution." *Research Bulletin*, 11. Bloomington, IN, Center for Evaluation, Development and Research, Phi Delta Kappa, 1993.

Shelton, Maria M. "The Americans with Disabilities Act: A Primer for Principals." *The Principal* 73, no. 2 (November 1993): 35–37.

Strahan, Richard D., and Charles L. Turner. *The Courts and Schools* (New York: Longman, 1987).

Valente, William D. *Law in the Schools*, 3rd ed. (New York: Macmillan, 1994).

Yodorf, Mark G., David Kirp, and Betsy Levin *Educational Policy and Law*, 3rd ed. (St. Paul: West, 1992).

Chapter 6

School Restructuring through Systematic Planning

*If you don't know where you are going,
it doesn't much matter what you do.*
—ALICE IN WONDERLAND[1]

Every effort to bring about change or initiate something new logically should begin with a plan. Good plans begin with a vision and goals. This chapter describes the systematic processes and tools that can assist you in successfully reaching both short-term problem resolution and long-term goal accomplishment. Techniques addressed include developing belief statements, goal setting, computer-assisted project management, force field analysis, Gantt charting, and action planning.

Good site-based planning involves the translation of concepts, ideas, and beliefs or values into operational processes and measurable outcomes or objectives—the accomplishment of which is believed to lead to the realization of predetermined goals. Principles of Total Quality Management (TQM) suggest that the attention to both the processes and the goals are critical to the success of the endeavor.

Beliefs, Goals, and Objectives

What is the purpose of schooling? What do you believe should be the major goals of education? What is the nature of educational excellence? Goals 2000: Educate America Act of 1994[2] calls for six major national goals for education as we move into the twenty first century. They include readiness to learn, graduation rates, student achievement, first in the world in math and science,[3] adult literacy, and safe schools. Which of these goals are the responsibility of the local school? What should you be doing about them? These are difficult problems to deal with, but a school must have a solid sense of direction if it is going to improve continuously and move toward greater quality.

Determining Direction and Purpose

Every school today must strive for quality. When improvement is seen in a school's quality, it is usually because the school has a vision of what quality represents and a sense of direction toward creating a quality program. The sense of direction can be developed for a school through the creation of a statement of beliefs (philosophy), a set of goals (vision), and specific objectives to be achieved (outcomes). Each of these three levels—beliefs, goals, and objectives—has a specific purpose in the planning process and each contributes in determining direction and showing interrelationships (see Figure 6–1).

A *statement of beliefs* can be thought of as a foundation or a philosophy for the school and should represent the collective thinking of the staff and community representatives. For example, the statement "Every child can learn and achieve mastery" is a statement of belief. It is part of one's philosophy of education.

A *goal statement* is a statement of intended direction relative to a belief statement. For example, a school goal could be "Successful learning experiences will be provided for every child each day." This is a specific statement of intent. A goal, however, is often something that a school strives toward but may never totally achieve.

Just as goals should be an outgrowth of a philosophy or belief, *objectives* should be extensions of goals. Objectives are more specific than goals and should be obtainable, often within a stated period of time. An illustration of a program objective is "Instructional objectives will be developed by the staff for the reading and math curricula this year."

Total Quality Management (TQM) speaks of performance goals and process goals.[4] These suggest that some goals or objectives will be stated in such a manner that they are measurable in some meaningful way. An example might be "that unit test

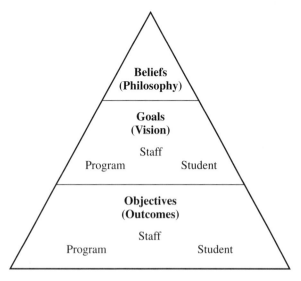

FIGURE 6–1   Determining Direction and Purpose for the School

scores when charted over time will show overall class improvement." However, Deming, in laying out the principles of TQM, cautions against setting work standards that prescribe numerical quotas.

Much of the literature on effective schools refers to their being both loosely and tightly coupled.[5] In excellent schools there exists a strong common sense of purpose (tightly coupled) while at the same time a great deal of freedom (loosely coupled) is given to teachers as to how this purpose is to be achieved. Well-articulated goals to which the faculty "buys in" are the keys to the loosely coupled–tightly coupled concept.

This loosely coupled–tightly coupled concept also applies to the restructuring ideas of site-based management. Properly done, the higher authority (school district or state department) should establish fairly specific goals with a school (tightly coupled). The method or process by which those goals are attained should be left with the local site to determine based on what works best for it (loosely coupled).

Focus on Purpose

A second consideration, a focus on purpose, must be made relative to beliefs, goals, and objectives. There are basically three types of goals used in the school: (1) program goals, (2) staff goals, and (3) learner goals. Program goals focus on the overall collective expectations for the curricular and instructional program of the school. Examples of program goals are "to improve the reading test scores in the second grade" or "to improve the articulation between science programs in the fourth and fifth grades."

Staff goals focus on specific improvements to be sought often by the individual staff members. Examples of a staff goal are "Developing procedures for increasing the amount and quality of student-teacher verbal interaction in my classroom," or "To tailor my questioning style to a different ability level in my classroom," or "To increase the involvement of students through the use of more student-centered teaching techniques."

Learner goals focus on the specific outcomes expected of students. An example of a learner goal is "At least eighty percent of the students will be able to answer correctly at least eighty percent of the problems on a four-place multiplication test."

The focus of this chapter will be largely on program goals. Using the concepts of TQM, these would be thought of as process goals. Staff goals will be discussed at greater length in Chapter 13, Human Resources Development, and learner goals will be discussed in Chapters 9 and 10, on curriculum and instruction. Restructuring the Curriculum and Restructuring Learning.

The Principal's Role

Schools really can make a difference in the achievement levels of students, but a school is most often only as good or bad, as creative or sterile, as the person who serves as the head of that school. The research on effective schools highlights the role of the principal in establishing goals and objectives for the school.

What do effective principals do?

Principals of effective schools are strong instructional leaders who know how to manage time and money effectively…they concentrate on priority goals…they set as their main goal the acquisition of basic skills…effective principals have high expectations for all students and they will enlist the support of others in meeting common goals.[6]

The principal is the one person in a school who can oversee the entire program because of his or her interest in the success of the entire school and all of its parts. Therefore, the principal is in the best position to provide the necessary sense of direction to the various aspects of a school. Research has shown that the most effective principals have a clear sense of purpose and priorities and are able to enlist the support of others toward these ends.

Many of the problems of direction within a school organization are very subtle, will be difficult to solve, and require great conceptual and technical knowledge of curriculum, instruction, and learning. The principal must have the necessary understanding to find proper and just solutions to these problems and many others like them.

Framework for Establishing Beliefs or Philosophy Statements

The beliefs and philosophy for a school should relate to societal expectations, wants and needs, and the individual differences of children. Such a list can best be organized with an outline or framework of concepts and ideas to be included. There are many different ways such a framework can be organized. Three different frameworks or structures are included in this chapter for consideration.

School Structural Framework

The structure of a school program requires that specific thought be given to each of several organizational components of the program: (1) curricular organization, (2) instructional processes, (3) student grouping practices, (4) staff organization, (5) the scheduling of learning time, and (6) facility utilization and design. Although the six components can be separated for discussion purposes, the program that results for any particular school must give detailed attention both to the contribution that each component makes to the achievement of the goals and objectives of the school and the development of each component in such a way that it is compatible with the other five components. For example, a belief statement may speak to the importance of meeting the individual needs of each child. From this belief statement a goal of individualizing instruction might be selected. This instructional format must then be supported with a student grouping plan, staffing plan, and schedule. In turn, if the staffing selection proposes team teaching, the facility utilization design should provide appropriate work spaces for teaching teams.

The organizational components are not equally important and should not be considered as equals, nor are they independent entities. Decisions regarding the organization of the curriculum and instructional program should be made first. These must logically be based on the beliefs and goals for the school. The other four components serve the first two.

Evaluative Criteria Framework

A second perspective of what approach should be used in developing a statement of philosophy or beliefs is drawn from the *Evaluative Criteria* guidelines of the national accrediting associations. They suggest considerations should be given to the following:

1. *Relevance of the statement of philosophy to the larger purpose of the American democratic commitment.*
2. *Attention to intellectual, democratic, moral, and social values, basic to satisfying the needs of the individual and his culture.*
3. *Recognition of individual differences.*
4. *The special characteristics and unique needs of elementary school children.*
5. *Concern for the nature of knowledge and for the nature of the learning process as they apply to learners and their total development.*
6. *Consistency of philosophy with actual practice.*
7. *Identification of the roles and relationships expected of the community, the student, the teacher, and the administration in the educational process of the school.*
8. *The role of the elementary school program of the school district and the importance of the articulation with other elements of the overall educational program.*
9. *The responsibility for making a determination as to a desirable balance among activities designed to develop cognitive, affective, and psychomotor demands.*
10. *The relationship of the school and all other educational learning centers.*
11. *The responsibility of the school toward social and economic change.*
12. *The accountability of the school to the community it serves.*[7]

Effective Schools Framework

The research on effective schools also suggest specific areas that might be considered for inclusion in a beliefs and goals listing. A summary of major areas includes the following:

1. Schoolwide measurement and recognition of academic success
2. A positive student climate emphasizing an orderly and studious school environment
3. A high emphasis on curriculum articulation
4. High support for good methodology
5. High expectations and clear goals for performance of students
6. Parental support for the education of students

These three frameworks for identifying beliefs statements obviously have some degree of overlap. But each also has a certain rationale for its own structure. The school might elect to use one of the three frameworks or create its own structure from a combination of them. One or more belief statements can be written for each of the areas on the outline.

Beliefs Development

The process of establishing a sense of direction in a school must be a dynamic one involving teachers, community members, and, in some cases, students. In reality, the interaction and debate of the processes in determining what the document is to include is more important than the product itself in that the beliefs and goals are important only if they are alive. Beliefs must be kept alive in the minds of staff and community, and those people must feel that the goals and objectives relative to those beliefs are appropriate.

The initial formulation as well as the regular reviews and updates of the belief statements should be done using a staff-community-student consensus model. The participants are divided into writing teams consisting of three to five members, including all members of the faculty. Each writing team should be structured to create maximum internal variability. This means that each team should have teachers from different grade levels, subject areas, and experience background. If community members and students (secondary) are participating, one or more should be assigned to each writing team.

Each writing team should be given a complete list of belief topic areas. The team's task will be to write one or more statements regarding what it believes for each of the topics. For example, if one of the topic areas asks the team to list its beliefs regarding curriculum, the members might ultimately write a statement such as "We believe that the school staff should collectively review the basic objectives and strategies for teaching and learning and periodically reexamine and reconstruct objectives in view of current curricular priorities."

Each writing team should develop statements for each aspect of the belief framework. This may require 6 to 12 or more statements from each writing team. Upon the completion of the initial writing task, each writing team is asked to select one representative member from the group to meet with a similar member from each of the other teams to form a consensus team to discuss the statements written down by each team on the first topic. A second representative should be identified for the second topic as well as a third and fourth until all writing team members are representing their team to a consensus team consisting of one member from each of the other writing groups. Figure 6–2 illustrates the writing team–consensus team structure.

These newly formulated consensus teams review the written statements on the assigned topic from each of the writing teams and select, combine, and rewrite the submitted statements until they have developed a series of statements on the assigned topic that their group accepts. Each team representative then takes the newly combined set of statements on the team's topic back to his or her original writing team for discussion, additional modification, or ratification.

If the original writing team feels that the rewrite of the consensus team does not reflect the original team's beliefs, team members should modify the consensus team's work. The consensus team would then be reconvened to consider the recommended modifications. If necessary, the statements may go back and forth several times. The other consensus teams are carrying out the same procedures for their topics. The final set of belief statements developed by a school using this process is shown in Figure 6–3.

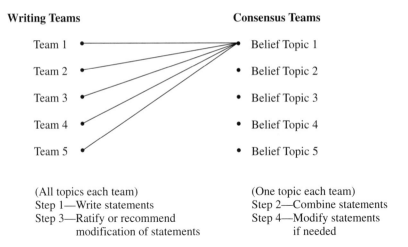

FIGURE 6–2   Writing Team–Consensus Team Structure

Developing Appropriate Goals for Improvement

Once the school's belief statement or philosophy has been developed, the next task becomes one of determining how well the beliefs are presently being implemented. Belief statements provide a sense of purpose for the school, but they often do not provide a specific sense of direction. For that reason, goals need to be stated to help the organization focus on improvement. One way to select goals is to conduct a needs assessment and discrepancy analysis to determine the extent to which those involved feel the beliefs are being carried out. The needs of the organization for improvement can then be defined using those beliefs that are least successfully achieved.

The Needs Assessment

A fundamental step in the planning process is the needs assessment. It requires a review of existing data and may require some surveying of clients and other appropriate reference groups.

There is always a certain risk in a needs assessment. In the process of uncovering needs, one may also raise expectations that all of the respondent's concerns will be addressed—and soon. Fundamental to good planning is priority setting and focus; thus, not all needs can be met immediately. Resources are in short supply and difficult, sometimes painful, decisions have to be made about which of an array of "pressing" needs requires attention.

Three reference groups are especially important to the needs assessment and planning process: students and parents, professional staff, and educational policymakers.

FIGURE 6–3 Sample High School Belief Statement

We believe that Manor High School is a unique educational environment. Its uniqueness is exemplified in certain aspects of its design. It is designed to meet the individual needs of a larger percentage of students than is possible in the traditional system; to avoid a mass-produced, molding effect; to provide a distinctly pleasant atmosphere for learning; to foster respectful relationships; and to serve the community.

We believe that all students have needs that must be fulfilled. We believe that all students are unique as individuals—that they develop at different rates and in different manners. We believe that students have a natural desire to learn independence, responsibility, self-assertion, democratic ideas, and the skills necessary to solve present and future problems.

We believe the role of the student is to involve himself or herself responsibly in the learning experience.

We believe that learning is evidenced by a behavioral change. It Is a continuous process that takes place in the home, community, and school.

We believe that the role of the teacher is (1) to design learning opportunities and (2) to provide each student for whom he or she is responsible the freedom to learn what the student needs to take a productive and rewarding part in society. The teacher is an advisor and sharer.

We believe that teaching and learning can best be accomplished through interaction and involvement of students, staff, administration, and community.

We believe that the administration is responsible for supplying and maintaining all the physical accouterments of the school. The principal is to be an instructional leader but shares with students, teachers, and community the task of facilitating and coordinating learning. His or her leadership should be participatory and not authoritarian.

Purpose: The purpose of Manor High School is to establish a student and community learning center with high expectations for student performance designed to facilitate stimulating learning experiences and harmonious social interactions in which each individual has the opportunity to realize his or her full potential.

It is our endeavor to develop the following qualities to a high degree through conscientious and dedicated guidance and instruction. These qualities are:

1. The self-evaluative ability of the individual
2. The positive attitude of the individual toward himself or herself and others
3. The independence and responsibility in the individual
4. The creativity in the individual
5. The ability to be self-assertive
6. The acquiring of knowledge relative to both the mental and physical needs and abilities of the individual
7. The critical thinking and decision-making ability of the individual
8. The ability of the individual to contribute to and to make his or her way in our society

Students and Parents

Much information about students is readily available in the myriad of reports a typical school system generates. Standardized test scores, attendance records, free lunch recipients, analyses of students with disabilities, transportation reports, among a host of other official and unofficial sources, serve as basic data sources when it comes time to develop a profile of the students in a school or school district. Informal discussions with colleagues, other professionals, and parents and community members about how former students are doing is another source—less objective perhaps, but nevertheless helpful for uncovering possible problem areas.

Judicious use of community and parent surveys can be very helpful to the school principal, as can community advisory groups. Such surveys are invaluable in the determination of parent and community expectations and attitudes as well as perceptions of educational needs of the community's young people. The diverse nature of most communities requires that in any survey care needs to be taken that the necessary degree of randomness exists. Concern for complete information as well as diversity of opinion should also be reflected in the composition of advisory groups.

Professional Staff

The professional staff of the school is another primary source of information about school needs, both with regard to instructional and curricular shortcomings as well as specific observations about the nature of the student body. Staff surveys, or any of a number of rational problem-solving processes, are useful in needs assessments. Good results frequently can be obtained by using some of these methods in combination.

For example, a faculty meeting—schoolwide, department, or grade level—may be given over to "brainstorming" such a topic as "This is a good school, but it could be better if…," following which the information is culled, recurring themes noted, and items generated for a survey to determine the perceived intensity and importance of the issues identified. The nominal group technique and the structured group creativity technique, discussed in Chapter 3, also offer possibilities.

Educational Policymakers

Some central office personnel of the school district may fall into this category. Local and state school board members, state departments of education, legislators, the federal Department of Education, among other agencies and agents that might come to mind, including the periodically constituted special education commissions, are policymakers.

Developing a Needs Assessment Instrument

A needs assessment instrument can be created by using the belief statements as a base. A series of items that can be rated on a five-point Likert-type rating scale, ranging from strongly disagree to strongly agree, are developed for each belief statement. An illustration of a needs assessment statement is as follows:

SA	A	N	DA	SD	
1	2	3	4	5	Programs and varied instructional techniques are provided in order to respond to each child's individual needs and differences.

Statements can be grouped into logical categories, weighted, and scored. For example, if belief statements were organized around concepts from the effective schools research including time, climate, basic commitment, staff, curriculum, leadership, and evaluation, several assessment items could be written for each of the categories. Responses can be divided by the number of items in the category in order to be viewed equally. This will allow comparison between categories for later priority determination. Figure 6–4 gives a complete illustration of a needs assessment instrument, including a weighted scoring sheet that is organized around effective schools concepts.

Although the development of the needs assessment instrument should be a major responsibility of the principal, other staff members should be contributors to the items included. Be sure the instrument offers the opportunity for written comments also.

Upon completion of the newly developed needs assessment instrument, it should be administered to all faculty members and also be completed by other reference groups that are knowledgeable about the school. Certainly include supervisory staff, but also include teacher aides, volunteers, and knowledgeable parents. When an ample number have been returned, they should be scored, weighted, and ranked by category. Areas of lowest weighted scores on the returned needs assessments are candidates for priority goal areas for the new planning period.

FIGURE 6–4   Needs Assessment

School Excellence Inventory

Directions—Rate the following Items on a scale of 1 to 5 to reflect your opinion of your school. (1 = Low…5 = High)

	(Low)				(High)
1. Students have favorable attitudes toward school and learning.	1	2	3	4	5
2. Student learning is frequently evaluated using curriculum-referenced materials.	1	2	3	4	5
3. The staff has high expectations for the students and adults with whom they work.	1	2	3	4	5
4. Student time on-task behavior is maintained at a high level because:					
a. A climate of order and discipline has been established.	1	2	3	4	5
b. Limited time is used in maintaining order.	1	2	3	4	5
c. Classroom management tasks have been "routinized" to maximize available instructional time.	1	2	3	4	5
d. The school staff has made a commitment to maximize learning time by reducing impediments to learning and interruptions of the school day.	1	2	3	4	5
5. Students and parents receive regular feedback regarding the student's progress	1	2	3	4	5
6. Student attendance rates are high.	1	2	3	4	5
7. There is a clear understanding of what the school believes in and stands for, which includes:					

Continued

FIGURE 6–4   *Continued*

School Excellence Inventory

a. An academic focus.	1 2 3 4 5
b. A belief that all students have the ability to learn.	1 2 3 4 5
c. An expectation that each student will learn.	1 2 3 4 5
d. High expectations for each student.	1 2 3 4 5
8. Teachers regularly utilize techniques to assure that all students are learning.	1 2 3 4 5
9. Staff members are evaluated regularly.	1 2 3 4 5
10. Programs and varied instructional techniques are provided in order to respond to each child's individual needs and differences.	1 2 3 4 5
11. Students feel valued and successful.	1 2 3 4 5
12. Individual help is provided to students when needed.	1 2 3 4 5
13. School staff members exhibit a high degree of concern and commitment for the achievement and well-being of each student.	1 2 3 4 5
14. The principal is effective because:	
a. He or she understands the process of instruction, and accepts the responsibility for being an instructional leader.	1 2 3 4 5
b. He or she is an able manager.	1 2 3 4 5
c. He or she has high attainable expectations for the students and adults with whom he or she works.	1 2 3 4 5
d. He or she has goal clarity (a clear sense of purpose and priorities) and is able to enlist the support of others in understanding, accepting, and accomplishing those ends.	1 2 3 4 5
e. He or she recognizes the importance of (and actively involves) the people who work in and who are served by the school.	1 2 3 4 5
f. He or she assists the school staff in implementing sound instructional practices.	1 2 3 4 5
15. Students receive prompt feedback on their work.	1 2 3 4 5
16. A high level of staff and student morale exists.	1 2 3 4 5
17. Members of the school staff are cooperative and supportive of each other.	1 2 3 4 5
18. The curriculum:	
a. Emphasizes mastery of basic skills.	1 2 3 4 5
b. Is well defined.	1 2 3 4 5
c. Is appropriately sequenced and articulated from grade to grade and from subject to subject.	1 2 3 4 5
d. Includes clearly defined learner goals.	1 2 3 4 5
e. Is regularly evaluated.	1 2 3 4 5
19. Techniques are used to pinpoint individual student's strengths and weaknesses.	1 2 3 4 5
20. The staff is competent and continues to grow and learn.	1 2 3 4 5
21. The school is open to and encourages participation and involvement by parents and other citizens.	1 2 3 4
22. Parents, students, and staff place a high priority on learning.	1 2 3 4 5
23. Students are instructed at the appropriate level of difficulty.	1 2 3 4 5

FIGURE 6–4 *Continued*

Summary Sheet
School Excellence Inventory

Time	Climate	Basic Commitment	Staff	Curriculum	Leadership	Evaluation
#4a = ____	#1 = ____	#7a = ____	#3 = ____	#10 = ____	#14a = ____	#2 = ____
#4b = ____	#6 = ____	#7b = ____	#9 = ____	#18a = ____	#14b = ____	#5 = ____
#4c = ____	#11 = ____	#7c = ____	#13 = ____	#18b = ____	#14c = ____	#8 = ____
#4d = ____	#16 = ____	#7d = ____	#17 = ____	#18c = ____	#14d = ____	#12 = ____
Total = ____	#21 = ____	#22 = ____	#20 = ____	#18d = ____	#14e = ____	#15 = ____
+4 = ____	Total = ____	Total = ____	Total = ____	#18e = ____	#14f = ____	#19 = ____
	+ 5 = ____	+ 5 = ____	+ 5 = ____	Total = ____	Total = ____	#23 = ____
				+ 6 = ____	+ 6 = ____	Total = ____
						+7 = ____

Campus Planning

The next step after the needs assessment is the development of the campus plan. A campus plan translates the results of the needs assessment into *targeted* areas for improvement. The word *targeted* is emphasized because it is frequently at this point that good intentions and good sense and a lot of heretofore energetic persons disperse and collapse in a gigantic pile of paper covered with statements of low-level objectives and quantifiable measures of attainment of low-level objectives. Care must be taken to focus on those aspects of improvement that carry the most impact on the quality of schooling. This requires priority setting and a recognition that not all things can be addressed. The limitations of resources—human, time, physical, and fiscal—must always be reckoned with.

Displayed in Figure 6–5 is a format for a campus plan. Each of the five functional aspects of the school operation is subjected to analysis. In the example, six aspects are revealed because "building maintenance" is most conveniently separated from "finance and budgeting." An analysis is made of the strengths and weaknesses of these aspects at the various levels of the school organization. It is here that the product of the needs assessment is most useful. The final column is designated for statements of proposed actions, most often stated as outcomes or objectives to be attained, to address targeted deficiencies.

What remains is to develop the proposed actions, outcomes, or objectives into an action plan. Action planning to achieve measurable results is the subject of the next part of this chapter.

FIGURE 6–5   School Self-Study

Campus: _____ Grade/Department: _____			
Aspects Studied	**Strengths**	**Deficiencies**	**Action to Take**
Instructional Program			
Staff			
Pupil Achievement			
Parent and Community Relations			
Finance and Budgeting			
Building Maintenance			

Action Planning/Project Management

Action planning is what professional planners label *programming an objective*, and that label is descriptive. The action plan contains

- A description of the several activities necessary to achieve an objective
- The relationship of these activities to each other
- The assignment of specific responsibilities to individuals who will see to the implementation of the activities
- A time frame and chronology of activities and events
- An evaluation process

There are no guarantees that the plan will succeed in solving the existing problem, of course, and that is why the last element of the plan provides for an evaluation. The activities in the plan may be best thought of as "hypotheses"—more than a hunch, perhaps, certainly more than a hope, but nevertheless, not certainties. Therefore, it is necessary to evaluate the efficacy carefully, not only of the total project but also of the specific activities comprising the project.

Once the action plan is developed, project management is in great part a monitoring process. The project manager may be the principal but not necessarily so. Any person on the staff with good administrative skills and an interest in the project may be a likely candidate to become the manager.

This becomes an excellent way for the principal to develop and capitalize on the leadership skills of staff members, including assistant principals, faculty, and resource or support personnel. It is important that adequate resources be provided to the person put in charge of managing a project. This may include released time and secretarial service, as well as a budget.

Problem Analysis

Care must always be taken that the presumed problem is adequately analyzed before moving into an elaborate action plan. It is at the problem analysis point that a force field analysis proves helpful.

Force Field Analysis

Kurt Lewin, applying certain physical laws to the organizational setting, concluded that things stay the way they are in organizations because a field of opposing forces is in balance. One way to think about a problem situation is to regard the situation as being as it is because of positive ("driving") and negative ("restraining") forces that are equal in strength. The driving forces are current conditions and actions present in the organizational environment (or in the community, or even in society as a whole) which are such that change is encouraged. Restraining forces are conditions or actions which are such that change is discouraged or inhibited. These can be thought of as negative, or "minus," forces in the developing equation.

The force field concept issues from the physical law that a body at rest (in equilibrium) will remain at rest when the sum of all the forces operating on it is equal to zero. The body will move only when the sum is nor zero, *and it will move only in the direction of the unbalancing force.*

It is not difficult to observe this phenomenon in organizations. The productivity of a school staff, the state of the school-community relations program, the success level of the intramural program, among any number of other observable situations are all subject to explanation (and change) by force field analysis. A thing is where it is because the sum of the *power* of the counterbalancing plus and minus forces is equal to zero—and the situation is "frozen."

Power is a key word here because equilibrium is not achieved by a simple equal *number* of forces. It is the strength of the force that is important. One overwhelming positive force (e.g., the infusion of huge amounts of federal or state dollars) may be quite sufficient to change dramatically the nature of a science program that had suffered from lack of equipment, inadequately prepared teachers, and lack of community concern. Similarly, a large, vocal, and interested religious group might impact mightily on the nature of a science curriculum in any particular community, despite research evidence about inquiry methods, adequate budget, well-trained teachers, or bright students, among any number of other forces that would otherwise be generative of good programming.

Movement (that is, change) will take place only when an imbalance is created. An imbalance will occur by eliminating forces, by developing new forces, or by affecting the power of existing forces. The imbalance "unfreezes" the current situation and the situation will change and a new state of equilibrium achieved. To recapitulate, an imbalance may be created by:

- The addition of a new force(s)
- The deletion of a force(s)
- A change in the magnitude or strength of any of the forces

Any plan that is developed after the force field analysis is conducted will probably make use of all three ways of creating an imbalance.

There is evidence, however, that attempting to increase only positive forces creates much tension in the system, and often the intensity of the restraining forces correspondingly increases. This leaves the organization no better off, and sometimes worse off, because of new tensions. The best results occur when the first effort is directed to reducing the intensity of the restraining forces. Also, there may be little or nothing that can be done about some of the forces—a few may be imponderables; others simply may be outside of the control of organization members.

Engaging in force field analysis focuses thinking and may result in a restatement of the problem. Often, what appeared to be the problem is really a symptom; one of the identified "restraining forces" is actually the problem that requires attention. Thus, a principal, project manager, and staff must have open minds at the early stages in order that energies are ultimately focused on the right issues and not dissipated on things that are only symptomatic.

A Case in Point

You are the principal of a middle school with an enrollment of 800 students. The composition of the student body is racially and ethnically heterogeneous, with perhaps few more children from families at the lower end of the community's economic continuum. The following describes the current state of affairs:

Case Study

You have become aware that all might not be well with the reading program in your school. The students in grades seven and eight do not seem to be reading as well as might be expected. There are a number troubling indicators.

As you review scores on standardized tests, the Iowa Test of Basic Skills among these, you observe that your students, in the main, are well below norms for the system as a whole and for the nation. Several of your teachers have also expressed concern about the reading skills of their students. The librarian has commented about a low circulation rate even among the usually more popular children's books. Senior high school principal colleagues have remarked to you that the incoming students from your school seem to have less well-developed reading skills.

As you examine the situation, you reach the conclusion that something is functionally wrong with the reading program, and the anticipated outcome—adequately skilled readers—is not being realized.

An example of a partial force field analysis of this problem appears in Figure 6–6. In any given real situation, many forces beyond those suggested in the example could exist. When conducting such an analysis, it is important to focus only on *what is*, not on what *might be* or on what one wishes were so. The purpose of the force field analysis is to get the problem under an analytical lens, so that a feasible solution (action plan) can be developed either to solve or ameliorate the problem.

Generating Action Plans

Once the force field analysis has been completed, it is time to generate ideas for activities that, if accomplished, could be assumed to help solve the problem. Creative thought is what is sought. To do this, a principal could lead the staff in any of the three techniques for "unstructured" problem solving described in Chapter 3. Brainstorming or the nominal group techniques most easily lend themselves to this. There is one caveat. If the solutions generated do not relate in any way to the pluses and minuses in the force field analysis, they probably should be discarded. Unless the activity is such that it would seem to reduce a negative or strengthen a positive, then that activity cannot be expected to help solve the problem. All project activities must be related to the force field. Figure 6–7 illustrates this.

FIGURE 6–6   Example of a Force Field Analysis

Problem: The pupils in Hughes Middle School are not developing good reading skills.

Facilitating Forces (+)	Restraining Forces (−)
Instructional Materials Center	Student transiency (over district average)
Full-time librarian	Bilingual population
Budgeted for 3 aides	Bimodal distribution of teachers (many first
Funded ESL program	year)
New reading series	New reading series program; no in-service
Assistant principal is a reading specialist	Parental involvement in school activities slight
State mandated and funded tutorial program	Little study room in homes—high number of
Most children walk to school (no bus students)	apartment and project dwellers
Expressed teacher concerns	Teacher turnover above district average
Flexible schedule	Single-parent and two-wage earner homes (people not readily available)
	No role models
	Staff overload

FIGURE 6–7   Action Planning: The Problem Resolution Document

Project: Improving the reading skills of seventh- and eighth-grade students at Hughes Middle School

Project Manager:	Kay Weise, Assistant Principal
Completion Date:	June 1*
Start Date:	August 15

Actions	Start/Complete	Relation to Force Field (What +/−)	Coordinator
Volunteers Program	10/1-cont.	#5(−)	Holland
After-school study program	11/1 cont.	#6(−)	Norris
"Why I Read" speakers	11/1–6/1	#9(−)	Carspecken
New teacher in-service program: Reading in subject areas	8/15–2/15	#6(+) #9(+) #3(−)	Craig
Reader of the Month Award	9/15–6/1	#1(+) #2(+)	Tanner
"Here's an Author"	2/1–3/1	#9(−)	Strahan
Story-Telling Time	10/5–5/15	#2(+) #3(+) #10(+)	Miller

*Actions #1 and #2 continue beyond June.

The Project Planning Document

Complex problems require the use of a planning document. The resolution of simple problems may not require an involved procedure, but the logic and steps in the project planning document are nevertheless applicable and should at least be a mental process. The document is the project manager's guide, and serves also as a monitoring device.

Figure 6–7 illustrates a comprehensive problem resolution document. Using the previous case as an example, the project goal is stated, activities are delineated, target dates are established, and specific persons are identified who have assigned responsibilities for the implementation of the activities.

In many instances, a specific activity may be especially complex and composed of several components to be carried out before the activity is accomplished. The responsible person would develop a similar document for use with his or her team and the project would be desegregated to another level. The point is, with such a document, tasks are clearly spelled out and all are made aware of precisely what it is that is being attempted, how, who is responsible, when, and for what.

Putting the Plan into Operation

The project has now been separated into a series of activities—complex activities have been subdivided into elements or events, the completion of which will conclude the activity, and responsibilities have been assigned and accepted. Before proceeding, there is need to establish realistic target dates, develop the project calendar, and put into place a monitoring and evaluation process. Project planning computer software is of great assistance in organizing and managing large projects.[8] Each of the activities and documents listed in this section can be efficiently developed with a good computer planning package.

Establishing Target Dates

Establishing precise starting and completion times for the project as a whole, as well as for each of the separate project activities, is critical.[9] In order to establish realistic completion dates, it is essential that those involved in the project understand: (1) the nuances of the problem; (2) certain organizational realities, including, for example, requisitioning and purchasing procedures and time lines; and (3) the capabilities of the staff. If these conditions are met, then it is possible to set realistic target dates. To do this, the project team raises two questions: "If unanticipated problems arose—strikes, floods, a championship basketball team—what is the most pessimistic date by which this project could be completed?" Then the question is asked: "If all went well—no one became ill, adequate resources were available, the purchasing department finally got its act together—what is the most optimistic date by which this project could be completed?" The realistic target date is a point midway between the pessimistic and optimistic dates.

The Project Calendar: Gantt Charting

Once the activities and tasks have been delineated, the specific elements of the more complex activities detailed, and responsibilities assigned, the master schedule needs to be developed and posted. This is developed in the form of a *Gantt chart*. Figure 6–8 depicts a Gantt chart for the case study presented earlier. In the Gantt chart, each project activity is listed, along with the elements or tasks composing each activity and an indication of the targeted starting and completion dates of every entry.

The Master Project Document
The preparation of a master project document is an important responsibility of the project manager. The document may simply be a loose-leaf binder within which is placed the comprehensive problem resolution document, key personnel checklist, Gantt chart, minutes of team meetings, and any diary entries or other notes that might help future project managers. Such a document is of great assistance in the monitoring and evaluation process.

Monitoring and Evaluating the Project
The project manager's responsibility is to help the project team stay on schedule. This does not mean daily, or even weekly, supervision; it does mean frequent conversations with individual activity coordinators and regular team meetings for the purpose of information sharing and "midpoint corrections."

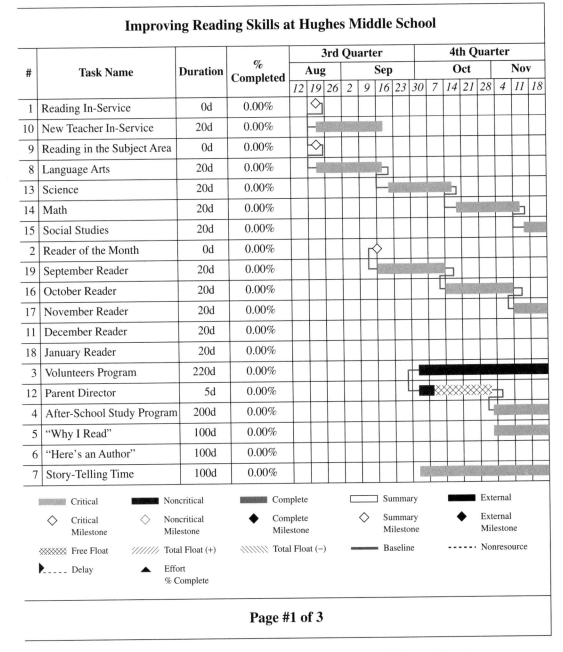

Improving Reading Skills at Hughes Middle School

#	Task Name	Duration	% Completed	3rd Quarter								4th Quarter						
				Aug			Sep				Oct				Nov			
				12	19	26	2	9	16	23	30	7	14	21	28	4	11	18
1	Reading In-Service	0d	0.00%															
10	New Teacher In-Service	20d	0.00%															
9	Reading in the Subject Area	0d	0.00%															
8	Language Arts	20d	0.00%															
13	Science	20d	0.00%															
14	Math	20d	0.00%															
15	Social Studies	20d	0.00%															
2	Reader of the Month	0d	0.00%															
19	September Reader	20d	0.00%															
16	October Reader	20d	0.00%															
17	November Reader	20d	0.00%															
11	December Reader	20d	0.00%															
18	January Reader	20d	0.00%															
3	Volunteers Program	220d	0.00%															
12	Parent Director	5d	0.00%															
4	After-School Study Program	200d	0.00%															
5	"Why I Read"	100d	0.00%															
6	"Here's an Author"	100d	0.00%															
7	Story-Telling Time	100d	0.00%															

Legend:
- Critical
- Noncritical
- Complete
- Summary
- External
- Critical Milestone
- Noncritical Milestone
- Complete Milestone
- Summary Milestone
- External Milestone
- Free Float
- Total Float (+)
- Total Float (−)
- Baseline
- Nonresource
- Delay
- Effort % Complete

Page #1 of 3

FIGURE 6–8   The Project Calendar: Task List and Gantt Chart

Other monitoring devices are available to the principal or project manager to help keep the project on target or to adapt to changes in the environment. Prominent posting of the Gantt chart will serve as both advertisement and stimulator.

Summative Evaluation

If regular monitoring has been occurring, then formative evaluation has been taking place. What remains to be developed is the summative evaluation. That is, how will the principal know if the project resulted in the desired outcome? Are things better? What worked? What did not work? What should be continued? What should not be continued?

To lend specificity, clarity, and form to the evaluation process, it is useful to think of the several activities as "hypotheses." In the case study, it was believed that if certain activities were carried out, students would evidence better reading skills. These hypotheses must be tested, for it is pointless to engage in a series of activities if there are no provisions to determine whether the results were sufficient to justify continued expenditure of resources.

At the beginning of any project it is important to state the indicators of achievement that the project staff is willing to accept as evidence of movement in the direction of the desired outcome. These indicators best come from restatements of the symptoms of the problem as originally stated. In the case study, some of those symptoms were

1. Standardized test scores were below system norms.
2. The circulation rates of library books was low.
3. Caustic comments were received from senior high school principals.
4. Teachers in the building expressed concerns.
5. There is high teacher turnover.

Changes in these conditions provide a basis for evaluating the effectiveness of the project. A review of test data, surveys of teachers and administrators, circulation rates, and formal and informal feedback from students and parents are all available tools for determining whether the project was successful. Moreover, it may be that certain of the activities were more productive than others. This, too, needs to be investigated and any changes made so that energies and other resources are focused for maximum benefit.

Summary

The subject of this chapter has been goal setting and systematic problem identification and resolution. Schools exist in an environment of change. The productivity of any particular school organization will depend in great part on the ability of leaders to analyze current conditions and future challenges, develop goals, and implement strategies for attaining the goals.

Instituting a process for identifying needs, and developing a campus plan to resolve these needs in a manner consistent with system needs is critical to effective building level leadership. Action planning and project management are fundamental skills that must be employed to meet this challenge satisfactorily.

Activities

1. Review Case Studies 1, 2, and 5. Apply the goal setting and strategic planning concepts expressed in this chapter. How might you proceed in addressing the problems cited in these cases? Set forth a strategy to overcome the problem.

2. Review the activities at the end of Chapters 13 and 15 for further planning activities.

Endnotes

1. Comments of the Cheshire cat to Alice (*Alice in Wonderland*) upon her request for directions after admitting she didn't know where she wanted to go.

2. *Goals 2000: Educate America Fact Sheet* (Washington DC: United States Department of Education, 1994).

3. The issue of international comparisons for education continues to grow along with the movement toward a global economy. An excellent resource to assist one's reflection on goal development is the NASSP publication edited by John M. Jenkins, *World Class Schools, an Evolving Concept* (Reston, VA: National Association of Secondary School Principals, 1994).

4. Chapter 1 outlines the concepts of Total Quality Management (TQM) and the 14 principles for TQM proposed by Edwards Deming.

5. T. E. Deal and L. D. Celotti, *Loose Coupling and School Administrators: Some Recent Research Findings* (Stanford, CA: Center for Educational Research, 1977).

6. *Good Schools—What Makes Them Work* (Washington, DC: National School Public Relations Association, 1980).

7. *Elementary School Evaluative Criteria* (Arlington, VA: National Study of School Evaluation, A Guide for School Improvement, 1973), pp. 39–40.

8. The Gantt chart illustration (Figure 6–8) uses *Project Scheduler 6 for Windows* by Scitor Corporation. There are many other good planning programs on the market, such as *Microsoft Project*.

9. In not all cases will the completion of one activity, or one component, depend on another, but sometimes this will be so. Even when this is not so, it is nonetheless vital that activities be completed on time. When a project is very complex and has many interrelated parts, it may be necessary to institute the Program Evaluation Review Technique (PERT). PERT will depict the order in which each of the activities and any subactivities must occur, as well as the relationship of one activity, event, or element to another. Especially good treatments of this technique applied to problem solving in the educational setting can be found in Saxe (1984, pp. 36–39).

Selected Readings

Buell, Nancy A. "Building a Shared Vision—The Principal's Leadership Challenge." *NASSP Bulletin* 76, no. 542 (March 1992): 88–92.

Carlson, Robert V., and Gary Awkerman (Eds.). *Education Planning: Concepts, Strategies and Practices* (New York: Longman, 1990).

Chance, Edward W., and Marilyn L. Grady. "Creating and Implementing as Vision for the School." *NASSP Bulletin* 74, no. 529 (November 1990): 12–18.

Duke, Daniel L. "What Is the Nature of Educational Excellence and Should We Try to Measure It?" *Phi Delta Kappan* 66 (June 1985): 671–674.

Gaynor, Alan K, and Jane L. Evanson. *Project Planning: A Guide for Practitioners* (Boston: Allyn and Bacon, 1992).

Goodlad, John I. "A Study of Schooling: Some Findings and Hypotheses." *Phi Delta Kappan* 64, no. 7 (March 1983): 465–470.

Herman, Jerry J. "School-Based Management: Sharing Resource Decisions." *NASSP Bulletin* 76, no. 545 (September 1992): 102–105.

Holt, Maurice."The Educational Consequences of W. Edwards Deming." *Phi Delta Kappan* 74, no. 5 (January 1993): 382–388.

Hughes, Larry W. "Organizing and Managing Time," in *Developing Skills for Instructional Supervision,* ed. James Cooper (Chapter 3) (New York: Longman, 1984).

Hughes, Larry W., and Gerald C. Ubben. *The Elementary Principal's Handbook: A Guide to Effective Action,* 4th ed. (Boston: Allyn and Bacon, 1994). Especially see Chapters 5 and 21.

Lewis, James, Jr. *Long-Range and Short-Range Planning for Educational Administrators* (Boston: Allyn and Bacon. 1983).

Martisco, Les, and William Ammentorp. "Take Five Strategic Planning Steps and Turn School Goals into Realities." *American School Board Journal* 173, no. 3 (March 1986): 38–39.

Rankin, Stuart C. "Total Quality Management: Implications for Educational Assessment." *NASSP Bulletin 76, no.* 545 (September 1992): 66–76.

Rhodes, Lewis A. "Beyond Your Beliefs: Quantum Leaps Toward Quality Schools." *The School Administrator* (December 1990): 23–26.

Rhodes, Lewis A. "Why Quality Is within Our Grasp…If We Reach." *The School Administrator* (September 1990): 31–33.

Saxe Richard. "Planning, and Goal Setting," in *Developing Skills for Instructional Supervision,* ed. James Cooper (Chapter 2) (New York: Longman, 1984).

Sergiovanni, Thomas J. *The Principalship: A Reflective Practice Perspective* (Boston: Allyn and Bacon, 1987). See Chapters 4 and 6 especially.

Snyder, Karolyn J., et al. "School Improvement Goal Setting: A Collaborative Model." *NASSP Bulletin 67,* no. 465 (October 1983): 60–65.

Valentine, Evelyn Pasteur. *Strategic Management in Education: A Focus on Strategic Planning* (Boston: Allyn and Bacon, 1991).

Vann, Allan S. "Setting Specific Annual School Goals." *Principal* 69, no. 5 (May 1990): 43–45.

Wilson, Richard B., and Mike Schmoker. "Quest for Quality." *The Executive Educator* (January 1992): 18–22.

Chapter 7

Creating a Positive Learning Climate

Student Control and Student Services

We have to assure these children that while they are with us they are safe and will be treated well. For some that may be all we can do but we must do that. We may not be able to control what goes on in any child's life before or after school. But here they will not be abused and they will be treated fairly. And they will be protected and they will be respected. And we're going to help them learn how life can be. —KARON RILLING[1]

High-performance schools invariably are orderly places. They are characterized by high standards, high expectations, and a caring environment. Misbehavior is dealt with quickly, fairly, openly, and without recrimination.

Analyses of leadership styles and support behaviors reveal that principals in high-performance schools are assertive and task and academically oriented. In effective schools, the discipline code is clear and the principal is viewed as "firm and friendly" but not as a "pal." Punishment for breaking the rules is certain. Good principals are mobile and highly visible in the halls, classrooms, and cafeteria. They spend much time monitoring behavior, troubleshooting and conferring with teachers.

It's No Secret

Study after study and myriad reports from practicing principals reveal four essential ingredients of the maximally productive environment for learning and positive student control:

- Clear, firm, and high teacher and administrator expectations
- Consistent rules and consequences that directly relate to breaking these rules
- A decided and well-implemented emphasis on the self-esteem of all students
- Public and private acknowledgment and rewarding of positive behavior by students.

The School as a Culture

Schools have a complex student society, and many things go on in a school that seemingly have little relationship to the curriculum. All of these things, including the curriculum, impact mightily on the learning climate of the school. Creating a positive learning climate requires a great understanding of the needs of learners. The needs of learners are varied and only partly addressed by a formalized set of classroom and cocurricular activities.

The real or perceived normative behavior of a student body will determine reward or punishment practices, teacher and administrator attitudes and behaviors, and even teacher and administrator attrition rates. Some schools in a community may be classified as "tough" schools; others as "good places to work"; most often, these references reflect normative student behavior patterns. And, it is easy to forget, normative behaviors and mass actions to the contrary, a student body is composed of many bodies and, while certain groups may determine in great part the "accepted" behavior, the student who walks through the door of the principal's office is an individual complex of forces that may or may not epitomize the student body.

The focus of this chapter is on student behavior and positive student control mechanisms to help students be successful. The chapter is organized into three parts. The first part contains a discussion of principles for achieving positive student control. Included are suggestions for the development of sensible rules and regulations. We conclude the section with an examination of gangs and violence. The second and third parts of the chapter include discussions about student counseling programs and other student services.

Positive Student Control

For more years than either of us care to think about, we have been actively engaged in working with principals and school faculties throughout the United States and other nations. Few things are universally true in this world but we have *never* been in a school that had a productive learning environment that was not also orderly. The schools were not always quiet, but they were always orderly. Students and teachers were going about the business of learning in an efficient, effective, and caring way.

People (staff, students, and parents) knew what the rules were and worked hard to see that they were abided by. Transgressions were dealt with quickly, fairly, and without lingering resentments. In these schools it was the uniform practice to follow the principles of substantive and procedural due process in spirit and in practice.

Five Premises about the School Environment and Students

Our discussion about schooling and student behavior is based on five premises:

1. Schooling occurs in a group context. Therefore, the behavior of any individual student will instantaneously have an impact on the behavior of other students.
2. Learning occurs best in an orderly environment.
3. An orderly environment can be best achieved by policies and strategies that promote self-regulation of behavior (internal control) rather than policies and strategies that try to force compliance with elaborate control mechanisms and overuse punishment (external control).
4. The environment is enhanced when the staff behaves in an orderly and internally controlled way.
5. The rules to guide behavior should be simple, well known, and continuously reinforced.

The Development of a Positive Program

The principal of a school has a particular responsibility to lead the staff in developing school policies to control student behavior. This is not to suggest that the principal personally should write the policy, but it is the principal who must develop the procedures by which the staff can establish a behavior philosophy, disciplinary procedures to be followed, and techniques for corrective action.

Fundamental to an orderly learning climate are well-understood, appropriate, and consistently applied rules and procedures. Once the rules are in place, there are two equally important conditions that must be met: The rules must be promulgated in a manner that ensures understanding by all affected, and there must be regular and systematic evaluation of the need for and efficacy of existing rules. Times change, needs change, and appropriate response patterns change. It is important that rules be examined routinely in view of whether they continue to serve the intended purpose in an effective and efficient manner.

Developing Good Rules

It is axiomatic that if staff and students are to be held accountable for certain standards, these expectations must be established and promulgated *ahead of their application* in a manner that makes them easily disseminated, learned, and understood. A principal has the responsibility to prescribe reasonable controls for the efficient day-to-day operation of the schools.

What is "reasonable"? A rule of thumb applied most frequently by the court is, "Does the regulation enhance the education of the children, promote their interest and welfare, and is it for the common good of education?" It is implicit that the regulations be within the legal authority of the school district. Regulations beyond the province of the school board are not enforceable. A long-standing decision has held that "boards are not at liberty to adopt according to their humor regulations which have no relevance to the schools' purposes.[2] This would be no less true in the matter of rules and regulations prescribed by the principal.

Moreover, while it is sound management practice to develop procedures and guidelines that provide for consistency of school operation, conscious parsimony will serve best. Developing long lists of do's and don't's in an attempt to cover every contingency can create a school climate in which the name of the game becomes beating the system—a climate in which staff and students derive a perverse joy from testing the limits.

Neither the extreme of rules for every occasion nor its opposite, no rule at all, is sensible. Principals within the school and teachers within the classroom have the right *and the obligation* to determine reasonable policies governing the conduct of their charges, not only to maintain a proper educational climate but also for safety.

Other Factors Influencing Behavior

There are other conditions well within the control of the school administrator and staff that contribute much to the learning climate. Disorder and lack of control in schools are frequently a result of the existence of large, impersonal masses of students. Students' feelings of alienation and teachers' feelings of helplessness must be recognized and can be addressed by the reorganization of schools into smaller learning communities. The "school within a school" concept *is* relevant.

It is also true that most of the severe disciplinary problems are caused by a very small percentage of the students. Special facilities and methods are needed to handle the more severely disruptive children if these cannot be handled effectively in the classroom. Crisis intervention centers, "adaptive behavior classes," and in-school suspensions, among a number of other common practices, respond to this problem.

The principal's own behavior and activities will help set the tone. A principal who helps teachers develop good disciplinary practices, a principal who maintains direct contact with students, and a principal who is visible and active in the hall, cafeteria, and library is critical to a good learning climate.

Actively Encouraging a Positive Learning Environment

A Promising Model

DuSable High School in Chicago is a good example of how one principal restructured his high school to address the impact that alienation and an inadequate social response system have on student behavior and the increasing incidence of violence in schools. DuSable serves an inner-city neighborhood that, at best, has been called "mean." It is not a huge high school—on any given day the number of students in attendance will be about 1,000—but the organizational framework at DuSable would work in any school, larger or smaller. With a combination of well-trained teachers and an organization characterized by a "house plan," serious discipline problems are significantly down and attendance is up.

The school is organized into 11 houses that operate under the philosophy of Theodore Sizer's Coalition of Essential Schools. DuSable is a member of the Coalition. The philosophic base is that anonymity and intellectual chaos are a concomitant of large schools—unless there are structural and instructional changes beyond simply adding more teachers, more sections of classes, and increasing the number of security personnel.

Sizer submits that large schools need to create clutches of students and teachers. The large school should be characterized by "a clutch of kids with a clutch of teachers. That's important because it's hard for any one of us to size up any kid well. If teachers have time to discuss these kids, they're liable to get a pretty good fix on them. They know them when they get into trouble.... At the same time, the students know they are cared for."[3]

At DuSable, each of the 11 houses has 8 to 10 teachers. Each of these teachers has undergone intensive and extensive training in curriculum planning, team building, and ways to assess student progress well beyond the usual standardized achievement tests. A learning community is created that at once contains the intimacy required to diminish alienation. The key ingredients are well-trained teachers, a restructured curriculum, block scheduling, and learners and teachers as teams.

Personalizing the School

The DuSable example has much relevance to creating an inviting school environment—an environment within which students take ownership of their school and behave in ways that are socially responsible.

Sizer states, "Personalization is the single most important factor that keeps kids in school."[4] And, no surprise here—staying in school is the single most important factor in student learning. In a study that examined data from all 50 states and the District of Columbia and focused on student outcomes, fiscal issues, and student persistence in schools (that is, not dropping out). Hashway reached the conclusion that "the most influential factor upon school persistence is school achievement." Very important and very pertinent to our discussion here, Hashway went on to write, "Students who view themselves as successful will stay in school."[5] To this same point, Achilles and Smith wrote, "Educators know that those who do best in school, who are rewarded by school participation, and who like school are also those who are most often not absent and not drop-outs."[6]

Positive learning environments are characterized by outward and readily recognized mutual expressions of appreciation and respect—from student to student, teacher to student, teacher to teacher, teacher to administrator, administrator to student—honestly given and graciously received. Positive learning environments are also characterized by mechanisms for the early identification of students who are drifting from the central purpose of formal schooling. Finally, positive learning climates are characterized by orderliness and a compassionate concern for the security of all members of the school family. Action-oriented programs are required to create the positive learning environment.

"Hoopla"

The efficacy of public rewards for achievement cannot be underestimated. "Hoopla" is not hokey; the most productive organizations—in private and public sectors—make much of measured progress toward goals and of individual accomplishment. Acknowledgment of achievement shouldn't be limited to only students; the entire school family, custodians, bus drivers, teachers, counselors, and all the rest, deserve public recognition for jobs well done.

Effective methods of acknowledgment abound: T-shirts, public ceremonies, special parking privileges, positive time-out, bulletin board exhibits, standing ovations at assemblies, stars and stickers, "Number One" clubs, prizes, badges, friendly taps on the shoulder, and the list could go on. The point is that praise, sincerely given, works!

"Hoopla" is also important to help individuals recognize their own achievements without benefit of others' approval. Self-approval is sustaining. Teachers can help students in this by asking them to share a personal accomplishment that they are proud of but that others may not know about. Principals can do the same with the staff.

Adult Visibility

Community volunteer programs that have increasing numbers of parents and other citizens in the schools are a great help in reducing the incidence of violence and gang activity. We are not referring here simply to "parent patrols" in the halls and the like, although this is one type of activity that has been used that has shown some success. Any of a variety of volunteer programs that increase the conspicuous visibility of adults—and particularly parents—in the schools will help. Children report feeling safer when adults are around.

Gangs

Policies and procedures that decrease gang activity may be best developed locally to meet local needs. Some general considerations can be found in the research and literature, however. Figure 7–1 identifies some steps a school staff can take if there is evidence of gang activity on the campus.

FIGURE 7–1   Is There a Gang in the House?

Steps to Be Taken if Gang Activity Is Suspected

School administrators should:

- Establish the school as neutral ground and adopt a "no-tolerance" policy for gang activity.
- Distinguish between youthful misbehavior and delinquent or criminal acts.
- Cooperate with other social agencies, including the police or sheriff's department, to train school personnel in how to identify and handle gang members.
- Create a mechanism for mediating student conflicts, including consideration of peer mediation.

Teachers should:

- Treat all students fairly and consistently.
- Incorporate gang issues into class lessons; address rights and responsibilities of citizens, decision making, and problem-solving skills.
- Establish good lines of communication with parents.
- Be aware of community resources that are available.

Achilles and Smith sum up the principal's responsibility: "The principal *must* ensure a safe environment that encourages learning. Pupils need to feel safe so they can attend to the school's learning goals; pupils who are trying to learn must be free from harassment, violence and external diversions that distract them from the tasks of learning. Teachers should be free to work at teaching rather than at order and control."[7]

Gangs are *not* loose social networks, however, and even though the attraction may be protection and friendship, *the goal of a gang is control and social intimidation.* Gangs operate outside of the civilized social fabric and in lawless ways.

Generally speaking, a gang is a group who meets all of the following criteria:

- The group has a name and an idenfiable leader or leadership structure.
- The group maintains a geographic, economic, or criminal activity "turf."
- Members associate on a regular and continuous basis in school and out of school.
- The group has visual symbols—insignia, greeting patterns, distinguishing dress, and so on—that readily identify one as either a member or nonmember.
- The group engages in delinquent or criminal activity. Delinquent and/or criminal activity is what differentiates a gang from organizations that often are otherwise visually consistent with stereotypic images of a gang.

School personnel need to become familiar with the symbols, terms, phrases, and other identifiers of gang presence. Figure 7–2 describes telltale signs suggesting the presence of gangs in the school.

The School as a Safe Haven

Schools should be safe places irrespective of the nature of the neighborhood from which the students come. This means a zero-tolerance policy for major transgressions. No weapons, no controlled substances, no graffiti—this must be the policy of the school, and all personnel and all students need to be advised of this and what to do when these are discovered. What should be done if this policy is violated? Report it, immediately. The principal's responsibility is to get the transgressor out of contact with

FIGURE 7–2   Is There a Gang in the House?

There May Be Gangs if...

Graffiti: Unusual or indecipherable signs, symbols, alphabets, and nicknames on walls, notebooks, papers, and clothing might be signals of gang presence.

Colors: Members of gangs often reveal a subtle or obvious choice of clothing or color of clothing, or wear specific brands or styles of clothing, hats, shoes, jewelry, or haircuts, or may wear their clothing in distinctive ways, such as one jean leg rolled up.

Handsigns, Handshakes, or Unusual Language: Members often have unusual ways of greeting or signaling each other.

Initiations: Otherwise unexplainable wounds, skin carvings, tattoos, bruises, or injuries may be the result of gang initiation ceremonies.

Behavior Changes: Sudden changes of moods or behavior, as well as unexplainable poor grades can signal gang involvement.

---

the rest of the student body—immediately. If it is a criminal act, then other agencies need to get involved as well.

Interagency Cooperation

Schools are not the only agency that has a stake in an orderly and safe environment. Large and small communities are depending more and more on an interagency approach. On any principal's phone list ought to be the numbers of the police juvenile division, Child Protective Services officers, juvenile court officials, Crime Stoppers organizations, and any departments of youth development, whatever they might be entitled. Additionally, the school records office needs to have the number and name of the responsible adult in the youth's home. Some success has be achieved in such cities as Chicago, Baltimore, and Knoxville, among many others where schools and mayors' offices have moved to develop formal councils and networks to provide for inter-agency cooperation.[8]

The Counseling Program

Counseling programs are too often thought of as an array of activities extended to the classroom by a designated person called a guidance counselor. Our position is that this is totally inadequate and at times counterproductive to the needs of students. A good counseling program needs to include teachers in a direct and organized way and avoid overreliance on guidance counselors.

Guidance counselors often suffer from highly unrealistic expectations of their colleagues. In these days of troubling anonymity in large school units, of drop-ins and spiritual drop-outs, an approach different from that which locates all counseling responsibilities in one office is required. The need is for a total school commitment to the counseling function.

A different mode of organizing counseling services in the schools is needed—not because trained guidance counselors aren't important, but because as presently organized in most schools, their skills are not being used maximally. The function of counseling is so critical to the development of students that a better approach must be employed.

Student advisement and guidance in the elementary and middle schools especially should remain the function of the classroom teacher, and a continued effort should be made to include teachers as part of a counseling team in the secondary schools as well. The main problem the classroom teacher faces in organizing an effective student advisement program is usually one of time. There are ways to gain time for student counseling however. Organizing activities and dividing some of the responsibilities with other appropriate personnel will assist teachers in this endeavor.

Nevertheless, the basic advisement and guidance functions to be performed for a particular student need to be in the hands of a single professional—someone who has a picture of the whole student. A person designated as school guidance counselor with the usually recommended student-counselor rates of 300 or 400 to 1 cannot be expected to develop very many such relationships; only perfunctory interpersonal encounters are probable. It would be absurd to think otherwise.

Advisor-Advisee Systems

A teacher-student advisement system can successfully combat the problem of identification and result in better student counseling. In one such system, each teacher assumes responsibility for the curricular decisions and learning goals for a particular group of students. The ratio of students to advisor is based on the total student-staff ratio in the school. Many schools involve every professional staff member in the school, including the principal, librarian, and specialists. Involving everyone reduces the ratio and also provides every staff member with direct student contact on an individual basis.

In this approach, a school is divided into clusters, with a counselor and a principal or assistant principal acting as administrative head. The counselor serves as a "Master-Advisor" for 15 to 20 teacher-advisors. The teacher-advisor has no more than 20 students for whom guidance services are performed.

The teacher-advisor's primary role is to work individually with students in much the same way that formerly was expected of the guidance counselor. The guidance counselor's role is that of expert-consultant to groups of teachers. The teacher-advisor is both friend and advocate and strives to know the student in ways well beyond what a teacher can with the usual classroom loads. He or she is a person to whom the student can talk freely about school problems and work through solutions.

Not all teachers are personally disposed nor equally able in such a role. Care needs to be taken to adequately prepare the staff for the role. In-service skill sessions will need to be developed and a good monitoring system maintained if the approach is to work well.

Among the many positive outcomes of such a system is the reduction of anonymity felt by many students in schools, both large and small. Shyness, transience, previous bad experiences with schooling, poverty among other symptoms of at-risk students and the simple human need of all of us for an anchoring friendship in times of need can be dealt with effectively with a teacher-advisor system.

Organizing Counseling Activities

Three basic counseling activities need to be carried out: group counseling, individual student counseling, and parent conferences.

Group Counseling

Group guidance activities can be of a variety of types, but the underlying concept is the advisor's responsibility to aid the students in developing good peer relationships, good personal problem-solving skills, and good attitudes about learning.

Individual Counseling

Individual counseling has two purposes. First, it provides the opportunity for each student to interact with his or her advisor as a friend and confidant. Second, it provides for frequent program planning and evaluation conferences. At least biweekly conferences are suggested, and these should function as the main stage for academic planning. The following comments of a teacher describing the preparation for and conduct of counseling sessions are illustrative:

For each of my students, I have a file folder in a box next to my desk. Every paper completed by that student is placed in that folder after it has been appropriately graded or reviewed. It remains there until the night before our scheduled appointment. Each night I take home the folders of the three students I am to see the next day and regroup and review their papers according to subjects. I also review my notes from earlier conferences with each student and look at the goals we established in previous weeks. I then write down tentative goals that I have in mind for the student for the next two-week period. The next day when that student comes to my desk for his conference, I review with him his schedule of activities and the amount of time that he has spent in each subject area. We then go over his papers and I ask if he is having any particular problems. I will note for him problems I have identified from my review. Next, we look to see whether previously set goals have been achieved and begin our discussion of which goals and learning activities should come next. I prefer that each of my students set goals for themselves rather than for me to always have to suggest them. We each write down the goals agreed upon and identify some of the activities to be done toward each. As might be expected, most are continuations of previously laid plans but if new interests or needs have developed, these are to be included. Finally, a cover letter is stapled to the entire collection of papers to be taken home to the parent.

Some teachers prefer to develop systems and forms with which to set and record goals. These can also be shared with parents and made a part of the student's yearly diagnostic file. An example of such a form is shown in Figure 7–3. Such record development and record keeping are greatly facilitated by only a modest use of any of a number of readily available data-based software programs formatted for the kind of microcomputers that the school owns.

FIGURE 7–3   Setting and Recording Student Goals

Advisement Conference Report

Student Name	Term
Advisor	Date

A. Goals set by student and teacher:

B. Adjustments/accomplishments
   toward previously set goals:

C. Additional teacher comments:

D. Additional student comments:

E. Next conference date: _____

Parent Conferences

Regular conferences with parents or guardians contribute to the development of a positive learning climate. In addition to as-needed "crisis" conferences, direct relationships between teacher and home should occur in the form of schoolwide planned parent-teacher conferences two or three times a year. These must be carefully organized and scheduled, however.

Numerous factors must be taken into consideration for these schoolwide programs to be successful. For example, two working parents in a home might preclude attendance at parent-teacher conferences scheduled during the normal school day. Similarly, single-parent homes present scheduling problems. Transportation may be a factor, too, especially if schools are organized on something other than a neighborhood basis. Magnet school programs, for example, present special problems. These and other constraints can be overcome if there is a sincere desire on the part of teachers and other school personnel to do so.

Organizing the conferences can be made a task of a joint community-teachers' group, perhaps the responsibility of a PTO task force. Again, one must be sure that the group that is assigned the task of organizing the effort is generally representative of the neighborhood or community that the local school serves. Also, the bilingual, multicultural norms of school-community members must also be considered.

Establishing a Good Advisement Program

Maximum flexibility in advisor assignments can be achieved by the expanded team concept. This will help keep the advisor-student ratio reasonable. Advisors should schedule meetings regularly with advisees, both on a group basis and individual basis. The total weekly commitment to advisor-guidance functions of an individual nature is approximately four hours per week during the school day while students are available and two hours after school, or when parents are available. Group guidance activities can be built into the regular school schedule, setting aside approximately 30 minutes each day, for a total of 2½ hours each week.

A regular appointment calendar on a two-week rotation should be established, with each student aware of the designated time well in advance of the conference. Figure 7–4 is an example of such a schedule.

Providing adequate time for teacher student or teacher-parent conferences is of top priority. The more flexible the school program, the easier it is to schedule conferences during the school day. An effective way to provide more conference time is to lengthen the school lunch period an additional 15 or 20 minutes. The provision of an expanded noon activities program, and opening the study and instructional media areas, will provide for those students who are not having conferences.

Selecting the Advisor

The advisor must be able to communicate with each student on a friendly, personal basis. In order for this to be accomplished, a good personality match between advisor and student is essential. This is best achieved if several choices for advisor assignment are available. Alternatives for advisor assignment for each student exist when the guid-

FIGURE 7–4   Student Advisement Schedule (week 1 in a two-week cycle; 15 minutes each conference)

	Monday	Tuesday	Wednesday	Thursday	Friday
8:00 Early bus arrivals	David Thomas	Mary Murphy	Richard Hooker	Cynthia Norris	Makeup
	Classes begin				
11:45	Lunch				Makeup
12:15	Douglas Edward	Patricia Holland	Anne Venditti	Kevin Arthur	
3:00	Classes end				
3:10 Late bus departing	Phyllis Selter	Lupe Hernandez	Rod Paige	Dennis Spuck	Makeup

ance program is operating on a team or expanded team basis. After staff and students have become acquainted in the fall term, each member is assigned an appropriate number of advisees, keeping in mind the needs of each individual student and which team member might best meet those needs.

A school organizational structure that greatly enhances the effectiveness of the advisement program is multiage grouping. This approach places students with a particular team for two or three years, each student keeping the same advisor during that entire period.

The Role of the Guidance Counselor

The guidance counselor has a particularly important function. In the system just described, the guidance counselor must assume six responsibilities:

- Become attached to a team and assume an advisor responsibility in order to keep in close touch with the program and with the other specialists within the school.
- Function as a school referral agent for problems identified by the advisor and faculty.
- Conduct diagnostic work beyond that possible for teachers to do.
- Administer and supervise the advisement program. The level of advisement activities proposed in this chapter far exceeds that typically carried out in school. In order for it to operate well, a good advisement program requires constant attention, encouragement, and coordination.
- Provide and direct staff development activities in the techniques of advisement, including teacher training for both group guidance functions as well as individual

student academic diagnostic work and techniques for personal counseling. A major portion of the guidance counselor's role should be spent directly in staff development activities.

- Assist the teachers in establishing and maintaining a good in-class student personnel record system. These are the records maintained by the teacher for day-by-day counseling and academic prescriptions.

Student Services

Student services include all of those special support functions outside of the curricular and cocurricular offerings at the building level that impinge on the development of the student. The array of services offered by a school district adds a necessary quality to the individual school operation. The student services professional provides technical services and additional professional insight in the diagnosis, prescription, and treatment of individual learner difficulties as well as balanced programs for all learners. The principal's role in this is crucial. It is the principal who must provide for the organization, coordination, and articulation of such services at the building level.

Student Referral System

Most school systems have a number of specialists available to the student to meet needs beyond those that can be met by the regular school staff. Each school should have someone designated to coordinate the special services needs for the school. The guidance counselor is an appropriate referral agent to determine needs for services, as well as for identifying the proper source for those services.

It is good practice for principals to prepare and disseminate a list of available services, and people to contact for those services, so that teachers, parents, and other community members will know to whom they can turn for help with particular problems. Included on such a list would be counselors, including guidance, special education, and attendance; school psychologists; special education resource teachers; pathologists; home-bound teachers; reading specialists; diagnosticians: and other special personnel provided by the district.

Principal's Role in Coordination and Articulation

With respect to the delivery of pupil personnel services, the principal is truly the person in the middle—not as a gatekeeper but as a facilitator. Referrals, if not routed directly through the principal, should at least be made with an information copy to the principal. Why? *Everything that goes on in and around the school is the responsibility of the principal*—and that includes the proper delivery of support services. The reason for centralizing many student personnel services is because of the systemwide impact of these services and because individual school needs vary widely enough to make it more efficient to centrally house some services to provide maximum access in time of need. Such a model works well, provided the principal recognizes a responsibility to continually be aware of student and teacher needs in the building, and to investigate whether their needs are being met in a timely and efficient manner by the student personnel services division.

Summary

For many children and youth, the school is the only stable thing in their lives. For some, it is the only place they can get a decent meal. For these and still others, it may be the only place they are safe from an otherwise marauding, hazardous, and unstable world. And for these and others, it may be the only place where they may be rewarded for behaving and succeeding in socially acceptable ways. School should be a place where every student can learn what a civilized world there can be. We like the words of Barbara Ries Wager: "We…faced the fact that we had forgotten what our forbearers of 50 years ago knew so well: that one of our most crucial missions is the civilizing process itself, that this historic professional mission had been eliminated from our intellectual repertoire."[9] At Ries Wager's school, that mission is being preserved.

And so we return to the thoughts of Karon Rilling that opened this chapter: "And they will be protected and they will be respected. And we're going to help them learn how life can be." That is what this chapter has been all about.

Activities

1. Review Case Studies 4 and 11. You are the principal. Assume that the data provided all relate to your school (that is, the school in Case 4 is the same one as described in Case 11). Given the information you have and any reasonable assumptions you make, how will you begin to address the issues raised in this case? Be sure to state your assumptions. What, if any, guidance do any of the concepts expressed provide?

2. Review Case Studies 12 and 21. Both of these incidents have occurred in the school for which you are the principal. (Yes, we know we have reported different enrollment data for each school; however, that is not important in this instance.) Your school is traditionally organized into the standard grade levels and teaching assignments. What approach will you take in each instance to resolve the issues?

Endnotes

1. Dr. Karon Rilling, Principal of Humble Middle School, Humble, Texas, to a graduate class of aspiring school principals at the University of Houston.
2. *State* v. *Fond du Lac Board of Education*, 63 Wis. 234, 23 N.W. 102, 53 Am. Rep. 282 (1985).
3. Reported in Maribeth Vander Weele, "Chicago Hope," *The Executive Educator* 17, no. 2 (February 1995): 23.
4. Reported in Roberta Shore, "How One High School Improved School Climate," *Educational Leadership* 52, no. 5 (February 1995): 76.

5. R. A. Hashway, "Does Money Make a Difference? An Econometric Analysis of School Outcomes," *National Forum of Applied Educational Research Journal* 2, no. 2 (1989–90): 59.

6. Charles M. Achilles and Penelope Smith, "Stimulating the Academic Performance of Pupils," in *The Principal as Leader*, ed. Larry W. Hughes (New York: Macmillan, 1994), p. 256.

7. Ibid., p. 259.

8. See, for example, Elizabeth Crouch and Debra Williams, "What Cities are Doing to Protect Children," *Educational Leadership* 52, no. 5 (February 1995): 60–62.

9. Barbara Ries Wager, "No More Suspension: Creating a Shared Ethical Culture," *Educational Leadership* 50, no. 4 (December 1992/January 1993): 37. Wager is Principal of an inner-city school in Rochester, New York, and was writing about how her school moved from "chaos to harmony" once disciplinary goals and processes were clarified and an "ethical culture" created.

Selected Readings

Armstrong, Coleen. "How About Some Creative Discipline." *Principal* 74, no. 33 (January 1995): 51–52.

Cantrell, Robert P., and Mary Lynn Cantrell. "Countering Gang Violence in American Schools." *Principal* 73, no. 2 (November 1993): 6–9.

Hughes, Larry W. (Ed.). *The Principal as Leader* (New York: Macmillan, 1994). See Chapter 10, especially.

Rogers, Carl R., and H. Jerome Freiberg. *Freedom to Learn*, 3rd ed. (New York: Macmillan, 1994). See especially Chapter 12.

Schreiber, Vicky D., and Martin Haberman. "Building a Gentler School." *Educational Leadership* 52, no. 5 (February 1995): 69–71.

Shore, Rebecca. "How One High School Improved School Climate." *Educational Leadership* 52, no. 5 (February 1995): 76–78.

Sullivan, Judy S. "Elements of a Successful In-School Suspension Program." *NASSP Bulletin* 73, no. 516 (April 1989): 32–38.

Vander Weele, Maribeth. "Chicago Hope." *Executive Educator* 17, no. 2 (February 1995): 22–24.

Wager, Barbara Ries. "No More Suspension: Creating a Shared Ethical Culture." *Educational Leadership* 50, no. 4 (December 1992/January 1993): 34–37.

Chapter *8*

Special Students, Special Services

Historically, special education has been synonymous with separate education. Fundamental changes in America's schools have resulted in education for special children becoming an integral part of the total schooling picture. And, all educators now share responsibility for teaching all children.
— MICHAEL BRADY[1]

Children may come to school with many problems that will make learning difficult. Some are hungry, some need decent clothing, some have been abused at home physically or psychologically, and others have physical or mental disabilities that make learning difficult. Often, the need for special assistance is first signaled by low attendance. In many cases, school personnel have a legal responsibility to provide the resources to improve students' learning opportunities. In other cases, school personnel may feel a moral responsibility to function as a quasi-social services referral agency in order for some of the children of that school to have an adequate "quality of life." This is often necessary before learning can take place.

The principal or designated members of the staff need to develop a network of contacts in the community where assistance can be obtained. Many communities are fortunate to have governmental agencies both within and outside the school system available to provide most needed services to children. Special education services are mandated nationwide by the Individuals with Disabilities Education Act (IDEA).[2] Section 504 of the Rehabilitation Act of 1973[3] and the Americans with Disabilities Act[4] (ADA) also impact on the kind of services that must be provided to children with special needs. All states have child abuse laws administered, most often as part of a social services agency or welfare department. Public health departments often are charged with providing special health services to needy children as well as providing health screening and immunization monitoring of school-age children. Many private agencies also have available services for needy children, such as the Lions clubs that provide eye care or church groups that have emergency food or used clothing available.

Although some will argue that these needs of children should not be the responsibility of the school, often the school—the gathering point for all children—is the first to become aware of problems. When the physical or emotional needs of children get in the way of learning, the school has a direct stake in seeking a solution. The principal, the guidance counselor, the school nurse, the social worker, the special education staff, the regular classroom teachers, as well as others, all have a part to play. But when reaching beyond those activities required by law, or when taking fullest advantage of services from available agencies, the leadership of the principal in setting the direction for the school in providing services to special children is critical.

Special Education and Related Services

The IDEA requires school districts to provide a free appropriate public education (FAPE), including special education and related services, in the least restrictive environment (LRE), as determined by a multidisciplinary team (M-team) and written in an individual education program (IEP). The term *inclusion* is not mentioned in the federal law; it is a state-of-the-art term that provides the least restrictive environment by placing children with disabilities in integrated sites. These services are mandatory for all children from age 4 to the end of the school year in which the student turns 22, or, in the case of a child who is deaf, age 23, who can be certified by an appropriate specialist as having a disability or exceptionality and verified by a multidisciplinary team of educators as needing special education services. Exceptionalities include:[5]

Mental retardation	Serious emotional disturbance
Learning disabilities	Visual impairment
Hearing impairment	Other health impairment
Orthopedic impairment	Speech impairment
Autism	Deaf-blind
Multidisabled	Traumatic brain injury
Developmental delays	

Due Process

The law requires that certain due process procedures be followed, assuming the right of the parent and child to be fully informed and included in the decision making at all steps in identification, child evaluation, planning, programming, and program evaluation. (See Chapter 3 for a more complete review of the law regarding special students.)

Step 1: Screening

The school has the responsibility to monitor the development of each child in order to know as early as possible if any child is having problems with his or her school work. Screening checks are to be made for the child's medical health record as well as the child's progress in school. Medical screenings are usually scheduled by the district special education departments or appropriate health agencies. Educational checks are initially the responsibility of the regular classroom teacher to observe and identify children with potential disabilities.

Step 2: Prereferral Actions

When a student presents a particularly unique problem, the classroom teacher often needs somewhere to turn for help. The problem may surface as a disciplinary problem, a learning difficulty, poor attendance, or what seems like a lack of interest in planned classroom activities. None of the strategies tried by the teacher have seemed to work. If the child is referred to special education, weeks can pass before a formal assessment is completed and a staff meeting is held to recommend a plan. In some cases, a formal referral may identify a student as disabled and recommend placement in a special education instruction program. Other students may be identified as mildly disabled, but not in need of special education programming, while others will not be identified as disabled at all. For these last two groups, the delay in providing immediate support to the teacher and student may not have been necessary at all.

It is suggested that prereferral procedures be developed that will allow for more immediate action and assistance in most cases and that would be less costly than the formal referral and assessment process. The prereferral procedure should begin with the collection and review of classroom data gathered by the teacher. Included should be attendance information, available standardized and classroom test data, teacher observations of student effort, attention, ability to follow directions, listening, social skills, self-confidence, peer relationships, and so on. Teaching strategies attempted should also be documented.

Step 3: Support Team Review

Each school should organize a school support team (S-team) to function as an intermediate step between the recognition of a problem by a classroom teacher and a formal referral for a comprehensive educational evaluation. For students who are obviously disabled, this support team review is bypassed and a formal referral is made immediately. On the other hand, the teacher who is experiencing less severe difficulty with a student should request the team's assistance. The information gathered through the prereferral action is received by this team. The team that meets regularly to discuss such cases considers the problem, generates possible remedial actions, and recommends specific intervention strategy. The support team (S-team) should be made up of experienced teachers qualified to teach that age child, possibly the special education teacher, and other appropriate staff members such as a Title I teacher or guidance counselor. One member should function as the S-team coordinator to schedule meetings, organize records, and ensure that the team's recommendations are implemented.

The S-team should be viewed as problem solvers, bringing to focus the expert resources of the school on those issues that fall just short of resulting in a formal special education referral. Those students deemed to have educational or emotional problems beyond the normal capability of the school staff and program to adequately address ultimately will be given a formal referral to the other education specialists for further evaluation.

Step 4: Formal Referral for a Comprehensive Evaluation

An evaluation to specifically determine the severity of it child's deficits is scheduled. An assessment team may include all or any of the following: school psychologist, occupational therapist, physical therapist, other special educators, physician, regular classroom teachers, and/or medical specialists. Parents have the right to obtain an independent evaluation at their own expense if they so choose; however, depending on the nature of the events, the school must sometimes eventually assume these costs. Ultimately, the assessment team determines if the student is eligible for special education. Eligibility is based on the child fitting the certification requirements for a particular special education category.

Step 5: The Multidisciplinary Team

The multidisciplinary team (M-team), made up of a group of at least three school professionals and the parent/guardian, is responsible for developing an appropriate educational program for the student based on a careful review of all diagnostic data. The M-team's responsibilities include: (1) reviewing the present level of educational performance as derived from the assessment data, (2) developing the individualized educational program (IEP), and (3) making a recommendation for placement.

The M-team approach is designed to ensure that decisions concerning a student's program will be made by a team of persons whose primary goal is to accommodate the interests, needs, learning styles, and abilities of that student. Careful consideration should be given to the selection of M-team members who are most qualified to contribute to the development and implementation of the IEP. Those individuals who must be part of the initial M-team include the principal or his or her designee; the teacher who recently or currently has the student in class; the assessment specialist(s), such as the psychologist or audiologist, who conducted the assessments as part of the evaluation; the parent/guardian of the student; and the student, when appropriate.

Principal's Role. For the principal, the M-team represents a very visible form of involvement with the special education program and the special needs children in the school. Although it is possible for the principal to designate a representative to serve on M-teams, direct participation by the principal in the M-team process signals an interest in this program to students, teachers, and parents. It also provides to the principal very direct feedback regarding the adequacy of the special education program in meeting the needs of the children in the school and an opportunity for leadership in improving the program where needed.

Individual Education Program (IEP). The individual education program, or IEP (or for preschool children, an individual family service plan [IFSP]), is a written record of the decisions reached by the members of the multidisciplinary team at the IEP meeting. It sets forth in writing the commitment of resources necessary for the child who has disabilities, functions as a management tool to ensure services, is the compliance/monitoring document for government monitoring of the law, serves as the evaluation device in determining the child's progress, and functions as the communication document with the parent. The IEP must contain the following components:

1. The present level of educational performance
2. Certification that student meets disabled requirements
3. Annual program goals and interim program objectives
4. Regular program participation and modifications

5. Special education placement and justification
6. Multidisciplinary team signatures of participants
7. Parent signature and statement of review/appeal rights
8. Indicated date for annual review

Recommendations for Placement.   It is required by the IDEA that the individual educational program developed by the M-team be provided in the *least restrictive environment*. Today, that generally means inclusion. *Inclusion* differs from *mainstreaming* in that the latter term usually refers to integrating children with disabilities and children without disabilities for only a portion of the day, which may be during nonacademic times. In a fully inclusive model, students with disabilities, no matter how severe, are taught in the regular education classroom of their home school with their age and grade peers for the full day with support services provided within the classroom.[6] In short, inclusion means bringing support services to the child rather than moving the child to a segregated setting to receive special services.[7] This means that each child should be placed in a setting where he or she can be with noneligible children as much of the time as possible. The act allows for 10 different placement options but demands that the least restrictive option appropriate for the child be used. The act requires that a continuum of service options be provided. A typical sequence of options would include the following:

1. Full time in the regular classroom with special supplies and/or equipment.
2. Full time in the regular classroom with consultative services for the teacher.
3. Full time in the regular classroom with additional instruction by a special education teacher in the regular classroom.
4. Part time in the regular classroom (as much as is appropriate) and part time in a special *resource program* coordinated with the regular classroom activities.
5. Full time in a special *comprehensive development classroom* (*CDC*) provided to meet the needs of the severely/profoundly involved students who require intensive planning and programming.
6. Part time in the regular school program with a special education aide supervising the child with disabilities while in the regular classroom.
7. Other related services, including transportation; speech pathology and audiology; psychological, physical, and occupational therapy; recreation; counseling; medical (for diagnostic and evaluation purposes); school health; social work; parent counseling and training; assistive technology devices and services; transition; nursing; interpreter; as well as others not specified.
8. Ancillary services provided by agencies outside the school to provide services a minimum of four hours a day in order to maintain the child in the regular program.
9. Residential services to provide for a child whose disabling conditions are so profound or complex that continuous intervention is required to meet his or her educational needs and no special education services offered in a CDC or self-contained program can meet these needs. While these programs are very costly, if the IEP calls for this service, the school system is responsible for the total program.
10. Home or hospital instruction may be provided to continue the educational advancement of eligible students who are unable to attend school.

Step 6: Implementing the Plan

Options numbered 1 through 6 from the preceding list are often implemented in the regular school, whereas the services of options 7 through 10 are more often provided by school district staff, by special schools, or by contract with outside agencies. The concept of *least restrictive environment* is being applied to greater and greater numbers of special education children, bringing more low-functioning and children with disabilities into contact with the regular education program. As a result, many more children with severe disabilities, previously housed in segregated special schools, are becoming part of the regular school and are spending at least a part of their day in regular classrooms, often accompanied by an attendant.

In some cases, building modifications are required to provide access for wheelchairs and health-related and other equipment required to support these special students and their program needs. Special Education Vocational Rehabilitation Laws (PL 93-113, sec. 504) require that buildings be made accessible to all children.

Often, the initial reaction of the staff to students with severe disabilities in their classrooms is one of fear because of the health concern for such a child and the concern that he or she will disrupt the normal classroom environment. A good in-service training program for the staff frequently turns the fear of special students into a learning opportunity. This is especially true when regular classroom children are taught about the classmates who are joining them. Often, a compassion and understanding develops in children that could not be taught as effectively any other way. Rather than children who are disabled detracting from the learning of other children, they often enrich it with the development of new values and understanding for all children.

The principal should take advantage of the opportunities provided by the special education program and its integration into the regular education activities and be very careful not to allow these to develop into separate programs.[8]

Program and Assessment Reviews

Each special education student's IEP is reviewed annually by the M-team for the purpose of determining the continuing appropriateness of the program placement, goals, and objectives. These review dates must be monitored so that the annual reviews take place on schedule. The intent of the review should always be to move the child toward a less restrictive environment with less special education assistance if this is appropriate. The effort should be to try to move the child back toward the regular program whenever possible. The evaluation process for each special education student must be repeated every three years. A new assessment plan must be developed and carried out, recertification must take place, and the M-team must once again develop a new IEP.

Safeguarding Special Education Records

Special education records must be maintained separate and apart from a student's regular school cumulative record folder. Access to the special education records is to be carefully controlled, with availability restricted to only those school personnel who have direct contact with the child or to whom the parents have given written permission for access, such as an outside psychologist. Sign-out sheets should be used and permission letters kept on file. Regular education records are not supposed to reference the existence of a special education file. The purpose of this regulation is to protect the special education student from later discrimination that might occur if it became known the child had some type of disability. This makes it extremely difficult for records maintenance, however, and it is easy to misfile or not be able to locate information. Some schools code their regular cumulative folders with some special mark to indicate the existence of a separate special education folder.

Rights of Parents and Due Process Requirements

The requirement of involvement of the parents of the potential or verified special education student has been noted through this entire section describing special education procedures. From the notification of the initial referral, through the assessment process, to the writing of the IEP,[9] and finally to the approval for placement, as well as future access to their child's records, parents must give their informed consent as participants in the process. Failure to notify or obtain this consent is a violation of the rights of parents under the law.

Disciplining Students with Disabilities

Discipline of children in school is an important concern of all principals. In most situations, the day-to-day decisions regarding the control of children has been the prerogative of the principal supported by the staff. However, in the case of children with disabilities, intricate federal and state regulations govern the administration of punishment of these students; these regulations are based solely on federal court cases interpreting the IDEA.

Attention Deficit Hyperactive Disordered (ADHD) children can now receive educational services and protection under Section 504 regulations. These children, by the nature of their disabling condition, often show up in the principal's office as discipline cases. Great care must be taken in establishing discipline procedures for these children because they often defy normal school behavior expectations. The results of these cases clearly establish a double standard. One cannot discipline children with disabilities in the unilateral fashion generally used for other students. In 1989, in *Honig* v. *Doe*,[10] the U.S. Supreme Court ruled that students with disabilities cannot be unilaterally suspended or expelled for more than 10 days without provision of due process. This case triggered a array of procedural restrictions on local schools. Figure 8–1 summarizes basic disciplinary actions often used in school and indicates under what conditions they may or may not be used for children with disabilities.

Dealing with Parents of Special Children

The identification of a child as a potential special education child is always stressful for parents, and the principal and staff must be prepared to deal with a variety of reactions from parents. The parent has probably been aware for some time that a problem

FIGURE 8–1   Conditions of Disciplinary Action for Children with Disabilities

Disciplinary Action	Conditions of Use
Verbal reprimand	OK
Written warning	OK
Payment for damages	OK as long as the child's behavior does not suggest IEP changes.
Time out	OK
Detention (lunch, recess, after school)	OK
In-school suspension	OK if supervised by a certified special education teacher and/or the child's IEP is being carried out.
Corporal punishment	Many states prohibit its use. If permitted, it must be administered fairly. It is not recommended for children with disabilities.
Aversive therapy/Devices	Only if specified in IEP.
Bus suspension	Counts as part of 10-day maximum if busing is included in child's IEP.
Exclusion from extracurricular activities	OK as long as it is not central to IEP goal.
Suspension/Expulsion	OK for 10 school days per offense so long as "pattern of exclusion" does not exist.* For longer periods, the M-team must determine the offense not to be related to the child's disability.
Alternate school placement	OK as long as the change is made through the regular IEP process.

Any disciplinary action must have no adverse effect on IEP goals and objectives and must not be applied in a discriminatory manner.

*In addition to the 10-day limitation imposed by *Honig* v. *Doe*, the Office of Civil Rights (OCR) reminds districts that Section 504 requires a student reevaluation prior to every significant change in placement. Therefore, any change in placement, including a suspension/expulsion, for more than 10 days or any consecutive 10-day suspensions must be evaluated by the M-team.

exists for his or her child. This knowledge may have been suppressed or the parent may already have a long history of dealing with the child and the school about the problems. There are at least four general patterns of parental reaction for which the school, the M-team, and the principal, whether part of that M-team or not, must be ready.

The Supportive Parent

This parent is understanding of his or her child's problems, is concerned about the child's education, and respects and appreciates the efforts of the school to develop an appropriate educational plan for that child. He or she generally is most supportive during M-team meetings, attending faithfully and asking how he or she might best support the school's efforts at home. Some always accept the recommendations of the school staff without question, while others may begin to question M-team recommendations if they feel services are not adequate. This latter type may become a demanding parent if the school fails to carefully present a rationale for its recommendations.

The Denying Parent

This is the parent who is unaccepting of the possibility that his or her child has a disability. He or she is offended by the request for a referral, often initially refusing to sign the permission for testing, and frequently demanding to submit outside independent evaluations to refute the school's claim that the child is disabled. In some cases, he or she begins to resist actions of the school by not attending meetings, by refusing to sign documents, and generally by becoming purposefully nonresponsive. The denial of the disability may be due to a feeling that the child's disability is a reflection on his or her own intelligence or on his or her ability as a parent to raise the child. In these cases, parent education must often be an additional consideration before meaningful assistance can be provided for the child.

The denying parent is often extremely frustrated with the child, and his or her demands of the child are often impossible, given the identified disability. It is sometimes helpful to counsel with the parent privately, reviewing assessment data and pointing out that disabling conditions know no social or intellectual bounds (Albert Einstein had a learning disability, the Kennedy family has a retarded sister, and President Roosevelt was confined to a wheelchair). Additional support needs to be provided to these families because these feelings of denial die slowly and new strategies for dealing with the disability at home must be learned if the home is to be a supportive environment. Parent education and counseling is an appropriate consideration in the development of the IEP for these situations.

The Nonresponsive Parent

The problem of the nonresponsive parent is probably the saddest of all. Notices are sent out, phone calls are attempted, and certified letters are sent in order to meet the due process informed-consent legal requirement for parent notification. Some schools will even attempt to arrange a home visit in order to elicit a parental response. In some cases, the work schedule of the parent interferes; in others, child care makes school visits difficult. If these are really the problems, the school should make every effort to arrange a schedule or situation that will allow the parent's participation. However, there are situations where there is little or no interest on the part of the parent in the child's schooling. In these cases, it is often appropriate to identify some other responsible adult to work with this child and to provide an adult advocate and educational support system outside the classroom environment.

The Belligerent, Demanding Parent

This parent is going to attempt to obtain more than the school (the M-team) believes is necessary to provide appropriate options for program placement. He or she will question the assessments provided by the school staff to the point of demanding independent evaluation or bringing in his or her own psychologist. He or she will challenge the recommendations of the M-team, and if his or her demands are not met, will threaten to or actually will bring his or her lawyer to the M-team meeting. He or she will sometimes contact EACH (Effective Advocacy for Citizens with Handicaps)[11] and bring a representative of that organization to the M-team meeting. As might be expected, this parent is very aware of his or her due process rights and will demand a hearing to contest the recommendations of the M-team if his or her demands are not satisfied.

When, as a principal, you see this type of parent, be prepared to participate fully in the M-team process yourself. Don't leave your teachers to deal with this situation without strong support. If you can see that a particular staffing is going to be very difficult or complicated, request that someone from the district-level special education office join the M-team. Remember: You must keep in mind the best interests of the child, tempered by the needs of the parents, staff, administration, and other children in the school. Your goal is to provide each child with an appropriate educational program in the least restrictive environment possible, given that child's disabling conditions.

Special Education and the Regular Classroom Teacher

Many students with special needs are in regular classrooms. The teachers in these classrooms have certain responsibilities for these children, including the following:

Identifying and referring potentially disabled children
Taking part in due process and M-team procedures
Collecting assessment data about children with disabilities
Assisting children with disabilities with special equipment
Participating in a team effort with special education staff
Helping all children work and play together
Communicating with parents

Whenever a child with disabilities is placed in the regular classroom, the responsibility of the regular classroom teacher for that child is the same as for any other child in the room. Because all children differ with respect to the amount, rate, and style of learning, minor modifications in methodology, curriculum, or environment are often necessary for children, disabled or not. When a child's IEP specifies modifications in methodology, curriculum, or environment from the regular class, the development of such specially designed instruction is the responsibility of special educators. Regular educators are responsible for assisting in carrying out the program. Overall classroom management remains the responsibility of the regular educator.

Educating children who are severely disabled in the regular classroom can often be difficult. It is here where problems sometime arise. Given the requirement of the law for providing programs in the least restrictive environment and inclusion, more children with severe disabling conditions are now being educated in the regular school setting, both in the regular classroom as well as in the special education classroom but housed in the neighborhood school. Regular classroom teachers are sometimes frightened by the responsibility they feel for children who have special physical or emotional needs. Wheelchairs and other special manipulative equipment to transport children are seen as problems. Assisting children with bodily functions—helping to place a child on a toilet, changing diapers, and monitoring catheterizations—is felt to be beyond their level of training or interest. With the onset of acquired immune deficiency syndrome (AIDS) and the need to wear laytex gloves as a precautionary measure, additional fears are generated. When difficult physical situations exist, the IEP should specify the need for special assistance for the classroom teacher both through special training and through the provision of a special education assistant in the classroom or one who is on call and immediately available.

Children with mental disabilities provide an even greater problem for many teachers. Many of the learning disabilities, though mild in a sense, cause great difficulty for the child and require great understanding and skill on the part of the teacher. Children who we used to say were just discipline problems and should be sent to the office or who we claimed were lazy and not motivated to do their work, we now know actually have a type of learning disability such as attention deficit disorder, dyslexia, dysnomia, or one of a host of others. In many cases, the problem has gone undiagnosed for many years and becomes compounded by the repeated failure to succeed on the part of the student who now has advanced to middle or even high school. Teachers often have not been trained either to diagnose these problems or know how to deal with them properly when they are known. Additionally, many teachers feel overwhelmed by the number of children and problems they face daily in the classroom.

Good staff development activities are needed by most school faculties in many aspects of working with children with special needs. Training in diagnosing and treating learning disabilities can be a help to virtually every classroom teacher. Knowledge in the use of supplementary aids and services such as brailled worksheets for students who are blind, provision of tape recorders or computer word processors for children who cannot write, or the operation of physical aids such as wheelchairs, walkers, and hearing aids is helpful. Skill in the use of cooperative learning techniques in conjunction with special educators or the management of disabilities in the classroom needs to be learned.

Most needed of all, perhaps, is the need for good human relations training for teachers to help them understand and deal with their own fears and biases concerning people who are disabled and how to help children in their classes to do the same. Finally, teachers need to be trained about their role in special education, state, and national special education policies, their role in referrals, evaluations, IEP development, due process, working with parents, and working with special educators regarding such things as student grading, scheduling, and record keeping.

Outside Public Agencies

A variety of public agencies in every community have direct access to the school. Local states and communities will have different names for these agencies and offer somewhat different services, but each school must recognize the demand and need to interact with these other services.[12] The three that are common to almost every school are public welfare or human services departments, public health agencies, and judicial systems (usually represented by police departments and juvenile court systems). Each of these agencies has certain legal responsibilities and authority. The authority of each of these agencies transcends the walls of the school, and the school principal is not always "master of the house." It is important not to get into a "turf battle" with the representatives of these agencies, but rather to develop a supportive network with them to serve the children of the community better. When the police come to pick up or question a child regarding a local crime, the principal is summoned to juvenile court to testify on a matter dealing with one of the school's children, or a representative of the protective services unit of the local welfare department shows up to investigate a child abuse case, not only is it important for the principal to know his or her rights and the rights of the children but also to have a good working relationship with the representatives of these other agencies so that all can work for the benefit of the children and the community.

The development of a network of contacts with private agencies and other public agencies is also important. Who should be in a principal's network is somewhat dependent on the nature of the local student clientele, but important network contacts for many schools would include groups that can provide clothing or food on an emergency basis, both emergency and nonemergency medical treatment, and both public and private mental health professionals.

Public Welfare or Human Services Agencies

Child abuse cases are one of the most common school-related involvements with public welfare or human services agencies today. A problem that a few years ago was normally considered "only a family matter" now is recognized as an area of responsibility for our society. Most states now require schools to report suspected child abuse cases to the appropriate authority for investigation. The classroom teacher who notices heavy bruising on a child or the pattern of absences along with extreme emotional behavior on the part of a child is required by law to report it. The school is, in fact, the one place outside the home where a child can take some refuge from an abusive home environment. Confidentiality regarding the reporter of abuse is generally guaranteed. However, it is this confidentiality issue, along with the sensitive nature of child abuse investigations, that sometimes causes some difficulty.

Child abuse investigators often consider the school to be an appropriate safe location to conduct initial interviews. It is a safe place to contact a child without alerting a suspected abuser, and it is a place where the child is more comfortable and hopefully willing to discuss the problem. The problem is that it can also disrupt the ongoing instruction in the school. The intrusion into the school by an outside investigator can also be taken as an interference in the school's domain.

Most state laws give authority to child abuse investigators from public agencies outside the school to interview children on school premises and, in some cases, to take them into their custody. These investigators also have the authority to conduct the interviews in private with no school official present and generally do not have to reveal the content of an interview after it is concluded. For some principals, this contradicts what they consider to be their responsibilities for their children. The first reaction may be not to want to take a child out of class, and, second, not to want to let an "outsider" conduct a private interview with a child for whom the principal is responsible. The laws of most states, however, give the public social services agency this authority if it chooses to use it. The following suggestions are appropriate ways to manage requests from outside investigators:

1. Always ask to see credentials.
2. Attempt to convince investigators of the importance of having a school representative present during any interview. Some workers will allow you to be present.
3. Control the time and place for the conference. You are generally allowed to protect instructional time.
4. Document the conference, noting date, place, names of persons present, and length of the conference.
5. Refuse to give access to student records without a signed release from the parent, guardian, or a court order.

In almost all cases, it is to the school's long-range advantage to develop a good working relationship with these outside agencies. They have a job to do and are also trying to safeguard the well-being of the children. Most often, you need each other.

Working with Law Enforcement Agencies

The major school involvement with law enforcement agencies will be requests by officers to interview children while they are at school. Of course, schools also often employ off-duty officers as security guards for ball games and other evening school activities. The basic suggestions listed for investigator procedures apply to police officers as well and are for the school's protection as well as the protection of the children.

Developing a good working relationship with police officers who work in the school zone can be most helpful to both the school and the police. The occasional informal discussion with them can sometimes cut bureaucratic paperwork and procedures and solve a problem where formal procedures could not.

The school principal will also be called on to testify in juvenile court in conjunction with children from his or her school. Every community has a juvenile court system ranging in size from a part-time judge in smaller communities to large buildings and multiple judges in larger communities. School children may be brought into juvenile court for three different types of situations. The first is for felony or misdemeanor charges similar to charges brought against an adult. However, juvenile court handles the disposition of a case somewhat differently: Publicity of juvenile crimes is kept at a minimum and prescribed treatment has rehabilitation as its purpose rather than punishment.

Status offenses, the second category, make up the largest number of cases that will involve school officials. *Status offenses* can be defined as actions that are considered violations of laws for children but not adults. Nonattendance at school (truancy) and running away from home are the most common. For school officials, instigating truancy charges becomes the last resort among efforts to obtain regular attendance from a child. In many cases, the real problem is the parents. Juvenile courts have the power to order certain action from the parents to improve or control their child's behavior, such as requiring the parent to ensure the child's presence at school each day or be held in contempt of court. A contempt charge against the parent could result in the parent being jailed. Once again, a good working relationship between the school principal and the juvenile court can be most helpful in solving such problems.

The third type of case dealt with by the juvenile court involves the problems of neglected and/or abused children. In these cases, the children are the victims rather than the offenders. School employees are often reporters of suspected child abuse and may be called on to testify in juvenile court regarding their observations. Testifying in these situations can be particularly traumatic. Reporting child abuse is generally kept confidential, or at least confidentiality is attempted. However, when the accused are the parents or someone else closely associated with the school, testifying can be difficult.

Outside Agencies and Closed Records

In an effort to protect the reputation of children and their families, many of the agencies who work with children are required by law to maintain strict confidentiality of the records they develop and maintain. This is true, for example, with the special education records maintained by the school. When a child has been in the custody of the juvenile court or has been a ward of the welfare department's Children's Protective Services unit and is then returned or placed in your school, it is extremely difficult, it not impossible, to get any information about the child's recent history. In some cases, this makes it extremely difficult to know how to deal with a child or even if the safety of other children should be a concern. Some local areas have developed coordinating councils for the several children's agencies in an effort to improve the communication among them. The individual principal will probably find his or her efforts to develop an informal network among the workers of the various agencies to be an extremely useful communication link to information not available through the formal channels.

Drawing on the Services of Outside Social Welfare Agencies

Mental health agencies, chemical abuse agencies, civic clubs, local churches, and so on, all have an interest and a role to play in the welfare of school children. Networking once again becomes the byword for the principal and staff. Situations always develop that fall short of eligibility for one or more of the formal service agencies to the school. It may be a parent who becomes aware that his or her child is doing drugs, or it may be the child who appears to be suffering from severe depression; however, until children take some overt act to harm themselves, there is no regular agency support available. It is in these situations that it is important to have contacts with professionals from other agencies from whom the principal can get advice and learn where the school or the parents might turn for help.

What can be done for middle school-age children who don't want to come to school, such as the boy who doesn't have any shoes or the girl who has had a front tooth knocked out and is ashamed of her looks? The best way to solve the attendance problem is to help solve the child's personal problem. If the school is fortunate enough to have a public agency that can meet these needs, that is wonderful, but often it must be met by the principal getting a pair of size eight sneakers from the local church clothing service or working out a deal with a local shoe store or the salesperson from whom the principal buys athletic equipment. For the girl who needs dental work, but the school does not have a formal procedure for obtaining assistance, the principal may call a local dentist, explain the problem, and ask for some free service. Obviously, a preestablished relationship with these community members and agencies is critical to the success of these attempts. Once again, the importance of establishing a network of contacts in the community is apparent.

Public Health Departments and Local Schools

The services provided by public health agencies directly to school children vary greatly throughout the country. In some states, the only contact may be to monitor immunization records to ensure the health of the general public, while in other areas, services may include provision for public health personnel to provide direct services to children in the school. Nurses stationed in the school, health presentations in classrooms, dental services, immunizations, and some emergency medical care may be provided. Once again, there may be more services available for the asking than the average school receives. It is up to the principal to make the contact, develop the relationship, and add these professionals to his or her network of available persons to be called on when needed.

Summary

Schools have many special children with many special needs. The quality of school life is dependent on the collective satisfaction of the needs of all the children. The principal cannot personally meet the needs of each and every child, but he or she can set the tone, develop the network of contacts who can assist in providing for the children's needs, and be a facilitator of resources for its achievement. Once again, the symbolic leadership of the principal in showing concern for all children will demonstrate to the staff the significance and importance of their efforts.

Activities

1. Review Case Studies 4 and 13. Analyze the problems presented and apply the special services concepts developed in this chapter. What approach would you use in addressing the problems? Set forth a strategy to overcome the difficulties faced by the school as well as ways to deal with individuals such as Ricky.

2. What are some ways the services required by special education laws can be implemented, while minimizing the time required of the regular classroom teacher for special education activities?

3. What are the agencies in your community that provide services to children? In what networks does your school participate to help link together these services?

Endnotes

1. Professor Michael Brady, University of Houston. Department of Educational Psychology, to a graduate class of aspiring principals, summer 1991.
2. The Individuals with Disabilities Education Act (IDEA) Part B and its amendments were passed in 1990 and 1991. It is located in 34 CFR Part 300 and 304.
3. 34 CFR Part 104, Section 504, has become a means of obtaining special attention or services for children who do not fit into one of the discrete IDEA categories of handicapping conditions. Children with a wide variety of disabling conditions such as acquired immune deficiency syndrome (AIDS), attention deficit disorders (ADD), or children with a temporary disability such as a broken leg can obtain services under this section.
4. The Americans with Disabilities Act, 42 U.S.C S 12101, et seg., basically indicates that a school district cannot discriminate against/ exclude an otherwise qualified individual with a disability on the basis of his or her disability.
5. As this material is being written, the U.S. Department of Education is considering a dramatic retooling of IDEA that would greatly modify the current funding system and eligibility categories. The intent of the 1995 proposed changes is to refocus the law from merely guaranteeing access to education to improving the results for students with disabilities. The most fundamental change proposed is the replacement of the 13 disability categories in IDEA with a disability definition similar to the one in Section 504 and ADA.
6. National Association of State Boards of Education, *Winners All: A Call for Inclusive Schools* (Alexandria, VA: NASBE, 1992).
7. See Joy Rogers, "The Inclusion Revolution," *Research Bulletin 11*, Phi Delta Kappa Center for Evaluation, Development, and Research, May 1993, p. 1.
8. In Chapter 9 will be found several suggestions to aid in the development of an integrated special education and regular education program.
9. A draft copy of the IEP should be developed in advance of the M-team meeting to be presented and explained to the parent. Following this meeting, and any appropriate parental modification, refinements are made and the document executed.
10. *Honig* v. *Doe*, EHLR 559:231 (U.S. 1988)
11. EACH (Effective Advocacy for Citizens with Handicaps) is a nationwide volunteer organization that provides assistance for disabled individuals to ensure their legal rights are met.
12. See J. P. Comer, *School Power* (New York: The Free Press, 1980). Comer presents a powerful thesis for developing integrated community services for inner-city children, with the school being the delivery point for these services.

Selected Readings

Anderson, Ronald J., and Robert H. Decker. "The Principal's Role in Special Education Programming." *NASSP Bulletin* 77, no. 550 (February 1993): 1–6.

Darrell, Larry D. "At-Risk Students Need Our Commitment." *NASSP Bulletin* (January 1989): 81–83.

Dixon, Virginia L., and David E. Greenburg. "Assessment in Special Education: Administrators' Perspectives." *Diagnostique* 10 (1985): 161–175. (ERIC Document Service No. EJ 334 426).

Dragan, Edward F. "Accountability and Special Education: Planning for Results." *NASSP Bulletin* 78, no. 565 (November 1994): 1–5.

Dubin, Andrew. "Through the Administrative Looking Glass: The Special Needs Child." *Thrust for Educational Leadership* 16, no. 4 (January 1987): 36–37. (ERIC Document Service No. EJ 347 177).

Ellis, Joseph and Daniel Geller. "Disciplining Handicapped Students: An Administrator's Dilemma." *NASSP Bulletin* 77, no. 550 (February 1993): 22–38.

Epstein, Michael H. et al., "Improving Services for Students with Serious Emotional Disturbances." *NASSP Bulletin* 76, no. 549 (January 1993): 46–51.

"Feds Eye Major Changes to IDEA." *The Special Educator* 10 no. 13 (February 4, 1995): 206–207.

Golden, Diane Cordry. "Discipline of Students with Disabilities: A Decision-Making Model for Principals." *NASSP Bulletin* 77, no. 550 (February 1993):12–20.

Greenburg, David. *A Special Educator's Perspective on Interfacing Special and General Education: A Review for Administrators*. Reston, VA: ERIC Clearinghouse on Handicapped and Gifted Children, 1987. (ERIC Document Service No. ED 280 211).

Jachard, Charles. "Researching the Underchallenged, Marginal, or At-Risk Student." *Clearing House* (November 1998).

Katsiyannis, Antonis. "Individuals with Disabilities: The Role of the School Principal and Section 504." *NASSP Bulletin* 78, no. 565 (November 1994): 6–10

Lasky, Beth, Belinda D. Karge, Suzan M. Robb, and Marjorie McCabe. "How Principals Can Help the Beginning Special Education Teacher." *NASSP Bulletin* 79, no. 568 (February 1995): 1–14.

McCarthy, Martha M. "Inclusion and the Law: Recent Judicial Developments." *Research Bulletin* 13. Phi Delta Kappa Center for Evaluation, Development, and Research, November 1994, pp. 1–4.

Newby, John. "Parent-School Partnerships: Breaking Down the Barriers," *The High School Magazine* 2, no. 3 (March 1995): 17–18.

Sires, Carolyn, and Sandra Tonnsen. "Special Education: A Challenge for Principals." *NASSP Bulletin* 77, no. 550 (February 1993): 8–11.

VanSeiver, James H. "From Intimidation to Participation: Making Parents feel Welcome at Special Ed Proceedings," *The High School Magazine* 2, no. 3 (March 1995): 19.

Chapter *9*

Restructuring the Curriculum

*The purpose of school is not merely to help students achieve aca-
demically in school, but to prepare them to lead fulfilling lives.*
—ELLIOT EISNER[1]

"Let's put in a Drug Abuse Resistance Education (DARE) program." "We need an
AIDS awareness program in our school." "Please incorporate a 'Tobacco and Respira-
tory Illness' unit into your health curriculum." "The fire department has a new unit on
fire safety." "The police department has a new Jr. Deputy program for you." "Junior
Achievement would like to assist you with a new 'hands-on' business economics unit
in social studies." "The U.S. Department of Energy is providing a Nuclear Waste
Awareness unit." "The U.S. Department of Transportation is offering a new interdisciplinary 'Intelligent Transportation Systems' unit." "We need a gifted education program!" "We need a special education program." "Don't forget the arts." "Our
textbooks don't match the new state testing program." "Our English literature curriculum has no relevance for inner-city children." "What are we going to do with the new
national curriculum standards?"

The pressures on the curriculum are many. The principal must take a proactive role
in dealing with these issues or be overwhelmed by the demands of others. There are
many curriculum tasks to be performed in the school that require the involvement of
the principal. He or she must be a major player and decision maker for many of these
tasks and certainly must provide the initiative and leadership for all of them. Curricu-
lum-related tasks can include:

- Analyzing what subjects, topics, knowledge areas, skills, and abilities should be
  taught in the school
- Designing, developing or modifying courses; selecting the knowledge, skills, and
  abilities to be included; and organizing content outlines, objectives, lesson plans,
  activities, test items, and so on

- Delivering the curriculum, determining the array of available courses, sequencing courses or units, scheduling courses with concern for balance, flexibility, availability, and the like
- Evaluating curriculum by determining the congruence among course objectives, content taught, and student evaluation, as well as a review of the relevance of the curriculum for the students and community served

Obviously, the major participants in some of these tasks will be teachers and possibly subject area supervisors. On the other hand, as the field continues to move more toward site-based management coupled with the concepts of magnet schools and school choice, the principal must take on major oversight responsibility for the restructuring of the curriculum for the local school.

Curriculum Analysis

The introductory paragraph of this chapter points out the pressures faced by every school in determining what is to be the curriculum of the school. The school staff must have an orderly logical way of going about the task of making these curriculum decisions. The first step is often one of determining if the curriculum decision is theirs to make. Many states have curriculum requirements imposed by their legislatures or state departments of education. In other cases, local boards of education determine what subjects are to be taught. In reality, few, if any, decisions on course offerings or the number of hours of instruction in a certain subject are left to the local school.

The local school's role in curriculum analysis generally has two domains. One is to select a few elective offerings for the schools curriculum; for most schools, this is a relative minor part of the overall curriculum. The more significant task is the responsibility to determine the content to be taught in almost every course in the school. Policymakers may determine course offerings by title, but rarely do they dictate the detail of the knowledge, skills, and abilities (KSAs) to be included within the courses. States often provide curriculum guides and some local school districts will provide prescribed content outlines, but usually the detail of what is to be taught is left up to the local school.

The responsibility for determining the detail of curriculum content for the school needs to be assumed by the professional staff of the school under the leadership of the principal. If the staff does not act collectively, it will go by default to the individual teacher or the author of the selected textbook.

The determination of the content (KSAs) of virtually every course and subject offered by the school should be as the result of a joint effort by two or more faculty members. Curriculum requests, such as the ones mentioned at the beginning of this chapter, should be submitted to the appropriate faculty curriculum team for consideration.

Curriculum committees can be organized around either a grade level or subject matter. Grade-level committees develop the content for the entire curriculum for a particular grade. This is a common elementary school approach, but it is becoming popular as a way to review middle school and high school curriculum as well. This approach emphasizes the *horizontal* dimension of the curriculum, which usually includes all the subjects available to a student at a given time. When a student participates daily or weekly in social studies, English, science, mathematics, health, art, music, and physical education, one is describing the horizontal dimension of the curriculum. The horizontal structure of most U.S. schools is relatively uniform, and curricular areas are almost standard among schools and among grade levels. The horizontal balance remains about the same from year to year, providing students with equal amounts of time in each subject area.

Schools that are departmentalized, such as some upper elementary and junior high schools, have an additional problem with horizontal organization. The departmentalization creates *compartmentalization*, and the several disciplines taught are often not well coordinated or integrated for the students but taught as separate and unrelated bodies of knowledge.

An interdisciplinary curriculum using combinations of subjects offers ways to reestablish the integration of school subjects. In the lower elementary grades, this is best represented with so-called whole-language programs. There is a pedagogical movement away from discrete skills sequencing in the teaching of reading, for example. This approach integrates listening, speaking, reading, writing, and critical thinking. The whole-language approach is literature and subject matter based and is heavily student experience based rather than issuing from teacher-prepared worksheets and other didactic materials.

Thematic units, also often literature based, offer interdisciplinary studies. Figure 9–1 is an illustration of an elementary school thematic unit outline. Note that it includes skill areas to be taught in reading, language, mathematics, research, and higher-order thinking. Applications to social studies, science, and art are part of the unit as well. The entire unit is organized around a book about Benjamin Franklin.

Subject matter curriculum committees develop the content for a particular subject area such as social studies. This group will review and plan social studies content for all courses within one discipline for combination of grades such as K–5, 6–8 or 9–12. This subject matter approach is effective in providing good vertical articulation for the curriculum.

The sequence of the skills or topics taught within a particular course of study over-time, week by week, semester to semester, or year to year, represent the *vertical* dimension of the curriculum. Many resources are available to provide suggestions to the school or system's staff in the development of curriculum guides, including objectives and test items for vertical organization.

The voluntary National Curriculum Standards developed by the U.S. Department of Education represent a major national resource for curriculum guides. National professional associations for the various disciplines—such as the International Reading Association (IRA), the National Council of Teachers of English (NCTE), and the National Council for the Social Studies (NCSS), as well as many others—have curriculum outlines available. Many states departments of education also have developed curriculum guides for their own state schools and will sell them to schools in other states upon request. For example, in 1985, California completed model curriculum standards for grades 9–12 in English/language arts, foreign language, history/social science, mathematics, science, and visual and performing arts[2] (see Figure 9–2). Textbook publishers often provide curricular management systems, including skills con-

FIGURE 9–1   Sample Interdisciplinary Unit

What's the Big Idea, Ben Franklin?
Novel Study
and
Integrated Unit for Grade 3
by Judy Rehder and Kaye Williams
Knox County Schools

Content and Skills Covered in This Unit

Social Studies/History
1. Reading and using maps—legends, distance scales, locating places, and tracing routes, latitude equator
2. Understanding of the duties of an ambassador
3. Understanding of the causes of the American Revolution and what it was
4. Understanding of the Declaration of Independence and the Constitution of the United States
5. Cities—organization, fire departments, libraries—how people work together
6. Understanding of occupations and apprenticeships then and now
7. Understanding of how cities grow based sometimes on physical location
8. Understanding of how latitude affects climate
9. Understanding of how water and warm water currents affect climate
10. Understanding of the printing process and newspapers—understanding the effect of newspapers, etc. on people
11. Learning to work together on group projects

Science
1. Understanding what electricity is
2. Understanding how electric currents work
3. Understanding what will conduct electricity
4. Understanding dangers and safety measures related to lightning and electricity
5. Understanding how electricity has affected life
6. Understanding of seasons and earth/sun relationships
7. Scientific method
8. Inventions and Inventors
9. Understanding how soap is made

Art
1. Printmaking—vegetable prints
2. Drawing illustrations for a how-to book
3. Looking at famous American artists of this period
4. Making candles

Reading
1. Main idea, sequencing, details, inference, cause/effect
2. Reading to learning how to do things
3. Reading to learning information

Language Skills
1. Letter writing
2. Report writing
3. Writing poetry and prose and understanding the difference between
4. Using capital letters in place of names and titles

Continued

FIGURE 9–1   *Continued*

---

5. Underlining titles of books
6. Use of the comma—series and dates
7. Use of a dash
8. Forming plurals
9. Forming possessives
10. Dividing words into syllables at the end of a line
11. Suffixes and prefixes
12. Oral communication skills

Math
1. Magic squares
2. Figure distances on a map
3. Figure ages and differences in time

Research Skills
1. Encyclopedia
2. Almanac
3. Maps
4. Other books
5. Gathering information
6. Organizing information
7. Utilizing information
8. Sharing information

Higher Levels of Thinking and Working
1. Comparing and contrasting
2. Cause/effect
3. Productive thinking
4. Analysis
5. Synthesis
6. Evaluation—decision making
7. Drawing inferences/conclusions
8. Application
9. Working together in a constructive manner in small groups
10. Self-discipline and management skills for independent work

Related Mini-Courses
1. WHAT A SHOCK!!!—Experiments and experiences with electricity
2. WEATHER OR NOT!—Observing, recording, and forecasting weather
3. BRIGHT IDEAS!!!—A look at inventions and inventors—becoming inventors

---

Reprinted by permission of Judith J. Rehder, Kaye Williams, Chilhowee School.

tinua, mastery tests, and tracking systems to support their materials. A number of local schools developed federally supported projects promoted through the National Diffusion Network and listed in the catalog entitled *Educational Programs That Work* which also includes curriculum guides.[3] Finally, the Instructional Objectives Exchange (IOX) has compiled lists of objectives and test items organized by subject area and difficulty level that provide an excellent resource for curriculum planners in the selection of objectives in matching test items.[4] The test items, many of which are classified according to Bloom's Taxonomy, make excellent contributions to test item banks.

FIGURE 9–2   High School Economics Model Curriculum

High-School Economics Course

In order to achieve this basic understanding, students should master the fundamental economic concepts, appreciate how the principal concepts of economics relate to each other, and understand the structure of economic systems.

The model curriculum standards are enclosed in boxes. The terms below them are useful in understanding the standards, and the activities are offered to assist the teacher in developing these terms and concepts in the classroom.

Philosophy and Prerequisites for Economics

Students should have:

- An ability to read and understand charts and graphs
- A capacity to understand the nature of resources and the human interest in acquisition of goods and services
- A basic familiarity with institutions of our economic system

MODEL CURRICULUM STANDARDS FOR ECONOMICS

> **1.** A course should demonstrate that the study of economics requires the understanding of certain fundamental concepts and terms. Among these are the terms with definitions that appear in the Glossary at the end of this section.

> **2.** A course should include a study of the tools of analysis, such as charts, graphs, statistics, and marginal analysis.

> **3.** A course should show that economists measure economic performance by using certain economic indicators.

- National Income Accounting
- Gross National Product (G.N.P.)
- Consumer Price Indexing
- Inflation
- Measurements of unemployment.

Activities:

- Discuss unemployment and how it differs between population groups, depending on age, sex, and race.
- Analyze the history of inflation in the United States since 1973.
- Compare the inflation rates among countries, i.e., Mexico, Switzerland, Brazil, Japan, and the United States; and discuss the impact of these rates on the domestic economies and world trade.
- Show how changes in the Gross National Product (G.N.P.) measure changes in production.

Continued

FIGURE 9–2   *Continued*

---

4. A course should make it clear that the basic economic problem facing society is the condition of scarcity, or limitation on productive resources relative to human wants. As a result of this scarcity, choices must be made, taking account of the opportunity costs of each choice.

- Scarcity
- Trade-offs
- Economic choices
- Opportunity costs
- Wants
- Productive resources

Activities:

- Discuss the trade-off between producing more consumer goods and more investment goods.
- Review the economic history of the United States with regard to the growth in our productive resources.
- Consider the opportunity costs of completing high school, taking a part-time job after school, or going to the movies instead of doing required homework.

---

5. A course should demonstrate that all societies have economic systems that enable them to make choices on what to produce, how to produce it, and for whom to produce it. The economic system of the United States relies primarily on the market to make these choices.

- Economic systems
- Market
- Market economy
- Traditional economy
- Command economy
- Role of government
- Income distribution
- Supply and demand

Activities:

- Compare the economic system of the United States with one or more other economic systems with regard to how choices are made on what to produce, how to produce, and for whom to produce
- Discuss the role of the government in the largely market economy of the United States. In particular, when does the government interfere in private choices as to what to produce and for whom to produce it?
- Compare and contrast the economy of the Rancho system operated by the Californios with that which the Anglo-Europeans brought to California after 1850.

Reprinted, by permission, from *Model Curriculum Standards: Grades Nine Through Twelve*, © 1985, California State Department of Education, Sacramento, pp. HS-52 and 53.

Curriculum Design and Development

Each school serves a unique community. Therefore, each school must ultimately take responsibility for the design and development of its own curriculum. The principal provides the leadership for these tasks working through the faculty. The faculty curriculum committees used for curriculum analysis can build on their earlier curriculum analysis efforts and continue with the design and development tasks.

Effective schools research identified the importance of a well-designed curriculum structure to the development of effective schools. The recommended structure included for each subject or course a list of knowledge, skills, and abilities; specific student outcomes to be accomplished; well-designed lesson plans with instructional strategies, activities, and resources identified and matched to expected outcomes; and evaluation items created for each objective with a recommended mastery level for the evaluation. Each of these components is coordinated to achieve congruence throughout the curriculum, as shown in Figure 9–3.

Objectives and test items developed for the various course structures should be analyzed for the depth of learning they require. A classification system such as Bloom's Taxonomy[5] provides a method to determine the level of learning being expected of students. Bloom's Taxonomy of Cognitive Objectives, which includes the domains of knowledge, comprehension, application, analysis, synthesis, and evaluation, is valuable in ensuring high-order skills are developed within the various disciplines.

The course outlines, objectives, and tests should be used by all the teachers in the school who might be teaching that particular subject at that grade level. These curriculum structures, in some cases, may be based on a state-approved curriculum, may be organized around a particular text series developed by a districtwide curriculum committee, or may be constructed by the teacher or teachers in an individual building. The prescribed curriculum should be at least the work of two or more professionals and determined in concert by their joint effort.

Any discussion of curriculum must pay heed to the effects of maturation on changes in student interests and needs. Several notions in particular are significant when considering the organization of a school. The first is that all children do not mature at the same rate and thus all are not ready for the same curriculum at the same time. The difference in maturation of boys and girls is quite obvious, both physically and mentally. The same variation in size, mental capacity, interests, and needs also

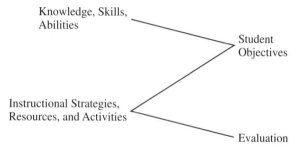

FIGURE 9–3   Curriculum Structure

exists within children of the same sex at a given age, only to be in a different balance or relationship after several more years of maturation. These differences should have a bearing on both instructional techniques and curriculum offerings, as well as on ways of grouping students.

Curriculum Delivery

Although curriculum delivery may seem to be largely the responsibility of the teaching staff, there are many major delivery tasks that encompass the entire school, thus requiring the leadership of the principal. These include determining which courses are to be offered, sequencing courses and/or units, and scheduling courses with concern for curriculum balance, continuity, flexibility, and availability. In addition, materials and equipment must be made available for quality instruction in today's world of changing technology.

An important aspect of curricular organization from the effective schools research is the concept of *curricular alignment*.[6] Once a structured curriculum has been adopted and supposedly implemented for each subject area, the questions become: "Are the teachers following it?" "Is the content presented to the students the same as indicated by the stated curriculum?" The teacher who takes the student only two-thirds of the way through the prescribed topics for the year is out of alignment with the planned curriculum. The classroom teacher who spends an inordinately large amount of time on his or her favorite topic and slights or ignores the prescribed topics is out of alignment with the agreed-upon curriculum.

The concept of curricular alignment is particularly significant when accountability for learning is important. If the school's evaluation system of either standardized achievement tests or criterion-referenced tests is matched to the anticipated curriculum, a serious curricular alignment problem could lower test scores significantly for children who were never given the opportunity to master the content measured by the tests. Curricular alignment includes, therefore, the alignment or coordination of what is taught with what is to be measured.

Curricular alignment, however, is more global than just the match between what is taught and what is measured. It also encompasses the articulation and coordination of the school's philosophy to goals, goals to objectives, objectives to instruction, and instruction to evaluation. For example, if the school's philosophy includes the statement "We believe critical thinking and decision making skills are important for every student to develop," then a goal should exist such as "to provide courses that help students develop critical thinking skills." Objectives also need to exist that speak to developing critical thinking skills. To illustrate, "a student will be able to demonstrate critical thinking skills by (1) defining a problem, (2) identifying and judging information relative to the problem, and (3) solving the problem and drawing conclusions." Instructional activities at a variety of levels of sophistication need to be incorporated into the several different courses and, finally, test items need to be utilized that are designed to measure critical thinking skills. The lack of any of these items may result in curricular misalignment.

If good teaching is an art, should classroom teachers have the freedom to change, adapt, and take advantage of unique opportunities for learning as they evolve? Freedom in the classroom certainly is desirable, but it can be thought of primarily as a problem of teaching technique or strategy and should not necessarily be a problem of content or curriculum unless a teacher drifts too far from a prescribed curriculum. If that occurs, then maybe it is time to evaluate the approved curriculum or otherwise indicate to teachers that they are expected to follow the agreed-upon plans.

Curriculum Flexibility

It is important to give adequate attention to individual differences and varying maturity rates and levels and to recognize that student interests and needs are broadly based. The organization of a school program must account for these needs, interests, and capabilities in all their diversity and provide learning experiences that will motivate all students.

If individual differences are to be recognized, both the vertical and horizontal dimensions of the curriculum require flexibility. Figure 9–4 illustrates the three different rates of learning. Since most children vary from the norm, the curriculum needs to be organized to allow each child to progress individually, as shown by lines A, B, and C.

The organization must allow both child B and child C access to appropriate information as it is sequenced according to the difficulty of concepts and materials. The achievement of the student overtime will depend, therefore, on the capability of the student to learn and the time committed to that subject.

In subjects such as reading and mathematics, where one has traditionally have assumed that all basic skills are taught in the elementary school, it is important to recognize that, because of their slow maturation rates, a large portion of children in fact have not learned these basic skills at a satisfactory level in each grade. Therefore, these subjects must be continued through the middle school years and on into high school.

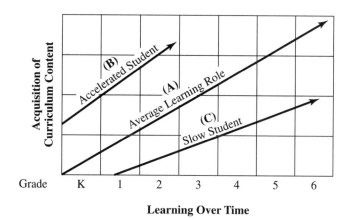

FIGURE 9–4 Impact of Individual Differences and Rates of Learning on Curriculum Needs

Curriculum Continuity

How much freedom should a student have to pursue needs and interests when curriculum selection is determined? Should a student have unlimited choice or should he or she be guided according to some plan? Should the student have few curricular choices and be expected to take all required subjects? How can the school arrange curricular opportunities for the student who can move rapidly up a vertical skill sequence ladder, for the student who progresses at a slower rate, for the student who wants or needs an extremely broad range of content areas, and for the student who must concentrate on basic skills? In the past, educators have not differentiated for individual students but have provided a very basic curriculum for everyone, allowing for little variation. This traditional curriculum included the same basic subjects in each year of a child's education.

Curriculum Balance

The school is under frequent pressure to expand its curricular offerings. However, the time available for instruction has remained relatively constant, although there is increasing interest in extending the length of the school year. However, only a limited number of hours each day are available for instruction. Difficult and sensitive decisions must be made to determine what alterations in the curriculum offer the best promise of an enhanced learning environment. Frequently, too, many aspects of the curriculum and the time allotted are mandated by state rules and regulations. But there are many aspects of the curriculum that are at the discretion of local boards of education and schools.

Each school should have guidelines to use in making good decisions about these discretionary aspects and to provide a balanced curriculum free from momentary fads or the wishes of this or that special-interest group. John Goodlad, in his book *A Place Called School*,[7] suggests that adequate attention be paid to each of the "five fingers" of the curriculum each year. His five fingers come from the Harvard report published in *General Education in a Free Society*.[8] The fingers are mathematics and science, literature and language, society and social studies, the arts, and vocational programs. Goodlad goes on to indicate that he feels elementary programs are too heavily directed toward language arts and mathematics.

Goodlad recommends that for high schools, literature and language and mathematics and science each be 18 percent of a student's program, with the other fingers comprising 15 percent each. Physical education, he believes should receive up to 10 percent attention, with the remaining time to be spent on guided individual choices.

J. Lloyd Trump,[9] in a much earlier work, suggested that all students receive at least some exposure to each discipline on a continuing basis each year they are in school, even though they may not at the time be taking a course in that discipline.

Curriculum Classification System

A curriculum materials classification system is also a desired curricular feature for all schools. School resources—the materials, books, pamphlets, worksheets, filmstrips, tapes, kits, software, and so on—that fit the curriculum structure of the school are many and vary significantly from school to school, even in the same district. The average school has over 20,000 curricular items in its holdings. Teachers seldom are aware of all the curriculum resources for particular topics or objectives they plan to teach and seldom are they able to remember the difficulty level or instructional format of these many resources.

As part of the overall effort to provide structure to the curriculum, concern must be given to organize curriculum resources through some type of materials classification system that matches the school's adopted curriculum and its instructional objectives. An excellent prototype to consider is the Annehurst Curriculum Classification System.[10] This system classifies materials on the basis of subject matter and appropriate student characteristics, such as age level, perception type, and so forth. A retrieval system is available for manual or computerized searches to match all available materials to particular courses, topics, and students. Most of the computerized library retrieval systems that provide for bar code identification of materials can incorporate the schools instructional materials as well. Using these systems places all school materials under one cataloging system, usually under the direction of the school media program.[11]

Test Item Bank

The secret of good curricular alignment often lies with the school's ability to monitor its progress through evaluation. The development of a test item bank or collection of test items that reflect the prescribed content of the curriculum guides to be used by the staff becomes a way of providing some of this monitoring ability. The bank consists of a minimum of three or four test items for each of the stated objectives for the course. Tests are then compiled to measure the mastery of students on each objective in the curriculum outline by including one or more test items for each objective at appropriate levels of difficulty. Test item profiles reflecting the percentage of items from each of the levels of Bloom's Taxonomy can also be prescribed for each test.

Teachers, having contributed the test items to the bank and knowing their students will be evaluated in all aspects of the content assigned to their particular course study, are motivated to maintain a high degree of curricular alignment with the prescribed course of study. By having multiple items in the test bank and drawing on them randomly for particular test administrations, reduction in the opportunity to "teach the test" can also be accomplished. The major change in the system is one of making the staff collectively responsible for curriculum and evaluation instead of allowing each individual teacher to function as an autonomous agent for those responsibilities.

A Curriculum Model

Consideration of the needs and interests of students throughout the curriculum should accommodate different maturity levels. Furthermore, curriculum must be divided into priorities with different weightings for each subject. Equal emphasis on all curricular areas is not necessarily appropriate for each year. For example, basic skills in language and computation are obviously needed in the early years of education. As a child matures and as interests broaden, the curriculum of the school should expand along with the child. By the middle of the elementary school years, the curiosity of most children is very broad in scope, and a child may participate in a great variety of different elective explanatory curriculum areas over the course of the year. Obviously, if the child participates in many different activities, covering most in depth is unlikely.

The pattern of elective curricular choices may need to be somewhat different for each child. For example, during one quarter, a particular child may select sewing, leisure reading, entomology (the study of insects), music appreciation, spelling skills, and math games. A second child may select topics on the basis of what friends select because of a real need to belong to a specific group. The following quarter the pattern for both children might be different This normal variation of curricular interests among children raises the important question of what areas of learning are common to all children.

Organizing curriculum around areas of importance rather than considering all curricular areas equally offers one solution. In this way, varying emphasis can be placed on different areas as appropriate during each segment of a student's school career. One well-accepted model clusters curriculum into four major areas:

1. Basic skills
2. Common learning
3. Exploratory areas
4. Specialization

Figure 9–5 shows the type of subjects to be included in each area.

Time-on-task studies demonstrate that the amount of engaged time a student spends in a particular discipline has a direct effect on the student achievement in that subject.[12] These studies on academic learning time (ALT) usually emphasize the importance of the efficient and effective use of time. However, the total amount of allocated time is probably an equally important factor. The most effective way to improve a student's achievement in any particular subject is simply to increase the amount of allocated time for the subject, recognizing of course that a corresponding decrease in

FIGURE 9–5   Major Curriculum Clusters

Basic Skills	**Common Learning**
Reading	Health
Arithmetic	Social studies
Psychomotor skills	Science
	Language

Exploratory Areas	**Specialization**
Social sciences	College prep
Science	Computer science
Art	Drafting
Music	Commercial foods
Mathematics	Distributive education
Typing	Horticulture
etc.	etc.

other subjects must occur unless the school day is lengthened. In other words, if school officials are under tremendous pressure to improve reading and math achievement scores, increasing the number of minutes spent each day in those subjects will generally result in improved achievement, assuming the quality of instruction is constant.

Society demands that children learn certain basic skills, which include skills in communication and computation and a knowledge of basic health care and physical education. U.S. society also requires basic familiarity with other more general areas, such as the knowledge of democracy and the way it works. A school can provide this information in many different ways. A real danger exists in curricular organization in regard to what to include as required common learning. It is easy to include so many topics that all of the available school time is utilized to teach this information and no discretionary time remains for exploratory and student-selected curriculum. Thus, areas of common learning must be kept to a bare minimum if other concepts are to have room in the program. The interrelationship of basic skills, common learnings, and exploratory or student-selected activities can be diagrammed as in Figure 9–6.

Initially, schools concentrate on basic skills development. This work consumes most of a child's time during the early years of school, gradually diminishing as a percentage of the total time spent on learning as other things are added to the program. Common learning curriculum may begin in small amounts during the child's early mastery of basic skills and increase as skills are learned. The exploratory or student-selected aspect of the curriculum should continue to broaden as a child matures. The curriculum will reach its greatest breadth at a point approximately midway through the school career when it is made up of many varied and diverse parts, including courses of the student's own choosing.

The time involvement of the child in the several parts of the curriculum varies, but the school year contains only a predetermined amount of time. In the early years, the curriculum has depth or concentration only in basic skills, with a relatively narrow scope of courses. By the time the child has reached the midschool point, time can be

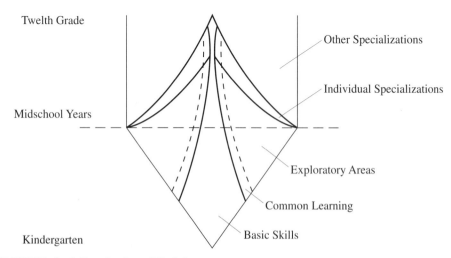

FIGURE 9–6 Curriculum Model

spent on more curricular areas. In other words, with so many curricular selections available during those middle years, students will spend less time on a particular subject. A child will be expected to learn some about many things rather than a lot about a few things.

By considering the natural motivation of the child, this expanding curricular organization better meets his or her growing curiosity during the elementary and middle school or junior high school days. In high school, the needs and interest of students begin to change. They begin to make tentative decisions relating to life as an adult. Puberty brings about emotional and psychological changes. The organization of the school system should take this into account. These changes have particular implications for curricular organization.

The interests and needs of children collectively continue to remain very broad and diverse, requiring a continued wide range of curricular offerings. On the other hand, the interests and needs of a particular child usually narrow as future life goals are sorted out. The curriculum of the school must allow students to begin to narrow their own curriculum into a specialization when they reach a maturity level that calls for it. The implications here for a flexible and active guidance program are also apparent.

During high school, the individual child begins to devote more and more time to an area of *individual specialization*, as shown in Figure 9–6. Specialization gradually replaces the exploratory phase of a student's curriculum. This individual specialization may entail a specific vocational program of one type or another. It may mean preparation for a particular vocation requiring continuation into a specific college program, or it may simply mean a decision to go to college.

For example, if a particular child is not progressing in reading skill development at a rate comparable to the majority of children that age, the child should probably spend a greater proportion of time in basic skills. The question then is what should give way? The choices probably rest between common learning and exploratory activities.

At first glance, it would seem that exploratory activities should probably give way to common learnings. But should they? Many children need strong motivation during the middle elementary years to keep up their interest in school. If exploratory activities are diminished for an increased skills emphasis, all interest in school on the part of the student may be lost. On the other hand, if the common learning areas are reduced instead, the interest in the exploratory areas might save the day (or the year), allowing a return to common learning later. One might even consider the content of the common learning areas as appropriate material for instruction in basic skills, providing a double-barreled program with the emphasis on the skills rather than on the common learning content.

Offering Curricular Breadth

Special Programs for Special Students

Students Who Are Gifted
Exploratory areas are one of the best opportunities to provide supplementary activities to gifted students and still have them participate with all children in the majority of curricular areas. Special programs in natural science, technology, mathematics, and other

areas can be made available on an interest basis or on a selective-qualification basis while still providing other programs for all children.

Students Who Are Disabled
In a similar fashion, students with one or more disabilities also need the opportunity for exploratory opportunities. Often, when these students have difficulty acquiring basic skills, opportunity for exploration gets a low priority and is replaced by additional basic skill activities. This presents a real dilemma in that well-taught exploratory activities often are a child's major motivator for the entire school program. Thus, the reduction in exploratory activities reduces the motivation that is so desperately needed for learning the basic skills.

Mini-Courses

Curricular breadth at the secondary level is also possible. A number of techniques are available. A *mini-course* is a short course usually offered for one marking period of six to nine weeks; it is frequently nontraditional in its content and organization. Mini-courses are a functional method of creating desired variety, flexibility, and open access to content within a high school curriculum.

The concept of the mini-course is to offer to students a learning experience either within one of the given disciplines or from a multidisciplinary approach in an effort to better meet their needs and interests. When a great variety of mini-courses are offered, the curriculum is broadened. When mini-courses are available on a nonsequenced basis, maximum access to the curriculum is obtained. When necessary, some sequencing can be accomplished through the use of an introductory course within a particular discipline, followed by a series of mini-course options. But in many cases, sequencing to meet individual student needs is carried out internal to course structures.

Honors Courses and Advanced-Placement Courses

Creating special courses for highly motivated or high-achieving students offers ways to meet special needs. Honors courses are generally restricted to students who have a grade-point average or achievement test score above a predetermined level. Often, too, students must maintain a grade of B or better to remain in the course. Assignment to a particular honors course neither precludes assignment to another such course, nor does it result in assignment to all other honors courses.

Advanced-placement courses are similar to honors courses but are available to juniors and seniors only. Successful completion of such courses, if they have been approved by the College Board, may result in college credit.[13]

Caution should be exercised in the use of advanced classes to not create a totally separate curriculum for academically talented students. It is important that heterogeneity also mark the student population of some classes. High-achieving students serve as good examples for lower-achieving students. Moreover, high-achieving students profit from working with all levels of the school population, socially and intellectually. The use of techniques for cooperative learning, discussed in the next chapter, work well when a range of student abilities are included in a class.

Action Learning

Some 400 seniors in a midwestern high school performed tasks in the community as part of their twelfth-grade social studies class. More than 90 percent of the senior class chose to do community service instead of writing a research paper. The students worked in a variety of endeavors, including political campaigns, voter registration drives, elementary and junior high schools, daycare centers, nursing homes, county recreation departments, and other places where they were needed. The only criterion for selecting placements was that the students work with people, not in clerical jobs. Finding placements for such a large number of students was facilitated by holding a community fair each fall. Those community agencies that desired student assistance set up tables or booths and the students shopped around for a volunteer opportunity that interested them and met their time and transportation limits. Students did their volunteer work during unscheduled time during the school day or after school.

Action learning is based on the concept of young people learning by doing and tying this concept into the idea of learning by serving. It is learning through a combination of direct experiences and associated instruction or reflection. The purposes that action learning can serve and the student experiences it can offer vary greatly from school to school. The emphasis can be on "service learning," which connotes activities focused on self-development. All the varied approaches, however, put the emphasis on the personal involvement of young people in the wider community and recognition that learning does and should take place outside the classroom. Actual learning situations can include volunteer services, internships, community surveys and studies, social and political action, shadowing a person to explore a career role, living in another culture, and work experience. Of course many of these activities are very common to some of out vocational programs, but in fields such as math, English, health, history, and government, the practice to go along with the theory is less common.

Schools that offer action learning identify a variety of objectives for their program, including:

1. Contribution to a young person's social development and his or her sense of responsibility for the welfare of others
2. Intellectual development—academic subjects take on added significance when students can apply their classroom knowledge to real problems
3. Career education—being able to see firsthand and participate in a variety of possible job roles
4. Benefits to the school—breaking down the barriers between the school and the wider community
5. Benefits to the community—the ability to provide many community services that would not have been possible without student volunteer help

Organizing for Action Learning

Many different action learning programs have been implemented, each with its own unique characteristics. Analyses of these different programs show five basic types of action learning situations, ranging from the minimum integration with the school program to almost total involvement. From least involvement to most, the action learning programs are described here.

A Volunteer Bureau

The school or the student identifies volunteer activities. The work is done during unscheduled time, study hall time, or before or after school. In some cases, arrangements are made for half-day release of all students participating in the volunteer program on a particular day of the week. The staff coordinator of volunteer programs is valuable in providing coordination to the program by identifying and placing students, following up, and reviewing the student's work. The student usually has the prime responsibility for initiating his or her community experience, with the school providing a coordinating function.

Community Service for Credit

The same basic plan arranged as a volunteer bureau can be carried out, adding to it some form of academic credit for student participation. The school may actively promote the program or the student may possibly still be the initiating agent.

Laboratory for Existing Course

Projects organized in conjunction with regular courses are used often in lieu of research papers or other assignments. Students may engage in community activity during school hours or after school, depending on their schedules. Often, as the students become more involved in community projects, course content begins to be altered toward the more practical useful information, emphasizing teaching systematic observation, data gathering, and community involvement.

Community Involvement Course

A formalized course in community involvement draws on the major features of the laboratory idea (from the previous model) along with the service for course credit concept. The course, though, has its entire structure organized around community involvement and draws all of its data for the course directly from the community. A course title such as "Student Community Involvement" might be appropriate.

The Action Learning Center

The center carries the students and teachers into the community, where they gain their total experience. This type of course is often interdisciplinary in nature and may be staffed by specialists who repeat the experience several times each year for different groups. Projects such as mountain camp-outs, canoe trips, rebuilding deteriorated homes, and other forms of community action are illustrative of this idea.

Action Learning Guidelines

Guidelines for directing action learning programs have been proposed by the National Association of Secondary School Principals:

1. The program must fill genuine needs of adolescents and of society in involving youth in tasks that are recognized as important by both young people and adults.
2. It must provide a real challenge to students, offering them an opportunity to extend their skills and their knowledge.
3. An opportunity for guided reflection on the service experience is necessary and this opportunity should be continued during the period of service.
4. Successful programs provide participants with the sense of community, that special feeling that comes from sharing a goal and working toward it with others.
5. A learning-by-serving experience should contribute to the knowledge that adolescents need regarding career options open to them in the adult world and offer some opportunities to work cooperatively with competent adults who are models for these options.
6. In format, the program must be both structured and flexible. Many projects have failed because they were too rigid to respond to changing conditions, and others have been unsatisfactory because they were too loosely structured to bring out a clear and continued sense of direction.
7. The program must promote a genuine maturity by allowing young people to exercise adult responsibility and be held accountable for their actions. This means, among other things, that students should actively participate in decision making and governance of the project in which they are learning by serving.
8. The stimulus for a worthwhile project or program can come from innumerable sources, so keep your eyes and minds open for leads as to needs, people, and places. Be particularly alert to hints that young people themselves may drop. They often are closer to the subtle but serious needs of the community than are school teachers and administrators.
9. Try to determine the optimal life span for a given learning-by-serving project and make this an element in planning and administration of the program. Probably more than most other aspects of secondary school curriculum, learning-by-serving programs have a constant need for new blood.

Summary

A variety of curricular concepts have been outlined in this chapter. In summary, these concepts are:

1. A complete curriculum structure, including concepts, topics, skills, behavioral objectives, recource lists, and evaluation instruments, should be developed for each content area.
2. Curricular alignment should be maintained for all areas and attention should be given to the density of the curriculum.
3. Improving academic learning time (ALT) is of critical importance to ensure that basic areas of the curriculum are given adequate attention.
4. Curriculum should be organized flexibly so that students can move to a sequence of learning experiences at different rates.

5. Curriculum should be organized so that varying amounts of time can be spent by students in specified content areas that meet special learning needs.

Activities

1. Reflect on the curriculum structure and offerings in your own school. Can you identify areas where restructuring should take place? Why do you believe so? Apply the concepts of this chapter to your school. How would you proceed to restructure your school's curriculum?

2. Review Cases Studies 5, 6, and 14. Analyze the problems presented and apply the curriculum concepts developed in this chapter. What approach would you use in addressing the problems? Set forth a strategy to overcome the difficulties faced by the school as well as ways to deal with individuals in the cases.

Endnotes

1. Elliot Eisner," What Is the Purpose of School?" *ASCD Update* 32, no.10 (December 1990):4.

2. California State Department of Education, *Model Curriculum Standards: Grades Nine Through Twelve*, 1st ed. (Sacramento: California State Department of Education, 1985).

3. National Diffusion, *Educational Programs That Work* (Lungmont, CO: Sopris West Inc. Network, 1984).

4. Instructional Objectives Exchange (IOX), Box 24095, Los Angeles, CA 90024. IOX has collections at the secondary level in language arts, including reading, comprehension, structural analysis, composition, reference skills, listening, oral expression; journalism; grammar, mechanics, and usage; and English literature. Other collections include general mathematics, business education, home economics, auto mechanics, electronics, general metals, mechanical drawing, woodworking American history, geography, biology, and Spanish. A current catalog can be obtained by writing to the above address.

5. Benjamin S. Bloom and others, *The Taxonomy of Educational Objectives: Effective and Cognitive Domains* (New York: David McKay, 1974).

6. W. Fredrick, "The Use of Classroom Time in High Schools Above or Below the Median Reading Score," *Urban Education* 11 (January 1977): 459–464.

7. John A. Goodlad, *A Place Called School* (New York: McGraw-Hill, 1983).

8. Report of the Harvard Committee, *General Education in a Free Society* (Cambridge, MA: Harvard University Press, 1945).

9. J. Lloyd Trump, *Images of the Future* (Washington, DC: National Association of Secondary School Principals, 1959).

10. Jack Frymier, *The Annehurst Curriculum Classification System* (West Lafayette, IN: Kappa Delta Phi, 1977).

11. D. J. Armor, P. Conry-Oseguera, M. Cox, N. King, L. McConnel, A. Pascal, E. Pauly, and G. Zellman, *Analysis of the School Preferred Reading Program in Selected Los Angeles Minority Schools* (Santa Monica, CA: Rand Corporation 1976).

12. Charles Fisher et al., "Improved Teaching by Increasing Academic Learning Time," *Educational Leadership* 37 (October 1979): 52–54.

13. *A Guide to the Advanced Placement Program,* The College Board, 45 Columbus Ave., New York, NY 10023-6992.

Selected Readings

Anderson, L. "Improving Instruction: Policy Implications of Research on School Time." *The School Administrator* (Arlington, VA: American Association of School Administrators, 1983).

Berliner, D. "Academic Learning Time," in *Effective Teaching for Higher Achievement*, ed. R. Brandt (Arlington, VA: Association for Supervision and Curriculum Development Videotape A, 1983).

Bloom, B. S. *Human Characteristics and School Learning* (New York: McGraw-Hill, 1982).

Bloom, B. S., M. B. Engleshart, E. J. Furst, W. H. Hill, and D. R. Krathwohl. *Taxonomy of Educational Objectives: The Classification of Education Goals. Handbook I. Cognitive Domain* (New York: Longmans Green, 1956).

Bolaños, Patricia. "Restructuring the Curriculum." *Principal* 69, no. 3 (January 1990): 13–14.

Bracey, Gerald W. "A Critical Look at Standards and Assessment." *Principal* 73, no. 3 (January 1994): 6–10.

Cauley, Kathleen M., and John T. Cauley. "Curriculum Reform in Middle Level and High School Mathematics." *NASSP Bulletin* 79, no. 567 (January 1995): 22–30.

Cawelti, Gordon. "Designing High Schools for the Future." *Educational Leadership* 47, no. 1 (September 1989): 30–35.

Chesley, Gary. "The Engineering of Restructuring: What Do We Do and How Do We Do It?" *NASSP Bulletin* 78, no. 565 (November 1994): 21–27.

Clinchy, Blythe McVicker. "Goals 2000: The Student as Object." *Kappan* 76, no. 5 (January 1995): 383–385.

Clincy, Evans. "Learning in and About the Real World: Recontextualizing Public Schooling." *Kappan* 76, no. 5 (January 1995): 400–404.

De Souza, Anthony R. "Time for Geography: The New National Standards." *NASSP Bulletin* 78, no. 564 (October 1994): 1–6.

Eisner, Elliot W. "Who Decides What Schools Teach?" *Phi Delta Kappan* 71, no. 7 (March 1990): 523–526.

Fisher, C., D. Berliner, N. Filby, R. Marliave, L. Chance, and M. Dishaw. "Teaching Behaviors, Academic Learning Time, and Student Achievement: An Overview." in *Time to Learn*, ed. C. Denham and A. Lieberman (Washington,

DC: The National Institute of Education, U.S. Department of Education, 1980).

Foriska, Terry J. "The Principal as Instructional Leader: Teaming with Teachers for Student Success." *Schools in the Middle* 3, no. 3 (February 1994): 31–35.

Fuller, Frank Jr. "The Arts for Whose Children? A Challenge to Educators." *NASSP Bulletin* 78, no. 561 (April 1994): 1–6.

Goodlad, John I. *A Place Called School* (New York: McGraw-Hill, 1984).

Hill, John C. "The Principal as Curriculum Supervisor." *Principal* 69, no. 3 (January 1990): 6–9.

Hough, David L. "The Elemiddle School: A Model for Middle Grades Reform." *Principal* 74, no. 3 (January 1995): 6–9.

Jacobs, Heidi Hayes, (Ed.). *Interdisciplinary Curriculum: Design and Implementation* (Arlington, VA: Association for Supervision and Curriculum Development, 1989).

Kanpol, Burry, and Eva Weisz. "The Effective Principal and Curriculum—A Focus on Leadership." *NASSP Bulletin* 74 (April 1990): 15–18.

Komoski, Kenneth P. "Needed: A Whole-Curriculum Approach." *Educational Leadership* 47, no. 5 (February 1990): 72–78.

Lewis, Anne C. "Getting Unstuck: Curriculum as a Tool of Reform." *Phi Delta Kappan* 71, no. 7 (March 1990): 534–538.

Resnick, Lauren B., and Leopold E. Klopfer, (Eds.). *Toward the Thinking Curriculum: Current Cognitive Research* (1989 ASCD Yearbook). Arlington, VA: Association for Supervision and Curriculum Development, 1989.

Shutes, Robert, and Sandra Peterson. "Seven Reasons Why Textbooks Cannot Make a Curriculum." *NASSP Bulletin* 78, no. 565 (November 1994): 11–20.

Vann, Allen S. "Curriculum and Textbooks: A Happy Marriage?" *Principal* 73, no. 4 (March 1994): 20–21.

Vann, Allan S. "How to Deal with a Bloated Elementary Curriculum." *Principal* 69, no. 3 (January 1990): 10–12.

Wagner, Tony. "What's School Really for, Anyway? And Who Should Decide?" *Kappan* 76, no. 5 (January 1995): 393–399.

Chapter 10

Restructuring Learning

Goals, strategies, learners, and objectives have styles.
Each style implies a different set of relationships
between the teacher, the learner, and the curriculum.
—R. W. STONG, H. F. SILVER, AND R. HANSON[1]

If curriculum can be defined most simply as *what* is taught in the school, then instruction is the *how*—the methods and techniques that aid students in their learning. The emphasis in instruction should be on student achievement, not on teaching, but obviously both are significant.

Instruction is the lifeblood of the school. It is the process by which content, or curriculum, is transported to the student. Instruction, however, requires a learner who gains insight, acquires information, and forms values not only from the content of the curriculum but also through the processes by which the content is presented—instruction. Therefore, the entire learning environment of the school constantly provides content for learning. This entwining of curriculum and instruction forces school administrators to look very carefully not only at what they teach in the school but at how they teach it, for the medium is truly the message.

Consideration of instruction as the process for providing content to the learner presents several major problems to the thoughtful organizer of the school program. These can best be presented as five questions:

1. What is the nature of the learner and how can students best be organized?
2. What instructional processes are available to be used?
3. How do these processes accommodate individual differences?
4. What are the implications of these instructional processes for the other organizational components of the school?
5. How can these processes be improved?

Answers to these questions are not always available, but principals should be aware of the implications of each.

How different are children from each other? What differences count when organizing a school? Differences can be found in children's abilities, height, weight, age, sex, interests, needs, ethnic backgrounds, learning styles, achievements, and personalities. But before determining which differences matter in school organization, we should consider what these differences really are. Obviously, as children mature, differences increase. Many characteristics can be measured against accepted fixed scales and spoken of in fairly concrete terms. Items such as gender or ethnic background remain fixed and can usually be described in specific terms, also. However, factors such as abilities, interests, needs, learning styles, and personalities are far more difficult to assess, for they are far more complex, varied, and changeable. As a result, efforts to classify people become more dependent on other constructs for definition and therefore less exact. For example, rarely will a single continuum suffice in a description of ability. Ability to do what? To be meaningful, ability descriptions must also be scaled in some way. Ability compared to what or to whom? Ability to do something or to do something better than someone else? Comparative information, then, is necessary in studying or determining differences in abilities because of the abstract nature of terms such as ability.

Individual Differences among Children

One reason for looking at individual differences is to determine the conditions they may set for organization. Individual differences obviously affect the way instruction and curriculum are organized. Contributing to these organizational decisions will be decisions relating to grouping children. *Achievement* is most often used as a basis for predicting *ability*. As a result, the two terms become inappropriately interchanged. Achievement can be measured with a fairly high degree of accuracy, but translating achievement into ability is fraught with danger because of the inability to always know of, or adequate place in the formula, those factors contributing to a student's opportunity to achieve.

For example, a child may have the ability to be an excellent computer programmer, but if he or she has never had the opportunity to even sit at a computer terminal, future performance is uncertain. Thus, to take past achievements with computers as a predictor of future success would be erroneous. More thought about the conditions or circumstances under which past achievement occurred needs to take place before making instructional decisions.

If one is going to look not at ability but at achievement as a determinant for organizing children for learning, what kind of differences should one expect to find in a school population? Studies done at the University of Minnesota in the early 1940s, that still hold today, established a simple rule of thumb to indicate an achievement range.[2] The rule is: The achievement range of an age group of children is equal to approximately two-thirds of their chronological age. A group of 6-year-old children will have an achievement range of four years; a group of 9-year-olds will have an achievement range of six years. In other words, the slowest 9-year-old will be approximately equal to an average 6-year-old (three years below), and the fastest 9-year-old will be approximately equal to an average 12-year-old (three years above). Figure 10–1 illustrates the formula for school-age children. Note particularly the overlap of achievement over any three-year age span. A group of 6-year-olds, a group of 7-year-olds, and a group of 8-year-olds have a broad range of achievements in common. The extremes contribute only fractional differences across the several years.

Grouping Students

Instruction in any normal school setting requires numerous decisions about the grouping of children. Basically, these decisions will relate to three variables: group size, group composition, and group flexibility. The basic purpose of grouping students is to bring about the highest quantity and quality of instruction possible. Grouping practices should be consistent with curricular decisions and should be compatible with each student's needs and interests. These lofty goals must be tempered by two factors.

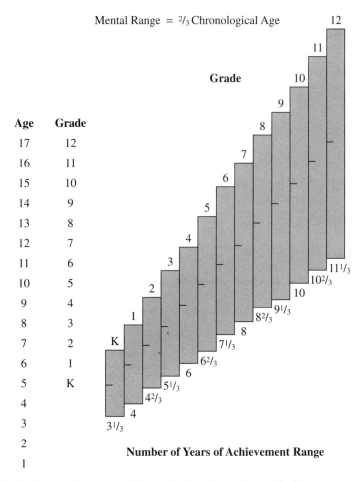

FIGURE 10–1   Achievement Formula for School-Age Children

The first factor is the variations of abilities within each learner making homogeneous grouping very difficult. The second factor is the practical consideration of the cost of a particular organization design in comparison with its related effectiveness. For example, group size usually suggests certain staffing patterns that can be converted into dollar costs. A school might conclude that a staffing ratio of three-to-one would give the best quality and quantity of learning per student but that it would be too expensive. Instead, grouping designs must consider more economical staffing ratios, most likely in the range of 15 to 30 students per 1 staff member.

Group Size

Over the years, research studies on class size have produced mixed results. Two meta-analyses of class-size, researched by Gene V. Glass and Mary Lee Smith, published by the Far West Laboratory, have been widely interpreted as providing convincing evidence that smaller classes are better than larger ones. The basic finding of analyses on class size indicated that smaller classes resulted in increased achievement. However, the study showed that in classes ranging from 20 to 40 pupils, class size made little difference in achievement. The major benefits from reduced class size were obtained as size was reduced below 20 pupils.[3]

A more recent study in Tennessee,[4] using over 70 classrooms in a well-designed four-year study of primary classes (K–3) size 13–17, 22–25, and 22–25 with an aide, produced conclusive results. Students in the small classes made higher scores on both the achievement and criterion-referenced tests. The greatest gains were made in inner-city small classes. The highest scores were made in rural small classes. Teachers reported that they preferred small classes in order to identify student needs and provide more individual attention as well as to cover more material. The findings also suggest a cumulative and positive affect of small classes in later grades. Students in grade 4 who had previously been in the project's small classes demonstrated significant advantages on every achievement measure over students who had attended regular classes.

Teachers who had the smaller classes were observed to cover their basic instruction more quickly, providing increased time for additional material. They used more supplemental texts and enrichment activities. There was more in-depth teaching of basic content. More frequent opportunities were available for children to engage in firsthand learning activities using concrete materials. In summary, teachers were better able to individualize instruction.

Group Composition

What should be the criteria for organizing children into groups? Obviously, efficient instruction requires groups. The question of group composition has intrigued educators for years. This section will deal first with some of the more controversial grouping practices, such as homogeneous ability grouping and retention, and their accompanying problems. Then, on a more positive note, alternative grouping patterns based on interest, age, skill, and achievement, as well as group flexibility and tenure will be discussed.

Ability Grouping in the Elementary and Middle School

A common practice is to organize or group students on the basis of their supposed ability, creating a tracking system with a two-, three- or four-group continuum consisting of high-ability, average-ability, and low-ability students. The basic assumption underlying this pattern of student organization is that by subdividing children from the extremely broad-ability continuum found in any normal school population, teachers will be better able to focus instruction on the needs of the children in any particular group. Thus, ability groups supposedly narrow the range of abilities within any group and make it more possible for the teacher to organize and prepare materials for a narrower range of abilities.

Criteria used to determine group composition have included achievement test scores, IQ scores, previous grades, and teacher opinion. Serious problems develop when any of these criteria or combinations are used as the basis of organizing students on a permanent basis or for extended periods of time. This method of grouping is usually not effective. No common denominator can be found for long-term grouping across disciplines or even within disciplines. For example, interest can greatly change productivity within a discipline, overriding previous supposed ability measurements.

Children can be grouped successfully according to one factor to obtain a degree of homogeneity, but the group remains heterogeneous in all other aspects of curriculum and instruction. For example, homogeneity in mathematics can be obtained by placing in a group all children who know their multiplication tables through 12, but they remain a heterogeneous group for the rest of the curriculum, including other areas of mathematics.

When the descriptors of homogeneity are based on previous math achievements, an IQ test score, or all previous grades, almost all useful definition of homogeneity is lost, for in almost any specific skill or knowledge, some children placed in the lowest group on one basis will exceed the knowledge level of other children placed in the highest group on another. Therefore, homogeneous grouping as a broad-based or permanent grouping design simply does not work, and the homogeneity is a figment of the imagination of the staff.

Many teachers and administrators have argued strenuously that ability grouping does work and that definite differences exist among students. Of course, differences can be seen, but the point is that the overlap in abilities is far greater from group to group than most of us imagine, and, most importantly, homogeneous grouping overlooks the individual child.

Several attitudinal factors must also be considered in a discussion of homogeneous grouping. The phenomenon of the *self-fulfilling prophecy* enters into the ultimate outcomes of ability grouping. This prophecy says that children become what others say they are or what they think they are.[5] Research about self-concept has shown that children's own attitudes toward themselves as people and their assessment of their own abilities represent major factors in their ultimate success or failure in school. Teacher attitudes, as well as the student's self-concept, contribute greatly to the child's ultimate success or failure in school. The placement of a child in a group on the basis of perceived ability can seem to prove itself correct by adjustments in productivity on the part of the child that in fact take place as a result of the placement, thus fulfilling the prophecy.

Over the past 40 years, numerous research studies have considered ability grouping. A massive review of many of these studies was reported in 1973 with the following conclusions:

1. Homogeneous ability grouping as currently practiced shows no consistent positive values for helping students generally, or particular groups of students, to achieve more scholastically or to experience more effective learning conditions. Among the studies showing significant effects, evidence of slight gains favoring high-ability students is more than offset by evidence of unfavorable effects on the learning of students of average and below-average ability, particularly the latter.

2. The findings regarding the impact of homogeneous ability grouping on affective development are essentially unfavorable. Whatever the practice does to build or inflate the self-esteem of children in the high-ability groups is counterbalanced by evidence of the unfavorable effects of stigmatizing those placed in average- and below-average-ability groups as inferior and incapable of learning.

3. Homogeneous ability grouping, by design, is a separative educational policy, made ostensibly according to test performance ability but practically according to socioeconomic status and, to a lesser but still observable degree, according to ethnic status.

4. In cases where homogeneous or heterogeneous ability grouping is related to improved scholastic performance, the curriculum is subject to substantial modification of teaching methods, materials, and other variables that are intrinsic to the teaching-learning process, and that, therefore, may well be the causative factors related to academic development wholly apart from ability grouping per se. Similarly, with respect to social development, evidence that points to variables other than ability grouping tends to relate substantially to personal growth or lack of growth.[6]

High School Grouping

In high schools, ability grouping functions somewhat differently than in the lower grades. Deficit and average students do seem affected by grouping but talented students achieve more and have better attitudes about subject matter when they are placed with others who are also talented. Ability grouping frequently occurs naturally in the selection of elective courses labeled "honors" or in advanced-placement courses. Advanced foreign language courses and higher-level mathematics courses also attract these students. More recent studies on grouping in the elementary school continue to support the position that heterogeneous grouping produces greater student learning than does homogeneous grouping.[7]

Retention

One form of ability grouping that is often overlooked is the result of the retention policies operating in many school districts. Retention places a child with a less intellectually and socially mature group based on the child's demonstrated ability or achievement. Therefore, it is actually an instance of ability grouping—adjusting the placement of the child to fit a curriculum and instructional level thought more appropriate, rather than bringing the appropriate curriculum and instructional level to the child.

Retention is as ineffective an approach to the grouping of children as the previously discussed method. A poorly achieving fourth-grader is not more like third-graders. That student is still more like his or her peers and will be more successful with them than if retained and placed with a younger group of children. At any grade level, the achievement range will spread over a number of grade levels. The Cook studies of the 1940s concluded that:

> *When pupils in the lower 10 percent of the classes are failed because of low achievement, they do not become better adjusted educationally or socially in the retarded position. The available evidence indicated that, on the average, they achieve as much or more by being given more regular promotions.*

The study went on to point out that:

> *When attempts are made to reduce the range of abilities and achievement in a school by retarding slow learning pupils and accelerating fast learning pupils, there is an increase in the proportion of slow learning pupils in each grade. Average grade achievement is lowered.*

The study concluded, somewhat tongue in cheek, that:

> *If the major concern of the teachers is to maintain grade level standards, the most effective way of increasing achievement standards in a school is to retard the bright and accelerate the dull pupils.*[8]

Recent research on retention continues to show its inappropriateness as a means of adjusting for individual differences.[9] Nevertheless, it continues as a very popular policy in many schools. It does not work as a method of maintaining standards. It does not work as a means of threatening children to perform. If you have become an advocate of TQM, retention violates the TQM principle of not setting outcome goals. It is much better if a school uses instructional process solutions to adjust for individual differences of children.

Appropriate Bases for Grouping

Groups are necessary for school organization, but retention and homogeneous ability grouping as semipermanent forms of student organization are not effective. What should be the basis for grouping? The following principles and techniques for organizing students are sound:

1. Regular classrooms and teams should be based on heterogeneous grouping. Some means should be taken to ensure that all teams have an equal portion of students on various achievement and ability levels.

2. Achievement grouping for math and reading is appropriate, particularly if these subjects are taught from a skill continuum. However, achievement groupings should not result in tracking. Primary identity for a student should still be with the heterogeneous grouping pattern.

3. The principal has the responsibility of sharing with teachers the research on retention and grouping practices. "Conventional wisdom" misleads in this case. The principal also needs to be responsible for developing grouping patterns that serve the needs of the unique student population and should monitor teacher implementation of these grouping plans.

4. Grouping patterns must be flexible and, as a result of individual student assessment, allow change in student placement as needed.

5. Within each classroom setting, subgroupings should be kept small enough to ensure individual instruction.

6. Children of various ages may be grouped together if some other appropriate criteria such as skill development is utilized.

7. Particular care should be taken so that grouping practices do not become damaging to the self-concept of the child or create stereotypes in the eyes of other students or teachers toward particular children.

Group Flexibility

How long should an established group remain intact? When groups are reorganized, how extensive should that reorganization be? At what level within the organization should decisions for group reorganization take place? These questions relate directly to the ultimate flexibility that can be obtained for grouping within any school organization.

Groups should remain intact until they have accomplished their skills objective. Once the original purpose for the grouping has been achieved, the group must be reorganized. This may be after one hour of instruction in a skills group, or it might be after three years together as a heterogeneous, multiage group. Skill groups, interest groups, and achievement groups should be designed so they can be reorganized daily, if necessary.

Problems of Regrouping

The need for frequent regrouping in the school presents several problems in school organization. First, it is impractical to refer all grouping decisions to the principal since the quantity and frequency of needed grouping decisions would overwhelm that office. More significantly, most of the information needed for intelligent grouping decisions is found at the teacher-student level.

To give teachers and students an opportunity to make flexible grouping decisions, a school is best organized into learning communities consisting of two or more teachers, their students, and an extended time block. With this arrangement, students and teachers can group students. The unit design for school organization with a team of teachers, aides, and a group of 75 to 150 students is a good example of this organization.[10]

The important concept here is that the principal has passed on the power of decision making regarding grouping directly to the teachers. Once the components of the learning community have been designated, the principal's role becomes one of giving advice to the teams for internal grouping decisions. The teachers, in turn, then organize the groups.

Grouping Guidelines

Student grouping is necessary for all school organizations.

1. For purposes of assigning students to individual teachers or teams, a heterogeneous or mixed grouping plan is usually best.
2. Homogeneous grouping should take place in the classroom and should be done by teachers. The basis for internal class grouping can be interest, achievement, skill, age, or designed heterogeneity
3. Homogeneous grouping should be kept flexible with several different grouping patterns used each day. All homogeneous groups are usually of short duration. Flexibility is necessary because of the changing nature of groups and the problems of negative student self-concept or poor teacher attitudes that can develop from rigid homogeneous grouping patterns.
4. Homogeneous groups should not be used for more than one-third of each school day.

Instructional Processes and Types of Instruction

Instruction can take place in a variety of formats. Types of instruction can be divided into several basic categories:

1. Lecture presentation or demonstration
2. Discussion
3. Laboratory activities
   a. Group or individual
   b. Independent study

Each category presents a different mode for student learning. The purpose of instruction and the expected outcomes should be major factors in determining which instructional type should be used. For example, if the purpose of instruction is to introduce or present an overview of a topic, a lecture presentation to a large group might be best. On the other hand, if the anticipated outcome is the modification of values, then an instructional format that directly involves the learner (such as a laboratory or discussion) is most often more effective. Figure 10–2 presents the major purposes of these four categories of instruction. Note that each category also has certain group size recommendations.

In reality, in most lessons, all four types of instruction should probably be used. For example, the model lesson design proposed by Madeline Hunter uses all four types. The Hunter model suggests seven steps for a sequential learning model as shown in Figure 10–3.[11]

Steps 1 to 3 of the Hunter model are usually in the form of a lecture to the entire group. Steps 4 and 5 are often in a discussion mode, initially with the entire group, but often with smaller follow-up groups as fewer and fewer children remain not having yet achieved mastery. Step 6 is a form of group lab activity, and step 7 is an individual lab or homework-type assignment.

FIGURE 10–2   Types of Instruction and Major Purposes

I. Presentation
Build concepts through
   information
Stimulate inquiry
Enrich course
Relate course to reality
Make assignments

Usually most efficient
   and effective in large
   groups

II. Discussion
Raise questions
Report experience
Discuss ideas
Generalize
Form opinions
Plan independent study

Usually most efficient
   and effective in small
   groups (7–15 persons)

III. Laboratory Activities

Individual Study	*Purpose*	*Independent Study*

Student
   performed
   directed
	Build concepts and
	   principles through
	   action and viewing
	Practice skills
		Student
		   directed
		   planned
		   performed
		   evaluated

Teacher
   directed
   planned
   evaluated
   managed
	Apply ideas
	Develop investigative
	   skills
	Develop problem-
	   solving techniques
	Develop evaluation skills
		Teacher
		   advised

These activities may be small group (2 or more) or individual in nature and
can be either scheduled or unscheduled.

FIGURE 10–3   Sequential Learning Model

1. **Anticipatory Set**
   The teacher prepares students for the lesson. The first five minutes of a lesson are the
   most critical as that is when the teacher has the greatest degree of student attention.

2. **Statement of Objectives**
   The instructor should inform students of the objectives for a particular lesson: namely,
   Robert Mager's three elements of an instructional objective:

   a. State the task.
   b. Identify how the task is to be completed.
   c. Identify minimum level of competency to be achieved, if the teacher wishes to
      identify a minimum level.

   Instruction in the deductive style is recommended for students experiencing academic
   difficulty. The teacher would state the rule and give students adequate practice until
   they could demonstrate mastery prior to introducing a new concept.
       Guiding questions, prior to independent completion of an assignment, are
   recommended.
       The teacher should clarify for the students how one day's instruction ties into
   what has academically preceded and how it will influence the next day's instruction.

FIGURE 10–3   *Continued*

3. **Instructional Input**
   The teacher should move among the students, while they are working, providing additional reinforcement when needed.

4. **Modeling**
   The teacher should be illustrating concepts taught, providing many and varied examples, and responding to student questions.

5. **Checking for Understanding**
   Students should demonstrate 75–80 percent mastery on a concept before being taught a new concept.

6. **Guided Practice**
   The teacher can have children working in groups of five to seven, carefully monitoring their achievement while they are working. Particular attention should be given to those children who, in the past, have demonstrated difficulty in working independently.

7. **Independent Practice**
   Such practice should consist of only ten to fifteen minutes for a particular assignment. Independent practice should not be used as a teaching strategy; it should be used as reinforcement for concepts that are understood by the students.

Research on Teaching

Research regarding instruction and the development of a consistent view of teaching represents one of the major changes in education in the past decade. This change has come about as education has made a major shift in its attention from focusing on teacher traits to focusing on instructional skills. Although there may never be a generic set of teaching skills, the research on effective teaching has produced a list of recommended instructional skills that, when implemented effectively by teachers, produces observable, measurable gains in student learning. A summary of the major teaching competencies, along with citations of their research, are listed for teacher competencies in planning, lesson implementation, cooperative learning, student motivation, evaluative feedback, evaluative methods, assigning grades, time on task, and individualized instruction.

Effective Planning Skills

Research on teachers' planning indicates that if teachers identify instructional objectives, set an appropriate level of difficulty for mastery, plan out matching instructional methods, procedures, materials, and student activities, and use good formative and summative evaluation techniques, the resulting preparedness can increase the probability of improving student learning as measured by test scores. Such planning also ensures teacher confidence, direction, and security.

Some of the success of this planning can certainly be attributed to the improved curricular alignment that occurs from the detailed planning around objectives drawn directly from a prescribed curriculum. However, the *planning* for instructional implementation is believed to be the major cause of the gain found in student test scores.

The research on planning also provides a clear understanding of the stumbling block to planning.[12] Teaching for mastery demands a well-developed statement of goals and instructional objectives as well as appropriate criterion-referenced tests.[13] Although this makes good sense to administrators and many teachers, it requires a tremendous amount of work for teachers. Most teachers, however, intuitively base their success in the classroom on student interest and attitudes and not on cognitive gain. Therefore, the teachers do not obtain the personal reinforcement from the results of the students' test gains.[14]

Effective Lesson Implementation

The effective implementation of a lesson planned by the teacher is as important as the planning itself. The high-gain teachers use a variety of instructional methods, including drill, explanation, discussion, inquiry, role-playing, demonstration, and problem solving. One important element of good lesson implementation is the use of advanced organizers, which gives the learner an overview of the lesson. Hunter's concept of an anticipatory set is an example of an advanced organizer.

Other important elements of effective lesson implementation include asking relevant questions, giving explanations, and doing demonstrations in conjunction with frequent feedback to the teacher regarding student understanding. Feedback techniques, such as signing (thumbs up, thumbs down) or "if you know the correct answer raise your hand," can provide this information to a teacher throughout the lesson.

"Electronic classrooms," equipped with a keypad at each students work station, with a monitor for the teacher to see student responses, provide a means for each student to respond to questions. Such systems have the capability to record all the answers for later review by the teacher. The major limitation of these systems is that the questions must be only those that can be answered with multiple-choice responses, true/false responses, or numerically.

Increased wait time, the amount of time a teacher waits after asking a question, also has shown positive effects on student performance. Untrained teachers often wait only one to two seconds after asking a question. A longer wait time produces longer more complete student responses, more student confidence in their responses, increased factual evidence used by students in their responses, a greater number of slow students participating, and reduced teacher-centered presentations.[15]

Research also has produced surprising results about questioning techniques. First, many teachers do not use questioning of students during discussion very much, but it has been demonstrated that the frequency of factual, single-answer questions is positively related to gains in achievement.[16]

Quizzing and reviewing also have been shown to be elements in successful lesson implementation. When teachers give regular quizzes one or more times a week, scores on final exams go up. Frequent testing influences study behavior positively.[17]

The most effective teachers also use homework to enhance study habits of students. Studies support the view that frequently assigned homework, in small amounts to provide independent practice on what has been learned during the instructional lesson, has a positive effect on achievement.[18]

Cooperative Learning

This instructional strategy delegates some control of the pacing and methods of learning to student groups, usually composed of two to six persons. Students in the groups work together on assignments, sometimes competing with other groups. Individuals in the group assume responsibility for sharing knowledge and tutoring each other. It is an active-learning approach and has been shown to offer great opportunity for the development of higher-order thinking skills in all participants.

Classrooms that are organized for cooperative motivation instead of competitiveness produce a better classroom climate. Competitive organization permits aggressiveness, cheating, lowered motivation, and failure-avoiding behaviors; whereas cooperative environments are linked to positive peer relationships, higher achievement, positive self-esteem, and interracial acceptance.[19]

Student Motivation

Motivation concerns the "why" of behavior. Bloom suggests that motivational factors can account for 25 percent of the variation in student achievement.[20] The high-gain teacher, in motivating students, has a classroom environment that evidences a warm acceptance of students along with consistent rules and high expectations for student behavior. A special environment or climate must be created in the classroom that ensures involvement and success. It should move at a brisk pace, monitor all students, stimulate attention, and ensure accountability by variety and unpredictability in questioning patterns.[21]

It is an important motivator to use students' ideas in discussions by acknowledging student responses, repeating the responses in different words, applying their ideas, comparing their responses, and summarizing their responses.[22] Promoting students' beliefs in their own competence by carefully matching students' abilities to learning assignments is also a powerful motivator. The ALT (academic learning time) studies[23] suggest that materials allowing high and middle SES students to achieve approximately an 80 percent success rate and low SES students a 90 percent success rate will maximize student motivation. Teachers need to plan for and treat all students as if they were winners.

A good way to identify factors that may be affecting achievement and motivation is by using the instrument Comprehensive Assessment of School Environments (CASE) developed by the National Association of Secondary School Principals. The instrument also provides information about parent satisfaction.[24]

Providing Students with Evaluative Feedback

This competency consists of several tasks, including providing written comments to students on their progress in addition to grades, returning tests as quickly as possible, holding individual conferences with students, and interpreting test results to students and parents.

The research evidence is extensive regarding the importance of the frequency and timeliness of effective feedback to students. Formative feedback, done while the lesson and learning are in progress, is best done orally rather than in writing and is most beneficial when correcting wrong answers, both to correct the student and to allow the teacher to modify the lesson to cope with the problem.[25]

Feedback in the form of praise should be used extensively but within certain parameters. Low-achieving students may require more explicit recognition for their classroom participation; however, indiscriminate praise may not motivate learning. What is desired is real recognition for real achievement.[26] Feedback on tests and assignments also provides information both to the students on how their work is being evaluated and to the teacher on how successful the instruction has been.[27]

A high volume of feedback from the teacher is of value for reinforcement, as well as its information content.[28] The research also shows that immediate feedback from the teacher is important, as is a high frequency of testing on content material in the classroom.[29]

Preparing Appropriate Evaluation Activities

The effective teacher begins instruction by making the methods of evaluation clear to students; basing the evaluation on specific goals, objectives, and content of the course; and using both pretests and posttests in order to measure student gain. Student progress is measured through a series of both formative and summative evaluation techniques.

Specific statements of instructional objectives, in measurable terms announced to the students, become the first step in projecting toward the evaluation. These objectives need to be closely aligned with the stated curriculum and should be reflective of some diversity, as shown by some classification system such as the work of Bloom (cognitive domain), Krathwohl (affective domain), or Samson (psychomotor domain).[30] Surveys have shown that teachers generally select most of their objectives from the cognitive domain and most from the lowest level (knowledge) of that domain.[31] Greater diversity of objectives is usually desirable.

Formative evaluation, while instruction is unfolding, should be frequent and have as its purpose monitoring and guiding students to the correct learning as well as providing the teacher with data for monitoring instructional effectiveness.[32] Summative evaluation should be used to determine if the student has achieved the objectives. Mastery learning is a graduated approach to summative evaluation. Here, instructional objectives are divided into small units with specific objectives whose mastery is essential for the mastery of the major objectives. In mastery learning, frequent testing and evaluation are crucial. The research indicates that mastery learning evaluation techniques produce superior student achievement, learning retention, transfer of learning, and positive affective outcomes.[33]

Assigning Grades

High-gain teachers recognize the importance of assigning grades and take the responsibility seriously. They keep in mind what parents want to learn from student report cards, and they use grades to accurately reflect student progress rather than as a form of behavior modification. Teachers must test often and consistently to achieve good reliability of evaluative data.[34]

Marking systems using a maximum of five to nine discriminations are best under-stood by parents; therefore, a 5-point, letter-grade scale is probably a better communi-cator than is a 100-point scale.[35] Pass-fail grading system appear to lead to lower achievement.[36]

Two general approaches are used by teachers in assigning grades. The first is grad-ing students on their performance relative to their classmates. The second is using an absolute scale of some type based on a standard, such as a predetermined number of objectives to be achieved. The first type, that of relative scores compared to other stu-dents, is commonly called *grading on a curve*. Students' grades are either based on raw scores drawn from posttest data only or gain scores based on the difference between pre- and posttest data. Gain scores logically provide a better measure of student achievement under the instruction of that particular teacher. However, this type of rel-ative comparison of student scores to one another is appropriate only if there are very large groups of students included, and the students are not tracked. This is rarely the case in the normal classroom setting.

The second type of grading, that of using an *absolute scale*, is common to crite-rion-referenced tests and to mastery learning. Proficiency tests with minimum accept-able levels of performance also use this logic. Grades are based on a predetermined level of achievement necessary to obtain a particular grade, such as 8 out of 10 correct for a B, or 9 out of 10 correct for an A.

Grading must reflect student performance and growth. When it reflects something other than academic achievement, it cannot be considered valid. High-gain teachers do not abuse the assigning of grades but consider it a significant part of their communica-tion with both parents and students.

Time on Task

The high-gain teacher uses the time allocated for the class in a highly efficient manner. Classwork begins promptly at the beginning of each period, management time and transition time are kept to a minimum, and the teacher reinforces students who are spending time on task. Studies report that low-achieving students are off task in excess of 50 percent of the time, whereas high-achieving students are off task less than 25 per-cent of the time.[37] Another study, of junior high students, showed that low achievers had engaged time of approximately 40 percent, whereas high achievers reached in excess of 85 percent engagement time.[38]

The research evidence demonstrates that time is a valuable resource in school, and when used efficiently, increases student performance.[39] The studies identify three lev-els of time used: allocated time—that assigned to a particular course or subject; engaged time—the amount of allocated time in which students actually are engaged in learning activities; and academic learning time (ALT)—a refinement of engaged time reflecting quality of learning. Factors included in the definition of *quality* are the appropriateness of instructional materials relative to the achievement level of the stu-dent, the best student's success ratio of learning (suggested is an 80 percent success ratio for most learners), and the amount of concentration the learner is actually contrib-uting to the instructional process.[40]

The high-gain teacher is punctual and begins instruction for each class promptly, leaving management details until later in the hour, if possible. During seatwork time, the teacher monitors students closely, encouraging more time on task. It is suggested that at least 50 percent of each class period be devoted to active, direct instruction. This is significantly higher than what is found in most classes. For example, one study demonstrated that math teachers on the average used only 14 percent of their time for direct instruction, with 34 percent going for written work, 8 percent for review, and the balance being assigned to off-task activities.[41]

Individualized Instruction

Where does individualized instruction fit, in light of all the research findings supporting direct instruction in the form of demonstration-practice-feedback? How does the finding of the need for whole group instruction impact on individualized methods?[42] Although direct instruction has shown great results for the acquisition of specific skills, it cannot do it all; in fact, for higher-order learning and thinking skills, direct instruction may be counter productive.[43] An effective classroom must solicit student involvement in learning activities under appropriate conditions for mastery. This demands a proper climate and opportunity for the child to achieve success. These requisites demand that teachers provide appropriate opportunity for individual differences if maximum student productivity is to be maintained. Teachers can accommodate individual differences in a variety of ways:

1. By varying the level of teaching internal to the class through adjusting the level of questioning and varying the length of wait time
2. By providing varying amounts of allocated time to different students
3. By grouping within or between classes, as has been discussed earlier in this chapter
4. By consideration of different learning styles of children
5. By selection of classroom organizational methods, including learning centers, tutors, or study groups[44]

Instructional Tools for Individualization
We have emphasized individualized instruction and the need to provide a variety of instructional activities for students in order to make such a system functional. The logical question is how to organize or create materials for self-instruction.

Excellent commercial materials are now available for individualized systems, and more are becoming available each year. In areas such as reading and math, schools can purchase an entire system for a wide range of student achievement levels. Other materials can be organized and coordinated for instruction by teachers using those materials. Teachers, of course, should also continue to use their own materials.

The real problem, however, is organizing materials in a systematic way so that they are adequately available to students when they need them, adequately self-instructional so that teacher time can be appropriately balanced, and adequately organized to assure proper instructional sequencing, recording, and evaluation. Today's microcomputers can aid greatly in managing records for individualized instruction. A number of methods of instruction have gained acceptance as ways to achieve individualization of instruction and to enhance learning. Among these are mastery learning, independent study, cooperative learning, and computer-assisted instruction.

Mastery Learning.   Mastery learning, as described by Bloom,[45] has been a very successful form of individualized instruction.[46] Although this form of mastery instruction, as a means of obtaining individualization, has many benefits and has shown good success for certain types of learning, primarily skills development, a number of difficulties exist:[47]

1. Alternate instructional materials and tests are needed for those students required to recycle to achieve mastery.
2. Management problems of the increasing spread of achievements are caused by early masters and the extended recycling of others.

Independent Study.   Two frequently stated goals for secondary student development are "the development of independence" and "the development of purpose." Traditional approaches to organization of instruction tend to limit, restrict, or inhibit these desired goals, however. Instruction that is heavily teacher directed, although it may be best for basic skill development, tends to foster dependence rather than independence. If student interdependence and independence with purpose are desired, then instruction must be organized to achieve it.

A variety of types of learning experiences may be considered as independent study program activities. Students may participate in homework and in-depth projects, walkabout challenge projects, enrichment courses, regularly scheduled classes, informal discussion, and other activities that are consistent with the purposes of the independent study phase of instruction.

Specific independent study objectives for students include the following:

1. Assume an increased responsibility for making decisions relative to his or her education.
2. Develop an increased control over his or her impulse behavior.
3. Become a more purposeful, independent learner by achieving a higher degree of interdependence, venturesomeness, resourcefulness, goal directedness, and persistence.
4. Develop an increased capacity to solve problems and learn to use critical and creative thinking processes.
5. Acquire relevant subject matter content.
6. Develop an increased interest in learning.
7. Achieve emotional independence of parents and other adults.
8. Achieve more and more mature relationships with peers of both sexes.
9. Desire and achieve socially responsible behavior by becoming more self-disciplined.
10. Acquire a set of values in an ethical system and a guide to behavior.

The implementation of an effective independent study program will be a new activity for many schools. Each student participating in advanced forms of independent study should sign an appropriate contract that states purpose, completion date, conference dates, and so on.

Computer-Assisted Instruction.   This methodology has existed in theory for many years. However, new technological advances in both software and hardware make its daily use in the classroom practical and affordable. The graphical user interface (GUI), used now by much of the new computer software, along with mass storage capabilities of compact discs make this possible with the addition of full color pictures and sound to programs. Added to this is the capability of the software to offer instruction to students on the basis of their individual needs, monitor and adjust that instruction based on progress, and maintain progress records for each student. Although cost will always be a factor, it continues to drop dramatically while capability continues to rise.[48]

Summary

In conjunction with any instructional system must come a plan for organizing and grouping students. Grouping considerations include group size, composition, and flexibility. A diversified system of instruction requires a new role for most teachers. Extensive preparation is needed to develop a variety of learning goals, objectives, and activities, so that appropriate instructional plans can be developed for all students.

Research on teaching indicates the importance of each teacher having skills in lesson planning, lesson implementation, student motivation, evaluative feedback, evaluative methods, assigning grades, maintenance of high time on task, cooperative learning, and individualization of instruction. The principal must have an understanding of diversified instruction and exhibit an expectation of such instruction from the teachers.

Activities

1. Review Case Studies 2, 12, and 18. Apply the instructional concepts expressed in this chapter. How might you proceed in addressing the problems cited in these cases? Set forth a strategy to overcome the problem.

2. Reflect on the instructional strategies and behaviors in your own school. Can you identify areas where restructuring should take place? Why do you believe so? Apply the concepts of this chapter to your school. How would you proceed to restructure your school's instructional program? How might you use the concepts of Chapter 13, Human Resources Development, to assist in your planning?

Endnotes

1. R. W. Stong, H. F. Silver, and R. Hanson, "Integrating Teaching Strategies and Thinking Styles with Elements of Effective Instruction," *Educational Leadership* 42 (May 1985): 9–15.
2. Walter W. Cook and Theodore Clymer, "Acceleration and Retardation," in *Individualized*   *Instruction, 1962 Yearbook of the National Society for the Study of Education*, ed. Nelson B. Henry (Chicago: NSSE, 1962), pp. 179–208.
3. Gene V. Glass and Mary Lee Smith, "Meta-Analysis of Research in the Relationships of Class Size and Achievement," in *The Class Size*

and Instruction Project, Leonard S. Chaen, principal investigator (San Francisco: Far West Laboratory for Educational Research and Development, September 1978).

4. Helen Pate-Bain, C. M. Achilles, Jayne Boyd-Zaharias, and Bernard McKenna, "Class Size Does Make a Difference," *Phi Delta Kappan* (November 1992): 253–256.

5. A study by Rosenthal and Jacobson investigated the concept of the self-fulfilling prophecy and found that teacher attitudes and expectations about a child do have a direct bearing on the child's performance. Robert Rosenthal and Lenore Jacobson, *Pygmalion in the Classroom* (New York: Holt, Rinehart and Winston, 1968).

6. Dominick Esposito, "Homogeneous and Heterogeneous Ability Grouping," *AERA Journal* (Spring 1973): 163–179.

7. R. E. Slavin, "Grouping for Instruction in the Elementary School," *School and Classroom Organization* (Hillsdale, NJ: Lawrence Erlbaum, 1989).

8. Walter W. Cook, "Effective Ways of Doing It," in *Individualized Instruction, 1962 Yearbook of the National Society for the Study of Education*, ed. Nelson B. Henry (Chicago: NSSE, 1962), Chapter 3.

9. Margaret M. Dawson and Mary Ann Rafoth, "Why Student Retention Doesn't Work," *Streamlined Seminar, NAESP* 9, no. 3 (January 1991): 1–6.

10. *IGE Unit Operations and Roles* (Dayton, OH: Institute for Development of Educational Activities, 1970).

11. M. Hunter, "Knowing, Teaching and Supervising," in *Using What We Know About Teaching* (Alexandria, VA: Association for Supervision and Curriculum Development, 1984), pp. 169–192.

12. P. L. Peterson, R. W. Marx, and C. M. Clark, "Teacher Planning, Teacher Behavior, and Students' Achievement," *American Educational Research Journal* 15 (1978): 417–432.

13. J. I. Goodlad, M. F. Klein, and associates, *Looking Behind the Classroom Door* (Worthington, OH: Charles A. Jones, 1974).

14. T. R. Mann, "The Practice of Planning: The Impact of Elementary School on Teachers' Curriculum Planning," *Dissertation Abstracts International* 35 (1975): 3359A–3360A.

15. M. R. Rowe, "Relation of Wait-time and Rewards to the Development of Language, Logic, and Fate Control: Part II—Rewards," *Journal of Research in Science Teaching* 11 (1974): 291–308.

16. J. Stallings and D. Kaskowitz, *Follow-Through Classroom Observation Evaluation*, 1972–73 (Menlo Park, CA: Stanford Research Institute, Stanford University, 1974).

17. P. Peterson and H. Walberg (Eds.), *Research on Teaching* (Berkeley CA: McCutchan, 1979).

18. J. D. Austin, *Homework Research in Mathematics 1900–1974*. Paper presented at the 1974 Annual Georgia Mathematics Education Conference at Rock Eagle, GA, 1974.

19. D. W. Johnson and R. T. Johnson, "Instructional Goal Structure: Cooperative, Comparative and Individualistic," *Review of Educational Research* 44 (1974): 213–240.

20. B. S. Bloom, *Human Characteristics and School Learning* (New York: McGraw-Hill, 1982).

21. T. L. Good and J. E. Brophy, *Looking in Classrooms*, 1st ed. (New York: Harper and Row, 1973).

22. B. Rosenshine and N. Furst "Research on Teacher Performance Criteria," in *Research in Teacher Education: A Symposium*, ed. O. Smith (Englewood Cliffs, NJ: Prentice-Hall, 1971), pp. 46–56.

23. C. Fisher D. Berliner N. Filby, R. Marliave, L. Chance, and M. Dishaw, "Teaching Behaviors, Academic Learning Time, and Student Achievement: An Overview," in *Time to Learn*, ed. C. Denham and A. Lieberman (Washington, DC: The National Institute of Education, U.S. Department of Education, 1980).

24. CASE is available from the National Association of Secondary School Principals. Inquire: Publication Sales, NASSP, 1904 Association Drive, Reston, VA 22091-1598.

25. "Florida Beginning Teacher Program," Office of Teacher Education, Certification, and Inservice Staff Development, Tallahassee, FL. 1982. M. Mims and B. Gholson, "Effects of Type and Amount of Feedback upon Hypothesis Sampling Among 7–8 Year Old Children," *Journal of Experimental Child Psychology* 24 (1977): 358–371. B. B. Hudgins et al., *Educational Psychology* (Itasca, IL: Peacock, 1983).

26. J. Brophy, "Teacher Praise: A Functional Analysis," *Review of Educational Research* 51 (1981): 5–32. W. Brookover, C. Beady, P. Flood, J. Schweitzer, and J. Wisenbaker, *School Social Systems and Student Achievement: Schools Can Make a Difference* (New York: Praeger, 1979).

27. M. Hunter, *Appraising the Instructional Process.* Presentation for California Advisory Council on Educational Research, November 1973. Appears in *Resources in Education* (Washington, DC: ERIC Clearinghouse on Teacher Education, October 1977). B. Rosenshine, *Teaching Functions in Instructional Programs*, Airlie House Paper (Washington, DC: NIE Conference, 1982).

28. R. Bardwell, "Feedback: How Well Does It Function?" *Journal of Experimental Education* 50 (1981): 4–9.

29. Peterson and Walberg, *Research on Teaching.*

30. B. S. Bloom, M. B. Englehart, E. J. Furst, W. H. Hill, and D. R. Krathwohl, *Taxonomy of Educational Objectives: The Classification of Education Goals. Handbook I: Cognitive Domain* (New York: Longmans Green, 1956).

31. Good and Brophy, *Looking in Classrooms.*

32. Peterson, Marx, and Clark, "Teacher Planning."

33. J. H. Block, *Schools, Society and Mastery Learning* (New York: Holt, Rinehart and Winston, 1974).

34. Clinton I. Chase, *Measurement for Educational Research* (Reading, MA: Addison-Wesley, 1978).

35. G. A Miller, "The Magic Number Seven, Plus or Minus Two: Some Limits on Our Capacity for Processing Information," *Psychological Review* 63 (1956): 81–97.

36. L. A. Gatta, "An Analysis of the Pass-Fail Grading System as Compared to the Conventional System in High School Chemistry," *Journal of Research in Science Teaching* 10 (1973): 3–12. W. L Claiborn, "Expectancy Effects in the Classroom: A Failure to Replicate," *Journal of Educational Psychology* 60 (1969): 377–383.

W. M. Stallings and H. R. Smock, "The Pass-Fail Grading Option at a State University: A Five Semester Evaluation," *Journal of Educational Measurement* 8 (1971): 153–160.

37. D. Powell and M. Eash, "Secondary School Cases," in *Evaluating Educational Performance*, ed. II. Walberg (Berkeley, CA: McCutchan, 1974), pp. 277–293.

38. C. Evertson, *Differences in Instruction Activities in High and Low Achieving Junior High Classes.* Paper presented at the Annual Meeting of the American Educational Research Association, Boston, 1980.

39. J. Stallings, "Allocated Academic Learning Time Revisited, or Beyond Time on Task," *Educational Researcher* 9 (1980): 11–16. W. Frederick, "The Use of Classroom Time in High Schools Above or Below the Median Reading Score," *Urban Education* (1977): 459–464. T. L. Good, "How Teachers' Expectations Affect Low Achieving Students," *American Educator* (December 1982): 22–32.

40. Peterson and Walberg, *Research on Teaching.*

41. J. Stallings and A. Robertson, "Factors Influencing Women's Decisions to Enroll in Elective Mathematics Classes in High School." Final Report to the National Institute of Education (Menlo Park, CA: SRI International, 1979).

42. W. R. Borg, "Time and School Learning," in *Time to Learn*, ed. C. Denham and A. Lieberman (Washington, DC: The National Institute of Education, U.S. Department of Education, 1980).

43. P. L. Peterson, "Direct Instruction Reconsidered," in *Research on Teaching*, ed. P. L. Peterson and H. J. Walberg (Berkeley, CA: McCutchan, 1979).

44. Good and Brophy, *Looking in Classrooms.*

45. Bloom, *Human Characteristics.*

46. B. B. Hudgins et at., *Educational Psychology.* Itasca, IL: Peacock, 1983.

47. Peterson and Walberg, *Research on Teaching.*

48. D. Stansberry, "Taking the Plunge," *New Media: Multimedia Technologies for Desktop Computer Users* (February 1993): 30–36.

Selected Readings

Adams, Buck, and Gerald D. Bailey. "School Is for Teachers: Enhancing the School Environment." *NASSP Bulletin* 73 (January 1989): 44–48. (ERIC Document Service No. EJ 382 023).

Berliner, David, and Ursula Casanova. "When Are Two Heads Better Than One?" *Instructor* 98, no. 4 (1988): 22–23.

Bracey, Gerald. "The Social Impact of Ability Grouping." *Phi Delta Kappan* 68, no. 9 (May 1987): 701–702.

Braddock, Jomills H. "Tracking the Middle Grades: National Patterns of Grouping for Instruction." *Phi Delta Kappan* 71, no. 6 (February 1990): 445–449.

Carroll, Joseph M. "The Copernican Plan: Restructuring the American High School." *Phi Delta Kappan* 71, no. 5 (January 1990): 358–365. (ERIC Document Service No. EJ 400 584).

Colvin, Shirley Beard. *Creating Effective Learning Environments for Disadvantage Learners: Implications for the Design of Educational Programs.* Paper presented at the Annual Meeting of the American Educational Research Association, New Orleans, LA, April 8, 1988. (ERIC Document Service No. ED 293 969).

Cruickshank, Donald R. *Research That Informs Teachers and Teacher Educators* (Bloomington, IN: Phi Delta Kappa Educational Foundation, 1990).

Davidson, Neil, and Pat Wilson O'Leary. "How Cooperative Learning Can Enhance Mastery Learning." *Educational Leadership* 47 (February 1990): 30–33.

Eisner, Elliot W. "The Ecology of School Improvement." *Educational Leadership* 45, no. 5 (February 1988): 24–29. (ERIC Document Service No. EJ 368 822).

Fennimore, Todd F. *A Guide for Dropout Prevention: Creating an Integrated Learning Environment in Secondary Schools* (Columbus, OH: National Center for Research in Vocational Education, 1988). (ERIC Document Service No. ED 298 323).

Grace, Linda, and Robert L. Buser. "Student Motivation." *The Practitioner* 14, no. 1 (September 1987): 1–12. (ERIC Document Service No. ED 286 284).

Gursky, Daniel. "On the Wrong Track?" *Teacher* (May 1990): 42–51.

Hillerick, Robert L. "What Does 'Grade Level' Mean?" *Principal* 69, no. 3 (January 1990): 47–48.

Howe, Geery S. "Expecting Miracles: How to Develop a Learning Consciousness in High School Classrooms." *Social Studies* 79, no. 5 (September–October 1988): 228–231. (ERIC Document Service No. EJ 379 343).

Johnson, D. W., and R. T. Johnson. *Learning Together and Alone*, 2nd ed. (Englewood Cliffs, NJ: Prentice-Hall, 1987).

Knapp, Michael S., and Patrick M. Shields. "Reconceiving Academic Instruction for the Children of Poverty." *Phi Delta Kappan* 71, no. 10 (1990): 753–758.

Lake, Sara. *Instructional Practices for Middle Grade Students: Developing Self-Directed Learners.* Sacramento, CA: California League of Middle Schools, 1988. (ERIC Document Service No. ED 304 232).

McPartland, James M., and Shi-Chang Wu. *Instructional Practices in the Middle Grades: National Variations and Effects* (Baltimore, MD: Center for Research on Elementary and Middle Schools, 1988. (ERIC Document Service No. ED 301 321).

Miller, William. "Are Multi-Age Grouping Practices a Missing Link in the Educational Reform Debate?" *NASSP Bulletin* 79, no. 568 (February 1995): 27–32.

Porter A. and J. Brophy. "Synthesis of Research on Good Teaching." *Educational Leadership* 45, no. 8 (1988): 74–85.

Rodes, Marcia, and Jody Scott. "The Promise of Cooperative Learning as an Instructional Strategy to Help Students Think and Work Together." *Curriculum in Context* (Summer 1988): 14–15.

Schulz, Elizabeth. "Smaller Is Definitely Better." *Teacher* 1, no. 3 (December 1989): 332–333.

Sharan, S., and C. Schachar. *Language and Learning in the Cooperative Classroom* (New York: Springer, 1988).

Sharon, Shlomo, and Yael Sharon. "Group Investigation Expands Cooperative Learning." *Educational Leadership* 47, no. 4 (December 1989–January 1990): 17–21.

Sikorski, Melanie F., Richard P. Niemiec, and Herbert J. Walberg. "Best Teaching Practices: A Checklist for Observations." *NASSP Bulletin* 78 no. 561 (April 1994): 1–6.

Slavin, R. E. "Are Cooperative Learning and 'Untracking' Harmful to the Gifted?" *Educational Leadership* 48 (February 1991): 63–74.

Slavin, R. E. *Cooperative Learning: Theory, Research, and Practice* (Englewood Cliffs, NJ: Prentice-Hall, 1990).

Strong, R. W., H. F. Silver, and R. Hanson. "Integrating Teaching Strategies and Thinking Styles with Elements of Effective Instruction." *Educational Leadership* 42 (May 1985):9–15.

Thomas, John W., Robert G. Curley, and Amy Strage. *Course-Related Impediments to Effective Study Practices.* Paper presented at the Annual Meeting of the American Educational Research Association, Washington, DC, April 1987. (ERIC Document Service No. ED 293 810).

Van Deusen, Jean Donham, and Robert van Deusen. "Don't Buy Computers Unless…." *Principal* 69, no. 2 (November 1989): 10–12.

Weaver, Rosa Lee. "Separate Is Not Equal." *Principal* 69, no. 5 (May 1990): 40–42.

Chapter *11*

Restructuring the Deployment of Instructional Personnel

*Inherent in any good staffing design is optimal utiliza-
tion of staff. Staff planning must take into account the
present needs and functions of the members of the organization, as well as the school's long-range goals and
plans that might modify hiring practices in the future.*
— *J. LLOYD TRUMP*[1]

One of the greatest responsibilities assigned to a principal is organizing and assigning
staff in the school. Included in normal staffing responsibilities is the deployment of all
employees and volunteer workers to the instructional program and service functions of
the school. Central office administrators and supervisors often have a hand in these
assignments, but especially with the advent of site-based management, the responsibility, and particularly the final decision, rest with the principal and staff. Inherent in any
good staffing design is optimal utilization of staff. Staff planning must take into account
the present needs and functions of the members of the organization as well as the
school's long-range goals and plans that might modify hiring practices in the future.

Professional employees in school organizations often have great insight and usually excellent ideas of how a school could be improved. They also have the need for
both personal development and professional growth through interaction with other professionals in the school. School organization, however, often works against this opportunity for interaction because of self-contained classrooms that isolate teachers for up
to six hours each day. The development and vitality of the organizational climate of the
school is also dependent on the opportunity and ability of the school staff to interact
with each other. One way for school professionals to interact with each other is to participate in management decisions at the building level that affect the school's curriculum and instruction.

Participation by Staff

Site-based management, to function successfully, requires greatly increased participation in school decisions on the part of staff members. An excellent way to involve the faculty is through the formation of a faculty council to improve the school's curricular and instructional program. If the school has a multiunit learning community design, as described later in this chapter, this faculty council should be made up of the head of each learning community and the principal (see Figure 11–1); otherwise, department heads or grade level chairpersons would be appropriate. Topics appropriate for consideration by this advisory council to the principal include virtually any significant decision that will require staff cooperation and is in their field of expertise. A quality circle approach is appropriate for some of the advisory council activities.

Matrix Management

In a similar fashion to the advisory council, special coordinating committees should be organized to deal with curricular areas such as reading, math, social studies, or any area that requires cross-unit coordination. These committees may be permanent or temporary in nature, depending on the assignment.

If a multiunit staffing design is used, these committees can best be formed with one teacher from each team (Figure 11–2). The curriculum committee, thus formed, provides representation from each of the teams as well as communication back to each team. Each staff member also shares in the schoolwide efforts to provide community and thrust to the curricular and instructional program. The major line of responsibility (vertical) in the matrix still rests with each team. The curriculum committees (horizontal) function only to coordinate the overall school program. If the school maintains a

The staff within the dotted line makes up the Principal's Advisory Council.

FIGURE 11–1   Principal's Advisory Council

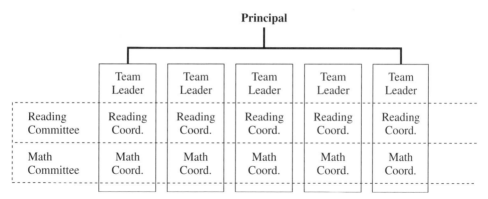

FIGURE 11–2   Multiunit Curricular Coordinating Committee's Matrix Management

more traditional staffing pattern, these schoolwide staffing designs can still be used. There will be some loss of representation, however. In any case, staffing must be viewed in the context of the total mission of the school.

Empowerment

Ultimately, what is wanted of teachers is quality instruction and for learning to take place between teachers and students. There are many functions within the school organization that must be properly balanced for this to be maximized. Too little attention on the part of administration regarding what goes on in each classroom can lead to lack of coordination of the curriculum, great variation in the quality of teaching, and great variation in the motivation of teachers. On the other hand, too much control or structure over teachers or centralization of authority over the classroom might produce some uniformity but take away teachers' autonomy, negatively affecting teacher motivation and thus reducing the quality of instruction among the better teachers.

What is desired is a fine balance that can adequately empower teachers to exercise appropriate professional judgment while still ensuring the coordination of the curriculum and supervision of instruction. The appropriate empowerment of teachers must lie in the amount of authority granted, methods of accountability used to ensure responsibility, and the organizational structures created to maintain the proper communication flow necessary to carry out these tasks.[2]

Team Staffing

Traditionally, staffing has been by simple unit-classroom analysis—that is, one teacher, one group of students, one room, sometimes one instructional format, and sometimes one subject. Staffing plans have been built and modified from year to year using this basic classroom unit. Such a procedure is very restrictive, particularly when used in conjunction with some of the curricular, instructional, and grouping ideas presented in previous chapters. Team staffing offers several desirable alternatives to single classroom units.

Team staffing has been used with varying degrees of success in schools for years. Persuasive arguments can be given both for team staff organizations as well as self-contained classrooms. Arguments favoring team teaching are:

1. A teaching team provides variation for the children because the students have contact with a set of teachers.
2. Teacher productivity generally increases under a team arrangement since teachers tend to support each other in the achievement of goals.
3. Flexibility of grouping becomes possible and building-level scheduling can be greatly simplified when teachers are working together in a team.
4. The advantages of both specialization and generalization can be obtained when teachers specialize in either or both the curricular and instructional dimension within the team and still have the opportunity to observe the whole child as that child works with the team over the major portion of the day.
5. Individualized instruction can more easily be attained with the team of teachers sharing the variety of instructional tasks necessary to successfully implement an individualized program.

On the other hand, some still argue that self-contained classes are better. Reasons favoring self-contained classrooms are as follows:

1. Teacher training and experience traditionally has been for the self-contained classroom. Many teachers favor it because they know it best.
2. Buildings are designed for self-contained classrooms, not for team arrangements, and they simply do not lend themselves to team teaching.
3. When placed on teams, teachers develop difficulties in interpersonal relationships because of different personalities, teaching styles, or philosophies.
4. Team teaching requires a great deal of additional time in planning on the part of the teacher that could be devoted to children or to preparation of lessons in the self-contained classroom.

However, when consideration is given to the overall management of instruction, the arguments favoring team staffing patterns are clearly superior.

Staffing Patterns for Elementary and Middle Schools

An elementary or middle school staff can be organized in a variety of different ways depending on its desired results. Organizational patterns that utilize teams of teachers with responsibility for a common group of students are favored by the authors. The integrated contributions of several teachers, the teacher growth enhanced by common planning and quality circles, and the collective team concern for the growth of their students generates a synergism that is difficult to match in the traditional self-contained classroom. Adaptation of the principles of site-based management and TQM strongly point in the direction of teaching teams.

FIGURE 11–3   Staffing Assignments for Self-Contained Classrooms

Grade	Students	Teachers	Class Size
K	75	3	25
1	80	3	26–27
2	95	3 or 4	31–32 or 23–24
3	85	3	28–29
4	100	3 or 4	33–34 or 25
5	90	3	30
6	75	3	25

Staff Teachers		21 or 23	
	Plus	1 Principal	
		1 Librarian	

	Staff Totals	23	overall ratio: 1–26.1
		25	overall ratio: 1–24.0

Different staffing patterns are possible for any situation, from the traditional self-contained classroom to a variety of team and differentiated staffing models. Given a basic student population of 600 for an elementary school, as shown in Figure 11–3, the following examples illustrate several basic staffing designs.

Traditional Self-Contained Classrooms

A traditional staffing pattern with total reliance on self-contained classrooms based on a student-teacher ratio for each classroom of approximately 30 to 1 is shown in Figure 11–4. As is often the case, tough dollar decisions determine when to exceed the 30-pupils-per-classroom figure and when to hire additional staff to reduce the ratio. For a totally self-contained program, the only additional support staff would be the principal and possibly a librarian.

FIGURE 11–4   Staffing for Grade-Level Teams

Grade	Students	Staff Team	
K	75	3	
1	80	3	
2	95	3 or 4	
3	85	3	Sp. Ed. 1
4	100	3 or 4	
5	90	3	
6	75	3	Sp. Ed. 1
Specialists	Art, Librarian, Music, P.E.	4	
Principal		1	

	Staff Totals	28	overall ratio: 1–21.4
		30	overall ratio: 1–20.0

Teachers Plus Specialists

Usually, a school prefers specialists in certain areas such as special education, art, music, and physical education. Figure 11–5 illustrates a specialist staffing pattern with two special education teachers each taking a class load of 10 to 15 students, thus reducing class size by approximately 1 or 2 students in each room. The art, music, and physical education specialists, on the other hand, either come into the classroom with the regular teacher once or twice a week or take the children from the regular teacher for several periods each week, giving the regular teacher a break. The total staff size is increased by the number of specialists added, increasing the total staff in this example to 28 or 30.

Team Teaching

Teaching teams can easily be implemented as an alternate pattern to those just outlined using the same number of students and staff positions (see Figure 11–5). Each team consists of three or four teachers in grade-level arrangements. The special education teachers attach themselves to either the primary or intermediate teams, dividing their time among the several groups. The art, music, and physical education specialist and the librarian also form a team for staff organization. Advantages as well as disadvantages of team organization have been discussed earlier.

Team Teaching with Paraprofessionals

Grade-level teaching teams can be enhanced if each team adds a paraprofessional. In many communities, aides can be hired for a minimum wage, or in some cases, volunteers can be used to support the team. The cooperative organization of a team approach permits sharing students. Teachers often prefer to employ paraprofessionals rather than additional teachers to reduce class size. If, as shown in Figure 11–5 grades 2 and 4

FIGURE 11–5   Grade-Level Teams with Paraprofessionals

		Teams	
Grade	**Level**	*Teachers*	*Paraprofessionals*
K	75	3	+ p.p.
1	80	3 Sp. Ed. 1	+ p.p.
2	95	3	+ p.p.
3	85	3	+ p.p.
4	100	3	+ p.p.
5	90	3 Sp. Ed. 1	+ p.p.
6	75	3	+ p.p.
Specialists: art, music, P.E., librarian		4	+ p.p.
Principal		1	

Staff Totals   28   8 paraprofessionals
overall staffing ratio: 1–16.7
Eight paraprofessionals can be hired for the salary of two teachers.

FIGURE 11–6   Staff Utilization in a Staff Organization

20 teachers (5 teams, 4 each)	5 instructional assistants
4 teacher specialists	3 clerical assistants
1 principal	8 paraprofessionals
2 special education	overall staffing ratio: 1–16.7.
1 librarian	
28	

could function with three-teacher teams instead of four, the salary dollars saved could pay the salary for eight aides (part time if necessary), one for each of the school's teams (see Figure 11–6).

Teaching staff to support these five groups would be deployed as shown in Figure 11–7. The organizational pattern illustrated in Figure 11–8 results in the same staff requirements but distributes responsibilities more evenly. This type of team organization, coupled with multiage grouping, allows for an extremely even distribution of students. Even when the enrollment numbers vary greatly or when staffing ratios are unfavorable, balance can be provided, ensuring uniform availability of instructional services.

Utilization of Staff Specialists

The addition of specialists for special education, reading, math, learning disabilities, physical education, art, and music has been a mixed blessing. Most schools have desperately needed the extra help but have not been able to make maximum use of the talents that specialists can provide.

FIGURE 11–7   A Multiunit Design for Staff and Students

FIGURE 11–8   Learning-Community Staff Assignments

Teacher A	Teacher B	Teacher C	Teacher D	P.E. Specialist
25 advisees	25 advisees	25 advisees	25 advisees	20 advisees
Team Leader Advisement Coordinator	Reading Coordinator	Math Coordinator	Learning Center Coordinator	
Reading (3)	Reading (3)	Reading (3)	Reading (3)	
Math (2)	Math (2)	Math (2)	Math (2)	
Writing	Science	Social studies	Science	
Crafts	Spelling	Library	Health	
Language	Learning center	Learning center		

Part of the problem of using specialists arises from single-classroom organization. The specialist in a "pullout" program is a fifth wheel and often is never fully integrated into the program. Many times, specialists have been set apart in little rooms by themselves to call children out of regular classrooms, disrupting the regular program for the child as well as using their own time very inefficiently.

A team organization leads to a variety of ways to use specialists. In some cases, specialists can best be utilized by dividing their time into fractional units and assigning them to teams for each unit. Following are three examples of how a team organization can utilize the services of specialists or the services provided by special programs.

School One: Resource Teachers

A school organized in a multiunit fashion similar to the school just discussed was allocated two additional reading and math positions out of federal funds. One was for remedial reading and the other for mathematics. The school decided to integrate these positions fully into the teams so that no specialist would work with more than one team. In order to do this, the specialist positions were divided into fractional units and student loads were adjusted accordingly. Instead of hiring new people for these positions, interested faculty from the existing staff were identified and given the special training necessary for the new assignments. The two positions were divided into four units of time and distributed among the existing staff. Each team was assigned a one-fourth-time reading specialist and a one-fourth-time math specialist. The released staffing money was used to hire two more regular teachers. Specialist services were integrated into each team to make the available instruction relate closely to the organized program. Federal guidelines were met by assigning designated students to these specialists for the appropriate times.

School Two: Special Education—Full Inclusion

In order to provide for full inclusion for children with disabilities within this school, organized according to a multiunit pattern, these children were assigned on an age basis to the appropriate learning community. The two special education teachers for the children with disabilities in this school worked together as a team with the instructional teams in the school. They attended team planning meetings when appropriate and scheduled their visits to coincide with the skill-grouped reading program of the team. During the reading schedule, they became part of the team and took the children with disabilities into expanded reading groups, thus bolstering the reading staff. The children of this school never identified and labeled these two specialists as special education teachers, even though they spent almost all of their time with certain children. A way to save time for the special education staff is to place all the children with disabilities into two or three learning communities, reducing the number of different teams with which specialists must work.

School Three: Art, Music, and Physical Education Specialists

In the third school, the art, music, and physical education specialists served two major functions: (1) They served as student advisors along with each of the other four teachers on the team to which they were assigned. They did this during the early minutes of the school day, the noon hour, and the last 30 minutes of the afternoon. (2) During an approximately 2½-hour block in the morning and again each afternoon, two physical education teachers, an art teacher, and a music teacher worked on a unit-rotating basis, taking half of the children from two of the units for instruction in their specialties. Thus, for 2½-hours once or twice a week, each team had a block of time with only half the children and could concentrate on small group instruction activities.

The full integration of a team's instructional program is the key to its success. All teachers must share in organizing the curriculum, preferably with an interdisciplinary approach with each teacher carrying a specific independent assignment. The teachers must share the children and together discuss their problems. Specialization in curriculum can be used to reduce the planning required of any particular teacher, but not to the extent that it causes departmentalization of the curriculum. Figure 11–8 illustrates how one learning-community staff divided the workload after much discussion and planning. All of the children were organized into 12 skill groups for reading and 8 for math. Thus, each of the 4 regular teachers had 3 reading skill groups and 2 math skill groups. In addition, each teacher took several other curricular responsibilities for learning-center development as well as for direct instruction. Each team member also assumed some administrative responsibility. The physical education teacher worked directly with the team only part of each day. Each week a schedule was planned.

Staffing Patterns for Secondary Schools

General ideas have been presented for staffing design, curricular arrangements, and instructional strategies in elementary and middle schools. How does a high school operating in a traditional mode begin to make the transition to incorporate some of these ideas into its operating model? Let us take an existing high school with a staff of 67 professionals and 1,260 students and show a number of staffing alternatives for their organization. Each staffing pattern takes into account some of the ideas previously discussed in the chapters on curriculum, instruction, and grouping of students. The first model shows how the school might be organized at the present time in a traditional departmental staff organization.

Departmental Staff Organization

The standard departmental staffing arrangement shown in Figure 11–9 divides the high school into nine departments: language arts; social studies; science; math; foreign language; physical education, health, and driver education; fine arts; vocational; and special services. The school is a comprehensive high school with a large vocational program. The special services department is somewhat unique. It includes guidance counselors, one vocational rehabilitation counselor, one special education coordinator, two instructional medial specialists, and one person to coordinate both the independent study program and action learning program. The three principals share the school's administration, with one of the assistants responsible for buildings, grounds, lunch-

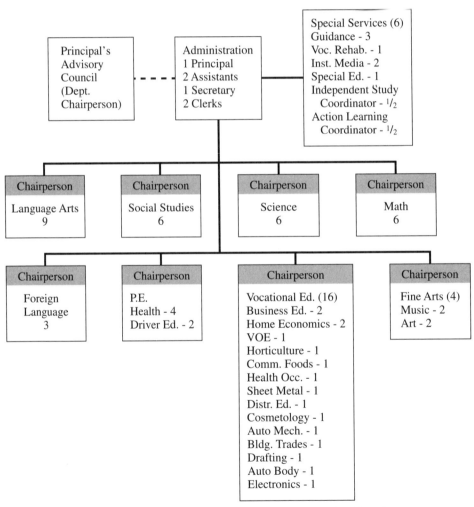

FIGURE 11–9   Standard Departmental High School Staffing Pattern

room, transportation, office management, and some discipline. The other assistant's major responsibility is the curricular and instructional program and the coordination of volunteer services.

Department Head—Role and Responsibilities

A department head coordinates the activities of each department and serves as a member of the principal's advisory council. Figure 11–10 lists possible department head responsibilities.

FIGURE 11–10   Department Head Responsibilities

Job Description—High School Department Head

1. Coordinate the inventory of textbooks and audiovisual materials.
2. Coordinate the development of an instructional budget for the department.
3. Provide the department staff with information regarding advances and subject matter and promising instructional materials.
4. Coordinate the placement and supervision of student teachers and interns in the department.
5. Recommend special resources and personnel needed to aid the department's instructional staff.
6. Direct department staff in selecting or preparing a written behavioral objective for each curricular area.
7. Seek the advice of a counselor or principal in handling special department problems.
8. Assume responsibility for completing routine reports.
9. Participate in the development of the school's in-service teacher education program.
10. Observe on request the instructional presentations of department staff and provide feedback aimed at improving instruction.
11. Provide individual assistance to new and beginning teachers.
12. Hold the staff accountable for student achievement.
13. Evaluate paraprofessionals assigned to the department.
14. Attend all meetings of the principal's advisory council.
15. Schedule and chair department meetings.
16. Channel information from a variety of sources to the department teachers.
17. Conduct demonstration lessons for department staff members using new materials and procedures.
18. Coordinate the assessment of students and the department based on individual objectives.
19. Plan with appropriate personnel to research activities for the department.
20. Schedule department meetings for goal setting, problem solving, and evaluation.
21. Coordinate the assessment of students' characteristics prior to any grouping.
22. Cooperate with other department chairpersons in coordinating schoolwide facilities and resources.
23. Confer informally with department staff members to discuss ways of improving instruction.
24. Facilitate communication between central office personnel, consultants, and department staff.
25. Participate in the selection of professional staff assigned to the department.
26. Participate in the evaluation of professional staff assigned to the department.

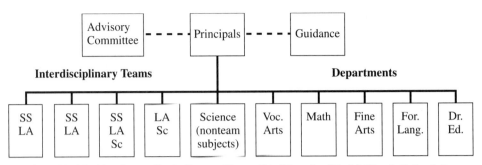

FIGURE 11–11   Interdisciplinary Team Staffing for Fluid Block Schedules

Team Staffing Pattern

The basic staff of a typical high school, as shown in Figure 11–11, can be used to create numerous variations in team arrangements. Appropriate team designs, however, must provide a good relationship with a planned curricular design, good instructional strategies, and desirable patterns for student grouping. A summary of previous information concerning good design for curriculum, instruction, grouping, and staffing includes the following: team members from two or more disciplines; a differentiated staff including a team leader, team members, aides, clerks, and so on; and a group of 75 to 150 students in a block of time appropriate in length to the number of subjects included in the team. The interdisciplinary team allows for the best options in integrating the curriculum, ease of schooling, flexibility in grouping, and student control.

Interdisciplinary teams can be organized in a variety of ways. One high school organized a series of two-subject, four-teacher teams, consisting of two language arts teachers and two social studies teachers in a three-hour block of time coordinated with a free-floating elective. Each team met with one group of approximately 120 students in the morning and worked with another block of students during the afternoon. The other half of the day for the students involved participating in a regular elective program.[3]

Using the staff outlined in Figure 11–11, the fluid block design organized language arts, social studies, and science teams. One of the main advantages of the fluid block design is its allowance for three basic styles of instruction, ranging from traditional, to team approaches, to individually paced labs.[4] Most of the teachers in the basic required subjects of language arts, social studies, and possibly science must be willing to work in a team arrangement for a fluid block schedule to work. Teachers in other subject areas may join teams, may wish to set up their instruction as an individually paced laboratory (typing, art, foreign languages, and certain math courses lend themselves nicely to individualized labs), or may operate in a traditional-type schedule as in the past.

Team Planning

Site-based management requires the active participation of staff members in decisions that affect their own areas of responsibility. This includes an expanded role in curriculum and instructional decisions, evaluation decisions, and the day-by-day organizing and scheduling functions. These tasks are most effectively carried out on a team or unit basis.

One of the most crucial factors in a successful team operation is adequate planning time and efficient utilization of that time. If at all possible, team planning should occur during the regular school day. Planning should be regularly scheduled; at least two hours per week are needed in a minimum of one-hour blocks. Building an agenda for team meetings needs to be an opportunity for all team members to share in the planning for the team. One good way is to place an agenda planning sheet in a central location for the team to list items they wish to discuss at the next scheduled meeting. Some principals have the teams prepare their agenda so that copies can be quickly reproduced and distributed to team members, as well as to other key people such as the librarian, special education teacher, or the principal, all of whom may want to attend the team meeting. Each meeting should have a designated chairperson, and a secretary for the team should keep minutes of the meeting. Figure 11–12 is an example of a form to be used for agenda building.

A variety of different planning tasks of both a long- and short-term nature need to be carried out by each team. Effective use of planning time can usually be enhanced by focusing on a particular purpose during a meeting. The following five types of planning meetings are suggested with recommendations regarding frequency:

1. *Goal-Setting Meeting.* One goal-setting meeting should be held each semester to look at the philosophy of the school, the curriculum guidelines existing for its direction, and the identification of goals for the particular group of students for whom the team is responsible. These goals would be long range in nature and would be things to work toward over a semester or year.

2. *Design Meeting.* A design meeting is a planning meeting to select instructional topics and develop instructional units. Principles and objectives as well as general ideas for the unit are considered. After the topic has been selected, one team member is usually assigned the responsibility of drafting the unit. When the draft is ready, the team modifies and builds on the design. Specific objectives are listed, overall responsibility for each member of the team is outlined, and the calendar of events is developed with specific target dates. Methods of student evaluation are also planned. One of these meetings is necessary for each new unit, and a minimum of one each quarter or marking period is essential.

3. *Grouping or Scheduling Meeting.* This planning meeting outlines activities for the next week or two, defining specific instructional plans, organizing students into appropriate groups, and constructing the weekly calendar and daily schedule. One of these meetings is needed at least once every two weeks, if not weekly.

4. *Situational Meeting.* This meeting focuses on individual children. Various children within the group are discussed by the various members of the team to coordinate information and develop plans for learning activities for that child. The teacher advisor for the particular child has the responsibility of carrying out team decisions. These meetings should probably be held each week, with each teacher advisor determining which children need to be discussed by the team.

Team: ___4 - A___   Date of Meeting: ___10/14___

I. Students

Name	Person Presenting	Concern	Est. Time Needed
Bill Fox	Mary	attendance	5 m.
Nancy York	Jane	uncomp. assign.	5 m.

II. Program Development

Area	Person Presenting	Est. Time Needed
Unit—election	Gary	20 m.
Unit—health	Mary	to next time

III. Staff Development

Area	Person Presenting	Est. Time Needed
accelerated learning	Pat	20 m.

IV. Administrative

Area	Person Presenting	Est. Time Needed
lunchtime	Pat	5 m.
Friday's assembly	Pat	5 m.

FIGURE 11–12   Form for Agenda Building

FIGURE 11–13   Schedule of Team Meetings

Two team meetings should be held each week.	
Prior to school year	• Goal setting for the semester • Design of units for the first grading period • Initial grouping and scheduling of students assigned to team
Week 1	• Situational meeting • Grouping and scheduling meeting
Week 2	• Situational meeting • Grouping and scheduling meeting
Week 3	• Situational meeting • Grouping and scheduling meeting
Week 4	• Situational meeting • Design meeting—plans for the next period meeting
Week 5	• Situational meeting • Design meeting
Week 6	• Situational meeting • Evaluation meeting (of teaching)
Week 7 (repeats Week 1)	• Situational meeting • Grouping and scheduling meeting

5. *Evaluation Meeting.* The major focus of this meeting should be the evaluation of the instructional program and units. Questions to be asked are: Did we achieve our goals? What were our strengths? What were our shortcomings? How well did we function together as a team? One of these meetings should be held each quarter immediately after the close of the quarter or immediately after the completion of a major unit.

Team Meeting Schedule

Assuming a planning schedule that allows for two planning meetings per team each week in a six-week instructional period, a schedule of team meetings for the period might look like Figure 11–13. Extra grouping and scheduling meetings as well as situational meetings are scheduled early in the year to work through changes in enrollment and to place children better as more data are available.

Summary

The principal has many plans to make regarding how best to utilize the staff. Many of these plans rest on earlier decisions regarding curriculum, instructional formats, and grouping of students. Teaching teams offer maximum flexibility for instructional programming but attention must be given to good team planning for it to work. The appropriate use of specialists must also be considered in elementary and middle school staffing. Secondary school staffing patterns can be designed with flexibility in mind as well. A variety of staffing patterns can be created using forms of teaching teams or departmental units. Schoolwide committee structures for overall management should take several forms, including a school management council and curriculum or grade-level committees.

Activities

1. How would you proceed to restructure your school's staff deployment? Why would it be important to integrate your plans on instructional and curriculum restructuring with your plans on staff restructuring?

2. Review Case Studies 1, 7, and 20. Analyze the problems presented and apply the staff deploy-ment concepts developed in this chapter. What approach would you use in addressing the problems? Set forth a strategy to overcome the difficulties faced by the school as well as ways to deal with individuals teachers.

Endnotes

1. J. Lloyd Trump, *Images of the Future*, Experimental Study of the Utilization of Staff in the Secondary Schools and the National Association of Secondary School Principals, 1959.
2. Gene I. Maeroff, "A Blueprint for Empowering Teachers," *Phi Delta Kappan* 69, no. 7 (March 1988): 472–477.

3. Gerald C. Ubben, "A Fluid Block Schedule," *NASSP Bulletin* 60 (February 1976): 104–111.
4. See the section in Chapter 12 on fluid block schedules.

Selected Readings

Armbruster, Barbara, and Clifford E. Howe. "Educators Team Up to Help Students Learn." *NASSP Bulletin* 69 (March 1985): 82–86. (ERIC Document Service No. EJ 359 248).

Brandt, Ron. "On Changing Secondary Schools: A Conversation with Ted Sizer." *Educational Leadership* 45, no. 5 (February 1988): 30–36. (ERIC Document Service No. EJ 368 823).

Chandler, Theodore A. "Here's What to Try When You Can't Shrink Class Size Enough to Matter." *American School Board Journal* 175, no. 10 (October 1988): 33–51. (ERIC Document Service No. EJ 378 765).

Charters, W. W., Jr., et al. *Change in the Governance of the School's Instructional Program: A Study of Multiunit Elementary Schools* (Eugene, OR: Publication Sales, Center for Educational Policy and Management, University of Oregon, 1986).

Costello, Ronald W. "Improving Student Achievement by Overcoming Teacher Isolation." *Clearing House* 61, no. 2 (October 1987): 91–93. (ERIC Document Service No. EJ 359 244).

Dobbs, Stephen Mark. "Generalists and Specialists: Teaming for Success." *Design for Arts in Education* 87, no. 6 (July–August 1986): 39–42. (ERIC Document Service No. EJ 341 1919).

Donaldson, G. A. "Working Smarter Together." *Educational Leadership* 2 (1993): 12–16

Donavel, David F. *Restructuring the High School: The Renaissance Program.* Written version of presentation at the Annual Meeting of the National Association of Secondary School Principals, San Diego, CA, February 1990. (ERIC Document Service No. ED 321 390).

Erb, Thomas O., and Nancy M. Doda. *Team Organization: Promise—Practices and Possibilities* (Washington, DC: National Education Association, 1989). (ERIC Document Service No. ED 313 339).

Feirsen, Robert. "A Model for Assessing Team Meetings." *Clearing House* 60, no. 8 (April 1987): 360–362. (ERIC Document Service No. EJ 352 209).

Flummerfelt, Dan R. "Getting the Best of Both Worlds." *NASSP Bulletin* 70 (December 1986): 118–119. (ERIC Document Service No. EJ 345 310).

Fullan, M. G., and A. Hargreaves. *What's Worth Fighting For: Working Together for Your School* (Andover, MA: Regional Laboratory of the Northeast and Islands, 1991).

Fullan, M. G., and C. Rolheiser-Bennett. "Linking Classrooms and School Improvement. *Educational Leadership* 8 (1990): 13–19.

Hallinan, Maureen T., and Aage B. Sorensen. "Class Size, Ability Group Size, and Students' Achievement." *American Journal of Education* 94, no. 1 (November 1985): 71–89. (ERIC Document Service No. EJ 329 033).

Harris, Kathleen C. "Meeting the Needs of Special High School Students in Regular Education Classrooms." *Teacher Education and Special Education* 10, no. 4 (Fall 1987):143–152. (ERIC Document Service No. EJ 367 423).

Hollifield, John H. "A Special Report on Middle Schools." *Principal* 67, no. 4 (March 1988): 26–31. (ERIC Document Service No. EJ 368 858).

Idol, L., A. Nevis, and P. Paolucci-Whitcomb. *Collaborative Consultation* (Austin, TX: Pro-Ed, 1994).

Ivarie, Judith J. "Leadership Strategy: Building Teams." *NASSP Practicioner* 2 (1994).

Jamgochian, Richard, et al. "Reform, Teacher Improvement and the Use of Paraprofessionals to Alter Traditional School Structures and Teacher Roles." *Teacher Education Quarterly*

15, no. 4 (Fall 1988): 55–63. (ERIC Document Service No. EJ 391 488).

Johnston, John M. *Relations between Reduced Class Size and Reduced Teacher/Pupil Ratio and Developmentally Appropriate Practice in Kindergarten through Third Grades.* Paper presented at the Annual Meeting of the American Educational Research Association Boston, April 1990. (ERIC Document Service No. ED 317 278).

Kenney, Jane L., and Jane M. Roberts. *Teachers as Instructional Leaders.* Paper presented at the Annual Meeting of the American Educational Research Association, New Orleans, LA., April 1987. (ERIC Document Service No. ED 242 699).

Kessler, R. "Shared Decision Making Works!" *Educational Leadership* 1 (1992): 36–38.

Maeroff, G. I. "Building Teams to Rebuild Schools." *Phi Delta Kappan* 7 (1993). 512–519.

McPartland, James M. "Balancing High Quality Subject Matter Instruction with Positive Teacher-Student Relations in the Middle Grades: Effects of Departmentalization, Tracking and Blocking Scheduling on Learning Environments." Report 15. (Baltimore: The Johns Hopkins University, 1987). (ERIC Document Service No. ED 291 704).

Raebeck, Barry Scott, et al. "Can We Improve High Schools and Save Money? Yes!" *Clearing House* 61, no. 8 (April 1988): 341–346. (ERIC Document Service No. EJ 370 177).

Salem, Philip J., and Robert D. Gratz. "Matrix Design: An Alternative Model for Organizing the School or Department." *Association for Communication Bulletin* 50 (October 1984): 69–77. (ERIC Document Service No. EJ 308 124).

School Staffing Ratios. Educational Research Service Report (Arlington, VA: Publication Sales, 1988). (ERIC Document Service No. ED 297 425).

Shanker, Albert. "Restructuring Leadership." *College Review Board* 149 (Fall 1988): 14–17. (ERIC Document Service No. EJ 382 419).

Restructuring Time
Scheduling

The school schedule is considered by many to be the command performance of the principal. It is here that the ability to conceptualize, to organize, and to carry out detailed planning is most visible. If well done, the schedule will strongly support the instructional and curricular program of the school. On the other hand, if poorly designed, the schedule will be a roadblock to a balanced curriculum and instructional flexibility.
— L. W. HUGHES AND G. C. UBBEN[1]

Scheduling can be defined as the plan to bring together people, materials, and curriculum at a designated time and place for the purpose of instruction. Its basic purpose is to coordinate the requirements laid down by previously reached decisions regarding curriculum, instruction, grouping, and staffing.

The effective schools research has much to say about the use of time in school. The concept of academic learning time (ALT), discussed in earlier chapters, describes scheduled time as its umbrella component from which the "actual" instructional time and "engaged" time are achieved. It is therefore imperative that scheduled time be maximized so that ultimately high amounts of instructional and engaged time can also be obtained.

Several important concepts in scheduling should be reviewed before actually beginning the construction of a schedule. The concepts are equally important for elementary, middle, and high school schedules. These include the flexibility, simplicity, and complexity of the schedule, the decision level at which schedule changes are made, efficiency in the use of time, and the timeliness of the schedule. Other concepts to consider are previously made decisions concerning the design of curriculum and instruction; staffing and grouping patterns; and space availability and utilization.

Schedule Flexibility

The schedule should have either the potential of being legitimately changed with great frequency or have the internal elasticity of meeting a variety of curricular and instructional requests within its regular structure. For example, the teacher who would like to take a group of children on a half-day field trip should be able to do so without disrupting the entire school schedule. Likewise, the group that needs an extra hour to complete a project should be able to have that hour with an easy adjustment in the schedule.

Simplicity and Complexity

The schedule needs simplicity to prevent interdependence of the components of the schedule, so that the modification of one component does not require the modification of several others. Complexity, on the other hand, is also needed in order to meet the demands of individual differences of students. To meet individual differences, intricate schedule designs need to be constructed. This seemingly creates a paradox, but it is another application of the loosely coupled/tightly coupled concept of organization. An analogy that seems fitting to describe this relationship is found in modularized electronics. The complexity of their circuitry is an amazing example of modern-day technology, but, on the other hand, this complex design is constructed in such a way that if a failure occurs, or a modification is desired, a circuit board can be removed and replaced very quickly, once the trouble spot has been identified or the desired modification determined, without having to disassemble the entire set. So it is with schedules: A good schedule must permit the complex construction required for individual differences while maintaining simplicity to allow easy changes.

Efficiency and the Use of Time

The effective schools research points out the need for time efficiency. There are many ways greater efficiency can be obtained within the schedule. Several specific suggestions are as follows:

1. Minimize the use of nonspecific study time during school hours. This means the reduction—or better yet, the elimination—of study halls. Too often study halls are where we put children we cannot get scheduled into any other class and are a reflection of the principal's inability or unwillingness to design a tight, efficient schedule. In a good schedule, study halls should be virtually eliminated. At the elementary and middle school levels, activity periods must be carefully designed so they do not also become holding areas for children otherwise not engaged in a supervised learning activity.

2. Minimize the time used for movement from classroom to classroom. Techniques will vary greatly depending on building arrangements and instructional design. Specifics might include the use of two- or three-hour blocks of time with no student passage required, as well as clustering of classrooms and lockers to minimize travel on the part of students for the development of efficient hall traffic patterns and the reduction of the time between classes.

3. Available instructional time can be enhanced with the development and implementation of an efficient policy regarding the use of the intercom system. Within the school, restrict its use to the first and last few minutes of the day so as not to interrupt potential instructional time.

Other efficiencies in the use of teacher and children's time in school may include good use of lunch time (including a duty-free lunch for teachers and the opportunity for students to relax as well) and the effective use of before and after school waiting time on the part of students (waiting for buses, parents, etc.). Every minute of the school day counts. The rule must always be "What is the best possible use of this time?"

Timeliness of Scheduling Decisions
Timeliness is part of flexibility. Schedules must be designed so that daily and weekly instructional and curricular needs can be met as they occur.

Decision Level—Loosely Coupled

The decision level is the point in the hierarchy of an organization where decisions are made. A basic rule for good decision making in most organizations is that decisions should be made at the lowest level within the organization where adequate information exists for that decision (loosely coupled). The application of this rule to scheduling suggests that students and teachers should have maximum involvement in scheduling decisions. At the building level, scheduling should be kept as simple as possible so that the various components can be changed without disrupting the entire school. Also, each building should have maximum control over its schedule and not be frequently subject to the schedules of other schools in the school system. Some traditional areas of conflict such as coordinating bus schedules between schools or scheduling shared teacher specialists require higher-level decisions. The major conflicts will arise over making up specialists' schedules within the school, in coordinating special areas such as gymnasiums and music rooms, and in scheduling schoolwide programs such as lunch.

Scheduling Techniques

There are several approaches to achieving a good schedule. Although the detail of scheduling certainly differs among elementary, middle, and high school, the basic tenets are largely the same. One of the best methods is to provide relatively large blocks of time unencumbered by outside influences to teams of teachers and groups of students so they can develop a detailed daily schedule to meet curricular and instructional needs. Such a schedule must accommodate a few special activities such as lunch, physical education, or music (see Figure 12–1).

Inside these large blocks of time, the team of teachers and students plans all of the learning activities. These internal schedules can differ from one day to the next as plans are made by the team reflecting the instructional format, curriculum, groupings, and staffing assignments. Because each of these instructional blocks stands alone, changes within them do not affect the remainder of the school.

Morning	Team Scheduled Block	Team Scheduled Block	T.S.B.	P.E. MUSIC
			P.E. MUSIC	T.S.B.
	LUNCH	LUNCH	LUNCH	LUNCH
Afternoon	Team Scheduled Block	P.E. MUSIC	Team Scheduled Block	Team Scheduled Block
	P.E. MUSIC	Team Scheduled Block		

FIGURE 12–1   Team Scheduled Block

Figure 12–2 illustrates a simple form of scheduling within the block of time that can be used by a team of four teachers following a basic rotating design. In this schedule, each teacher has access to each group of children operating in a semi-departmentalized school-within-a-school design. The schedule does not meet all of the curricular, instructional, and grouping recommendations made in the previous chapter, but nor does not preclude further development to meet the additional criteria. The team has a high degree of autonomy to plan its schedule as it sees fit and can modify it as frequently as every day if it chooses.

Numerous schedule variations can be created from this basic design. It offers an excellent opportunity to create groups that vary in size as well as the ability to group students according to a variety of special interests and skills patterns.

At the elementary level, a team might create small groups for reading instruction by assigning children to instructional groups on a skills basis. Each team member can

Period	Group A	B	C	D
1	R	SS	SC	M
2	SS	SC	M	R
3	SC	M	R	SS
L	L	L	L	L
4	M	R	SS	SC
5	P.E.	P.E.	Music Alternate Days	

R   Reading
SS   Social Studies
SC   Science   Four teachers responsible
L   Lunch   for groups A–D
M   Math

FIGURE 12–2   Block Rotating Schedule

FIGURE 12–3   Staffing for Small Skill Groups

	Teacher A	Teacher B	Teacher C	Teacher D
9–9:30	Reading Group 1, 10 children	Reading Group 2, 10 children	Reading Group 3, 10 children	90 children, direct instruction

teach a small group of children by sharing activities and placing children in several different learning activities. To have reading groups of a reasonable size, three teachers of a four-member team can each take 10 children in their reading group while the fourth teacher supervises the other children in some form of teacher-planned instructional activity (see Figure 12–3). Sharing responsibility among teachers within a schedule permits the group variation necessary for good instruction. During additional periods, the schedule can shift so that each teacher has some large-group direct instruction time as well as small reading groups for skills instruction (see Figure 12–4). An instructional aide could assist in supervising computer centers and independent study activities while the regular staff does direct instruction.

Grouping patterns can remain flexible. As the team's planning develops, the internal schedule can change as frequently as needed. Variations for math, the addition of science, social studies, or language arts activities (including independent study work), and the scheduling of field trips can be built in and designed by teachers without requesting approval from an outside authority. Only when special teachers, facilities, and services for these activities are needed must the team consult and coordinate with the principal at the building level.

Ultimately, how the block schedule is to be used depends on the decisions regarding curriculum, instruction, grouping, and staffing. If teachers are organized in teams, the curriculum has a broad base of subjects, the instructional program is individualized,

FIGURE 12–4   Reading Skills Group Schedule

	Teacher A	Teacher B	Teacher C	Teacher D	Aide
9:30–10	R–4 10 children	R–5 10 children	Direct instruction, (30) children	R–6 10 children	Learning centers, (60) children
10–10:30	R–7 10 children	Direct instruction, (30) children	R–8 10 children	R–9 10 children	Learning centers, (60) children
10:30–11	Direct instruction, (30) children	R–10 10 children	R–11 10 children	R–12 10 children	Learning centers (60) children

Twelve groups, including those in Figure 12–3—30 minutes directed instruction of each group plus a small reading skills group.

and the grouping is designed to allow change frequently, the block schedule may be designed to accommodate those needs with ease.

Team Planning Time

One of the most important features of any schedule involving a team of teachers working together is the provision of adequate team planning time. Every teacher should have a minimum of five hours each week for planning and materials preparation. Much of this time should be in common with other members of the team. Teachers usually prefer to arrange this time in several large blocks rather than divide it into many small segments. Teachers and aides can occasionally alternate supervision, giving each team member some time for planning or materials preparation. However, extended planning sessions where all team members are present is also a must.

Parallel Scheduling

Team planning can usually be best arranged on a schoolwide basis using parallel scheduling. Parallel scheduling provides large blocks of planning time through the use of specialists. The elementary school or middle school staff must include three or four full-time specialists such as music teachers, art teachers, and physical education teachers. These teachers are scheduled in a design paralleling that of the regular teaching staff so the specialists can replace each of the regular teaching team members, freeing them from all of the children in their learning community for a given block of time. The specialists then work in rotation with these children from one team for a period of one or more hours (see Figure 12–5). Specialists can handle additional children if there are more specialists available or if an aide can work with a specialist and increase group size. The specialists work with each group of children so that, within a one- or two-day period, they replace each team (the team organization used here is the one shown in Figure 12–3).

	Monday	Tuesday	Wednesday	Thursday	Friday
Morning	Specialists Replace Team A	Replace Team C	Replace Team E or Specialist Planning	Replace Team B	Replace Team D
Afternoon	Replace Team B	Replace Team D	Replace Team A	Replace Team C	Replace Team E or Specialist Planning*

FIGURE 12–5   Team Weekly Parallel Schedule

*In a five-team school, the specialists use an extended duty-free lunch for planning.

These examples of schedules are meant only to be suggestions to generate ideas. Many variations can be developed from these different models. Each school and each team must develop a schedule of its own, tailored to meet its individual needs. It is important to let the schedule follow the demands of the curricular and instructional program and the student grouping and staffing patterns and not allow the schedule to dictate the rest of the program.

Elementary School Schedules

Self-Contained Elementary Classrooms Compared with Pullout Programs

There is renewed interest in one-teacher, self-contained classrooms. This has occurred as a reaction to what is considered by some to be overspecialization, "pullout" programs such as Chapter 1, and the seemingly myriad other special programs that fragment the activity of the regular classroom. It is true that the special programs and the utilization of instructional specialists have often been uncoordinated and apparently directionless. As noted in an earlier chapter, eliminating many of the specialists and converting these staff lines to regular classroom instructional lines in order to reduce class sizes to 15 or fewer has seemed to make a difference in student achievement in some schools.[2]

The drawback to doing this is that many teachers do not have the requisite skills to meet the very special needs of many of the children in their classes. Moreover, a good case can be made on other grounds for the use of specialists as a part of the school team. It is neither useful nor productive to operate at either extreme. Clearly, though, there is a need for great coordination when large numbers of specialists are to be found on a school staff.

An alternative to pullout programs is the integrated team approach. Here, the specialist is integrated into the regular instructional team and the team itself develops the schedule and instructional activities for the students assigned to it. Block scheduling, discussed in the previous section of this chapter, is consistent with this kind of staffing arrangement.

Block Scheduling—Elementary

A sample internal block schedule is shown in Figure 12–6. It is designed to meet the time needs based on the following major tenets:

1. A flexible curriculum (different subjects with varying amounts of allocated time for different students)
2. Individualized instruction (use of mastery learning, cooperative learning, small skills groups, independent study, and student interest groups)
3. Varied and flexible grouping (skills groups of 10 to 15 for reading and math instruction, interest groups with student advisor direction for learning centers, large heterogeneous grouping for directed instruction, such as in science, social studies, and health)

Time	Teacher A	Teacher B	Teacher C	Teacher D	Teacher E	Aide
8:00	PREPARATION FOR DAY AND FINAL TEAM COORDINATION					
8:30	Children Arrive Group Advisement					Lunch Count Attendance
9:00	Reading 1 (10)	Reading 2 (10)	Social Studies Large Group (50)	Science (50)	Learning Centers (30)	Science
9:30	Writing (25)	Learning Centers (95)	Reading 3 (10)	Reading 4 (10)	Reading 5 (10)	Learning Centers
10:00	Reading 6 (10)	Reading 7 (10)	Social Studies Large Group (50)	Science (50)	Learning Centers (30)	Science
10:30	Writing (25)	Learning Centers (95)	Reading 8 (10)	Reading 9 (10)	Reading 10 (10)	Learning Centers
11:00	Reading 11 (10)	Reading 12 (10)	Social Studies Large Group (50)	Social Studies Large Group (50)	Learning Centers (30)	Science
11:30	Writing (25)	Learning Centers (95)	Reading 13 (10)	Reading 14 (10)	Reading 15 (10)	Learning Centers
12:00	Lunch (duty free)	Lunch (duty free)	Lunch (duty free)	Lunch Supervision	Lunch Supervision	Supervision
12:30	Playground	Playground	Playground	Lunch (duty free)	Lunch (duty free)	Lunch (duty free)
1:00	Math 1 (15)	Math 2 (15)	Math 3 (15)	Health (25)	Learning Centers (80)	Learning Centers
1:30	Learning Centers (55)	Spelling (15)	Learning Centers (50)	Math 4 (15)	Math 5 (15)	Learning Centers
2:00	Math 6 (15)	Math 7 (15)	Math 8 (15)	Health (25)	Learning Centers (80)	Learning Centers
2:30	Learning Centers (55)	Spelling (15)	Learning Centers (50)	Math 9 (15)	Math 10 (15)	Learning Centers
3:00	Group Advisement Cleanup					
3:30	Dismissal	Dismissal	Dismissal	Dismissal	Room Supervision	Bus Load
4:00	PREPARATION TIME					

FIGURE 12–6 Sample Daily Schedule

Note: The number in parentheses indicates the number of children for that activity. Learning centers are supervised by the teacher indicated but all teachers contribute to their preparation.

223

4. Organization of the staff, a team of five teachers, and an aide in a learning community

This schedule is meant only as an illustration of a particular day. The reading and math schedules are fairly constant for the teachers each day, but the groups change for the children as they master their skills and are regrouped in both math and reading.

The schedules for the other subjects change frequently as instruction is planned and group sizes are determined. Students use learning and computer centers for drill and practice activities previously assigned during directed instruction when they have not scheduled group activity.

A child's daily schedule is based on skills groups. Since children are grouped in the morning on a skills basis for reading, reading then becomes the grouping basis to direct children to all other subjects during the morning. In the afternoon, the math groups become the organizational block in which children are directed to the other group activities. This provides homogeneous grouping according to skills in reading and math and heterogeneous grouping in all other subject areas. The only exception to this rule occurs when children are grouped on an interest basis for other activities while not in reading or math.

The schedule can be simplified or made more complex as the situation changes. Teachers' skill in scheduling these internal team activities evolves with practice and time. Adequate team planning is an essential component to making the schedule function properly.

Middle School Schedules

Middle schools have unique problems in scheduling students and staff. Greater subject area specialization on the part of teachers is required than is generally the case in the elementary school. However, it is preferred that each student have a limited number of teacher contacts. This means that each teacher still must be capable of teaching several subjects.

The range of differences in the achievement levels of middle school children is also greater. This means that to meet the individual skills needs of the children, greater efforts must be made to individualize instruction either through skills grouping, cooperative learning, or some other technique. Care must also be taken not to overuse homogeneous grouping because of its detrimental effects on student attitudes and achievement when overused.

The block schedule shown in Figure 12–1 is probably the best design for a schoolwide schedule in the middle school, along with the following ideas to be used for the internal team schedule.

Achievement grouping is recommended for use in reading and math instruction because of the relatively large span of abilities in the middle school. The fact that curriculum tends to be organized according to skill levels in these two subjects makes them the best candidates for this technique. Most other areas of the curriculum should use heterogeneous grouping.

Homogeneous grouping is more successful in improving learning when the curriculum is modified for the homogeneous grouping (i.e., when reading and math skills learning continues). When homogeneous grouping is used, the criteria for grouping must specifically match the curricular area (e.g., total reading scores for reading groups and math scores for math groups). Grouping on the basis of an IQ score, for example, is much too general and should not be used.

It is almost impossible from a scheduling standpoint to group more than two subjects if each teacher teaches a separate subject. The schedule shown in Figure 12–7 will allow homogeneous grouping in reading with good flexibility in assigning and moving students because all four teachers will be teaching reading at the same time. In this schedule, the math teacher homogeneously groups children during periods 2 through 5 into four or eight levels for mathematics. However, this schedule fails to meet the specification of heterogeneity for social studies, science, and language arts because the math grouping spills over into these subjects, allowing the good math students to stay together in science, period 3; social studies, period 4; and language arts, period 5.

Additional refinements to the schedule can help solve the problem of homogeneous grouping carrying over in an undesirable manner, however. In order to create heterogeneity, a matrix must be designed that will undo the grouping created by a subject such as math that runs parallel to social studies, science, and language arts. The matrix must reassign the math groups to bring about the desired heterogeneity. This can be done by assigning each of the math classes a series of scheduling numbers and placing children in groups of four or five (called *modules*). These subgroups for the math grouping can then be dispersed through the other classes in an orderly manner.

The first column (math) of Figure 12–8 assigns each succeeding group of five math students a number. The top five math students are assigned number 1. The lowest five

Teacher Period	A	B	C	D
1	Reading Groups A–E	Reading Groups B–F	Reading Groups C–G	Reading Groups D–H
2	Math 1	Science	Social Studies	Language Arts
3	Math 2	Science	Social Studies	Language Arts
4	Math 3	Science	Social Studies	Language Arts
5	Math 4	Science	Social Studies	Language Arts

FIGURE 12–7   Middle School Team Schedule with Tracking

math students are given number 24. This number assigned to them in math class is then used to disperse them, thus creating heterogeneous grouping in the other three subjects.

A schedule for a four-teacher middle school team might carry the following specifications. Many variations of these assignments are possible, however:

Home Base: Heterogeneous groups   2 subjects each teacher
Reading: Skill groups—8 groups
Math: Skill groups—each math module contains 5 students—120 total
Other Subject: Heterogeneous groups

Teacher Period	Home Base Heterogeneous		Home Base Heterogeneous		Home Base Heterogeneous		Home Base Heterogeneous	
1	(Heterogeneous groups are created by rank ordering on reading scores with each home base receiving every fourth card.)							
2	Reading Skill Groups A,E		Reading Skill Groups B,F		Reading Skill Groups C,G		Reading Skill Groups D,H	
3	Math Homogeneous Groups 1 2 3	4 5 6	Language Arts 7 10 13	16 19 22	Science 8 11 14	17 20 23	Social Studies 9 12 15	18 21 24
4	Math 7 8 9	10 11 12	Language Arts 15 18 21	24 3 6	Science 13 16 19	22 1 4	Social Studies 14 17 20	23 2 5
5	Math 13 14 15	16 17 18	Language Arts 20 23 2	5 8 11	Science 21 24 3	6 9 12	Social Studies 19 22 1	4 7 10
6	Math 19 20 21	22 23 24	Language Arts 1 4 9	12 15 17	Science 2 5 7	10 14 18	Social Studies 3 6 8	11 13 16

7,8 Lunch-activity period—Art—Music—PE—Health—Guidance—etc.

**FIGURE 12–8   Middle School Team Schedule: Four-Teacher Team—
Heterogeneous Grouping**

*These numbers are based on the math groupings of 5 students each and are used to recreate the heterogeneity for Language Arts, Science, and Social Studies.

All teachers teach reading—reading is divided into eight skill levels.
One teacher teaches math—math is divided into four or more skill levels.
One teacher teaches social studies. ⎫ These classes are to be grouped heteroge-
One teacher teaches science.   ⎬ neously and not reflect either the math or
One teacher teaches language arts. ⎭ reading grouping.

Secondary School Schedules

Secondary school schedules, while becoming somewhat more complex, can often be viewed as extensions of elementary or middle school schedules. The secondary school schedules can be classified under the following types: group schedules, mosaic schedules, and block schedules.

Group Schedules

A group schedule of single subjects is most often used to place in groups those students who are registered for the same subjects and where the elective offerings are very few. Students are scheduled by groups and stay together through the day. Only two steps are required for this scheduling procedure: Determine the number of students taking the same subjects and identify how many sections are needed; and arrange the classes into a schedule according to their groups, rotating through the subjects in a similar fashion to Figure 12–2. Only physical education and music or some other elective would also rotate.

The group schedule is used most often for traditional junior high school schedules. Its major advantages are its ease in scheduling and simplicity of design. Disadvantages are that students do not mix outside of their basic assigned groups and all classes are single-teacher responsibilities with very limited time flexibility. The block schedule, also discussed in this chapter, is a variation of the group schedule.

Mosaic Schedules

The most popular form of secondary school scheduling, mosaic scheduling is designed to allow the scheduling of a large number of student electives. It is based on the concept that students register for courses first and then a schedule is built that fits *all* their requests. The term *mosaic* comes from the method of schedule construction. Each course to be offered is written on a small card or tile and moved about on a scheduling board so that it can be assigned a teacher, a time, and a room that is free of conflicts from other parts of the schedule. When the board becomes full of these small squares, it resembles a mosaic. The steps in building a mosaic type schedule are as follows:

1. Determine the educational offerings of the school. Each year, a needs assessment is conducted to determine what the curricular offerings for the following school year should be. New courses may be proposed by new district or state requirements or by the requests from students and staff. The initial list should consist of courses that are desired and for which there is some probability that they can be taught. With computer scheduling, all possible courses can initially be put on request.

2. Provide an appropriate means for students and parents to review the curricular offering and to select courses for students to take with appropriate guidance from teachers and counselors. A booklet listing all courses with a brief description can be prepared. The booklet can also list requirements for graduation and suggested courses of study. Tentative planning worksheets for each year of a student's school career may also appear in the booklet so that complete programs can be worked out. Figure 12–9 shows a sample planning sheet for individual high school curricular planning. Student requests should be gathered on a standard registration sheet that allows for easy tallying. A form such as the one in Figure 12–10 can be used for either manual or computer scheduling.

3. Tabulate student choices by subject to determine the number of students in each subject as a basis for the needed number of sections in each subject. The tabulating can be done either by hand, placing the tallies on a sheet similar to the ones the students have used for registration, or by preparing input data for the computer indicating the student's request. The computer can provide an accurate total listing of all subjects and the number of requests for each.

4. Determine the number of sections needed for each subject. This can be determined by selecting a maximum class size for each subject and dividing the total students by that number. In the case of small enrollments, a determination must be made of adequate staff numbers to offer all requested courses. In some cases, small enrollments may require dropping some electives and asking those students to select another option. The feedback from the computer can aid the principal in rapidly determining the enrollment feasibility of offering a particular course. The computer specialist can assist the principal in reviewing course offerings. The number of small enrollment electives that can be offered is ultimately determined by the total student-staff ratio.

5. Determine the teaching staff needed and compare with the teaching staff believed to be available, considering areas of certification, budget, and so on. Teaching staff available can be determined roughly by multiplying the number of classes taught by each full-time teacher plus the number of sections taught by part-time personnel. This can then be compared to the number of sections indicated as being needed in the course tallies calculated in step 4.

Sections needed based on student requests	350
Teacher sections available based on total staff........................	<u>335</u>
Sections that must be cut from student request tabulations or provided for by the employment of three additional teachers............	15

A more detailed analysis must now be carried out to properly match teacher assignment requests and certification areas to student course tabulations. This is done

FIGURE 12–9   Senior High School Course Guide

Instructions: Use this form to plan your three years in high school. Circle the courses that you tentatively plan to take each of your three years in high school. Record next years courses on the registration form and return this sheet to your homeroom teacher.

Sophomore	Junior	Senior
English 10 (Required)	English 11 (Required)	English 12 (Required)
American History (Required)	World History (Required)	Creative Writing
World Geography	World Geography	Social Studies (Required)
Physical Education (Required)	Elementary Algebra	World Geography
Elementary Algebra	Integrated Mathematics	Humanities
Integrated Mathematics	Plane Geometry	Elementary Algebra
Plane Geometry	Higher Algebra	Integrated Mathematics
Biology	Biology	Plane Geometry
French I, II, III	Chemistry	Higher Algebra
German, I, II, III	French I, II, III, IV	Trigonometry/Advanced Algebra
Latin I, II	German I, II, III	Advanced Mathematics
Russian I	Latin I, II, III	Biology
Spanish I, II, III	Russian I, II	Chemistry
	Spanish I, II, III, IV	Physics
		French II, III, IV
		German II, III, IV
		Latin II, III, IV
		Russian II, III
		Spanish II, III, IV
Art I	Applied Physical Science	General Mathematics
Commercial Art I	Art I	Applied Physical Science
Typing I	Art II	Art I
Beginning Business	Commercial Art I, II	Art II
Electricity I	Typing I	Commercial Art I, II
General Metals	Office Skills	Typing I
Power I	Secretarial Skills	Office Skills
Wood I	Shorthand I	Secretarial Skills
General Graphic Arts	Bookkeeping & Accounting	Sales and Merchandising II
Home Economics I, II, III, IV	Architectural Drawing	Office Education
Journalism	Electricity I, II	Shorthand II
Speech	General Metals	Bookkeeping and Accounting
Gym & Choir (Alt. Days)	General Graphic Arts	Law/Sales
Gym & Band (Alt. Days)	Machine Drawing I	Architectural Drawing
Gym & Study (Alt. Days)	Machine Shop I	Electricity II, III
Orchestra	Power I, II	Machine Drawing I, II
	Wood I, II	Machine Shop I, II
	Home Economics I, II, III, IV	Power II
	Journalism	Wood II, III
	Speech	Home Economics I, II, III, IV
	Band	Journalism
	Choir	Speech
	Orchestra	Drama
	Boys' Physical Education	Band
	Girls' Physical Education	Choir
	Sales and Merchandising I	Orchestra
		Boys' Physical Education
		Girls' Physical Education

Graduation Requirements

1. English 10, 11, 12
2. American History
3. World History
4. Social Studies
5. One mathematics course
6. One science course
7. Passing grade in 10th grade phys. ed.
8. Total of 14 credits plus 10th grade phys. ed.

FIGURE 12–10   Registration Code Sheet and Teachers Tally Sheet

Student Course Requests

Student's Name:

Directions: Encircle the code number, *in red,* of all subjects for your next year's schedule as approved on your Proposed Program of Studies sheet. Recheck for accuracy. The homeroom teacher may reserve the responsibility of checking those subjects where ability grouping is involved.

Miscellaneous
___060 Unassigned
___065 Driver Education
___067 Library Training

Work Periods
___071 First
___072 Second
___073 Third
___074 Fourth
___075 Fifth
___076 Sixth
___077 Seventh

Special Education
___081 & 082 Spec. Educ.
___083 Individual Acceler.
      Prog.

Coop. Voc. Training
___091 Job not yet assigned
___092 Dist. Ed. (assigned)
___093 Ind. Coop. (assigned)
___094 Ind. Coop., Part G.

Mathematics
___321 Alg. 2R
___330 Analysis A
___331 Analysis R
___351 Analy. Geom. (1/2)
___352 Probability (1/2)
___354 Comp. Prog. (1/2)
___355 Comp. Prog. (1)
___356 Comp. App. (1/2)
___358 Trig. (1/2)
___360 Calculus
___361 Calculus AP

Science
___400 Spec. Ed. Biol.
___430 BSCS Biol. A (1/2)
___431 BSCS Biol. B (1/2)
___435 Botany (1/2)
___440 Biol. 2A (1/2)
___441 Biol. 2B (1/2)
___445 Radiation Biology (1/2)
___430 BSCS Biol. A (1/2)
___450 Chemistry A (1/2)
___451 Chemistry B (1/2)
___454 Chemistry 11 A
___455 Chemistry 11 B
___461 Physics A
___462 Physics B

Business Education
___604 Typing IV (1/2)
___605 Office Practice
___606 Pers. Use
      Typing (1/2)
___608 Voc. Off. Ed.
      —Jr.
___610 Shorthand I
___611 Shorthand II
___612 Voc. Off. Ed.
      —Lab.
___613 Voc. Off. Oc.
      —Coop
___620 Acct. 1
___621 Adv. Acct.
___631 Bus. Law (1/2)
___632 Off. Mach.
      (1/2)
___641 Bus. Arith.
___642 Cons. Ed. (1/2)
___643 Bus Comm.
___099 Cl. Off. Aide

Homemaking
___681 Homemaking
      1A (1/2)
___682 Homemaking
      1B (1/2)
___683 Homemaking
      2A (1/2)
___684 Homemaking
      2B (1/2)
___685 Homemaking
      3A (1/2)
___686 Homemaking
      3B (1/2)
___687 Chef's Course
      (1/2)

by comparing specific subject section needs with available staff. Some flexibility is usually available in determining staff assignments where additional positions are to be filled or staff turnover exists. Figure 12–11 is an illustration of the matching teacher specialties and student requests.

Assignments may need to be moved around in order for all to be matched with qualified staff. In some instances, modifications may be made based on appropriate assignments for staff yet to be hired or yet to be employed by putting together logical assignments for new faculty (i.e., math-science, social studies-physical education-coaching, etc.). Ultimately, job descriptions for new staff can be formulated from these data.

6. Determine the number and length of class periods and the time for extracurricular activities. The number of periods in the school day should now be determined. Six or seven periods is usually typical for mosaic-type schedules. Additional school periods over and above the number of classes taken by the average student usually become study halls or early dismissal opportunities. In most cases, experience has shown that unless students are on work assignments of some type, these additional hours are not used productively. Therefore, it is suggested that the number of periods in the school day match fairly closely the number of courses for which each student registers. It is somewhat more difficult to build a no-study-hall or limited-study-hall schedule requiring students to take courses each hour, but the productivity for a student is usually improved; thus, such tightly organized schedules are worthwhile. A five- or six-period day is recommended, which includes a large block of time plus several hour-long elective classes.

Extracurricular activities are most often scheduled after the regular school day. This works well when the students either walk to school or provide their own transportation. When a large number of students ride school buses, an after-school activity period greatly restricts the number of students that can participate. A number of schools have had good success in establishing midday activity periods during the early afternoon. All students are then expected to select and participate in an activity, club, or intramural program, or they may use the period as a study period if no other opportunities are available.

FIGURE 12–11   Teacher Assignment Worksheet

Staff Roster	Desired Assignment	Areas of Certification	Proposed Assignment
Bailes, Cris	English 10–11	L.A.	L.A. 3–10, 2–11
Bray, Gail	S.S. 10	S.S., L.A.	5–10th
Brewer, Max	Sc. 11–12	Sc., Math	2–Chem.
			1–Phys.
			1–Biol.
Crockett Reba	Typing, Bkk.	Business Ed.	4–Typing
			1–Bkk.
Dietz, Pat	SS. 10–11	S.S., P.E.	S.S. 5–11
Edison, Freda	Algebra	Math, Spanish	Alg.–4
			Germ.–1

7. Make a conflict chart to determine the subjects that must not be scheduled at the same time if pupils are to have the program they have selected. Subjects, for which only one section is offered, that are placed in the schedule at the same time prevent students from taking more than one such course. Therefore, in order for single-section subjects not to conflict, they must be scheduled at different hours of the day. Two-way conflicts can also frequently occur. This happens when two single-section offerings are matched with a request for a double-section course offered the same hours as the singles. Three-way conflicts are also possible, but the probability is relatively low (see Figure 12–12).

The underlying philosophy of a good mosaic schedule is to design a schedule that is capable of honoring all student requests and to then build a schedule that eliminates all possible conflicts. The smaller the number of unsolvable conflicts within the schedule, the more perfect the schedule is considered to be.

A well-designed mosaic schedule should be able to reduce unsolvable conflicts to around 2 percent of the total student population. An *unsolvable conflict* is defined as a set of student course requests that cannot be honored because of conflicts within the schedule and that requires the student to select one or more alternate courses in order to complete a program.

A conflict chart sets up a matrix of the least single-, double-, and triple-section offerings and shows how many students have signed up for the various possible combinations. The conflict matrix in Figure 12–14 shows that three students want to take both courses 107 and 111.

While a conflict matrix is a vital part of the mosaic scheduling procedure, it is also an extremely time-consuming task if done by hand—particularly in a large school. It is accomplished by taking each student course request and comparing it to the other courses also requested by that student. The comparison is indicated by placing a tally mark on the matrix at the bisecting point. Up to 15 comparisons could be required for six course requests from one student if they were all single subjects. Computer-assisted scheduling will produce a complete conflict matrix for all subjects generated from the same data that were used to determine student tallies. The computer scheduling consultant will often circle those conflicts that he or she feels to be particularly significant.

FIGURE 12–12   Conflict Mastery

Course No.	107	111	121	142	451	455	621	697	704
107		3	2	78	17	17	2	9	0
111			1	0	2	0	12	22	0
121				1	2	7	9	4	0
142					8	0	0	1	
451						3	2	0	
455							54	14	
621								0	12
697									2
704									

8. Assign classes to the master schedule in terms of the conflict matrix. Even where computer-assisted scheduling is being used, this is a necessary manual task. A small card, approximately one-inch square, should be prepared for each section of each subject to be offered in the schedule. It is often desirable to color code the card by predominant grade levels, also reserving an additional color for classes that draw heavily from all or several grades. The mosaic cards should contain the course title and the section designation such as 1–1, 1–2, or 2–3, indicting which section the card represents in the number of sections of that type. The mosaic cards are now to be placed on a scheduling grid, listing all proposed teacher positions and the periods of the day.

The following order is usually helpful in constructing the schedule with a minimum of conflicts. Use the conflict chart for all decisions.

a. Assign 12 grade sections, proceeding downward in grade order. This is desirable because often the greatest number of singletons are twelfth-grade courses. Also, it is often thought desirable to design the twelfth-grade schedule first to ensure no conflicts since it is the seniors' final year in high school.

b. Assign subjects having only one section, scattering them throughout the school day. The scattering will reduce conflicts. Next, check each single-section course against other single sections offered during that hour to ensure no conflicts. If some exist, move sections until all are free of conflict.

c. Be careful not to assign two or more classes to one teacher during the same period.

d. Classes having double or triple periods should be assigned next. Included are the core classes, vocational classes, team-taught block classes, and so on. Because of the larger block of time for these subjects, fewer options exist for scheduling; therefore, it is necessary to place them in the schedule early.

e. Subjects having only two or three sections should be scheduled next, checking each placement against the conflict matrix. By now, some moving of earlier placed sections will probably be necessary. Be sure to follow each through an analysis on the conflict matrix with other sections offered that hour.

f. Finally, multiple-section subjects should be filled in, taking care to properly balance teacher load. Care should be taken to assure reasonable balance each hour for teacher preparation time, as well as to ensure adequate availability of staff for teaching purposes. Each time a previously placed mosaic is moved, care must be taken to check out all other ramifications of that move on the conflict matrix. Consideration must also be given to available special facilities each hour, such as music rooms, science rooms, typing rooms, and so on.

9. A room assignment sheet is prepared to prevent the assignment of two or more classes to the same room the same hour. A chart can be used simply by replacing the top row of teachers' names with classroom numbers and entering each room assignment on the appropriate mosaic of the master schedule.

10. Students may now be assigned to the classes of the proposed master schedule. As each student is assigned to a class, the information needs to be recorded on the student's individual assignment sheet, as well as on the separate class tally worksheet in order to balance class size. Each student must be scheduled individually for each of his or her course requests. Previously undetected conflicts will now come to light if the information from the conflict matrix was not completely adhered to or if certain conflicts were overlooked.

Computer Scheduling

Computer-assisted scheduling procedures can save hours of clerical time by electronically loading students into a manually planned master schedule. Excellent scheduling software is also available for microcomputers that will actually construct a master schedule.[3] However, a particular advantage of using only computer loading is the opportunity for the scheduler to maintain greater control over the schedule design. Trial runs can be processed with computer printouts indicating any problem with student requests that cannot be scheduled. These student conflicts can now be reviewed by the schedule designer and result in additional scheduling modifications to avoid previously overlooked conflicts. All schedule modifications at this time are to the master schedule only. Until the master schedule is perfect, no individual student schedules should be changed. Unsolvable conflicts are reviewed later.

A good master schedule should result in required schedule changes on an individual basis for no more than about 2 percent of the students. The scheduling specialist, if used, frequently will offer additional suggestions as to how the schedule can be improved. Any number of simulated runs of the schedule can be made with additional schedule modifications each time. This method will finally confirm its soundness with minimum conflict levels before all other forms are printed.

In addition to the tally lists and conflict matrix previously mentioned, computer packages can include study hall control; common course scheduling (the same students in more than one class); simulated runs; alternate course schedules in case of conflicts; balanced class enrollments as to size; and class lists of students for each teacher for each hour of the day, as well as generation of the master schedule itself. Costs of these software programs range from several hundred to over one thousand dollars, but it is generally believed that when a school reaches an enrollment of three to four hundred, the clerical and administrative time saved by the use of a software program more than offsets the cost.

Student and teacher schedules can be electronically transferred directly into the student record database each year, saving the clerical time necessary for data entry (see Chapter 15). The individual student schedules can be printed in multiple copies on paper as well as on cardstock, providing one copy to the student, one for the office, and additional copies for school files such as attendance, counseling, and the like. Individual schedules can also be printed with home addresses for summer mailing if this is desired (see Figure 12–13).

Block Schedules (Middle and High School)

The traditional six- or seven-hour day schedule of the typical middle or high school creates a very hectic, fast-moving, disruptive day for most teachers and students. Frequent class changes constantly disrupt available academic learning time (ALT). An excellent alternative to the traditional six-or seven-period day is the use of block sched-

13939	WILBURN	ANGLIA	R	10	F	96-97	MARYVILLE	
STUDENT NAME				GRADE	SEX	NUMBER	HIGH SCHOOL	
PERIOD	SUBJECT NUMBER	SUBJECT		ROOM NUMBER	SEM.#	TEACHER	028	
1	121	ENG 2 COL PR		014	3	014	HOME ROOM	TELEPHONE
2	606	GEN BUS 1/2		013	1	117		
2	605	PERS TYP 1/2		017	2	117		
3	925	PHYS ED 1/2		025	1	106		
3	929	DR ED SFM 2		105	2	105		
4	821	HOME ECON 2		001	3	001		
5	211	ALGEBRA 1		020	3	020		
6	311	BIOLOGY		023	3	023		

13940	WILBURN	DAVID	M	10	M	96-97	MARYVILLE	
STUDENT NAME				GRADE	SEX	NUMBER	HIGH SCHOOL	
PERIOD	SUBJECT NUMBER	SUBJECT		ROOM NUMBER	SEM.#	TEACHER	028	
1	211	ALGEBRA 1		020	3	020	HOME ROOM	TELEPHONE
2	925	PHYS ED 1/2		025	1	104		
2	929	DR ED SEM 2		005	2	205		
3	121	ENG 2 COL PR		014	3	014		
4	311	BIOLOGY		023	3	023		
5	491	LATIN 2		015	3	115		
6	021	BAND		026	3	026		

FIGURE 12–13   Computer-Printed Student Schedule

uling. Block schedules generally increase the length of a class by doubling it and reduce the number of classes a student and teacher participates in on a given day usually by one-half. To achieve this one-half reduction, classes generally meet every other day or are one semester in length.

Block schedules offer a number of distinct advantages over traditional schedules. They reduce the number of class changes that students must make during any one school day. They reduce the number of students for whom a teacher must prepare each day and/or term. They also reduce the number of assignments, tests, and projects that the student must address at the same time, and decrease the fragmentation inherent in single-period schedules. Block schedules also provide teachers with blocks of time that

FIGURE 12–14   Alternate Day Six-Course Block Schedule for Five-Day Schedule

Days/Per.	Monday	Tuesday	Wednesday	Thursday	Friday
1	1	2	1	2	1
2	2	2	1	2	1
3	3	4	3	4	3
4	4	4	3	4	3
5	5	6	5	6	5
6	6	6	5	6	5

allow and encourage the use of a variety of teaching strategies. Students have extended amounts of time for learning. In addition, the schedule provides the opportunity for interdisciplinary teaching, which is a much sought after curriculum goal of the middle school.

Academic learning time is also enhanced with the use of block scheduling. Chapter 10 discussed the ALT concept and the importance of reducing the amount of "start-up" and "close-down" time at the beginning and end of each lesson. Two-period classes reduce by more than one-half the lost time by eliminating a class change. Block schedules are also relatively easy to implement. They do not require student assignment procedures much different from those already on place for a six- or seven-period schedule. Only the relative changes of hours and days that classes meet must be modified.

Alternate-Day Schedules

Alternate-day block schedules may be adopted to meet the needs of schools that offer six, seven, or eight courses per year. In schools where six or eight classes have been taught, half of the classes are taught every other day. Classes might have a Monday-Wednesday-Friday schedule one week and a Tuesday-Thursday schedule the next; or Monday could be maintained with single-period classes and double-period classes operate on Tuesday-Thursday and Wednesday-Friday. The seven-course block schedule uses six courses that meet in double periods while one course meets as a singleton. Often, the singleton is scheduled in conjunction with the lunch hour. Figures 12–14 and 12–15 illustrate the six- and seven-course alternate-day block schedules.

The 4/4 Semester Plan

In the block schedule semester plan, the school day is divided into four instructional blocks of approximately 90 minutes each and the school year is divided into two semesters. Each semester, students are enrolled into four courses that meet daily for a full 90-minute period. Instruction that was previously stretched out over 180 days is now taught in 90 days. The two-period block reduces the lost academic learning time more than enough to make up for shorter assigned minutes of instruction. In fact, it is argued that more instructional time is really available under this 90-minute, one-

FIGURE 12–15   Alternate Day Seven-Course Block Schedule for Six-Day Rotation

Days/Per	Day 1	Day 2	Day 3	Day 4	Day 5	Day 6
1	1	2	1	2	1	2
2	1	2	1	2	1	2
3	3	4	3	4	3	4
4	3	4	3	4	3	4
5	5	5	5	5	5	5
6	7	6	7	6	7	6
7	7	6	7	6	7	6

semester plan than the traditional two-semester, one-period schedule.[4] Figure 12–16 illustrates the basic 4/4 model. Proponents of the 4/4 semester plan suggest that the plan has the following advantages:

1. Teachers have to work with only 50 to 90 students at a time.
2. Teachers have only three classes and maybe fewer preparations.
3. Students are responsible for only three or four subjects at one time.
4. Students failing a course may have the opportunity to repeat it immediately the next semester.
5. Students have opportunities to accelerate their study in specialty fields.
6. More elective opportunities exist for high school students who now have as many as 32 choices over a four-year period of time.
7. As many minutes of instruction (ALT) can be built into the schedule as single-period schedules.

Variations in block schedules are many. Lunch schedules, single-schedule needs for subjects that need to meet for the entire year, vocational programs that require blocks of time for "school-to-work" activities—all of these represent special impacts to the schedule. There is no available space in this chapter to provide the answers to each of these variables. An excellent resource, however, is the work of Canady and Rettig,[5] who provide a great number of schedule adaptations illustrating their book on block schedules.

FIGURE 12–16   The Basic 4/4 Two-Semester Block Schedule

Period	Semester 1	Semester 2
1	Course 1	Course 5
2	Course 1	Course 5
3	Course 2	Course 6
4	Course 2	Course 6
5	Course 3	Course 7
6	Course 3	Course 7
7	Course 4	Course 8
8	Course 4	Course 8

Summary

Scheduling has as its basic purpose the bringing together of curriculum, staff and students for the purpose of instruction. It must be kept flexible, allowing for changes in group size and instructional time. Schedules must also provide for adequate staff planning and allow major scheduling decisions to be made by the team. Block-of-time schedules assigned to the team and parallel scheduling for team planning offer good solutions to scheduling demands.

This chapter has developed several different concepts of scheduling a high school, from a simple group schedule to the complex modular schedule of some of our more experimental institutions. Complexity is not always best, however. More traditional mosaic schedules, when properly constructed, are most functional. When all aspects of school organization are considered, such as staffing, student grouping, curriculum, instruction, and student advisement and control, the block schedule must be given a high rating.

Under all circumstances, scheduling is a major determinant of the school program. While it should not control, it must be designed in such a way as to not limit the desired instructional program for the school.

Activities

1. Reflect on the use of time and the schedule in your own school. Can you identify areas where restructuring should take place? Why do you believe so? Why is it important to consider the planned decisions for curriculum, instruction, and staffing along with rescheduling decisions? Apply the concepts of this chapter to your school. How would you proceed to restructure your school's use of time?

2. Review Case Studies 4 and 20. Analyze the problems presented and apply the concepts of restructuring time developed in this chapter. What approach would you use in addressing the problems? Set forth a strategy to overcome the difficulties faced by the schools in these cases.

Endnotes

1. L. W. Hughes and G. C. Ubben, *The Secondary Principal's Handbook* (Boston: Allyn and Bacon, 1980), p. 173.
2. Elizabeth Ward et al., "Student/Teacher Achievement Ratio (STAR)," *Tennessee's K–3 Class Size Study 1985-1990* (Nashville: Tennessee State Department of Education, 1990).
3. Isabelle Bruder reviews six microcomputer-based administrative software programs that handle scheduling, grade reporting, and attendance tasks—(1) Alpha II, (2) Harts III, (3) Mount Castor, (4) the Osiris System, (5) the School System, and (6) STARS (Student Academic Records System)—and lists companies producing the programs, the systems they run on, and price information. (Isabelle Bruder, "Users Speak Out: A Look at Six Administrative Software Programs," *Electronic Learning* 7, no. 8 [May–June 1988]: 54–56.)
4. See Chapter 2 of Robert Lynn Canady and Michael D. Rettig, *Block Scheduling: A Catalyst for Change in High School Scheduling,*

Princeton: Eye On Education, 1995. Canady and Rettig present an interesting rationale for longer classes providing more than twice the academic learning time of that provided by 50-minute classes. (Robert Lynn Canady and

Michael D. Rettig, *Block Scheduling: A Catalyst for Change in High School Scheduling* [Princeton: Eye On Education, 1995]). See especially Chapter 2.

5. Ibid., p. 300.

Selected Readings

Alam, Dale, and Roger E. Seick, Jr. "A Block Schedule with a Twist." *Kappan* 75, no. 9 (May 1994): 732–733.

Association for Supervision and Curriculum Development. *With Consequences for All: A Report From the ASCD Task Force on Increased High School Graduation Requirements* (Stock No. 611-85418) (Alexandria, VA: Author, 1985). (ERIC Document Reproduction Service No. ED 182 465).

Blair, B. J. "Educational Reform: It's About Time." *Educational Reform* 60 (September 1988): 38–40.

Bloom, B. S. "Time and Learning." *American Psychologist* 29 (May 1974): 682–688.

Braddock, Jomills Henry, II, and James M. McPartland. "Alternatives to Tracking." *Educational Leadership* 47, no. 7 (April 1990): 76–79.

Canady, Robert. "A Cure for Fragmented Schedules in Elementary Schools." *Educational Leadership* 46, no. 2 (October 1988): 65–67.

Canady, Robert L. "Parallel Block Scheduling: A Better Way to Organize a School." *Principal* 69, no. 3 (January 1990): 34–36.

Canady, Robert Lynn, and Joanne M. Reina. "Parallel Block Scheduling: An Alternative Structure." *Principal* (January, 1993).

Canady, Robert Lynn, and Michael D. Rettig. *Block Scheduling: A Catalyst for Change in High School Scheduling* (Princeton: Eye On Education, 1995), p. 300.

Canady, Robert Lynn, and Michael D. Rettig. "Restructuring Middle Level Schedules to Promote Equal Access." *Schools in the Middle* (Summer 1992).

Carroll, J. M. (October 1994). "The Copernican Plan Evaluated: The Evolution of a Revolution." *Phi Delta Kappan* (October 1994): 105–113.

Conway, M. A., G. Cohen, and N. Stanhope. "On the Very Long-Term Retention of Knowledge Acquired through Formal Education: Twelve Years of Cognitive Psychology." *Journal of Experimental Psychology: General* 120 (1991): 395–409.

Edwards, C. M. "The Four-Period Day: Restructuring to Improve Student Achievement." *NASSP Bulletin* 77 (1993): 77–88.

Fredrich, W. C., and H. J. Walberg. "Learning as a Function of Time." *Journal of Educational Research* 73 (1980): 183–194.

Glasnapp, D. R., J. P. Poggio, and J. C. Ory. "End-of-Course and Long-Term Retention Outcomes for Mastery and Non-Mastery Learning Paradigms." *Psychology in Schools* 15 (1978): 595–603.

Goldberg, J. A. Research Plan for the Study of Senior High School Alternative Scheduling Systems in the Montgomery County Public School System, 1983. (ERIC Document Service No. ED 230 633).

Karweit, N. "Time-on-Task Reconsidered: Synthesis of Research on Time and Learning." *Educational Leadership* 41 (May 1984): 32–35.

Karweit, N. "Time-on-Task: A Research Review." Report 332 (Baltimore: The Johns Hopkins University Center for Social Organizations of Schools, 1983).

McGuire, Kent. "School Size: The Continuing Controversy." *Education and Urban Society* 21, no. 2 (1989): 164–174.

Olson, Lynn. "A Seattle Principal Defies the Conventional Wisdom." *Education Week* 7 (April 1988): 1–5.

Roberts, Jack L., Fran Reinhold, and Bill Morgan Gosewisch, (Eds.). *An Administrator's Guide to the Business of Education* (Special Supplement). *Electronic Learning* (New York: Scholastic, 1989).

Semb, G. B., J. A. Ellis, and J. Araujo. "Long-Term Memory for Knowledge Learned in School."

Journal of Educational Psychology 85 (1993): 305–316.

Slavin, Robert E. *Using Student Team Learning*, 3rd ed. (Baltimore: The Johns Hopkins University, The Team Learning Project, 1986).

Vann, Allan S. "Let's Pull in Pullout Programs." *Educational Leadership* 46 (March 1989): 88–89.

Walberg, H. J. "Synthesis of Research on Time and Learning." *Educational Leadership* 45 (March 1988): 76–85.

C h a p t e r 13

Human Resources Development

Any lasting change in a school will occur only because the staff itself changes norms of expectations, appropriate role defini-tions, standards of accountability and patterns of behavior.
— *S. K. MILLER, S. R. COHEN, AND R. H. SAYER*[1]

Human resources development (HRD) is a process that uses developmental practices to bring about more quality, higher productivity, and greater satisfaction among employees as organization members. It is a function of both an individual's *knowledge, skills*, and *attitudes* and the *policies, structure*, and *management practices* that consti-tute the system in which the individual works. The goal of HRD is to achieve the high-est quality of work life for employees and to produce the highest quality of instruction and service possible for the school.

The development of human resources in the school organization is a complex pro-cess and sometimes not a very well accomplished one. Often, it seems, the effort lacks focus and becomes simple responses to either organizational culture expectations or spur-of-the-moment enactments of state legislatures. That being the case, no one should be surprised if any particular school staff responds unenthusiastically when issues of in-service training arise. It shouldn't be this way and it doesn't have to be this way and it isn't that way in good schools.

The focus of this chapter is human resources development in the broadest sense— from personnel in their first years to those who may be considering retirement. Our premise is that everyone wants to succeed; no one deliberately performs unsatisfacto-rily. We are realists too; not everyone who enters a particular workplace or workstation is suited for the job, either by personal disposition or by skills level. And some never seem to be able to develop the level of skill necessary to adequately perform the assignment. But in most organizations, public or private, not enough is done to help persons improve their performance. Even less is done to help those who cannot improve to understand their deficiencies and find jobs where they might succeed outside the school organization.

Human resources development requires more than training programs, however, even though well-developed skills training events are a part of any HRD program. The most important resource in an organization is its staff. When the staff is congruent with organizational needs, well trained, adaptive, and motivated, great things can happen. To achieve this requires attention to the variety of ways in which human potential can be realized and to the variety of needs that any particular person may have at any particular stage of growth.

A Human Resources Development Model

Recent years have been characterized by renewed interest and excitement about the "human dimension" of the organization. The growing interest in W. Edwards Deming's work on TQM (Total Quality Management) and his emphasis on training and cooperatively established work goals, the success of such works as *The One Minute Manager, Megatrends*, and *In Search of Excellence*, among others, has directed much attention to the human resources development focus that successful organizations maintain. If anything typifies such successful efforts, it is the diversity of programs available within any given organization.

The model we are about to present describes why the HRD program must be so diverse. Attention needs to be directed to four factors: the nature of the adult learner; the different kinds of learning required of effective staff members; the varying amounts of time required to effect different kinds of behavior change; and the application of the appropriate training or development process given factors 1, 2, and 3. Figure 13–1 displays the model.

Human resources development is a continuous process and, as suggested by the model, depending on the type of development needed, organizational responses must vary. Unsuccessful personnel development programs tend to be unfocused in approach, and the model explains why these types of programs do not work very well.

As teachers and administrators enter the school organization (point "A" in the model), they bring with them some already acquired knowledge about the nature of their work. In the instance of beginning teachers, they have been students of the technology of teaching, have acquired some degree of subject matter competence, and probably have had intern experiences as student teachers. Incoming veterans will also bring with them perceptions and skills acquired in previous positions.

Two immediate needs would seem readily apparent: a clear understanding of the formal organization requirements and certain housekeeping information (such as when payday is, room assignments, who to call when ill, etc.). It is appropriate that there be "new teacher" orientation sessions and a well-developed personnel handbook.

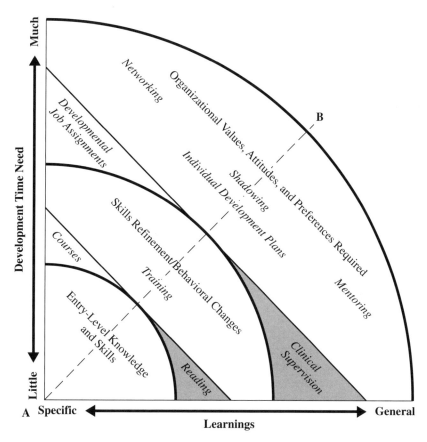

FIGURE 13–1 A Human Resources Development Model

Organizational Socialization

A critical but less apparent need is an organizational socialization process. This is not accomplished nearly as quickly nor as easily as other needs. Here, one is dealing with attitudes, values, and organizational preferences. Mentoring and networking are among the appropriate techniques. Such approaches require careful planning, matching, monitoring, and time.

The use of the "buddy system" in some schools is sound and consistent with this need. When employed by the principal with first-year teachers, it does speed up the socialization processes substantially, although not completely. Judiciously applied, involving only the best veterans on the faculty, such a technique also establishes an organizational support system that will provide the basis for both a peer supervision approach and a mentoring process.

In many organizations, the socialization needs are not met in any formal kind of way. The result is unnecessary blunders by new staff members as they stumble from one organization or public relations *faux pas* to another. Misunderstood directions and faulty perceptions, as well as a "survival of the fittest" mentality, send the neophyte home by Christmas and the veteran to a university placement office.

Individual Behavior Change

How should the human resources development program be organized to help individuals respond to new challenges in the system? And how can persons be helped to improve existing skills? In other words, how can behaviors be changed? *Knowledge* is a start, but it is insufficient to cause or even reasonably predict behavior change. Knowledge can be acquired either by reading or taking courses. Such practices *are* efficacious with adults when they are self-directed and for the purpose of learning, something the adult has decided he or she wants or needs to know.

But knowledge does not equate to ability or even desire. There is a chasm between "knowing how to" and "being able to," or "wanting to." One of the most difficult human resources development problems is behavior change. This aspect requires a good appraisal system and sophisticated follow-up. It also requires a considerable investment of personnel and time. Short courses and systematic reading may help but more is required.

Commonly used successful techniques include clinical supervision, employing behaviorally anchored appraisals; on-the-job training, developmental job assignments; "shadowing," or systematic observation of another person deemed to be expert in the skill being learned; and workshops. Each of these techniques—and none is mutually exclusive from the others—requires organizational flexibility and policies that permit released time from daily duties. Once the developing person engages in the prescribed activity, there is, of course, a need to reappraise, rediagnose, and continue the development, if necessary, and if it is believed to be ultimately fruitful.

The HRD model also indicates that activities appropriate to one phase in the employee's development are not necessarily to be excluded from subsequent stages (e.g.. those activities suggested in the shaded areas between development stages). In any organization, new demands and new research will require updated or new skills on the part of reorganization members. Thus, there will continue to be a need for skills development workshops, taking courses, and systematic reading, among, other techniques, irrespective of how long the staff member has been in the organization in a particular job.

Implementing a Staff-Development Program

Assuring the quality of a school staff has always been more than an occasional concern of the successful principal. Recently, it has increasingly become a concern of educational reformers and state legislators as well. The result has been myriad legislative outpourings and an even greater number of literary outpourings, all designed to "improve teachers." Emphasis is being placed on competency testing, career ladders, and demonstrated entry-level subject matter competency, among a number of focused efforts.

Although it is foolish to argue against the intent of these efforts, it remains doubtful that the quality of anything as complex as learning can be improved by legislative fiat. However, given an adequate degree of funding from these same state legislators, and given less prescriptive and categorical "advice," an uncommonly good opportunity exists for the school system and school building subsystem to implement a sound human resources development program. Certainly, the external interest and influence are there and one might even presume a modicum of support from the private sector, given a reasonably persuasive principal or superintendent.

Characteristic of such programs will be the implementation of a model analogous to that presented in the first part of this chapter with a focus on subject matter expertise and on pedagogical skills. Such programs require an organized array of organizational responses: clinical supervision, peer supervision, developmental job assignments, in-house diagnostic and remedial programs, and development of systematic cooperative relationships with local or area four-year institutions of higher education and community colleges.

The model HRD program would begin with individual staff needs assessments, progress through systematic review of the demonstrated levels of individual professional expertise, and on to designated programs of remediation and development. Such practices are occurring with increasing frequency across the nation.

HRD at the Building Level

It is not the responsibility of the principal to develop an in-service program that will examine the competency of the professional staff with regard to academic skills and subject matter proficiency. This is a shared responsibility between district, state, and university, and any systematic programs designed to identify and address these needs should issue from and be administered at those levels.[2] It is in the "higher-order" staff-development needs that the principal plays the most important part. This includes providing for staff needs assessments, engaging in clinical supervision, helping staff members initiate individual development plans, and organizing school-based in-service programming.

Discovering Staff Needs, Interests, and Skills

How well does the principal know the staff? In order to have a good staff-development program, it is necessary to have more information than is contained in the typical personnel folder. Normal attrition of staff—because of transfer, retirement, resignation, or termination—makes keeping track of staff difficult enough. Moreover, the ordinary difficulty present in any organization of becoming professionally acquainted with all of a large staff, even over a period of years, often inhibits the effective deployment of personnel and even more so the organization of a relevant in-service program. Staff inventories can help in this.

Inventories can be used to find out special skills and interests that staff may have that are unrevealed in other sources. Such an inventory would include an array of teaching and organizational skills and knowledge areas, using any of the commonly used teaching "frameworks" and local district needs. Figure 13–2 displays a sample page of such an instrument with some representative headings and items. A similarly constructed instrument can be used to discover the skills, interests, and needs of the noncertificated support staff, as well.

Title/Position _____   Date _____

Years of Employment _____   Degree _____

Directions: Please place a check in both Columns II and III for each area. Blank columns at the end of the instrument may be used to add special areas you may wish to list.

SECTION A

I. Area	II. Experience				III. Interest		
	Expertise in: experienced and can serve as consultant	Worked with: in many situations	Knowledge of: extends beyond definition but have not worked with	No knowledge of: extends to no more than simple definition	Desire further training in	Desire training in	Do not desire training in
(DIAGNOSTIC AND PRESCRIPTIVE TEACHING)							
Assessing the Classroom Climate							
Teacher-Made Tests							
Standardized Tests							
Grading							
(CLASSROOM MULTIDISCIPLINE)							
(MULTICULTURAL AWARENESS)							
Community Analysis Field Study							
Cultural Communication							
Multilingual Teaching Team							
(DEVELOPING INSTRUCTIONAL MODULES)							

FIGURE 13–2   Professional Staff Interests/Needs Questionnaire

Clinical Supervision

Clinical supervision is supervision devoted to diagnosis and prescription and formative, rather than summative, evaluation. It is a behaviorally anchored appraisal consisting most frequently of established objectives and desired instructional patterns; systematic observation and recording of teaching behaviors; and postobservation conferences during which any appropriate corrective actions are prescribed and future standards of performance established.

Clinical supervision is a collaborative process. The term *clinical supervision* gained national prominence in the 1960s through the writings of Robert Goldhammer and Morris Cogen.[3] Originally, the model was proposed for use with student teachers. Its applicability in the formative evaluation of practicing teachers was soon recognized.

Five steps comprise the model. Each step helps both the supervisor and the teacher in focusing on the teaching-learning process. An examination is made of the strengths and weaknesses of a lesson and then the process involves identifying specific activities to improve future lessons or teaching practices. The final step is formal feedback to the teacher.

Step One: The Preobservation Conference

The purpose of the preobservation conference is to provide focus to the upcoming observation. The teacher outlines for the principal the plans for the lesson and helps identify specific aspects to which attention will be directed during the observation. The teacher's plan is expected to contain learner objectives, introductions, teaching strategies to be employed, resources to be used, evaluation plans, and lesson closure.

During this discussion, there is opportunity for the principal to clarify the various components of the lesson and to offer suggestions about other possible approaches. The discussion about the initial observation should focus on specific areas of interest or concern to the teacher rather than areas or concerns of the principal. Later observations and discussions will provide ample opportunity to address principal concerns.

It is important that the teacher understand the purpose of each step in the clinical model. The teacher needs to know that the observer will be taking notes during the observation and that this is for the purpose of giving accurate feedback. Before the conclusion of the preobservation conference, both a time for the classroom visit and a time for the postobservation conference should be established.

Step Two: The Classroom Observation

The teacher's task is to teach the lesson as planned. The observer's task is to record those items specifically identified in the preobservation conference as well as the events surrounding the lesson. Specific happenings should be scripted and in the language of the teacher. Activities relating to the lesson—student verbal and nonverbal behavior, for example—should be noted. Opinion and summary statements need to be avoided; the language of the participants and specific events are what the principal needs to provide useful feedback. It is important to be on time and to stay for the entire lesson.

Step Three: Analysis of the Lesson

To prepare for the postobservation conference, script notes need to be analyzed. Were the objectives obtained? How did the various intended teaching strategies work? What unusual circumstances were observed? What seemed to work? What didn't? What comments can you make about the teacher's verbal and nonverbal (physical) behavior? How about student verbal and nonverbal behavior? What did the teacher do well? What specific aspects might be improved? What should the teacher work on for the next observation?

Step Four: The Postobservation Conference

The conference needs to take place in a comfortable and private location. The teacher's classroom itself is often appropriate. A good opening line, after the amenities, is: "What do you think went well?" Then, the teacher should be asked to clarify the objectives of the lesson, review what happened, and assess whether the objectives were attained and to what degree. At this point, the principal will relate some of his or her specific observations supported by the notes that were taken. Successes will be discussed.

Agreement should be reached about what went on. Together, the teacher and the principal should decide on some strategies that might be worth trying. Information should be solicited from the teacher. Every conference should conclude with some growth objectives and some agreed-upon plans for improving any deficiencies.

Step Five: Postconference Analysis

The final step in the clinical model is an evaluation of the process and the outcome. Information is solicited from the teacher. How could the process be improved? Are the growth objectives clear? What assistance is available to the teacher? After the teacher leaves, the principal needs to reflect on the process and his or her own behavior and skill. Did the conference go well? Why or why not? The process is intended to promote both improved instruction and supportive relationships. One likely will not occur without the other.

Teacher Appraisal

In recent years, many states have mandated forms and processes by which teacher appraisal will take place. Many of these mandates have resulted in standardized rating scales and designed checklists. Care must be used in basing an entire appraisal system on this or any other specific model. There is danger that the criteria will become too narrow to encompass the teaching of subjects that incorporate higher-order thinking skills or that require a high level of creativity on the part of students.

Tom McGreal has proposed alternatives to the rating scales appraisal designs to make them more useful as a clinical tool.[4] He suggests that an appropriate appraisal be based on a cooperative goal-setting model, and that the appraiser and the teacher identify specific instructional improvement goals on which to work together. In working together, the techniques of clinical supervision are used and a supportive environment is established. Appraisal thus is the basis for staff development. The collaborative goal setting based on the formal appraisal that ensues at the postobservation and later conferences is critical to the development process.

Several authors[5] have suggested that supervision and teacher appraisal styles become situationally specific; that is, situational factors determine the approach used by the principal in working with each staff member. This situational approach is similar to the situational leadership model proposed by Blanchard.[6] Glatthorn,[7] describing a differentiated system of situational supervision, suggested four levels.

1. *Clinical supervision,* as described in the previous section
2. *Collaborative professional development,* as a collegial process in which a small number of teachers work together for professional growth (the quality circle idea from TQM will integrate well with this approach.)
3. *Self-direction* in which the teacher prepares an individual development plan (IDP) with the assistance of the principal who serves as a resource person
4. *Administrative monitoring* where the principal makes a series of brief, usually announced visits as "quality control" assurance

The fourth approach, commonly used by administrators, is one that should not be considered a supervisory method because it does not provide improvement opportunities to the teacher being observed. However, each of these approaches has its appropriate place in certain circumstances, depending on the maturity and needs of the teacher. The chart shown in Figure 13–3 points up many of the differences in the three supervisory approaches from the preceding list.

Staff development and evaluation are essential activities of the elementary school principal. Just as a teacher manages student learning by using a diagnostic prescriptive model, so can the principal direct staff development using staff evaluation as a diagnostic tool and an evaluation-by-objectives approach as a prescriptive tool. For proper staff development and evaluation, the principal must take an initiating, rather than reacting, role, and the comprehensive plan for staff evaluation must be based on a sound rationale.

Staff evaluation has two basic purposes: (1) to improve the performance and provide direction for the continued development of present staff and (2) to provide a sound

FIGURE 13–3   Situational Models of Supervision

	Clinical	**Collaborative**	**Self-Directed**
Teacher Initiative	Low	Moderate	High
Supervisor Initiative	High	Moderate	Low
Approach	Formal, systematic	Collaborative	Self-directed
Goal of Learning	Create rationality/order	Problem solving	Goal directed
Knowledge	Predefined set of life-survival skills	Concrete results that "work" for individuals	That which is discovered
Learning	Condition individual by outer environment	Outcome of learner/environment interaction	Unfolding process within learner
Foundation	Behaviorist	Cognitivist	Humanist
Learning Theory	Conditioning	Experimentation	Self-discovery
Teacher Risk	Low	Moderate to high	Moderate to high

Adapted from A. A. Glatthorn, *Differentiated Supervision* (Alexandria, VA: Association for Supervision and Curriculum Development, 1984).

basis for personnel decisions such as awarding of tenure, promotions, transfers, or dismissals.

These two purposes create a dilemma for many administrators. even though both support quality education. Staff improvement is largely a helping relationship most effectively carried out when built on trust between the teacher and the principal. Personnel decisions are judgmental in nature and can cause teacher apprehension.

The Staff Evaluation Cycle

Staff evaluation and development is a cyclical process. Staff evaluation leads to a staff-development prescription that is checked once again through evaluation. Seven basic steps in the evaluation cycle focus on the ultimate purpose of improving instruction. The cycle begins when the teacher and principal plan goals and targets for the year and include other people in the evaluation process during the year (see Figure 13–4). The seven steps of the evaluation cycle are as follows:

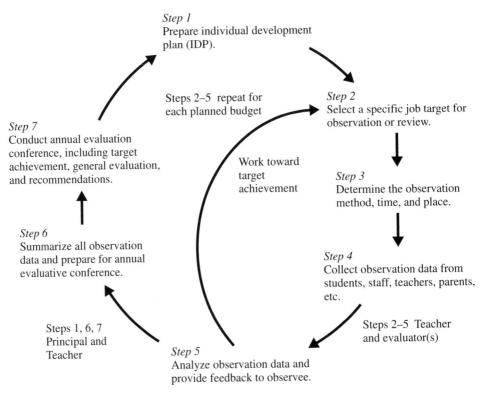

FIGURE 13–4   Staff Evaluation and Development Cycle

Source: Larry W. Hughes and Gerald C. Ubben, *The Elementary Principal's Handbook: A Guide to Effective Action,* 4th ed. Boston: Allyn and Bacon, 1994, p. 261. Used with permission.

1. Prepare an individual development plan (IDP).
2. Select specific objectives or activities for observation or review.
3. Determine the observation method, time, and place.
4. Observe and collect data.
5. Analyze data and provide feedback.
6. Summarize and interpret collective observational data.
7. Report evaluation results, target achievement, and make recommendations for individual and staff development at an annual conference.

Individual Development Plans (Step 1)

An IDP is a written schedule of experiences designed to meet a person's particular goals for development. It is a method of systematically planning for training and other experiences in order to develop necessary skills and knowledge. Rather than haphazardly chancing time and money on what may not be a useful learning experience, the IDP gives both staff member and administrator an opportunity to set reasonable objectives and then plan experiences that support those objectives.

The IDP is realistic and feasible because its construction includes both administrator and staff member perspectives. The staff member's personal and professional goals are considered insofar as these are organizationally feasible. The staff member also gets information and feedback so that goals can be set that are organizationally necessary and reasonably achievable.

Individual development is a joint responsibility of the administrator and the staff member. As such, it is a logical extension of the clinical supervision and appraisal process. The principal's responsibility is to arrange the work environment to capitalize on the skills and interests of the staff so that the important tasks get accomplished in the most efficient and effective way. To do so requires that the principal and staff member work together to identify skills deficiencies (developmental needs), strengths, and professional and organizational goals. The IDP is a joint commitment to address these issues.

The IDP includes first a self-assessment. The individual staff member reviews his or her professional qualifications, skills, and interests. A personal judgment is made about how these skills may be capitalized on in the organizational setting and how any skill deficiency can be best addressed. The second step in this process is for the individual to think about his or her professional career and begin to establish long-term career goals.

The responsibility of the principal is to conduct an analysis of the staff member's strengths and weaknesses as well. This analysis is always conducted from the perspective of what is good for the school. It frequently occurs that an individual's self-assessment will overlook important organizational demands and skills needs.

Following the two analyses, a development conference is held and the IDP begins to take specific form. Important information is exchanged at this conference. The two parties may not see all things similarly. Congruence is never likely to be achieved without a discourse about job-related expectations. At this time, the principal becomes aware of the goals of the staff member and, where possible and feasible, may provide job situations, special assignments, and professional opportunities so that both individual and organizational needs can be obtained.

The conference serves two other purposes. It provides an opportunity for the principal to point out skill-development areas and organizational goals about which the staff may have been unaware. These expectations become a part of the IDP as well. It is also at this time that the principal can point out things that the organization *cannot* do to help the individual. Figures 13–5 and 13–6 display two approaches to IDPs.

Preobservation Conference

The preobservation conference has two basic purposes: (1) selecting a particular topic for observation and (2) planning the details of the observation.

Target Selection (Step 2)
A teacher's job targets are usually too many or too varied to be observed and evaluated properly all at one time. Individual job targets should be selected one at a time for observation and evaluation.

Planning the Observation (Step 3)
Once the particular target has been selected, plans should be made for data collection regarding its achievement.

FIGURE 13–5   School-Based Individual Development Plan

Name: _____   Dept.: _____

  I. Instructional Target(s)
    Individualize instruction in mathematics.

    Indicators of Achievement:
    1. Develop self-instructional modules for units 1–4
    2. Revise preinstruction assessment instruments for sixth-grade math
    3. Devise at least four enrichment activities or games for low-interest students

  II. Curriculum Target(s)
    Integrate one unit of first semester math and science.

    Indicators of Achievement:
    1. Initiate interdepartmental study group
    2. Develop objectives for courses
    3. Identify potential students
    4. Develop syllabus

  III. Professional Growth Target(s)
    Improve diagnostic and prescriptive skills.

    Indicators of Achievement:
    1. Review Buros, *Mental Measurements*
    2. Successfully complete EPSY 6310 at University of Houston
    3. Revise preinstruction instrument for math (same as 1–2 above)

---

1. EMPLOYEE NAME (LAST, FIRST, MIDDLE INITIAL)	2. CURRENT POSITION	3. BUILDING AND GRADE OR DEPARTMENT

4. SHORT-RUN DEVELOPMENT GOALS
   (IMMEDIATE, WITHIN A YEAR)

4A. DEVELOPMENTAL OBJECTIVES (KNOWLEDGE, SKILLS, AND ABILITIES NEEDED)	4B. DEVELOPMENTAL ASSIGNMENTS (IDENTIFY TYPE, DATES, LENGTHS, AND LOCATIONS, IF POSSIBLE)	4C. FORMAL TRAINING (IDENTIFY SPECIFIC COURSES, LOCATIONS, AND DATES IF POSSIBLE)

5. LONG-RANGE DEVELOPMENTAL GOALS
   (NEXT FIVE YEARS)

5A. DEVELOPMENT OBJECTIVES	5B. DEVELOPMENT ASSIGNMENTS	5C. FORMAL TRAINING

FIGURE 13–6   School-System-Based Individual Development Plan

Observers.   A preobservation conference should include the teacher to be evaluated and those responsible for data collection. The principal should *not* attempt to conduct all observations personally. Sometimes the principal is an appropriate data collector, but students, other teachers, parents, and other supervisors are also available. Numerous research findings support the position that others besides a principal who come in contact with the teacher at work can make valid and reliable judgments about that work.[8] Also, a good data collection for evaluation takes time—usually more time than most principals have available.

Observation Tools.   A variety of observation instruments are available or can be created for various types of data collection for teacher evaluation. Elementary students, for example, can provide data on certain types of teacher behavior through the use of the smiley-face questionnaire (Figure 13–7). During the actual observation, students might be questioned about their degree of involvement in planning, and samples of student-planned activities could be collected. Some of the responses can be recorded directly by the students if they are mature enough.

Time and Place.   The time and place for the observation also need to be arranged during the preobservation conference.

Collection of Observation Data (Step 4)

Data collection is simply the carrying out of the plan outlined in Step 3. Observations need not be long, particularly if the job target is narrow in scope. Making separate

Categories of the Evaluation

This evaluation was designed to evaluate the role of the teacher in setting a classroom atmosphere in which the child feels important and has an active part. It was designed to check those areas that make a child either like or dislike the classroom. The statements cover these categories:

I.   STUDENT'S ATTITUDE TOWARD TEACHER: Statements 1, 4, 10, 13, 25.

II. TEACHER'S ATTITUDE TOWARD STUDENTS AS PERCEIVED BY THE STUDENTS: Statements 7, 17, 19, 22.

III. TEACHER'S INTEREST IN STUDENT'S OUT-OF-SCHOOL LIFE: Statements 2, 8, 15.

IV. TEACHER'S ROLE IN CREATING STUDENT PARTICIPATION IN CLASS: Statements 9, 14, 16.

V.   TEACHER'S INTEREST IN STUDENT'S PROBLEMS: Statements 3, 6, 18, 20.

VI. TEACHER'S FAIRNESS IN DEALING WITH STUDENTS: Statements 12, 21, 23.

VII. TEACHER'S AWARENESS OF THE CLASSROOM ENVIRONMENT: Statements 5, 11, 24.

Fill in the face

1. When my teacher helps me with my work, I feel . . .
2. When I talk to my teacher about my family, she looks . . .
3. When my teacher is busy and I raise my hand to tell her about a problem, she looks . . .
4. When my teacher talks to the class, it makes me feel . . .
5. When I walk into my classroom and look around, I feel . . .
6. When I do not understand something and I ask my teacher about it, she looks . . .
7. When I talk to my teacher about my work, she looks . . .
8. When I talk to my teacher about what I do at home, she looks . . .
9. When I have a good idea and I tell my teacher about it, she looks . . .
10. When my teacher talks to me, I feel . . .
11. When I tell my friends how my classroom looks, I feel . . .
12. When I ask my teacher if I can take the TV out of the room, she looks . . .
13. If my teacher came to visit my home, I would feel . . .
14. When I answer a question in class, my teacher looks . . .
15. When I talk to my teacher about what I do on Saturday, she looks . . .
16. When I bring in things to share with my class, my teacher looks . . .
17. When I talk to my teacher about myself, she looks . . .
18. When I do not understand what to do on paper and I ask my teacher to tell me again, she looks . . .
19. When I do some of my work wrong, my teacher looks . . .
20. When I have a problem and I tell my teacher about it, she looks . . .
21. When I ask my teacher if I can get milk for snack time, she looks . . .
22. When I do good work, my teacher looks . . .
23. When I ask my teacher if I can take the lunch report to the office, she looks . . .
24. When I look at the walls and bulletin board in my classroom, I feel . . .
25. If I had my teacher next year, I would feel . . .

FIGURE 13–7   Elementary Student Classroom Atmosphere Evaluation Form

Source: Larry W. Hughes and Gerald C. Ubben, *The Elementary Principal's Handbook: A Guide to Effective Action,* 4th ed. Boston: Allyn and Bacon, 1994, pp. 265–268. Used with permission.
Note: Repeat smiley faces for each of the 25 statements.

observation cycles for different job targets is often better than trying to combine a whole series of observations into one command performance. Fifteen minutes is usually adequate time to observe one technique or activity. The observation should take place at a scheduled time and place and should maintain as normal an atmosphere as possible so the data will be reliable.

Postobservation Conference (Step 5)

The observer should report and analyze the observation and provide feedback to the person observed. The postobservation conference should be conducted by the person in charge of data collection. In some cases, it will be the principal; often, it will be another teacher. Information gathered from students or parents is returned to the principal or other designated person. Confidentiality of responses should be maintained.

Appraisal Schedule

The planning schedule of the evaluation process is completed with the scheduling of the activities and the selection of dates for the completion of the various targets. Figure 13–8 illustrates the appraisal cycle time schedule. Upon completion of the planning document, the staff members proceed to initiate the plan, carrying out the activities as

FIGURE 13–8   Calendar for Appraisal Cycle

By June or end of September for new staff (principal and teachers):
  Plan goals, targets, and activities (Step 1)
  (This can be an extension of the Annual Evaluation Conference for returning staff.)
By end of November (teachers and evaluators):
  Achieve at least one job target using a preobservation, observation, and post observation conference (Steps 2–5)
By end of January (teachers and evaluators):
  Achievement of additional job targets (Steps 2–5)
By March 1 (teachers and evaluators):
  Achievement of additional job targets and submission of all evaluative data to principal (Steps 2–5 for Step 6)
By March 15 (principal and nontenured teachers):
  Completion of all annual evaluation conferences with nontenured teachers. All appropriate evaluation forms and recommendations forwarded to personnel office (Steps 6 and 7)
By April 1 (principal and teachers):
  Completion of all other annual evaluation conferences where transfer or termination is to be recommended. All appropriate evaluation forms and recommendations forwarded to personnel office (Steps 6 and 7)
April 15 (principal and teachers):
  Completion of all other annual evaluation conferences for all tenured staff. All appropriate forms and recommendations forwarded to the personnel office (Steps 6 and 7)
End of the school year (principal and teachers):
  Planning conferences to set goals, targets, and activities for returning staff (Step 1)

Source: Larry W. Hughes and Gerald C. Ubben, *The Elementary Principal's Handbook: A Guide to Effective Action,* 4th ed. Boston: Allyn and Bacon, 1994, p. 268. Used with permission.

outlined. The process of clinical supervision is often used for this. As the first target date approaches, the teacher plans for an evaluation of that target, beginning with a pre-observation conference.

A Cyclical Process (Steps 2–5)

Steps 2 through 5 of the evaluation cycle may be repeated numerous times during the year for different job targets or for repeated evaluations of a particular job target. The relationship of the steps to each other over time is illustrated in Figure 13–4.

Preparation of the Annual Individual Development Report (Step 6)

At the end of each annual evaluation cycle, and in time to meet the legal deadlines for contract renewal or termination, the evaluative data gathered during the year should be summarized. Each teacher should be sure that all the necessary data collection has been done for each target established. The actual task of analyzing and summarizing the evaluative data belongs to the principal.

Each set of goals and targets should be evaluated for the degree of achievement. The principal should not expect teachers to meet all targets, however. Teachers should work toward goals through the completion of set targets, but if they must achieve all targets each year, teachers will very quickly learn to set only achievable targets and will never reach out to challenging ones. Therefore, some targets may not have been reached. Each case, of course, must be judged on its individual merits.

Comments should be written about each job target and its degree of achievement. Recommendations should be considered as proposals for job targets for the following year. This evaluative summation can be recorded on a form similar to the one on which job goals, targets, and activities were entered earlier (see Figure 13–5).

Annual Evaluation Conference (Step 7)

The annual evaluation conference, held usually in March or April with each teacher, includes four distinct tasks:

1. A review of the year's IDP and the determination of the degree to which they have been achieved, using a form such as the one shown in Figure 13–5.
2. A summary evaluation by the principal of each teacher's overall performance, preferably in a narrative form but using a summary checklist if required.
3. The final personnel recommendation. using a form like the one in Figure 13–9.
4. Recommendations for next year's IDP. This should be the beginning of the new evaluation cycle. Plans made in the spring have the advantage of a full 12 months, including the summer, for fulfillment. Plans made in the fall allow for only 6 or 7 months for completion.

Recommendations for staff development should take two forms. The first is the identification of a proposed set of individual targets or goals as recommended improvement points for the next cycle of staff evaluation. These recommendations

FIGURE 13–9   Personnel Recommendation Form

Person evaluated _____
                          Last   First   Middle

School/Department _____

Grade, subject, or position _____

Period of evaluation _____to _____

Total years teaching experience _____

Total years teaching in present school _____

Total years teaching in this school system _____

Overall Rating

_____   Teacher performance is outstanding and exceeds district expectations

_____   Teacher performance is satisfactory and meets district expectations

_____   Teacher performance is unsatisfactory and fails to meet district expectations

Recommendation

(Check as many as are applicable. Comment when appropriate.)

_____   Reemploy

_____   Do not reemploy

_____   Recommend dismissal

_____   Transfer

_____   Reevaluate next year

_____   Conditional reemploy

_____   Recommend for Tenure

_____   DO NOT recommend for tenure

As signature below indicates, this conference has been held and the person has been evaluated. The person evaluated does not necessarily agree with the evaluation.

_____   _____   _____
Signature of Person Evaluated   Evaluator's Signature, Title   Date

become the basis for generating new goals. The second major thrust focuses on staff development on a schoolwide basis. Gathering the criticisms and target recommendations for teachers in a school portrays a particular pattern of staff training needs. This is a most useful planning tool for outlining group staff-development activities (see Figure 13–10). If, for example, a staff needs profile indicates a need for learning-center development or improvement, it would be helpful to organize a collective improvement program in that specific target area.

Teachers	Group Interaction	Learning Centers	Small Group Instruction	Discipline	Record Keeping	Reading Skills Instruction	Team Skills	Other
Abbot, C.		X	X	X		X	X	X
Carson, B.			X	X	X			X
Dole, J.	X	X		X			X	X
Goff, R.	X	X			X			X
Harris, S.		X	X	X		X	X	X
Henderson, F.	X	X		X		X		X
Jones, B.	X	X		X			X	X
Nance, D.		X	X	X	X			X
Periera, A.	X		X				X	X
Smith, L.		X			X	X		X
Wall, S.		X	X				X	X

FIGURE 13–10   Staff-Development Needs Survey

Source: Larry W. Hughes and Gerald C. Ubben, *The Elementary Principal's Handbook: A Guide to Effective Action,* 4th ed. Boston: Allyn and Bacon, 1994, p. 271. Used with permission.

A collective staff-development program can also be used on a school-district level if similar evaluation programs are used in each individual building. The more teachers available for the various parts of a planned, personalized in-service program, the greater will be its efficiency and effectiveness.

Mentoring

The focus to this point has been the relationship between the principal as supervisor and individual staff members. Mentoring proposes a relationship between peers—however, generally not peers of equal stature and experience. Mentoring is often used to assist in the orientation of new employees.

The term *mentor* comes from Greek mythology. Mentor was the friend and counselor to whom Ulysses entrusted his son when Ulysses set off on a 10-year odyssey. It was a complex role: Mentor was protector, advisor, teacher, and father-figure to the inexperienced boy. The relationship was one of trust and affection.

In today's organizational setting, a formalized mentor program typically involves a relationship between a veteran employee of some stature and a younger inexperienced colleague. When it is an aspect of a human resources development effort, the focus of the relationship is on career counseling, advanced skills development, and learning the culture of the organization from a broadened perspective. Less formal relationships, which are conceptually similar, are typified by labels such as *sponsor, coach,* and *senior advisor.*

Mentoring has come to take on a more precise role than that suggested by the other labels. Often, the practice is reserved to those who have been identified early as "fast trackers" or potential leaders. However, the concept is easily applied at the building level, albeit perhaps not quite as formally, but nevertheless to good effect. It can substantially improve the clinical approach to supervision and become a very sophisticated *peer* supervision program. It does require a cadre of excellent experienced staff, however.

As in any relationship, both parties in the mentoring process have important responsibilities. It is critical that the relationship be managed so that maximum benefit is achieved. The responsibilities of the mentor include:

- *IDP Counseling.* Specific guidance and suggestions are given for developmental experiences to be included in the protégé's IDP to strengthen competencies.
- *Monitoring and Feedback.* An active role must be taken by the mentor in monitoring the progress and performance of the protégé. Regular feedback sessions need to be held at which time the IDP is reviewed, clinical observations made, and formative evaluation considerations discussed.
- *Career Strategy Advisement.* The mentor provides general guidance and insight regarding the kinds of opportunities available in the organization and the career background and path necessary to qualify for such positions. In this capacity, the mentor brings to bear an extensive knowledge of the history and culture of the system, as well as of projected trends. Many school systems, for example, have differentiated staffing patterns, extended-year contract opportunities, special assignments for staff with special qualifications, different salary arrangements depending on certification, interesting opportunities for those whose teaching areas are in high demand/short supply, as well as the usual administrative positions with opportunities for broadened leadership responsibilities. The mentor advises about these.
- *Sponsoring and Mediating.* This aspect of the mentor's responsibility is to provide direction and assistance in arranging particular developmental assignments and promotion opportunities. The second dimension is to serve as a mediator in any conflicts that may arise that involve the advisee and others in the organization, including the "boss."

The developing person has responsibilities as well. Any productive relationship is mutually supportive and requires the active attention of both parties. The advisee needs to take the lead in several ways: by initiating meeting and actively seeking advice, by remaining open to the advice and suggestions of the mentor, and by a willingness to share personal and professional problems and aspirations.

Developing a Productive Relationship

Productive relationships are not automatically obtained. There is always the issue of the "interpersonal chemistry" of the involved individuals, for example. This notwithstanding to the contrary, there are several other factors that can greatly facilitate the relationship. Administrators interested in developing productive mentoring arrangements need to consider such aspects is careful matching, good initial orientation, and a feedback and monitoring system.

Careful matching of individuals is essential. The administrator should develop an initial list of potential mentors before considering the process further. Important factors that result in a good mentor include willingness to act as a mentor, personal commitment to helping others develop, commitment to the school, extensive knowledge and insight about how things get done in the organization, solid experience, good professional relationships beyond the immediate building or system, and a proven record of success.

For example, when using a mentoring system as part of the orientation of new teachers, it is often best to select as mentors relatively young but experienced teachers. As mentors, they will generally relate well to entering members of the profession having enough experience to share good advice, including a good memory for the problems of a first-year teacher.

Fundamental to a long-term relationship is an early orientation to the program at which the involved parties can, within a school system and school building policy, work through role definitions and expectations of each other. This process will clarify initial commitments to help foster the climate of trust and openness important to success.

The establishment of a regular feedback and monitoring system is essential. This must be encouraged and supported by organizational mechanisms. One approach is to schedule regular monthly luncheons, in addition to other spontaneous sessions, at which lengthier discussion can take place in a more relaxed atmosphere away from the usual interruptions.

Organizational Development

Organizational development (OD) is a process designed to improve the interaction and productivity of work groups. The work group may be a team of teachers, the staff of a particular school, or some other configuration of employees. OD methods work well as initial activities for newly formed teams or with established groups that are refocusing their efforts. Quality circles as part of a Total Quality Management (TQM) program can use OD methodology to facilitate their interaction.

Although HRD and OD are different and are employed for different outcomes, they are related. An OD intervention frequently results in the development, or improvement, of the human resources development program. Frequently, as well, a well-functioning HRD program will bring about conditions that result in a better-functioning work group—an intended outcome of organizational development. Some theorists may argue otherwise, but for the practitioner and the student of management it is most useful to view the two approaches as parts of a whole.[9]

Healthy organizations systematically and regularly engage in introspective analyses of organizational activities, the purpose of such introspection is to maintain viability—to continue to effectively respond to client needs. Three questions must be asked:

- *Why are we doing what we are doing?* This is a goals question. Healthy organizations have well-developed and well-understood goals and objectives, From time to time there is need to reexamine these in the light of changing conditions—to reaffirm them, add to them, or modify them.
- *What are we doing?* This is a question about the nature and kind of processes that are being implemented to achieve the goals and objectives. This has to do with such things as the nature of the curriculum, scoping and sequencing of subject matter, policy and procedures, and a host of other things that comprise the formal organizational structure and deliver, systems.
- *Can it be done a better way?* This is an evaluation question. Once the goals have been clarified, and reaffirmed or modified, and once the processes have been identified and analyzed, it is necessary to decide what, if anything, could be done differently to achieve the goal more efficiently. Such issues as decision-making practices, communication practices, allocation of resources and/or additional resources needed (personnel and material), changes in organizational structure and curricular delivery, systems, staffing arrangements, and any individual developmental activities are among the processes that must be examined.

As with any complex process issuing from the behavioral sciences, there is not complete agreement about just what organizational development is. Nevertheless, there are some common characteristics about which most in the field would agree.

Organizational development is systematic and involves a total organizational system *or* subsystems. The entire organization need not be involved. Any unified subsystem—a school building or a decentralized school system unit, for example—could engage in such a process *provided* the unit was relatively autonomous (i.e.. free within wide bounds to determine its own long-range plans), and *top* management was aware and committed to the effort.

It has as its main focus that of changing the attitudes, behaviors, and performance patterns of work groups rather than individuals. The emphasis is on realistic group goal setting, systematic planning, and problem solving. Such aspects of effective work groups as how best to work together, how to capitalize on the skills of members, how to communicate effectively, and how to manage and resolve intra- and intergroup conflict are among problem areas addressed.

OD is an ongoing and long-term process. People learn to work effectively together only as they face real problems and develop effective problem-solving skills. This cannot be accomplished quickly; behavior change and the skills needed are acquired only after much practice. Frequently, it is best to have a process consultant facilitate the work of the group. This person can be from within the parent organization but should be external to the target work group.

An OD process relies on action research and experiential learning. The data that are of most use are data about the ongoing system—its characteristics, issues, problems, and resources. This information is collected, analyzed, and returned in summary form to the work group. It forms the basis for problem identification, goal setting, and systematic problem resolution. The survey-feedback method of data collection/data analysis action planning is most frequently employed to facilitate this process.

Survey-feedback methods have a rich history. The method is essentially a systematic way of collecting information about the entire organization across several organizational dimensions. The process involves the development of an organizational questionnaire that is administered anonymously to organizational members.

The usual approach is to include questions about worker demographics and work group characteristics, as well as items that provide insight about such organizational dimensions as the nature of communication practices, organizational goal setting, decision-making practices, motivation and reward systems, and control practices, among other possible dimensions. In the often used survey of organizations, there is space for the organization to add its own questions about purely local issues and concerns.[10]

Once the data are collected, a computer analysis is performed and the information, appropriately categorized, is returned to the organization for the feedback/problem-solving effort to begin. Usually a consultant will feed the information back to the top administrative team first and then move through the organizational hierarchy. The process involves discussing the data, what the information means, and what might be done about it. Each administrator then meets with his or her own work group to interpret the data further and to develop corrective action plans.

Thus, just as HRD is far more than a cafeteria list of in-house seminars and on-the-job training, so is OD more than a few problem-solving groups working with a process consultant. Understanding and providing for the complexities of these two approaches brings sophistication and productivity to the staff and organizational development effort.

Implications for Leaders

The role of the principal in human resources and organizational development is a crucial one. Even if the school district is not operating on an enlightened development model, there is much that can occur at the school building level to address staff development systematically and provide for a responsive organization.

The Needs Assessment

What does the staff need? What does the staff want? Where is this expertise available? It is appropriate to survey the staff formally and such surveys should be more than a once-in-a-while activity.

A formal survey is not the only source of information about staff needs. If principals have been regularly and routinely engaging in clinical supervision, then they clearly will be in a good position to know what some of the important needs are on the faculty. Moreover, reviewing data in a systematic way about such things as pupil progress, demographic aspects of the community, changes in state law, federal programming, and impending curricular changes, among any number of other impinging forces, will be suggestive of current or impending development needs. The point here is that a principal must not feel bound to a survey when it is clear that there are pressing needs other than those recognized immediately by the staff.[11]

Making staff aware of changes on the horizon is one way to elevate a sense of need. Moreover, if the principal has been engaging in the postobservation feedback sessions essential to a clinical supervision process, this too is an awareness-raising activity. Urick and his colleagues prescribe the ARC model. The acronym stands for Awareness, Readiness, and Commitment, and the point of their manuscript is that these are the sequential building blocks to the success of any in-service development activity.[12]

Structuring and Monitoring the Development System

Whether the aspect of the human resources development program that is being addressed is individual in nature or is focused on the work group, there is a need for administrative support, an appropriate structure, and a monitoring system. Administrative support begins with needs assessment, of course. It continues when the expectations are established. It is buttressed by a willingness to engage others in the planning of the development efforts and a willingness to secure time and dollar resources to support the effort.

The nature of the need, who is to be involved, and whether the development is to be work group focused or individually oriented will, for the most part, determine the structure of the programs. If the program is an individually oriented one, then the IDP is probably the best approach. If the program is focused on the work group (school-wide, department, grade-level, teaching team, or whatever), then the structuring of the experiences becomes somewhat more complex. Once it is clear what it is that the group needs to know, and assuming that the group is at the stage of commitment, it is probably best to turn the planning of the development events over to the group itself. The principal's role then becomes one of facilitation rather than direction.[13]

Monitoring progress at regular intervals is important. In the instance of the IDP, regular conferences with the individual and/or the mentor, if there is one, is essential. This keeps the process a formative one and allows for appropriate adjustments. In the instance of group-development programs, it is equally essential that formative evaluation practices be present. All human resources development programs need regular assessment.

Positive Reinforcement

Learning and development—whether adult, adolescent, or child—are facilitated by positive reinforcement. Among a number of findings reported in a research synthesis about effective school practices was the following characteristic of leaders in these schools:

Leaders set up systems of incentives and rewards to encourage excellence in student and teacher performance; they act as figureheads in delivering awards and highlighting the importance of excellence.[14]

These findings highly correlate with those about successful management in the private sector:

The excellent companies have a deeply ingrained philosophy that says, in effect, respect the individual," "make people winners," "let them stand out," "treat people as adults."[15]

In sum, then, there are four implications to the principal who wants a well-developed, highly motivated staff:

- Development needs of the staff must be accurately assessed. Self-assessment is a starting point, but the principal must also conduct an investigation, using clinical observations in classrooms, student data, and current and foreseeable school and community concerns among other data sources.
- High standards of performance must be established and advertised. Setting performance standards in cooperation with staff members has been revealed to be the most effective practice.
- Human resources development systems require careful planning and a variety of approaches. IDPs as well as group development events must focus on recognized needs and be regularly monitored.
- Positive reinforcement techniques need to be consistently and continually employed. Public pats on the back, award ceremonies, private thank yous, bonuses for jobs well done—what Peters and Waterman call "hoopla"[16]—all serve to keep people congruent with the needs of the organization, and productively motivated.

Summary

Negative responses to organized efforts in the name of staff development are the result of a history of bad experiences with activities that have gone on in the name of inservice training. However well-intended such activities may have been, too frequently they have not addressed either the needs of the individual staff members or the needs of the organization.

Better approaches exist, and these approaches issue from a model of human resources development that recognizes the varied needs of individual organization members; the needs of the organization; the nature of adult learners; the time and effort required, depending on the nature of the knowledge, skill, or attitude to be acquired; and the impact that individuals have on the very nature and culture of the workplace.

Activities

1. Review Case Study 4. Apply the goal-setting and strategic planning concepts of Chapter 6 and the human resources development concepts expressed in this chapter. How might you proceed in addressing the problems cited in this case? Set forth a strategy to overcome the problem.

2. Review Case Study 7 and 12. Analyze the problems presented and apply the concepts of human resources development presented in this chapter. What approach would you use in addressing the problems? Set forth a strategy to overcome the difficulties faced by the schools in these cases.

Endnotes

1. S. K. Miller, S. R. Cohn, and R. H. Sayre, "Significant Achievement Gains Using Effective Schools Model." *Educational Leadership*, 42 (March 1985): 38–43.

2. Nevertheless, it is the responsibility of the principal to monitor these programs. Routine observations of staff members who exhibit less than adequate pedagogical skills or poor human relations skills or apparent deficiencies in knowledge of subject matter or bad communication skills, any or all, should be the basis for a conference, counseling, and prescribed remediation.

3. See Robert Goldhammer, *Clinical Supervision* (New York: Holt, Rinehart and Winston, 1969); and Morris Cogen, *Clinical Supervision* (New York: Houghton Mifflin, 1973).

4. Ronald Brandt, "On Teacher Evaluation: A Conversation with Tom McGreal." *Educational Leadership* 4, no. 7 (July 1987): 20–24.

5. A. A. Glatthorn, *Differentiated Supervision* (Alexandria, VA: Association for Supervision and Curriculum Development, 1984): and Carl D. Glickman, *Developmental Supervision* (Alexandria, VA: Association for Supervision and Curriculum Development, 1981).

6. K. Blanchard, D. Zigarmi, and P. Zagarmi, "Situational Leadership: 'Different Strokes for Different Folks.'" *Principal* 66, 4 (March 1987): 12–16. EJ 349–202.

7. Glatthorn, *Differentiated Supervision.*

8. An excellent reference for client-centered evaluations is the publication of the Educational Research Service, *The Evaluatee Evaluates the Evaluator* (Washington, DC: American Association of School Administrators and Research Division, NEA, No. 5, 1970).

9. A good treatment of the relationship of individual development organizational development can be found in Edgar H. Schein, *Career Dynamics: Matching Individual and Organizational Needs* (Reading, MA: Addison-Wesley, 1978).

10. The Institute for Social Research at the University of Michigan has a "Survey of Organizations" designed specifically for schools. A good source to learn more about survey-feedback methodology is David G. Bowers and Jerome L. Franklin. *Data-Based Organizational Change* (La Jolla, CA: University Associates, 1977).

11. The Survey should not be discounted, however. Commitment to improve is always more easily obtained when the individual to be improved personally recognize the need.

12. Ronald Urick, David Pendergast, and Larry W. Hillman, "Pre-Conditions for Staff Development." *Educational Leadership* 38, no. 7 (April 1981): 546–549.

13. As always, it is important to establish the ground rules when delegating such tasks. The principal will want to work with the group at the beginning to set the essential conditions that any development process must meet. Such things as budget, impinging systemwide policies, and so on that must be lived with in order for the plan to be implemented should be discussed and understood.

14. Northwest Regional Educational Laboratory, *Effective Schooling Practices: A Research Synthesis.* (Portland, OR: The Laboratory, 1984), p. 8.

15. Peters and Waterman, *In Search of Excellence,* p. 240.

16. Ibid.

Selected Readings

Acheson, Keith A. and Meredith, Gall. *Techniques in the Clinical Supervision of Teachers,* 2nd ed. (New York: Longman, 1987).

Bernstein, H. T., L. Darling-Hammond, M. W. McLaughlin, and A. E. Wise. *Teacher Evaluation: A Study of Effective Practices* (Santa Monica, CA: Rand, 1984).

DePasquale, Daniel, Jr. "Evaluating Tenured Teachers: A Practical Approach." *NASSP Bulletin* 74 (September 1990): 19–23.

Educational Research Service. *Teacher Evaluation: Practices and Procedures* (Arlington, VA: Educational Research Service, 1988).

Educational Resources Information Center. *The Best of ERIC on Educational Management: Teacher Evaluation.* NASSP Edition (Eugene, OR: Clearinghouse on Educational Management, College of Educational, University of Oregon, October 1989).

Goldstein, Irwin L. *Training in Organizations: Needs Assessment, Development and Evaluation*, 2nd ed. (Monterey, CA: Brooks/Cole, 1996).

Glatthorn, Allan. *Supervisory Leadership* (Glenview, IL: Scott, Foresman, 1990).

Glickman, Carl D. *Supervision of Instruction* (Boston: Allyn and Bacon, 1989).

Gordon, Bruce G. "Making Clinical Supervision a Reality: Steps Toward Implementation." *NASSP Bulletin* 76, no. 542 (March 1992): 46–51.

Harris, Ben M. *Supervisory Behavior in Education* (Englewood Cliffs, NJ: Prentice-Hall, 1985).

Hartzell, Gary N. "Avoiding Evaluation Errors: Fairness in Appraising Employee Performance," *NASSP Bulletin* 79 no. 567 (January 1995): 40–50.

Herman, Janice L., and Jerry J. Herman. "Defining Administrative Tasks, Evaluating Performance, and Developing Skills." *NASSP Bulletin* 79, no. 567 (January 1995): 16–21.

Hughes, Larry W., Mary Murphy, and Martha Wong. "Quality Assurance: Positive Approaches to Teacher Improvement." *Record in Educational Administration and Supervision* 5, no. 2 (Spring 1985): 11–13.

Hunter, M. "Knowing, Teaching, and Supervising." in *Using What We Know About Teaching,* ed.

P. L. Hosford (Alexandria, VA: Association for Supervision and Curriculum Development, 1984), pp. 169–192.

Joyce, B., and B. Showers. *Student Achievement Through Self Development* (New York: Longman, 1988).

Katims, David S., and Richard L. Henderson. "Teacher Evaluation in Special Education." *NASSP Bulletin* 74 (September 1990): 46–52.

Lane, Bruce A. "Personnel Evaluation: From Problems to School Improvement." *Journal of Research and Development in Education* 23, no. 4 (Summer 1990): 243–249.

Millman, Jason. *Handbook of Teacher Evaluation* (Beverly Hills, CA: Sage Publications, 1981).

Murphy, J., and P. Hallinger. "The Characteristics of Instructionally Effective School Districts." *Journal of Educational Research* 81, no. 3 (1987): 175–181.

National Association of Elementary School Principals. *Effective Teachers: Effective Evaluation in America's Elementary and Middle Schools* (NAESP, 1988).

Olthoff, Richard J. "The Principal as Instructional Coach-Providing Quality Education." *NASSP Bulletin* 76, no. 542 (March 1992): 6–12.

Pope, Carol A. "Indirect Teaching and Assessment: Are They Mutually Exclusive?" *NASSP Bulletin* 74 (September 1990): 1–5.

Scriven, M. "Validity in Personnel Evaluation." *Journal of Personnel Evaluation in Education* 1, no. 1 (1987): 9–23.

Shelton, Maria M., Kenneth Lane, and Patt Yuhasz. "Great Beginnings." *The Executive Educator* (January 1992): 27–29.

Sikorski, Melanie F., Richard P. Niemiec, and Herbert J. Walberg. "Best Teaching Practices: A Checklist for Observations." *NASSP Bulletin* 78 no. 561 (April 1994): 1–6.

Stufflebeam, Daniel L., Chair. *The Personnel Evaluation Standards: How to Assess Systems for Evaluating Educators.* The Joint Committee on Standards for Educational Evaluation (Beverly Hills, CA: Sage Publications, 1988).

Thorson, J. R., et al., "Instructional Improvement Through Personnel Evaluation." *Educational Leadership* 44 (April 1987): 52–54.

Wood, Carolyn J. "Toward More Effective Teacher Evaluation: Lessons from Naturalistic Inquiry." *NASSP Bulletin* 76, no. 542 (March 1992): 52–59.

Zumwalt, K. *Improving Teaching* (Arlington, VA: Association for Supervision and Curriculum Development, 1986).

Chapter 14

Staffing the School

Recruitment, Selection, and Termination Processes

*Selecting quality teachers may be the single most important
thing you do as an administrator. A beginning high school
teacher who stays in the class room for a thirty-year
career can have had almost 5,000 students under their
instruction by the time they retire. —G. C. UBBEN*[1]

Recruitment and selection policies of local schools vary. The principal's involvement
in the recruitment and selection process will depend on local district practice and policy. Central office personnel often assume the initial responsibility for the recruitment
and screening of applicants for teaching positions. The principal should maintain a
major role in the process and aggressively pursue it, if necessary. Central offices, often
as a means of expediency and sometimes as a policy of control, tend to limit the input
of principals and staff in the selection process. Under the concept of site-based management, if the principal is to be held in any way accountable for the quality of instruction in his or her building, he or she must have a major voice, if not the final voice, in
the selection of personnel.

Recruitment

The major recruitment efforts of the principal begin with good position and person
descriptions. Figures 14–1 and 14–2 depict sample position and person descriptions. If
the principal finds it difficult to locate appropriate candidates, central office personnel
should be contacted to review the recruitment process. For example, if the principal, in
an effort to diversify the staff, has asked for a teacher from somewhere other than the

FIGURE 14–1   Person Description

Lakeview Schools
219 Lakeview Ave.
Lake City

Person Description
Position: Elementary Teacher
Sex: Prefer male
Teaching Experience Necessary: None
Training Requirements: BS; prefer graduates from other than local college
Certification: Elementary, K–3
Teaching Strength: Strong reading training; interest in social studies
Other Skills: Prefer someone with training or experience with team teaching or cooperative
    learning
Other interests: Prefer someone with a vocational interests that would appeal to young boys
    such as camping, hiking, model airplane making, and so on

Source: Larry W. Hughes and Gerald C. Ubben, *The Elementary Principal's Handbook: A Guide to Effective Action*, 4th ed. Boston: Allyn and Bacon, 1994, p. 238. Used with permission.

FIGURE 14–2   Position Description

Lakeview Schools
219 Lakeview Ave.
Lake City

Position Description
Position Title: Teacher (team) grade-level elementary 1–3
Purpose of Position: To plan, organize, and instruct primary children
Starting Date:
Salary Range: Beginning teacher,   B.S.—$25,000
                                        M.S.—$30,000
Principal Duties: The teacher will be a member of a four-teacher team working with six-to-
    eight-year-old children. Instruction is organized on an interdisciplinary basis with coopera-
    tive planning units. The team has four assigned classrooms and schedules children in a flex-
    ible manner into these spaces. Major instructional responsibilities will include reading and
    mathematics as well as participation in the integration of other subjects.
Performance Responsibilities:
   I. Instructional Skills
      A. Knowledge and Training
         1. Is academically competent in assigned teaching areas.
         2. Keeps abreast of new findings and current trends in the field.
         3. Remains open-minded and willing to grow and change.
         4. Provides opportunities for all students to experience success.
      B. Classroom Environment and Management
         1. Maintains a classroom environment conducive to learning (by using special interest
            areas, learning centers, units, themes, furniture arrangements, proper lighting, heat-
            ing, ventilation, and structured rules and regulations understood and accepted by all).
         2. Monitors individual pupil progress and adapts the pace of instruction accordingly.
         3. Uses democratic procedures that show consideration for the rights of others.
      C. Methods and Techniques
         1. Uses a variety of stimulating instructional techniques (such as the lecture method,
            demonstration, self-directed activities, both small and large group activities [drill

Continued

FIGURE 14–2 *Continued*

and rote activities], and community resources, audiovisual aids and individualized programs).

2. Demonstrates and fosters the growth of communication skills.
3. Presents subject matter in a functional manner.
4. Makes homework assignments for meaningful instructional purposes.

   D. Planning
1. Establishes short- and long-range goals with well-defined objectives and identifies appropriate procedures to accomplish them. (Example: A minimum competency and curriculum guide.)
2. Provides opportunities for all students to experience success.
3. Has a well-defined alternative plan for substitute teachers.

   E. Evaluation
1. Provides feedback to students on their accomplishments and progress with positive and effective reinforcements.
2. Uses instruments based on activity, objective, or goal-oriented criteria.
3. Guides students toward self-motivation, self-evaluation, and self-direction.

II. Student Attitudes and Performance
   A. Demonstrates consistency, firmness and impartiality in dealing with students in a professional manner.
   B. Appreciates individuality.
   C. Shows positive attitudes toward students by helping all children experience success, possibly through the use of tutorial and counseling activities.
   D. Promotes desirable standards of work and behavior within the classroom.

III. Personal Qualities
   A. Demonstrates a positive and enthusiastic attitude and a genuine interest in students, colleagues, curriculum, and the education field in general.
   B. Recognizes and capitalizes on his or her own assets, thereby projecting a good model for students in dress, demeanor, and speech.
   C. Is able to profit from constructive criticism.
   D. Shows qualities that reflect the importance of punctuality, efficiency, dependability, accuracy, and congeniality.

IV. Professional Growth and Development
   A. Participates in enrichment activities, including such activities as study in his or her field and/or travel.
   B. Actively pursues avenues of personal and professional growth through workshops, classes, professional organizations, and seminars.
   C. Establishes personal goals for professional development.

V. Teacher Relationships
   A. Teacher-Parent
1. Establishes an effective line of communication between home and school via notes, conferences, written reports, work samples, telephone conversations, and meetings of groups such as the PTO that stress discussion of students' strengths and weaknesses.
2. Encourages parents to form a partnership with the teacher in the total education of their child—mentally, emotionally, physically, and spiritually.

   B. Teacher-Community
1. Works effectively with legitimate community organizations and identifies and utilizes community resources to augment the educational opportunities of the children.
2. Projects a positive image of the total school program to the community; liaison function is served.

   C. Teacher-Teacher
1. Cooperates fully with colleagues in shared responsibilities.

FIGURE 14–2 *Continued*

    2. Shows tolerance for peer differences.
    3. Shares experiences, ideas, and knowledge with peers.
    4. Communicates effectively with other teachers who have shared or will share the same students for the purpose of developing smooth continuity between grade levels and subject matter.
  D. Teacher-Administrator-Supervisor
    1. Understands and adheres to the chain of command.
    2. Participates in decision making when appropriate.
    3. Demonstrates cooperation in performing both classroom and extra duties.
    4. Seeks advice and counsel when needed.
    5. Forms a partnership to develop good public relations in the school district.
  E. Teacher-Student
    1. Recognizes the uniqueness of all students.
    2. Guides and encourages students in a friendly, constructive, and impartial manner.
    3. Initiates procedures that will invite regular feedback for students.
    4. Maintains a classroom atmosphere conducive to mutual respect, one that adequately establishes appropriate roles.

Source: Larry W. Hughes and Gerald C. Ubben, *The Elementary Principal's Handbook: A Guide to Effective Action*, 4th ed. Boston: Allyn and Bacon, 1994, pp. 238–240. Used with permission.

local college, and the personnel office has not posted vacancies at other colleges, the recruitment drive will be ineffective. The principal must assume responsibility for seeing that recruitment policies are broad enough to meet personnel needs.

The selection of personnel should be a cooperative effort between the district personnel office and the local school. The central-office role should be to screen applicants and then to send those best matching the position descriptions to the principal for final selection. In some large school districts, a personnel office may employ teachers unassigned to specific buildings, but even in this case, the building principal should have the final decision regarding who works in the building.

The greatest problem in the selection of new staff members often comes from the need of the central office to place "transfers." These are generally tenured employees who must be moved from a previous assignment in the district. Since they are tenured, the school district must place them ahead of any new hires. Although there may be many legitimate reasons for the transfer of employees within a school district, some school districts have a bad habit of playing "pass the trash." This is the practice of allowing the transfer of poor or incompetent teachers from school to school rather than going through the process of dismissal. Once again, as a principal, you must evaluate each candidate for a position in your school on the basis of what you think is best for your school.

The principles of site-based management and the concepts of teacher empowerment strengthen your position in employing new members of your staff. Involve the leadership team in setting policies for the selection of new staff members and involve members of your teaching staff in the interview and selection process. This will increase the principal's power base in resisting undesirable placements of staff by a central personnel office.

Federal Regulations to Prevent Employment Discrimination

Care must always be taken to abide by the federal laws regarding recruitment and selection of staff. The Civil Rights Act of 1964 and the Equal Employment Opportunity Act of 1972 and their several amendments as well as the more recent Americans with Disabilities Act (ADA) of 1992 make it unlawful to discriminate on the basis of race, color, religion, sex, age, national origin, or disabling condition.

EEOC Regulations
It is unlawful to ask about the following on either a written application or during an interview.

1. Complexion or color of skin.
2. Applicant's religious denomination, affiliation, church, parish, pastor, or religious holidays observed.
3. Applicant's sex, marital status, name or other information about spouse, or ages of children if any.
4. Whether applicant has a disability or has been treated for any of certain diseases. However, you may ask if the applicant has any physical impairments that would affect the ability to perform the job for which the applicant has applied.
5. If the applicant has ever been arrested. You may ask if the applicant has been convicted of a crime.
6. Any previous name that the applicant has used. You may ask if he or she worked for your organization under a different name, (e.g., a maiden name).
7. Birthplace or birthplace of applicant's parents or spouse; birthdate or certificate of naturalization papers, and so on.
8. Require the applicant's photograph before hiring.
9. Whether the applicant or a relative is a citizen of a foreign country. You may ask if the applicant is a U.S. citizen, intends to become one, or has a legal right to be in the United States.
10. The applicant's native language. You may ask which languages the applicant speaks and writes.
11. Questions or information about the applicant's relatives. Prior to employment, you may not even ask the name of a person to contact in case of emergency.
12. The clubs, societies, and lodges to which the applicant belongs. You may ask the applicant to list organizations he or she believes to be pertinent to the job.

After the individual has been employed, many of these items of information can then legally be asked on an employee information form but cannot appear or be asked on an application or during an interview.

Americans with Disabilities Act (ADA)
The Americans with Disabilities Act prohibits employers, public and private, from discriminating against any individual with a disability. The law covers the full range of employment activities, including recruiting and hiring, terminations, compensation, job assignment and advancement, and training. The law requires that employers make

reasonable accommodation in the workplace to enable the individual to perform fundamental job duties of a position. This may require providing properly positioned chalkboards, or new technology to allow the disabled person to function successfully. Often, the workplace itself is more of a barrier to the physically challenged than job skills and knowledge. Care must be shown to not exclude anyone from consideration for employment because of his or her disabling condition if he or she is capable of performing the essential functions called for by that position.

The Selection Process

The selection process for employing staff has several steps.

Screening

The first step is application clarification. Prior to an interview, the principal should carefully review the candidate's application file, comparing the application with the personal description. Few candidates will possess all the qualifications that have been specified, but the principal should try to find candidates with most of them.[2]

Discrepancy Analysis

The second step in the selection process should be a discrepancy analysis of the application materials. Applicants present themselves in the best manner possible, minimizing weak points. One technique used to uncover discrepancies is to search the file for missing information. Common problem areas are efforts to conceal unfavorable past activities by excluding dates and not listing appropriate reference sources. Other things to check for include health and legal problems.

The reviewer should look particularly at references from previous employers to make sure each employment situation is represented. Read between the lines on health records. Look for gaps in employment or school records. The interviewer can request more detailed explanations concerning those areas where possible discrepancies have been identified. Most often, candidates will give perfectly acceptable explanations regarding the discrepancies, but occasionally interviews uncover serious problems by a discrepancy review.

Reference Check

If the job candidate has had previous teaching experience and is one of the final candidates being considered for the position, a personal telephone contact with the previous principal or some other school administrator who is acquainted with the candidate is usually helpful. Often, interviewers can obtain more information during a phone call than from a written reference.

Care must be taken, however, in the manner in which questions are asked. Similarly, you must be careful, in answering any questions asked of you regarding a previous employee. The courts have held that in cases of employee nonreemployment where no charges have been officially brought and where no dismissal hearing has been held, an employer is restricted in the negative comments he or she may make about a previous employee. This is based on the concept that such comments could limit the opportunity of that former employee to obtain employment elsewhere and therefore place a limit on that former employees "liberty," a right that is protected under the amendments to the federal Constitution.[3] Therefore, employers must use care in stating opinions regarding former employees' performance.

These court decisions, however, do not prevent you from either asking for references or in answering questions. Nevertheless, they do signal that you must stick to the facts rather than delving into opinion or gossip. Similarly when asking for information from a previous employer, recognize that this individual is under the same limitation, and should hesitate in answering questions of a speculative nature. Ask for factual information about the previous employee. One very telling question that the former employer can answer is: "If the person in question would seek a job in your school again, would you rehire him or her?" If the answer is anything but extremely positive, it should raise a caution flag for you.

The Job Interview

The job interview has several basic functions. It provides an opportunity for the candidate to clarify any apparent discrepancies found in the written job application. The job interview, however, goes beyond the written application by allowing the principal to gather information in greater depth than can be obtained from written materials only.

The interview also allows the principal to gain insights into the personality and interpersonal skills of the applicant. Teaching is a "people" business, and teachers must be able to relate well to other adults and children. Research has shown that good verbal skills are particularly significant in determining the quality of a teacher. These skills call best be assessed through an interview. Whenever possible, an employment recommendation should be based on group interaction with the principal and the existing staff.

Interviews should be arranged to involve teachers, department heads, and team members in the process. This is one additional way to empower teachers. Some will argue that under the concept of site-based management, your local site board should also be involved. It is the authors' belief that staff selection is a task to be delegated to the professional staff based on policy set by the local site board, but that board members should not be involved directly in the selection process. The one exception to this might be if the central office continues to dictate personnel placements for your school. Then the clout of your site-based management might be needed to veto unwanted placements.

When staff members are asked to participate in the interview process, they also are obligated to follow the EEOC guidelines regarding appropriate questions. It is usually wise to hold a short refresher course before staff members interview candidates to remind them of appropriate and inappropriate questions.

Interviews can be conducted using a variety of different formats. Here is an interview agenda that is well accepted:

1. *Establish the atmosphere.* Open the interview slowly and try to create a warm, pleasant relaxed atmosphere that will reduce the candidate's anxiety.

2. *Ask focused questions.* Such questions will elicit the knowledge and information you need about the candidate. You want to learn of his or her perceptions of personal strengths and weaknesses, his or her understanding and philosophy of education, his or her verbal fluency, and his or her ability to project enthusiasm. The use of "what if" questions often works well to get the candidate indirectly to share these beliefs and attitudes with you.

3. *Be an active listener.* Ask open-ended questions rather than yes-no questions. Support the candidate verbally with "uh-huhs," or "tell me more." He or she should be contributing about 70 percent of the conversation to your 30 percent during the interview.

4. *Share school information with the candidate.* Remember the candidate also has a decision to make ("Do I want to come to work for you?"). Tell him or her about the specific job vacancy; with whom he or she may be working, particularly if those individuals met the candidate; the kinds of children enrolled in the school; particular programs that the school may have; and information about the school community if the candidate is not from that area.

5. *Close the interview.* Thank the individual for his or her time and openness. Share the next steps in the selection process including when he or she might expect to hear from you or how he or she might keep up with the decision process.

6. *Write out your notes.* Gather information from the others who participated in the interview process. Often a team discussion works well. If several candidates are to be interviewed before a decision is made, the use of a checklist or some formatted method of recording your perceptions is wise so that later comparison can be more objective.

Employee Probationary Status

The selection process for staff continues through the probationary phase. Most states have a one- to three-year probationary period during which the employee is on a continuing contract before receiving tenured employment. During this period, the principal and department head must reaffirm the original decision to employ a particular staff member. Usually, the contract renews automatically around April 15 unless notification is given to the teacher for nonrenewal. Through the continuation of the orientation phase and evaluation of instructional competence, which is discussed in more detail in a subsequent chapter, the emphasis for staff development is on improving the quality of teaching. The selection process is usually considered complete only when tenure is granted. During this probationary period, the principal must consider the possibility of termination or nonrenewal of the contract when there is reason to suspect that the original selection was not wise.

Teacher Tenure

One of the most misunderstood concepts in education is tenure. It is not, as often believed, a guarantee of a job from which dismissal is all but impossible. Rather, in most states, tenure is simply a statement of the guarantee of due process assuring exercise of academic freedom for the teacher by allowing dismissal only for specific causes listed in the tenure law. Tenure does not guarantee the right to a job. If the job is abolished or a teacher is found to be incompetent, insubordinate, or guilty of a variety of socially unacceptable behaviors, that teacher can be dismissed, with proper due process.

In the last few years, federal courts have broadened their decisions regarding due process and human rights to the point that due-process guarantees, including many of the guarantees found in the tenure laws, have been extended to most employees. As a result, probationary teachers are now guaranteed many of the same due-process rights afforded tenured teachers in the past.[4]

Involuntary Termination

An extremely poor or incompetent teacher should never be kept on the staff of a school simply because dismissal is difficult. The law establishes definite rights for employer and employee. Procedural due process is guaranteed, but due process does not mean that teachers cannot be dismissed. What it does mean is that teachers have specific rights, such as the right to a hearing, the right to be treated in a fair and nondiscriminatory fashion, and the right to require that just cause be shown for a dismissal action. The law may be more specific about the causes and process of dismissal for teachers under tenure, but dismissal can still be accomplished.

Every dismissal action should be carried out on the assumption that it will ultimately go to court. This attitude is the best way to prevent court action. Rarely will an attorney engaged by a dismissed teacher or provided by a teacher association take a case to court if the school district has prepared its action carefully. When the courts reject the dismissal and order reinstatement of a teacher, it is most often because of improper procedure on the part of the school district and less likely due to teacher behavior.

Preparation for Dismissal

Dismissal decisions should not be made quickly. A tentative decision not to rehire a first-year teacher for the following year should be contemplated three to four months before the deadline for contract renewal. For a tenured teacher, often two or three years are needed to build a case defensible in court to reverse earlier recommendations that were positive enough to have resulted in tenure, even though the recommendations may have been a mistake. Unfortunately, poor personnel records and poor evaluation procedures are common in school districts.

The defense attorney will often demand to see the entire personnel file for a teacher being dismissed. If positive evaluations have been given in the past, even though they were unjustified, a greater collection of data of a negative nature is required to offset them. Evidence that the teacher received specific notice of inadequacy and was offered help is important.

In a hearing, the courts will try to answer the following questions: Was procedural due process used? Is the evidence appropriate and supportive of the case? Was the employee discriminated against? Were efforts made to help the employee? Did the employee have prior knowledge that his or her work was unsatisfactory? Was the employee provided time and the opportunity to improve or correct whatever deficiencies existed?

Due Process

Teachers must be given timely notice of the decision not to rehire. If contract renewal comes on April 15, with a two-week hearing notice deadline, employees should be notified by April 1. A certified letter is the best way of assuring a record of such notification. Employees must be informed that they have the opportunity for and the right to a hearing. The hearing time, date, and place should be stated in the letter. If the teacher is tenured, the letter should also include the specific causes or charges for dismissal. Recent due process decisions from the courts in some cases make it highly advisable to provide this opportunity for a hearing to nontenured teachers as well as to those who have tenure.[5, 6, 7]

Appropriateness of Evidence

Evidence should be firsthand, factual, and documented accurately with appropriate dates. If the offense is cumulative in nature, the collection of data should also be cumulative. Descriptive notes of supervisory meetings and conferences—for example, expressing agreed-upon outcomes and a statement describing the extent of the implementation or the lack thereof on the part of the teacher—should be included. The statements should be objective. Rather than stating, "This teacher did a poor job of teaching today," the note should state that in presenting a lesson on the Civil War the teacher did not hold the interest of the class, the students did not understand the lesson as presented, and the class became unruly while under the teacher's direction. Include the date; the time; the events that led up to the conference, such as the previous involvement of a supervisor; and any immediate follow-up action that was taken. A note might simply read, "Mr. Smith arrived at school at 8:30 on December 2, 3, and 4. His designated time of arrival is 8:00. He has been notified of this deficiency." This is not a judgmental statement but a simple statement of fact. Such items, properly collected, can be used to support a claim of incompetence, neglect of duty, or insubordination. The important thing to remember is to record facts, not opinions, and to do this in a timely fashion.

Equal Rights

Was the employee treated in a fair and nondiscriminatory manner? Was anything done to or for this employee that was not done or available to other employees? Was the assignment unfair? Was the teacher asked to do more or less than the rest of the staff? Was supervision uniform? A grossly unequal schedule for supervision, for example, can be construed to be harassment. When problems arise, however, it is not unreasonable for supervision to increase as long as the time sequence can be demonstrated. Supervisory appointments and documentation included only in the file of the teacher being dismissed with no evidence of supervision included in the files of the other members of the staff, however, will often be looked upon as discriminatory action by the courts.

Were Efforts Made to Help the Teacher?

The courts will want to know what was done to make this individual an effective employee. Was adequate supervision of a helping nature developed? Was adequate time given for the improvement effort? If not, the courts may not uphold the dismissal action but may reinstate the employee, suggesting that the supervisory staff provide assistance.

Most often, when the principal is well prepared and has central-office support, teacher dismissal, while serious, will take place quietly. A teacher who knows that school officials are well prepared most often will not request a hearing and will simply resign. Most cases resulting in the failure to dismiss are a result of poor preparation and improper procedure on the part of the school district. See Figure 14–3 for a flowchart for employee dismissal procedures.

Voluntary Termination

Each year staff members will resign from a school for a variety of reasons: retirement, transfers, better jobs, starting a family, going back to school, and incompetence. In every case the principal should hold a termination interview before that person departs. Several basic purposes exist for such an interview. Of primary concern is the help the school might offer the individual in adjusting to a new life situation.

Second, the interview should be an opportunity to investigate the perceptions of the departing employee regarding the operation of the school. At times, principals have difficulty getting good information about the operation of the school and the existing climate within the staff. Often, departing employees will be very candid about their perceptions concerning existing problems. They may even identify some previously hidden reason for leaving.

Finally, the interview can be useful in identifying prospects for substitute, part-time, volunteer, and future employment when the departing employee is planning to remain within the community. Retired teachers, or those who are staying home to rear a family, are particularly good candidates for part-time employment or volunteer positions.

Summary

The search for and the employment of new staff members is one of the most important tasks of a school administrator. The process begins with the determination of staff needs—including recruitment, selection, orientation, and staff development—and culminates with the placement of the employee on tenure.

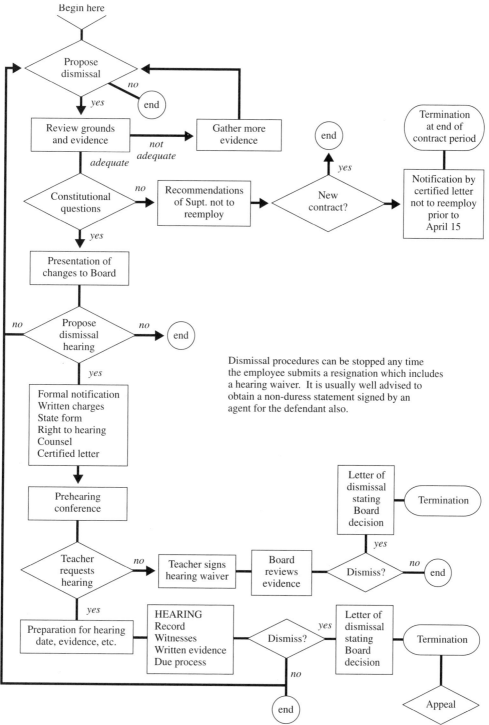

Begin here

Propose dismissal → *no* → end

yes ↓

Review grounds and evidence → *not adequate* → Gather more evidence

adequate ↓

Constitutional questions → *no* → Recommendations of Supt. not to reemploy → New contract? → *yes* → end

New contract? → Notification by certified letter not to reemploy prior to April 15

Termination at end of contract period

yes ↓

Presentation of changes to Board

no ← Propose dismissal hearing → *no* → end

yes ↓

Dismissal procedures can be stopped any time the employee submits a resignation which includes a hearing waiver. It is usually well advised to obtain a non-duress statement signed by an agent for the defendant also.

Formal notification
Written charges
State form
Right to hearing
Counsel
Certified letter

↓

Prehearing conference

↓

Teacher requests hearing → *no* → Teacher signs hearing waiver → Board reviews evidence → Dismiss? → *no* → end

Dismiss? → *yes* → Letter of dismissal stating Board decision → Termination

yes ↓

Preparation for hearing date, evidence, etc. → HEARING Record Witnesses Written evidence Due process → Dismiss? → *yes* → Letter of dismissal stating Board decision → Termination

Dismiss? → *no* → end

Termination → Appeal

FIGURE 14–3   Steps in Dismissal Procedures

Source: Larry W. Hughes and Gerald C. Ubben, *The Elementary Principal's Handbook: A Guide to Effective Action*, 4th ed. Boston: Allyn and Bacon, 1994, p. 248. Used with permission.

Termination of employees, voluntarily or involuntarily, will occur in most schools each year. The principal needs to conduct exit interviews with all terminating employees. Involuntary termination is usually a difficult, but sometimes necessary, task. An important point in staff dismissal is following due process and ensuring that the employee's rights have not been violated.

Activities

1. Review Case Studies 7, 12, and 16. Analyze the problems presented and apply the concepts of staff evaluation developed in this chapter. What approach would you use in addressing the problems? Set forth a strategy to overcome the difficulties faced by the individuals in these cases.

2. Develop a plan for the evaluation of the staff in your school. Over what portion of the year should it run? How much of your time will it take to conduct an evaluation of your faculty members? Should you evaluate all teachers each year? If not, which teachers get priority evaluations? What about other nonteaching staff members? What is your responsibility for their evaluation? How much of your time will this take?

Endnotes

1. G. C. Ubben, class lecture, University of Tennessee, Knoxville, October 1995.
2. Gerald C. Ubben, "Selecting Personnel." *Principal's Audio Journal* 1 (December 1974). Cassette Services, St. Paul, VA.
3. *Board or Regents* v. *Roth*, 92 S. Ct. 2701 (1972). This case dealt with the nonreemployment of a nontenured teacher who had difficulty obtaining another job because of comments made by the administrators of the nonreemploying school. The teacher charged that his right to "liberty" was violated by his inability to obtain other employment because of his lack of opportunity to defend himself against unheard charges. The Supreme Court found that his due process rights were violated and ordered that he be given a hearing and back pay.
4. See Chapter 5 for information about the steps in procedural due process.
5. See Chapter 5, especially the reference to *Illinois Education Association* v. *Board of Education*, 320 N.E. 2nd 240 (Ill. App. 1974).
6. Cases Related to Due Process—Teacher Dismissal
   a. *Board of Regents* v. *Roth*, 92 S. Ct. 2701 (1972) and *Perry* v. *Sunderman*, 928 Ct.

2694 (1972). These are the precedent-setting cases regarding due process just as *Brown* v. *Board of Education* set the precedent for discrimination cases.
   b. *Paul* v. *Davis*, 424 U.S. 693 (1976); *Bishop* v. *Wood*, 246 U.S. 341 (1976); and *Meachum* v. *Fano*, 427 U.S. 215 (1970).
   c. 7th Cir., the Court of Appeals in *Confederation of Police* v. *City of Chicago*, 547 F. 2d 375 (1977).
   d. *Codd* v. *Velger*, 97 S. Ct. 882 (1977).
   e. *Arnet* v. *Kennedy*, 416 U.S. 134 (1974).
   f. *Peacock* v. *Board of Regents*, 510 F 2d 1324 (9th Cir.)
   g. *Withrow* v. *Larken*, 421 U.S. 35 (1975).
   h. Hortonville 96S Ct. 2308.
   i. *Mt. Healthy City School District* v. *Doyle*, 97 S. Ct. 568 (1977).
7. Although most state tenure laws and continuing contract laws in and of themselves do not require a hearing for nontenured staff, the federal Constitution and the Civil Rights Act of 1964 might. According to a series of court decisions over recent years, a teacher is considered to have certain rights under the First and Fourteenth Amendments to the Constitution. While

nonrenewal of a contract does not require a hearing, dismissal does. If a denial-of-freedom-of-speech claim is made, a hearing is advisable, and if the case is receiving much publicity so as to endanger the individual's opportunity for other employment, a hearing should be held. Also, if discrimination is charged, a hearing should be held. If an opportunity for a hearing is not granted, the teacher may later file a complaint charging violation of due process.

Selected Readings

Beckham, J. *Legal Aspects of Teacher Evaluation* (Topeka, KS: National Organization on Legal Problems of Education, 1981). ED 207 126.

Bridges, E. M. *The Management of Incompetence* (Stanford, CA: Institute for Research on Educational Finance and Governance, Technical Report, 1983).

Bridges, E. M., and P. Gumport. *The Dismissal of Tenured Teachers for Incompetence* (Stanford, CA: Institute for Research on Educational Finance and Governance, Technical Report, 1984).

Carey, W. C. *Documenting Teacher Dismissal* (Salem, OR: Options Press, 1981).

Castetter, William B. *The Personnel Function in Educational Administration*, rev. ed. (New York: Macmillan, 1986).

Dolgin, A. "Two Types of Due Process: The Role of Supervision in Teacher Dismissal Cases." *NASSP Bulletin* 65, no. 442 (February 1981): 17–21.

Frels, K., and T. T. Cooper. *A Documentation System for Teacher Improvement or Termination* (Topeka, KS: National Organization on Legal Problems of Education, 1982). EDRS ED 228 725.

French-Lazovik, G. "Peer Review," in *Handbook of Teacher Evaluation*, ed. J. Millman (Beverly Hills: Sage Publications, 1981), pp. 73–89.

Hooker, Clifford (Ed.). *The Courts and Education, 77th Yearbook of the National Society for the Study of Education* (Chicago: University of Chicago Press. 1978). Especially see the chapter entitled "Frontiers of Law."

Kaufman, H. G. *Professionals in Search of Work* (New York: John Wiley and Sons, 1982).

Larson, D. H. "Advice for the Principal: Dealing with Unsatisfactory Teacher Performance." *NASSP Bulletin* 65, no. 442 (February 1981): 10–11.

Maslinowski, A. A. "An Empirical Analysis of Discharge Cases and the Work History of Employees Reinstated by Labor Arbitrations." *Arbitration Journal* 36, no. 1 (March 1981): 31–46.

Martin, Cynthia. "Hiring the Right Person: Techniques for Principals." *NASSP Bulletin* 77, no. 550 (February 1993): 79–83.

McDaniel, S. H., and T. R. McDaniel. "How to Weed Out Incompetent Teachers without Getting Hauled into Court." *National Elementary Principal* 59, no. 3 (March 1980): 31–36.

O'Reilly, C. A., and B. A. Weitz. "Marginal Employees: The Use of Warnings and Dismissals." *Administrative Science Quarterly* (1980): 467–484.

Pawlas, George E. "The Structured Interview: Three Dozen Questions To Ask Prospective Teachers." *NASSP Bulletin* 79, no. 567 (January 1995): 62–65.

Vann, Allan S. "The Pre-Employment Interview: Asking the Right Questions." *Principal* 73, no. 3 (January 1994): 38–41.

Chapter 15

Computer Applications for School Management

As Jim came into his office, he flipped on his computer. It had become almost as automatic as turning on the lights. Sitting down at his desk, he reviewed his e-mail to see if any messages had been downloaded to him overnight from the district office. But only a reminder that his new budget proposals for next year were to be in the district business office that day had been sent.

Reaching up and touching one of the keys, Jim brought his "daily reminder" to the screen for today and added the budget reminder as item 8 to those previously listed. Touching another key, his "daily calendar" for today appeared before him, and Jim noted that his 8:30 appointment that morning was with the parents of Maury McDonald. Realizing he needed to review Maury's case, he accessed the student database, entered his password, and requested the discipline file for McDonald. He printed out the dates of incidents of the past year from Maury's discipline file as well as the detailed reports that had been entered by the counselor at Maury's suspension several days earlier.

In his few remaining minutes while waiting for the 8:30 conference, Jim penciled in several modifications to rough drafts of letters his secretary had typed for him the previous day. In past years, he might have allowed the letters to go unmodified because he didn't like to put the extra burden of retyping on his already overworked secretary; but now with word processing, corrections were easy and did not require total retyping if modifications were desired.

Later, upon completion of his conference with the McDonalds, Jim returned to his computer and entered into the discipline record a short note indicating the result of Maury's conference. Jim next loaded his electronic spreadsheet into the computer on which he had been preparing his new budget. He entered the several changes he had been contemplating, checked his updated totals, and printed a copy of the revised budget document to share with his department heads in his afternoon meeting.

Continuing his perpetration for his afternoon department head's meeting, Jim loaded his presentation graphics program. He quickly created four bulleted slides to illustrate the major points he wanted to emphasize in his meeting and moved them to a floppy disk to load into the computer in the conference room.

The initial tasks completed, Jim now turned to a draft of the new student handbook. It was being produced on the office computer with desktop-publishing software and would be produced with a laser printer. The result would be professional looking and complete with graphics.

Does this scenario seem farfetched? Every one of the functions identified during Jim's busy morning on his computer is already available and in common use by administrators today. Electronic mail as a part of a local area network (LAN), word processing, desktop publishing, daily reminders and calendars, student record systems, and spreadsheets, as well as many more useful applications, are available for school principals. Software and hardware are available and the cost is not high. The potential saving in time can be great, and the access to more information for more effective administration is tremendous.

How to Get Started

By now, most schools can boast of having at least several computers. Chances are the first computer acquisition, as well as those that followed, went for instructional use directly by the students. It has not been uncommon for schools to then add a computer for teacher use, or possibly for use in the office. Often, the new computer purchase is of the same type and model purchased for the students. This may not, however, be the correct machine for office use. If many of the functions carried out by the principal in the beginning of this chapter (Jim) are to be implemented, equipment with greater capacity and more features than instructional computers may be needed.

It is best to plan for the development of computer applications in three distinct steps:

1. Review and determine the potential computer applications for your office.
2. Identify the software that can accomplish these applications.
3. Select hardware that will run the selected software, giving consideration to needs of capacity of the system and compatibility with other users.

Ultimately, the school is probably going to want to link together several computers for the principal, secretary, teachers, and guidance staff as well as develop the ability to communicate with remote sites such as the district office.

A Review of Potential Computer Applications for a School Office

Word Processing

Word processing is a computer application that allows the machine to be used to produce text documents as would a typewriter. However, the document is created on the screen and stored electronically in memory. Documents can be produced, edited, stored, printed, or sent electronically to another computer. A document can be recalled at any time when further editing is desired or additional copies are needed.

The typical school produces many documents that require periodic updating, demanding in many cases that the entire document be retyped in order for it to be properly formatted. Documents such as student handbooks, policy manuals, staff rosters, standard memos, and curriculum guides are generally modified and updated each year. These items are great candidates for the efficiencies of word processing. In addition, many form letters are used regularly in most school offices for discipline reports, absence notices, scheduling appointments, and the like, usually with blanks to be filled in with the name of the student or parent, or meeting time, or whatever. These documents can be prepared very efficiently with a professional look using the "data merge" capability of the word processor.

The merge feature allows form letters to be personalized with individual names, addresses, and any other data desired directly into the body of the letter or the document. Some of the better programs will allow either the combining of a database such as a name and address file with a form letter, or screen entry into the occasionally used form letter that is needed infrequently or in few copies. A suspension or discipline letter such as the one found in Figure 15–1 is an illustration. The code names called variables found between the "&" symbol are replaced with the data for the particular person or persons who are to receive that letter. For example, for each of the three lines shown in Figure 15–2, a copy of the letter would be typed inserting the proper parent name, address, student name, date, and time in each letter.

Desktop Publishing

Desktop publishing can be used for the many documents schools produce in multiple copies and distribute to faculty, students, parents, and other community members. There are many font styles and sizes and the capability exists to produce graphics and photographs. A variety of page layouts for multicolumn pages is available. The result is professional-looking booklets, newsletters, and forms.

Database Management Systems

A *database management system* is a computer application that allows the user to enter information into the computer to be later sorted, selected, listed, recalled, manipulated, or printed. The information entered usually is of a uniform nature (such as a series of names, addresses, and phone numbers) and is probably currently filed on one of the

FIGURE 15–1   Merge Letter Illustration

&DATE&

&NAME&
&ADDRESS&
&CITYSTZIP&
Dear &NAME&:

Regular attendance at school is very important to children if they are to do their best work. It is also important that your child establish good attendance habits in preparing for future employment.

The state of Tennessee recognizes the importance of attending school regularly and has a law requiring children to attend from their seventh until their seventeenth birthday.

According to the law, you are held responsible for &STUDENT&'s school attendance. I know you are interested in &STUDENT&'s education, and those of us who have the responsibility for teaching and administering the educational program for your child want to assist in any way we can.

I have scheduled a conference in my office on &APPDATES&, &APPTIMES& so that we can discuss the absences of &STUDENT&.

If you have any questions concerning this conference, please call me at 555-5942.

Your cooperation with us in the interest of your child will be appreciated.

Sincerely yours,

Randall Jones
Assistant Principal

FIGURE 15–2   Variables Used in Personalized Form Letters

&NAME&, &ADDRESS&, &CITYSTZIP&, &STUDENT&, &APPDATES&, &APPTIMES&

Mr. & Mrs. Jones, 1234 56th St., Birmingham AL 52318, Mary, "Monday, April 14, 1996," 9:15 AM

Mrs. Sally Snyder, Rt. 2, Jacksboro TN 38024, Robert, "Wednesday, April 16, 1996," 10:00 AM

Mr. & Mrs. Tom Jones, 121 So. 1st St., Sheffield IA 21233, Peter, "Friday, April 18, 1996," 8:30 AM many forms or cards that are maintained somewhere within the school. What the computer does best is to *sort* entries into a particular order, such as alphabetical or numerical, and/or select records that meet certain criteria from a larger set of records.

Schools generally maintain a tremendous number of record forms that are organized and maintained so that information can be retrieved when needed. Many of these files can be greatly enhanced when served by a computer and its ability to manipulate information. Examples of appropriate applications for the school office range from a simple list of staff names and building keys that they have been issued to a complex file of student cumulative records. Figure 15–3 is a list of possible applications for the school office.

Student Records

Schools collect and maintain a great deal of information on each of their students. This information is usually filed in the student's cumulative record folder, on an emergency card in the office, in the counselor's or teacher's file, or elsewhere. For each application, it is often collected again because there is no easy way to retrieve the information from the existing files and transfer it to the new user. A computerized student records system would allow for easier record updating or maintenance, transfer of data to the new various users, and the preparation of many reports that require student counts, lists, and other forms of information organization. Such things as "How many Title 1 students do you have?" "How many special education LD students are there in your school?" "Which children ride bus 342?" and "We need alphabetical class lists for each ninth-grade homeroom!" can be answered quickly and accurately, saving many hours of clerical time. Management can improve because of the availability of accurate, up-to-date information.

There are several different approaches to establishing and organizing the computer database applications. They are all dependent on the purchase of a software program designed to accept and manage records of this type. The simplest and usually least expensive of these programs are the "file managers." The most elaborate software systems available for microcomputers are the relational database management systems tailored specifically for school records.

FIGURE 15-3   Data-Based Applications for the School Office

Attendance	Student Record Files
Student Grades	Calendar of Events
Student Emergency Contact Information	Cost Accounting
Student Test Score File	Maintenance Records
Student Club Membership Lists	Bus/Transportation
Student Activity Accounting	Mailing Lists
Scheduling	Sports Accounting
Equipment Inventories	Staff Data Base
Building Key Assignments	Building Key Record

File Managers

A *file manager* is a program capable of organizing the information for a particular topic into a single file or flat file.[1] Within this particular file, it is necessary to organize all of the information needed for that database because it is not capable of interconnecting with any other files. In other words, when constructing the file, care must be taken to think through all the needed fields, both as to what data are to be stored, and as to how big each file is to become. For example, a basic file for a student record might consist of the following:

Field Name	*Field Length*
Student Name	25 characters
Studnet ID	9 characters
Student Address	30 characters
Parent Name	25 characters
Home Phone	8 characters
Homeroom Number	3 characters
Total	100 characters

If this information is to be used as part of an emergency card file for all students in the school, additional information such as parent's work phone number, doctor's name and number, and serious medical problems needs to be listed as well. On the other hand, if the file is to be used to identify important in-school information such as homeroom teachers, which bus the student rides, and whether the child receives any special services such as special education or Title 1, then this information needs to be included in the file.

Small files with from 500 to 1,000 records will run on lower-capacity computers, using floppy disks. Programs such as dbase work well. Most schools, however, have a need for much more elaborate records systems. For these, relational databases are required as well as a more powerful computer system.

Relational Databases

Relational database management software allows a number of files to be related to one another by some key field placed within each file. This type of database management system is called *relational* because of its ability to relate separate files to one another on this key field. For example, each student's ID number might be the key field in both the name and address file as well as the grade file. Using the ID number to make sure the correct records were accessed, the parent's address could be pulled from one file and the grades from another file. Together, they could be printed out for the report card to be sent home.

With this plan, a series of files can be created with each file including the student ID number as the key field. One file could include basic student descriptive information, another grades, a third standardized test scores, and a fourth emergency medical information. Each record is relatively small in size but can be accessed by other files as needed. A total systems approach using relational data files can be created. It also allows for flexibility, expansion, and modification. As new needs develop, additional files can be created as long as they key on a common field from one of the other existing files. Powerful software such as a relational database management system generally requires more computer memory on which to operate than the simpler file handling programs.

Several database management systems that can be designed by a principal, interested staff member, or student without any previous computer programming experience are available on the market. Consultants are generally available to provide assistance in this design if desired. Many commercial programs for particular applications are available that create a ready-made records system. Each approach has advantages and limitations. For a school to configure its own records system from a purchased database management system will take some time and energy to learn and implement. A school might not realize the full potential of its software nor develop as efficient a system as possible. To hire an outside consultant to assist the school in software development will probably result in the best product but will require a greater outlay of dollars. The purchase of a prepackaged program may or may not give the school a product that is totally functional.

Management Information Systems

A well-designed management information system should be able to provide the principal, as well as other personnel in the school, rapid, accurate access to a wide variety of data stored in the school computer. These data may relate to students, staff, finances, materials, athletics, grades, or any other part of the school. Although a school might develop its own system from one of the database management packages, it usually is more efficient to purchase one of the commercial programs designed specifically for school use.[2]

These programs have many standard features—such as scheduling, class lists, and grade reporting—but the better ones also allow the principal to design reports for specific needs. The standard reports and forms provide for efficient data processing in the school, but it is often the special reports that provide the opportunity for the principal to use these electronic data for management decisions. The following special reports could serve this management decision role:

1. *Community Parent Profile*. This is a summary profile of all the parents of the children in the school, showing the percentage of each educational level, number of single-parent homes, type of occupations, percentage originally from outside the area, number of children in the family, and so on. The analysis of this type of information is very useful in developing a better understanding of a student population and its needs.

2. *A New Enrollee Analysis*. This report consists of a listing of the new enrollments for each year by month, with information regarding each student's previous school, condition of transfer, and success in your school using GPA or test score comparisons.

3. *Departing Student Analysis.* This is similar to the enrollment analysis.
4. *Excessive Absence List.* This is a list by name of all students with more than X number of days absent, showing total days enrolled and days absent. Also, dates and days of the week of each absence are indicated. The report might include which absences were not excused and if a disciplinary file, particularly truancy, exists on the student. A cross-check on the attendance of siblings is possible as well. If the list is to be used to contact parents, then their names, phone numbers, and addresses could be included as well to speed the follow-up process.[3]
5. *Excessive Tardy Report.* This report could be similar to the excessive absence report. It might also be the basis for notification letters sent home using the merge feature on the word processor (part of good information management is keeping parents informed as well).
6. *Exceptional Student Report.* This is a list by grade and teacher, at the end of each grading period, of all students with a grade point average greater than 3.5, 3.0 to 3.5, and less than 1.5. Special notations can be included for those who were not in these categories during the previous reporting period.
7. *Proficiency Test Report.* This is a list of those students by grade, teacher, and subject area who have not passed certain components of the proficiency test.[4]
8. *Student Disciplinary Report.* A student disciplinary report can be a list of recent disciplinary cases by student and offense, or perhaps only a summary report indicating the number of cases, stating offense category and case disposition.
9. *Achievement Test Analysis.* This is a list of students showing achievement test score gains higher than expected over previous achievement test scores. It is also a list of all students showing achievement test scores lower than expected from previous achievement test scores reported by subject area and teacher.[5]

Financial Accounting Procedures

Financial accounting is one of the most common applications for computers. With the increasing demand for highly detailed accounting, the computer becomes a natural solution as a highly accurate labor-saving tool. Specialized packages for accounting are available from most computer stores. These packages are generally designed for business use, however. Most often, only the general ledger component is needed for school accounting and in many cases can be purchased as a separate component. Simple accounting procedures can also be created from a database management system or formulated on spreadsheet software.

Media Center Materials and Equipment

An excellent computer application for schools is the development of a computerized checkout system for library materials and media equipment. An inexpensive bar code reader attachment to a computer allows for easy processing of student and teacher requests. A file is created on the computer, listing all of the material and equipment items to be organized. A bar code label (similar to those used in grocery stores for product identification) is placed on each book or item of equipment.

Each student and staff member is also assigned a bar code number with a label attached to his or her ID card. To process a book or piece of equipment, the media clerk simply scans the book and the student ID card with the bar code reader to record the proper numbers. The date needs to be entered only at the beginning of each day. From this, lists can be generated for the identification of overdue materials. Equipment inventories can be similarly organized for identification and processing. Inexpensive, battery-powered portable computers with bar code attachments can be carried around the building to verify equipment placement at inventory time.

Document Retrieval System

Document imaging and management systems, along with document scanning hardware, allow a school to create a computer document file of records it receives as "hard copy" and retrieve it to the computer screen. Medical records, parent letters, certificates, and even student art work can be stored in such a system. Document descriptors are entered by which the document can be retrieved, sorted, or selected, just as one would do with a regular electronic database.

Management Planning

A variety of tasks and projects are carried out in school each year that involve many people, numerous resources, and detailed planning. Principals often find a key staff member to head up these annual projects and rely on his or her experience for a successful operation each year. The project may be the annual spaghetti supper, school yearbook, or planning the senior prom, but nevertheless, it requires a significant planning or coordination effort. The major difficulty for the principal often comes when the project advisor changes and the new director is not sure what to do.

Project planning software is available to assist in the organization and planning of major projects. It is useful for projects with as few as 15 to 20 steps and can be used for projects up to the size needed by the contractor planning for the construction of a new building. The program guides the user through a series of steps asking for the events, times, people, resources, and relationships to be carried out for the project. It then builds a Gantt chart or a critical path network (CPN) to highlight the necessary steps for project completion. Figure 6–8 in Chapter 6 is an example of a report generated by planning software.

For financial or numeric planning for items such as budgets or attendance projections, spreadsheet software is available. It uses the column-and-row format of an accounting sheet, but formulas can be entered for automatic recalculations as the numbers entered on the spreadsheet change. For example, the program could be used to show enrollment projections for future years based on a predetermined enrollment formula. Each year it could be easily updated to show new enrollment projections. Budget projections are also possible using a previous year's budget with new data. Some of these programs also have the capability of generating graphs from the data that have been entered to improve the visual impression. See Figure 15–4 for a budget example

FIGURE 15–4   Budget Spreadsheet

DEPARTMENTAL BUDGET, 1996
  Mathematics Department   Month <u>October</u>
  Southeast Elementary

Budget Area and Item	Allowable	Exp. This Month	Exp. to Date	Remainder
TEXTS (B-4)				
5th Modern Math	$ 500.00	497.00		3.00
Programmed Texts and Temac				
Binders 21 @ $10.50	220.50		220.50	—
Supplementary Texts	450.00		275.00	175.00
EQUIPMENT (D-4)				
Volume Distribution Set (1)	60.00		60.00	—
Graph Board (multipurpose) (1)	35.00			
Tightgrip Chalkholder (6)	6.00	1.00		5.00
Rack of Compasses	12.00		12.00	—
Rack of Protractors	15.00		15.00	—
SUPPLEMENTARY (B-6)				—
Universal Encyclopedia of				
Math (2)	20.00	20.00		
Other References	50.00			
AUDIOVISUAL (D-7)				—
Overhead Projector	175.00		175.00	
DISCRETIONARY SUPPLIES	100.00			
SUBTOTAL	$1,643.50	518.00	757.50	368.00
PERSONNEL (A-3)				
2 Consultants 2 days each for in-service expenses	900.00			
SUBTOTAL	$ 900.00			
TOTAL	$2,543.50	518.00	757.50	1268.00

on a spreadsheet. Figure 15–5 shows a computer-generated graph created using MS-Excel.

School Calendar

Calendar software is available for most computers to ease the task of scheduling events and producing graphic calendars on which to post daily, weekly, monthly, and yearly school activities. Keeping schedules clear of one another and the proper people notified is a monumental task in many schools. While master schedules can be posted on a planning board, producing calendars that are readable and that can be modified easily allows the entire school to have up-to-date schedule information. Figure 15–6 is an illustration of such a computer-generated calendar.

Achievement Test Scores — Kennedy Middle School

FIGURE 15–5   Computer-Generated Graphic

Standardized Test Scoring

Most schools have standardized tests scored and analyzed through their district office, through the state department of education, or by the publisher of the standardized test. For most situations, this may continue to be the preferred approach because of the need for these agencies to use the test data from each school in an aggregate manner for comparison purposes. However, test scoring and analysis programs are available along with low-cost, optical scan readers that will allow local schools to efficiently score these tests if they desire. To do so, the school will want to obtain scoring and norming data from the publisher. There are several advantages to local scoring of standardized tests. The results can be back the same day if desired . Also, additional analysis of the collective results of the school's scores are now readily possible with the data available in an electronic format.

Presentation Graphics

Teacher and administrators alike are constantly giving presentations for which illustrations, graphs, major bulleted points, or pictures or drawings are needed. Presentation software provides an easy, quick means of producing such illustrations with a very professional look. Backgrounds and formats are provided. Output can be to a regular printer for black and white transparencies or paper. Color transparencies can be produced even with a low-cost color ink-jet printer. A disk can be sent to a photo finisher to produce 35 mm slides or the output can be displayed through a LCD panel on an overhead projector or large computer monitor. Hard-copy printouts with a place for speaker notes or three-to-a-page printouts for participants can be produced also. Additionally, the more powerful packages can have sound or short movie segments associated with them.

NOVEMBER

Sunday	Monday	Tuesday	Wednesday	Thursday	Friday	Saturday
				1	2	3
4	5	6 ELECTION DAY Student Holiday	7	8	9	10
	3:20—Faculty Meeting					
11	12	13 NUTRITION DAY WORKSHOP	14 MAKE-UP DAY FOR PICTURES	15 STUDENTS FROM LITTLE WORLD TO TALK TO K–5 9:30–12:00	16	17
	3:20—Faculty Meeting	3:20—Leadership Team Meeting				
18	19 9:15—K & 1 Program Marty Silver Environmentalist	20 End of Third Month 9:00 2nd Grade Play K, 1, 3, & Multi-Age 9:15—4 & 3 Program Marty Silver Environmentalist 1:00 2nd Grade Play K, 4	21 End of Six Weeks 9:15—2 & 3 Program Marty Silver Environmentalist 10:30 Singers leave for Gatlinburg 2:00 Singers Program at Gatlinburg	22	23	24
	3:20—Faculty Meeting			THANKSGIVING HOLIDAYS		
25	26	27 The Clue That Turned Blue 10:00—K, 1st, 2nd Multi 10:30–3rd, 4th, & 5th	28 Progress Reports go out 8:30–11:30 Bledsoe—Ijani's Park Bivens—Airport	29	30 Kindergarten— "Nutcracker"	
	3:20—Faculty Meeting	3:20—Leadership Team Meeting				

FIGURE 15–6   Computer-Generated Calendar

Computer-to-Computer Communication

Within the Building

Serious consideration should be given to linking together several computers within the building where there is a desire to share information. Consideration of this linking needs to be made during software as well as hardware selection. The introductory illustration of "Principal Jim" calling up a student file at his desk implied that his secretary, assistant principal, or maybe the counselor could also access the same files, from other terminals. If this is desired for present or future use, it should be taken into account when software is being selected. This can be done by purchasing software that is designed to run on a network. This usually also has a cost benefit with only one copy of the application software required to run off the server.

Local area networks (LANs) are the way computers are wired together within a building. These networks generally require additional electronics to be placed inside each computer as well as the addition of special software to manage data sharing (see Figure 15–7)

Outside the School

There are several desirable applications for computers in schools to communicate with other computers over phone lines. These include electronic mail, fax, bulletin boards, national databases, file transfers, and the Internet (see Figure 15–8).

Electronic Mail
Memos, notes, letters, and documents can be sent electronically from one computer to another. The sender prepares the document on the word processor, but rather than sending it to the printer, it is sent over phone lines to another computer at the receiving end. Electronic addresses are used so that only the proper individuals receive the mail. The receiver can read messages from the screen or have them printed out on paper. The major advantage of electronic mail (e-mail) is speed and cost.

Electronic mail service is provided by several national companies that allow the user to send documents all over the world to other individuals who are also members of that service, or to a company receiving terminal where it is printed and delivered. Within an area, local e-mail represents an excellent method of communication between a district office and its member schools. The service can be established on a computer in the central office with automatic message delivery during the night for reading in each school the following morning. In a similar fashion, messages can be collected from each school over night for transfer to the central office the next day. Figure 15–9 is an illustration of an e-mail letter with its electronic address.

Fax Transmission
Facsimile transmission, or the process of sending graphic images as a digital signal over phone lines, represents yet another form of computer-to-computer communication. Fax machines can be either stand-alone units hooked directly to a phone line or

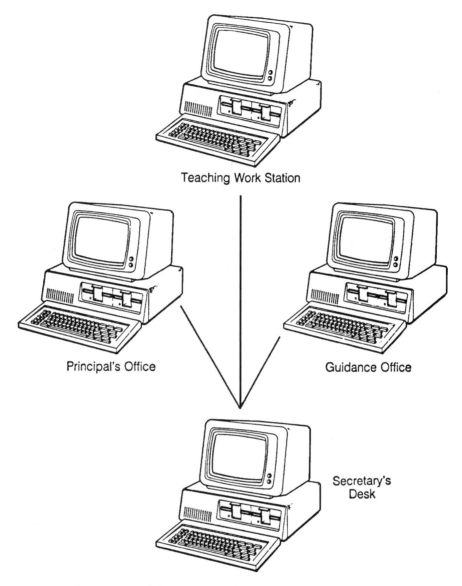

Teaching Work Station

Principal's Office

Guidance Office

Secretary's Desk

At least one of the computers is equipped with a hard disk and functions as a file server to the others in the system

FIGURE 15–7   Local Area Network (LAN)

built into your computer. Regardless of what your hardware configuration might be, the potential for school use is great where immediate information is needed. Student records for the transferring student, a transcript of courses completed for the graduated senior, and documents to or from the district office are only a few examples of its potential use. If the school already has a computer and printer, additional equipment

FIGURE 15–8   Computer-to-Computer Communication Using Modems and Telephone Lines

requirements are a scanner (also useful for desktop publishing), a fax board placed inside the computer, and the use of a phone line when sending or receiving images.

Electronic Bulletin Board

An electronic bulletin board functions somewhat like electronic mail. However, its messages are available to anyone with access to the system. Bulletin board software can allow messages to be placed and received by anyone with password access to the system. Messages can be classified and deleted by the system operator. In a school set-

FIGURE 15–9   Example of E-Mail

Date: Wed, 01 Mar 1996 14:58:06 -0500 (EST)
From: DIGH@utkvx.utk.edu
To: ubben <ubben@utkvx.utk.edu>
Subject: EdA&S Offering

Hello Professor Ubben,

I was planning out my course schedule for the next academic year and did not see Educ Admin 535 on the schedule for next fall or spring. I just wanted to check with you and see if that was correct, because I was interested in taking the course in the future.

Thanks,
Andy Digh

ting, it would be useful to post general messages and announcements to teachers and administrators to survey on a daily basis.

National Database

Hundreds of national databases are available for use by computer users. They range from general services through groups such as Compuserve and the Source to specialized services for education such as Special Net or Ed Net. These services generally provide electronic mail service, bulletin board service, and a topic database appropriate to their focus. For example, Special Net, a database service for special educators, has available on line information on national policy, early childhood education, multihandicapped vision, deafness, litigation, employment, and many other topics of interest to this group.

These services also generally provide a "gateway" into other database libraries for their members. For example, the massive Dialog database is where the ERIC (Educational Research Information Center) and CJIE (Current Journals in Education) electronic libraries are located. These gateways provide direct search capability for materials within these databases without going through a university or public library.

File Transfer

The simplest form for information transfer from computer to computer is the movement of files of information previously prepared. This might be the weekly attendance report sent to the district office, a copy of the budget information to be compiled by the school business manager, or a manuscript to be sent to the company that does typesetting and printing. In each case, sending this material electronically allows the recipient to continue processing the information without rekeying it into the computer. The attendance file can be merged directly with the report to go to the state. The budget information can be loaded directly into the business manager's spreadsheet, and the manuscript to be typeset can have type code added without the entire document being rekeyed. Time is saved, costs are lowered, and accuracy is greater. For example, the district office computer could be programmed to call each of the district schools during the night; send files, mail, and bulletins to the schools; and request any files to be transferred to the central office. If the district had 40 schools, it could take 10 hours at 15 minutes per school to communicate with each building in the system. By morning, when the staff arrived, the messages of the day would be waiting. The modem needed to support these functions is an auto/answer modem along with terminal software.

The Internet

The Internet and its ultimate successor, the Information Super-Highway, offer tremendous new opportunities for schools and computer communication. The e-mail system, file transfers to another computer, network news, and information browsing through a never-ending collection of information resources are all available through the Internet. Weather reports, electronic information databases, curriculum resource materials, and electronic journals are available—free to anyone with access to the Internet. With high-speed modems—or better yet, an ISDN connection—access to the World Wide Web and its graphics capabilities can be available to schools. Almost all universities have Internet servers that local schools can often access. Some State Departments of Education are providing state-supported access to all schools within the state.

Terminal Software

Each of the communication applications described requires at least one particular piece of software called a *terminal program*, as well as a hardware addition called a *modem*. The terminal program configures the computer to send a signal out of the serial port through the modem, into the phone lines, to a modem in a computer at the other end.

This terminal program should be what is called a *smart* terminal package. This means the program makes use of the computer's ability to store information on disks as well as to initiate commands automatically or remotely from another computer. This capability (smart) is necessary if previously prepared information is to be sent as opposed to simply typing the desired message at the time it is to be sent. This software and hardware also allows your computer to be called from a remote location so files can be transferred automatically. This is often used for overnight transfer.

Hardware Considerations

It is impossible to offer timely, specific recommendations for hardware with the technology that is changing as rapidly as the computer industry. School needs, however, vary only to a degree from one another so that certain concepts of hardware selection remain fairly constant. The following list of suggestions should be considered as guideposts to the school administrator in making hardware decisions.

1. Be sure the hardware selected is compatible with the software applications you wish to use. Also, check that your computer has the memory necessary to support some of the more standard software applications.
2. Be sure the hardware selected has the storage capacity to support the quantity of data that will be collected by the school. The more, the better.
3. Buy state-of-the-art hardware produced by a major manufacturer. Be more inclined to select for office use what is currently most popular with corporate business purchasers.
4. Try to purchase all of your hardware and as much software as possible from one dealer. Preferably, purchase from a dealer in your immediate area who will be able to provide setup and support for the purchase.
5. Place your first administrative computer in an easily accessible workstation available to several people.
6. Consideration should be given to multiple administrative computer stations connected with a LAN. Schools will soon have computers on the principal's desk, one for word processing on the secretary's desk, one for general use (such as attendance), one on the counselor's desk, and several at teachers' workstations, all connected through the LAN and running off the server. The particular configuration, of course, will depend on the size of the school.
7. Provide training for the principal, secretary, guidance counselors, teachers, and other interested users on the staff.

Software Selection

The basic application software used in the school office should be selected from the available choices of quality business software. Although it is suggested that software be selected before hardware choices are made, in reality this must be done somewhat in concert—that is, identifying a particular piece of software and then checking to see what its hardware requirements are.

Initial software purchases for many schools include:

1. Word processing
2. A quality database manager
3. A spreadsheet
4. A presentation graphics program
5. A terminal, fax, and e-mail program

General considerations for software selection include:

1. Does it have the features needed for your office?
2. Is it a popular choice of other buyers? (Lists of the most popular software are available in most computer stores and can be found in computer magazines. Popularity rankings allow one to draw on the judgment of other purchasers as well as having a greater assurance that the company will provide good technical support. You will also find that more popular programs generate ideas from other users for additional potential applications.)

A number of integrated office software programs on the market include a word processor, a spreadsheet, a database management program, a presentation graphics program, and an e-mail program if you are operating on a LAN. Features you should seek in reviewing specific programs include:

1. Word Processing
   a. What the computer creates on the screen is what it produces on paper
   b. The ability to handle lengthy documents—at least 50 pages
   c. The ability to merge with a database to produce form letters
   d. Desktop-publishing capabilities

2. Database Manager
   a. Ease of use—menu driven
   b. Large capacity—at least 64 fields, 10,000 records
   c. Relational or file linking ability
   d. Capable of sharing data with other programs (i.e., word processing or spreadsheets)
   e. The ability to modify program code
   f. A global change function

3. Ledger
   a. Ease of use
   b. Menu driven
   c. On-screen prompts
   d. Ability to print out reports at any time
   e. Reports amount budgeted, amount encumbered, amount invoiced, percentage of budget invoiced
   f. Subtotals by function as well as grand totals

4. Spreadsheet
   a. Ease of use
   b. Ability to provide some data manipulation similar to a database management system
   c. Graphics capabilities
   d. Data exchanged with your word processor and database management system

5. Presentation Graphics
   a. Ease of use
   b. Slide show with fades and wipes, transparencies masters, speaker notes
   c. Good supply of clip art for graphics

6. Student Scheduling
   a. Package that builds alternate schedules, allowing you to select a particular schedule based on its simulation performance
   b. Ease of data entry—optical scan, card entry, or keyboard with automatic repeats for required courses.
   c. Prints out schedule, room lists, class lists, teacher lists by hour, individual student schedules
   d. Interfaces with attendance program, grade reporting program, and student records files

7. Grade Reporting and Attendance
   a. Allows for optical scanner bar code data entry
   b. Interfaces with student record file and scheduling program (if used)
   c. Prepares all necessary report cards for mailing home, including attendance data, average grades for honor roll, and so on; prepares monthly district or state attendance reports allowing electronic dump to central office if service is available

8. Staff Personnel
9. Media Center Materials and Equipment Processing
   a. Capable of handling the quantity of materials in your Instructional Materials Center
   b. Bar code or similar data entry
   c. Ability to generate bar code
   d. Proper report capabilities for shelf lists, special subject requests, overdue materials by homeroom, and so on

10. Terminal, Fax, and E-Mail Program
    a. Allows for connection to other computers over phone lines or a LAN
    b. Must be used with a modem or ether-net LAN connection.

Hardware Security

Computer equipment, being expensive but relatively lightweight and compact, is highly vulnerable to theft, particularly in the open setting of a school. Particular caution needs to be taken to reduce this threat. The following actions are recommended to reduce this loss:

1. Record all serial numbers on microcomputers and related equipment. This will assist police in their investigation should equipment be stolen. Serial numbers further allow the police to place listings of stolen property in the NCIC (National Crime Information Center).
2. Stencil or burn the school name and location on the exterior surface of the computer in plain view. Also place identification markings on an unexposed area of your equipment.
3. Obtain security anchor pads, if available, from your vendor at the time of purchase, noting that time and effort will be involved in removing a device. This will prevent equipment from disappearing from open offices or classrooms during the day.
4. Be security conscious but be careful not to be so restrictive that it becomes inconvenient to use the equipment.

Summary

The areas of word processing, student records, financial accounting, scheduling, grade reporting, attendance, staff personnel, presentation graphics, media center materials and equipment, management planning, and standardized test scoring represent areas to consider when planning for the computerization of the school office. Although it would probably be overly ambitious to attempt all of them simultaneously, adequate consideration for future use should be given to each. This will help in both software and hardware selection so that program compatibility can be maintained and hardware expansion made possible.

Activities

1. Review Case Studies 15 and 20. Analyze the problems presented and apply the concepts of computer utilization developed in this chapter. How might these problems have been prevented if a good computer system had been in place? What approach would you use in addressing the problems identified in these cases? Set forth a strategy to overcome the difficulties faced by the school in each of these cases.

2. What are the greatest impediments to full computerization of our schools? Apply the concepts of strategic planning set forth in Chapter 6 and the ideas on human resources development outlined in Chapter 13 to the impediments you have identified. Outline your plan of action.

Endnotes

1. A database management system organizes information into three levels: files, records, and fields. A field is usually one piece of information for which a specific amount of space is allocated, such as a space for the name of an individual. A record is a collection of fields for one case, such as the name, address, and phone number for a particular individual. A file is a collection of records entered into the computer, all organized with the same format.

2. There are many kinds and brands of commercial software on the market for school record keeping, class scheduling, and to assist in project planning. Both IBM-compatible systems and Macintosh-compatible systems are available.

3. Automated phone-calling programs are available that can use the electronic absence report to call each home of the absentees during the evening hours to inform parents that their child was absent that day.

4. A proficiency test is the term for a state or locally administered criterion-referenced skills test often given in reading, math, language, and occasionally other areas, such as social studies and science.

5. Any attempt to use these test score data to review teacher performance must be done with extreme care. Using raw gain scores such as suggested here must be enhanced by special statistical treatments such as analysis of covariance, or some other means of adjusting gain scores.

Selected Readings

Alluisi, John C., and James Lee Staggs. "A Student Information System Based on Relational Technology." *T.H.E. Journal* 18, no. 4 (November 1990): 72–74.

Bruder, Isabelle. "Users Speak Out: A Look at Six Administrative Software Programs." *Electronic Learning* 7. no. 8 (May–June 1988): 54–56. (ERIC Program Service No. EJ 376 643).

Burton, P. "Microcomputers as Innovation: Policies for Implementation in Libraries and Information Services." *The Electronic Library* 65 (1987): 210–219.

Circulation Plus Demo/Tutorial Manual (Crystal Lake, IL: The Follett Software Company, 1987).

Collins, G. "From Catalog to Database: Preliminary Steps." *School Library Journal* 32 (1985): 123.

Gordon, Jeffery, and Rick Anderson. "Lotus 1-2-3: An Administrative Tool." *AEDS Monitor* 23, no. 11–12 (May–June 1985): 12–13.

Kearsley, Greg. "What Should Today's School Administrators Know about Computers?" *Technological Horizons in Education* 16, no. 4 (November 1988):65–69. (ERIC Document Service No. EJ 386 110).

Lavin, Richard J., and John Phillipo. "Improve School-Based Management through Intelligent Networking." *T.H.E. Journal* 18, no. 4 (November 1990): 69–71.

Loertscher, David. "High Technology in School Libraries." *Media and Methods* 25, no. 1 (September–October 1988): 21–24. (ERIC Document Service No. EJ 382 466).

Mecklenburger, James A. "Technology in the 1990s: Ten Secrets for Success." *Principal* 69, no. 2 (November 1989): 6–8.

Miller, Harold. *An Administrator's Manual for the Use of Microcomputers in the Schools* (Englewood Cliffs, NJ.: Prentice-Hall, 1988).

Pakieser, Ruth A, and Cynthia L. Corritore. "A Computer System for Student Program Advisement." *T.H.E. Journal* 18, no. 4 (November 1990): 75–78.

Richards, Craig E. *Microcomputer Applications for Strategic Management in Education* (White Plains, NY: Longman, 1989).

Roberts, Jack L., Fran Reinhold, and Bill Morgan Gosewisch (Eds.). *An Administrator's Guide to the Business of Education* (Special Supplement). *Electronic Learning* (New York: Scholastic, September 1989).

Waring, Michael G. "The Educator, the Spreadsheet and Site-Based Management." *T.H.E. Journal* 17, no. 10 (June 1990): 49–50.

Winnebago CIRC/CAT (Caledonia, MN: Winnebago Software Company, 1988).

C h a p t e r **16**

Budgeting, Accounting, and Building Management

Sounds emanating from the school business office:

"Gary, Art has overspent his budget again."

"And all it will cost for this supplemental reading program is $1,125 the first year. Sign here."

"The school band needs new uniforms."

"But you said the science program was high priority. So how come you're not approving this purchase order?

"The commodes in the second floor girl's restroom are clogged again."

"You spent Title I monies for *what*?"

"I dunno, these accounts just don't balance."

"Miss Hoke, the auditor's office just called. Something about some misappropriated funds...."

"I don't care what it costs—get the maintenance department over here and get those swings fixed."

"Dr. Karpicke, the Citizens for Economy committee is here for their appointment. They look grim."

A headache begins.

Budgeting, fiscal accounting, and building management are all functions of the principalship. When the budget issues from the needs of the instructional program, when accounting procedures withstand audit, when the building is well equipped and maintained, great things can happen in the school. Although usually it will not be the principal who determines the monetary needs of all of the instructional units, or who personally keeps the books, or who fixes the toilets, it is the principal who ultimately is responsible for all of these things occurring in a timely and efficient manner.

In research syntheses about practices in high-performance schools, two findings that relate to resource and facility management are evident. In high-performance schools, resources were allocated to maximally support instructional and curricular improvement. Good financial planning and good budgeting were apparent. Also, schools that were excellent were invariably clean and physically attractive, inside and outside. There was obvious attention to the impact the physical environment has on educational outcomes.

This chapter contains four parts. In the first part, important concepts about financial planning and budgeting are discussed. There is much attention given to ways to engage the staff in fiscal planning that has an impact on the instructional program. In the second part, good accounting and record-keeping practices are examined. The focus of the third part is on supplies and equipment management. The-chapter concludes with a discussion about the care of the school plant, including a review of custodial schedules.

The Budgeting and Planning Process

There are four sequential steps to the budget development/budget implementation process: program planning and tentative allocation of resources by category; analysis and adoption of a final budget; administration and coordination of the budget, including record keeping; and review and appraisal of budget implementation with regard to the instructional goals of the school program. The budget process is continuous and cyclical. Figure 16–1 depicts this process.

Responsible financial planning rests on good program planning. It requires, as well, a substantial database about the nature of the student body; population projections and housing patterns; estimates of personnel needs; and historical information about average daily attendance (ADA) or average daily membership (ADM), whichever is the basis for the state reimbursement program, and reasonable projections thereof, among other information that would help determine the financial demands of the next fiscal period.

Three Common Budgeting Processes

For the principal in school districts committed to decentralized (i.e. site-based) decision making, the budgeting process takes on critical importance. Three major techniques for budget development have emerged over the years, none of which is based on assumptions of decentralized decision making but any of which may be employed at the site. Two of these clearly are conducive to much staff participation in budget development and implementation. One is such a "mechanical" approach that only minimal staff participation would seem called for.

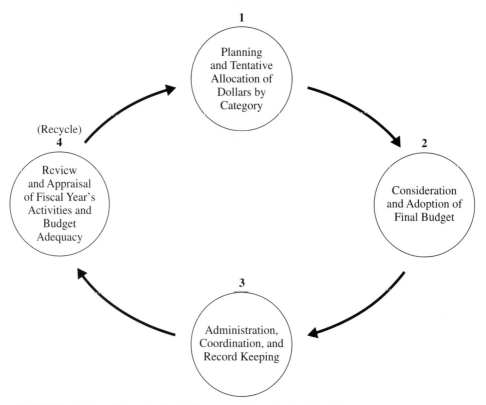

FIGURE 16–1   The Cyclical Nature of the Budgeting Process

Incremental Budgeting

Incremental budgeting begins with the current year's budget and in its pure form is largely an "add-on" (or "subtract-from") process. It assumes stasis: stasis in the nature of the needs of the student body, stasis in curriculum organization, and stasis among line items. Within line items there may be shifts in proposed expenditures, to be sure, and staff decisions with regard to this might be encouraged.

Fundamentally, however, the next school year is assumed to be very much like the current year. Often, certain fixed charges that can be anticipated are excluded from building-level planning. That is, the district may do its own projections with regard to such things, for example, as utility bills and provide for uniform maintenance. These most often will remain centralized and accounted for in the district business office.

At the school site, however, the principal will be expected to project needs for the next year on a formula that most often is based on the number of students anticipated to be enrolled. This becomes the primary factor for anticipating the number of teachers needed, supplies required, support staff permitted, among other expenses that can be expected that go along with an increased or a decreased enrollment. Frequently, the student enrollment figure is based on average daily attendance or average daily membership for the current year and any changes that might be anticipated because of new housing starts, for example.

Special requests such as needed building repair or special facilities for special programs housed in the building are most often considered separately. Programs such as those funded by such outside sources as the federal government—"Title" programs, vocational programs, lunch programs, and the like—are handled separately.

When the totals are calculated, preliminary decisions are made with regard to the appropriation for the school for the next year. This is budget development at its simplest. It is also budget development at its most inadequate—because it assumes that what exists is working well enough. It does not take into consideration any changes in the nature of the students to be served, or changes in instructional technology, for example. It is status-quo driven, and structural, curricular, and instructional innovations are less encouraged than would be desirable. The amount of money to be spent is viewed as finite and dependent on the school allocation.

Zero-Based Budgeting

At the other end of the budget development continuum is so-called zero-based budgeting. In its purest form, this technique assumes a new year, every year. The school organization is divided into program or budget units. The mere fact that a program was funded during the current year or in previous years is no assurance that it will be funded in subsequent years. The program unit and ultimately program heads are expected to justify their program and the dollars needed to support that program on an annual basis. The budget is "zero" until this is done.

Justifications are made on the basis of curriculum evaluations, demographic realities, research about instructional technology, shifting priorities in the light of the former, the established school and program goals. One important advantage of zero-based budgeting is that it forces continuous reevaluation of program objectives, needed resources, and the establishment of new priorities or reestablishment of existing priorities. A downside is that this is a very time-consuming process.

Planning, Programming, Budgeting System

This can become a reasonable alternative to either of the other two processes. At its best, PPBS recognizes that there are needs for a consistent base of support and that a per-pupil allotment may best provide for a baseline. That is, there is enough experience in the district to know that irrespective of individual learner needs, demographic realities, changes in instructional technology, and curriculum revisions, certain per-pupil costs of an education can be anticipated.

Beyond this, however, PPBS begins to take on the elements of zero-based budgeting. Some planners and analysts insert an *E* between the *B* and the *S* to stand for *evaluation*. The PPBES approach explicitly emphasizes that the goals and processes used to address these goals are subjected to evaluation. We believe this is implicit in a PPBS approach, but if it makes the point more telling, that's all the better.

The PPBS technique requires the establishment of specific program goals and processes to achieve these goals; projections of needs—students to be served, new technology, and so on; the generation, analysis, and projection of data about program element costs; alternative processes to achieve the goals; other sources of funding; and any additional personnel or additional facilities needed and what that would cost.

Implementing a Planning, Programming, Budgeting System

At its simplest, PPBS involves five steps:

1. Establishing the general goals to be achieved
2. Identifying the specific objectives that define this goal
3. Developing the program and processes that it is believed will achieve the objectives and goals
4. Establishing the formative and summative evaluation practices
5. Implementing a review and recycle procedure that indicates whether or not, or the degree to which, the program and processes resulted in the achievement of the objectives and the goals, and, if not, to help determine other procedures, processes, and programs

PPBS is designed to help a staff decide specifically what is to be accomplished and how to go about it. The focus is on goal accomplishment. When sensitively and sensibly applied, an efficient expenditure of monies results.

Too often, educational planning has primarily been concerned with the "inputs" of education. PPBS differs substantively from other budget-building procedures because PPBS focuses on desired "outputs" of the effort (goals and objectives) and afterwards considers the numbers of staff, books equipment, and buildings that must be engaged to obtain the desired end.

There are other values to a PPBS plan, however. The process provides great opportunity for staff involvement and staff development about an issue that many may be interested in and all are affected by. At the initial stages, individual departments, teaching teams, grade levels—however the building is operationally organized—essentially will be engaged in a "GII" decision process.[1] Later, as tough decisions need to be made—initial budget proposals almost outstrip available funds—the principal may find the "CI" or "CII" process more appropriate. In any of these instances, good use has been made of the collective wisdom and subject matter expertise of faculty to arrive at a budget which all will work hard to implement.

Moreover, as PPBS is implemented, data are being collected about the productivity of distinct elements of the program. As the school enterprise has become more complex and more diversified, and more demanding of public funds, personnel, and time investments, there has been a resultant anxiety about results. There is a pressing desire on the part of the various publics to know more precisely what this investment is producing and where changes should be made. PPBS helps provide this important information and forms a solid basis for gaining public support. Among the outcomes of such a budget development process is a concern for the future and a continuous assessment of current curricular and instructional practices.

Step 1: The Five-Year Plan

The planning process begins with the development of a five-year plan well in advance of any specific budget proposals for the next fiscal year. This is not a document that is developed quickly. The process does provide a good basis for in-service workshops with staff and lends a substantive focus to faculty meetings and workshops held throughout the school year.

The process may begin by organizing the preschool workshop to focus on planning for the future. Several schoolwide or department sessions are held, at which time the topics to be addressed are often stated as: "What a student at the end of grade 6 should know" or "What this school needs is" or "What the outcomes of the 7–12 social studies program should be," or any number of other topics that are generative of ideas that focus on curricular or student outcomes.

Following the idea gathering, staff members convert the product of these sessions into a series of goals and objectives by a process of synthesizing, summarizing, and combining. Once the staff has refined the statements of objectives and goals, they identify the processes, materials, and personnel that will be necessary in order to implement these goals and objectives over the next five years. The tentative five-year plan has four major components:

1. A written description of the current state of the discipline. The staff simply describes, briefly, where the department, or subject matter, or curricular field is at the present time in relation to what the literature and research reveal is the ideal state.
2. Statement of goals, objectives, and the indicators that will be accepted as evidence of achievement of objectives for the department. It is important to establish objective indicators of achievement. However, this does not have to be done at this time; it can be done later. A staff could bog down at this point and become fatigued at developing long lists of performance objectives based on lower-level cognitive achievement. The five-year plan is subject to modifications through the formative evaluation that will occur as it unfolds.
3. A list of processes to implement the objectives.
4. A statement of needed equipment, materials, personnel, and other resources supportive of the processes.

Component 4 is the culmination of the five-year plan development. The plan is subjected to refinement and modification and is ultimately submitted for executive review and discussion. It does not contain any dollar figures at this point. Although care should be taken not to hurry the process, definite time lines must be established for the completion of this process. Otherwise, it may become a cumbersome intellectual exercise that never gets completed.

Step 2: The One-Year Plan

While the five-year plan for the school plots a general direction, the one-year building plan provides budgetary substance. The one-year plan is a proposal that specifically identifies what needs to happen next year if the five-year plan is to be realized. Figure 16–2 provides a suggested format for the one-year plan.

The one-year plan describes equipment needs, supplies, supplementary materials, immediate changes of personnel or addition of personnel, remodeling, and other

Department (or Grade Level): _____

Fiscal Year: _____

Prepared by: _____

Amount Requested: _____

Amount Allocated: _____

Request (indicate after each item which long-term objective it supports)	**Estimated Cost**	**Suggested Source of Supply**	**Suggested Source** (federal funds, local funds, donation, state experimental funds, etc.)
1. Needed personnel			
2. Needed equipment and materials			
3. Needed other resources (e.g., travel monies, consultants, etc.) N.B. list above in descending order of priority.			
Total Requested _____			

4. Attach a brief statement describing how this proposed budget is consistent with and supportive of the five-year plan.

FIGURE 16–2   The One-Year Plan

needed resources. Justification for each specific item is available in the one-year document. This justification need not be elaborate; it is a brief statement about how the budget proposal is consistent with the five-year plan. An additional feature is that the departments or grade levels are asked to list needs in order of priority. If it is necessary to reduce budgets because of insufficient dollars, such cutting begins with lowest priority items in each of the proposals.

Subsequent Steps

Subsequent steps involve submitting the budget and the curriculum proposals of the department or unit to the principal and the administrative staff for its approval or return for clarification or modification. Ultimately, the preparation of a total school budget in summary form is made by the principal and the staff for submission to the central office. Following this, there are negotiations and approvals of the individual school budgets in some form by the ultimate fiscal authority in the school district.

Eventually, an approved budget is returned by the principal to each department or unit—a budget from which requisitions throughout the year will be submitted to the principal and purchase orders issued. Each month a recapitulation of purchases to date is returned to the department.

Expectations and Product

Involvement of instructional staff in budget building does not make the principal's job any easier. In fact, after going through the initial process, team leaders, department heads, and other instructional staff can be expected to develop formidable and well-conceived arguments in defense of their budgets. Needless to say, however, the principal will be supplied with much of the data needed in order to go to the superintendent or the board of education to justify an adequate budget. Moreover, the central office and the school board will become well informed as to outgo and the reasons behind the outgo.

The budget-building process just described attempts to accomplish three things. It gives the appropriate personnel a large measure of authority for initial budget preparation in their areas of instructional expertise. Second, it causes foresighted curriculum planning. Third, it provides substantiation to the central office, school board, and the community that tax dollars are being spent in an efficient and effective manner.

Accounting for Financial Resources and Expenditures

General Issues

In school districts, resource allocation and expenditures are generally divided into three broad categories: capital outlay, long-term and short-term debt payment and interest, and current expenses. It is the latter category that is of greatest concern to the principal, although certain items that appear in a capital outlay account also require consideration. Let us first examine what goes into each of these accounts.

Capital Outlay
An item with a life expectancy of over a year generally goes into a capital outlay account. The account will therefore contain equipment and all permanent additions to the buildings and school site. Plant and site maintenance expenditures are not reported here—only those expenditures that represent an extension to the existing school building and site. Relative permanence is the key determinate.

Debt Service
All short- and long-term loans and the repayment of those, including the interest payments, are reported in these accounts.

Current Expenses
Current expenses include all expenditures made for things that are consumable during a single fiscal year. This includes such expenses as textbooks, supplies, and salaries—known as *operating expenses*. Most often, these expenses can be found in the district budget classified under four categories: *Instruction*, which includes all of the programs—regular, special, and adult; *Support Services*, which includes transportation, food service, student services, and student activities; *Nonprogrammed Charges*, which include any payments to other governmental agencies for services, including rentals; and *Community Services*, which include recreation programs and nonpublic school services.

Accounting for Financial Resources at the School Site

Once the budget is developed and approved, it becomes the responsibility of the principal to see that it is managed properly. Schools are big businesses. In many communities, the school system is the single largest employer of personnel and the largest industry in terms of capital flow. School districts receive and disburse huge amounts of money for a variety of services and materials over the period of a year.

Similarly, at the individual school buildings, principals have the responsibility for administering sizeable financial resources—resources that come from the central district office as a result of local, state, and federal support programs, as well as much smaller sums that come from places such as PTOs, school clubs, plays, and so on. Managing financial resources is a major responsibility of most school principals.

All school systems have a prescribed accounting procedure, and a principal will need to become familiar with it in order to properly oversee income and expenditures. Figure 16–3 displays a typical array of accounts for a high school, and Figure 16–4 is a similar display for an elementary school.

FIGURE 16–3   Outline of Typical Accounts for a Secondary School

General Activity Fund Restricted	
INSTRUCTIONAL FEE	Class, Junior
Towel Fee	Class, Senior
INSTRUCTIONAL FEE & SHOP	Combined Studies
Art	Debate Club
INSTRUCTIONAL SHOP	DECA
Auto Mechanics	French Club
Machine Shop	German Club
Wood Shop	Gymnastics
OTHER INSTRUCTIONAL	Home Economics
Music	International Relations Club
Band Uniforms	Key Club
MERCHANDISING SERVICE	Leader's Club
Bus Tickets	Leo Club
PROFIT EARNING	Literary
Coke Fund	Magazine
Concessions	Masquers
SPECIAL PURPOSE	Music: Band
Hospitality	Music: Choir
Library	Musical Production
College Credit Course	National Honor Society
Sports Camp	Oak Leaf
Senior Trip	Oak Log
Scholarship	Pep Club
Science	Red Cross
Training & Technology	Ski Club
STUDENT ORGANIZATIONS	Spanish Club
Anchor Club	Student Council
Bridge Club	Tennis Club
	TOEC
	VICA

**FIGURE 16–4   Outline of Typical Internal Ledger Accounts for an
Elementary School**

MERCHANDISING SERVICE
  Bus Tickets
  Insurance
  Workbooks
PROFIT EARNING
  Coke Machine
  Pictures
  School Store
SPECIAL PURPOSE
  Field Trips
  Assemblies
  Hospitality
  Instructional Supplies
ORGANIZATIONS
  Faculty Club
  Student Council
  PTO
  Intramural Program
  All-School Chorus

In general, school principals need to keep a journal of receipts and disbursements and provide proper monitoring of these (see Figure 16–5). The principal may also have federally funded projects located in the building and will be expected to maintain appropriate records for these. Certainly, too, the principal will be responsible for securing supplies and materials, either by requisition from a central warehouse, perhaps using a system of transfer vouchers, or directly from a supplier. Probably most, if not all, of the principal's accounting responsibilities will occur in the operations" (supplies, equipment, etc.) part of the budget. Figure 16–6 displays a purchase requisition flowchart in common use in schools. (Principals are not usually required to account for capital income and expenditures. These accounts are commonly handled in the central office.)

In most schools, there will be a clerk on whom will rest the responsibility for keeping the books. Under the principal's direction, this person will generally make the journal entries and keep the records in order. This does not relieve the principal of executive responsibility, however. Regular review is essential, and we recommend an annual independent audit of all records.

For the first few months on the job, the principal is best advised to be involved directly in the accounting process to learn intimately the business side of the enterprise. Proper accounting and budget procedures are essential to a well-managed school. The accounting system exists in order that the school may expend its funds efficiently and in accordance with the plan incorporated in the budget document. It also provides a history of spending and may be used to evaluate how the plan developed in the budget document is proceeding.

Financial resources are always in short supply, and it is not likely that all of the budgetary requests in support of the instructional objectives and school goals can be

FIGURE 16–5   Monthly Report Form

Statement of Receipts and Disbursements

Report for_____ 19_____   Prepared by _____

                                                                                 Central Treasurer

Account	Cash on Hand 1st of Month	Receipts This Month	Total	Disbursements	Balance End of Month
TOTAL $_____	$_____	$_____		$_____	$_____

Reconciliation of Bank Statement

Bank balance as of _____ $_____
   Plus deposits not shown on statement_____ $_____
   Plus others_____ $_____
   Minus outstanding checks_____   TOTAL $_____
   _____ $_____
   Book balance as of _____ $_____
   _____ $_____

met in any one year. Thus, it becomes most important for the principal to keep a close record of outgo, making sure that this outgo is consistent with the budget plan and that sufficient funds remain for the purchase of high-priority items throughout the school year. It is a sad fact that improper accounting procedures have too frequently resulted in an adequate amount of money in April for the purchase of routine supplies necessary to complete the school year. Under such a system, teachers tend to overpurchase and hoard supplies in their rooms. These practices are neither healthy nor necessary in a well-ordered school.

Most school districts use an accrual accounting system, which means that as soon as a purchase order is initiated or a requisition for anything is approved, it is encumbered in the account book. Through such a process, the principal knows immediately how much money remains to be expended in any particular account. Under such a system, it is not likely that financial obligations will be made beyond the actual amount of money available.

It cannot be expected, however, that faculty and nonacademic personnel will understand the intricacies of the accounting system, and sometimes individuals on the faculty may view the entire process as a hindrance to the instructional program. Thus,

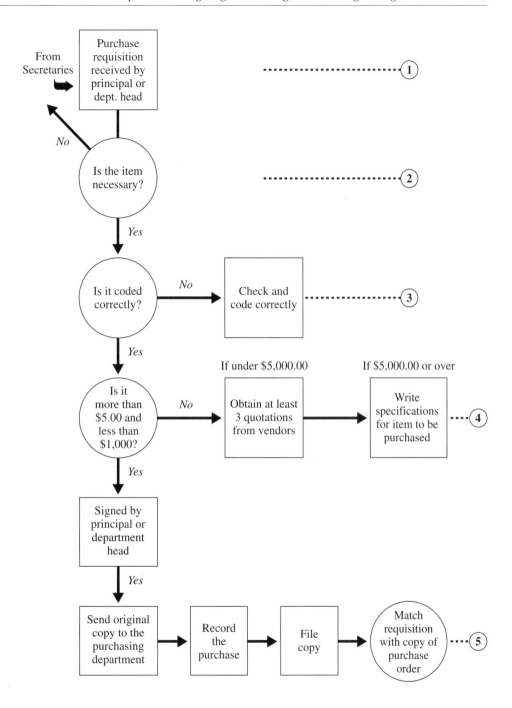

FIGURE 16–6   Purchase Requisition Flowchart for Principals and Department Heads

the wise principal will spend some time in faculty and staff meetings generally informing the staff about the reasons why good record keeping and accounting procedures are important to an instructional program.

Beyond this, it is the responsibility of the principal to make sure the practices being followed are, in fact, efficient and do provide for quick delivery of materials and other services to the classroom. It is also the principal's responsibility to make sure that his or her decision making, with respect to expenditures, is consistent with the preestablished instructional budget.

Regular Review

Once systemized, the accounting procedures need not absorb a vast amount of time but will require only regular monitoring by the principal. Care should be taken that materials ordered are received and properly inventoried. Keeping a separate set of books for district funds will provide the principal with a good check on expenditures against the accounts of the school that are kept in the central business office. Mistakes do get made and when this occurs, it is to the principal's advantage to be aware of it and able to rectify it.

In many school systems, the central business office will supply the principal with periodic financial reports in the form of ledger sheet printouts. These are easily checked against the school's set of books for accuracy. After reconciliation with the school's books, these will provide sufficient record of the financial aspect of the educational enterprise.

Activity and Other Funds

Most schools receive and distribute funds other than those disbursed by the district office. Such sources and accounts commonly include PTO funds, classroom accounts, insurance monies, candy sales, athletic funds, club treasuries, petty cash, funds from charity drives, gifts, and so on. Individually, the accounts may be quite small, but collectively they often amount to a considerable sum.

A separate set of books should be maintained for these funds. No less precise bookkeeping procedures are required for these than for the district funds. Many states have passed special legislative acts that require the establishment of orderly procedures for the administration of school activity funds. Some states, as well as local school districts, have developed policies and procedures to guide individual schools in such financial accounting. The absence of such policies and guidance in any particular school district is no excuse, however, for a principal to be any less careful—to the contrary, more care is required.

In general, specific procedures must be established to control the collection and disbursement of the variety of activity funds. The following procedures provide a good guide:

1. Official receipts should be issued for all money received.
2. All money expended should be expended by check, except for small cash purchases paid from the petty cash fund.
3. Supporting documents should be kept for all expenditures made.

4. Bank reconciliation statements should be made each month.
5. Monthly and yearly financial statements should be prepared.
6. An audit should be made each year, and copies of the audit should be filed with persons having administrative authority for the school.

Consistent with good financial practice is that each group having an account that the school is administering should file a simplified budget indicating anticipated income, anticipated expenditures, and persons designated to approve monies to be expended from the account. Further, all school employees who are responsible for handling funds should be bonded, the amount of the bond to be determined by an estimate of the amount of money that the school will manage. Many school districts provide a bond covering all employees in the school system who are responsible for such funds. Whether this is so in any particular district should be verified by the principal.

In some school districts, the principal is required to make a monthly report about the state of the internal funds in the school. Such a report commonly contains specific and general conditions of the accounts and expenditures. Regardless of whether this is required by district policy, it is an important procedure to be carried out by the principal and appropriately filed. It provides substantiation of the careful expenditure of funds and will assist in the annual audit. Figure 16–7 illustrates a monthly reporting procedure for an activity account.

The Audit

The internal account books should be audited annually by an external accountant. The product of this audit should be filled with the district office. One should not misunderstand the purpose of the audit—it is not an attack on anyone's integrity. It has two primary purposes: It will provide good information for improving the accounting procedures, and it protects all of those who have been responsible for handling school funds.

Before accepting the position, the incoming principal should insist on an audit of all funds as a means of being informed about current practices and improving on these as necessary. The audit also establishes the state of the accounts before a person has responsibility for them. It red-lines the accounts, and the new principal starts with clean fiscal air.

Supplies and Equipment Management

A major responsibility of the principal is securing, making an inventory, and allocating supplies and equipment necessary to the educational program. It is essential that adequate quantities of soft goods(supplies) and the appropriate kinds of hard goods (equipment) be provided and available ahead of educational needs and secured in the most economical manner possible. It is equally important that a management system be provided that will not require an inordinate amount of supervisory time.

If the school is operating under a budget-development system as described earlier in this chapter, the selection and purchase of needed supplies and equipment in support of educational goals is easily routinized. At most, it should require a regular review to

School _____   Report for month of _____

Bank Reconciliation

Bank _____

Balance per bank statement _____ $ _____
                                             Date

Add
   Deposits in transit   _____
   Other (specify)   _____
Total $ _____
Deduct
   Outstanding checks

$ _____

Balance per general ledger _____ $ _____
                                             Date

_____   _____   _____
    Principal   School Treasurer   Date

FIGURE 16–7   Monthly Financial Report of the School Activity Fund

see that anticipated needs are being met on schedule; estimated costs are remaining within budget; advantage is being taken of the appropriate discounts allowed by suppliers; inventories are adequate; and equipment is being appropriately tagged, recorded. conveniently stored, and used.

Storage and Inventory Control

The daily needs of instructional staff are such that amounts of common educational supplies (art paper, chalk, etc.) can be predicted and kept in sufficient reserve to meet needs over a period of a few months. Responsibility for ensuring that the appropriate amount of day-to-day supplies are available can become that of the school clerk or another designated person. This task need not and should not require much attention by the principal. An inventory control procedure set up by the principal working with the designated individual will permit routine replenishment of supplies. Adequate inventories of educational materials and supplies unique to special aspects of the program can be maintained by the person who is responsible for that special aspect of the program.

Inventory control is greatly facilitated by using the school computer. Specialized programs can be written easily, and there are any number of commercial programs to which inventory control requirements may be readily adapted. All equipment, irrespective of where it is housed, should be tagged or identified in some manner and listed in the inventory.

Things break and wear out and disappear. Equipment must be kept in good repair and staff members made aware of their responsibility to report immediately any malfunction of equipment so that necessary action can be made. Routine ways to address these realities so that teachers are able to teach and learners are able to learn unencumbered by malfunctioning or missing equipment need to be established. The form depicted in Figure 16–8 uses a light touch to get the job done and done quickly.

Central Warehousing

The responsibilities for supply management in school systems are frequently handled at the central office level. Even if the principal has a considerable amount of responsibility with respect to supply management, large systems will have a central warehouse from which most supplies and equipment are secured. There is considerable advantage to this because systems can develop standardized lists of materials, with precise specifications. These need to be reviewed periodically to provide maximum use of school system dollar resources.

Certain kinds of educational materials may also be housed centrally in the school district. Materials such as film, filmstrips, audio and video tapes, and so on, which have use throughout the system but are not required in any individual unit of study except on an infrequent basis, are often cataloged and housed centrally in the school district. Where this is the case, teachers must understand the need for more lead time in requisitioning and securing these for classroom use. This is not to say that last-minute requests should not be acted on to the degree possible. It is an unhealthy school system that is not responsive to an unplanned "teaching moment," but in general it will be necessary for staff to anticipate the need for centrally housed educational materials.

Care of the School Plant

This building is clean and we keep it that way. It's not a new facility as you can see but that doesn't mean it shouldn't look good. And, that makes a difference on how our students and their parents feel about this place We ask everyone—students, staff, parents—to help out. "If it drops on the floor, pick it up." "If you see

HI!
CLAMOR HERE,
YOUR MAINTENANCE MOLLUSK

It's my task to hammer away at any jobs that need fixing in your room.   Is there anything that requires attention?

Don't clam up now.
We want a smooth–sailing ship.

Please fill out this form and leave at the custodial desk for quick service.

Room: _____

Service Required: _____

_____

_____

_____

_____

For immediate needs, please call the office.

White: office
Pink: staff

FIGURE 16–8   Maintenance Form

it on the floor, pick it up. " Graffiti in the restrooms? It doesn't happen much anymore, and when it does our custodians have it erased within the hour. Does this make a difference? You bet it does. We like this place. And for a lot of our kids, this is the most stable and pleasant thing in their world.[2]

Properly housing the educational program and equipping the school presents some management priorities for the principal. Innovative programs can be housed in traditionally designed buildings. Whether the building represents the latest in school design or reflects architectural thinking in the 1950s, the principal's responsibility is the same: to ensure the maximum efficient use of the school plant for the educational program. An inefficiently used building, a poorly kept building, a building with unpleasant, colorless rooms, or a poorly maintained site all inhibit the development of a good educational program. These have a negative impact on staff and student morale and productivity.

The principal has two important support groups: classified employees who are assigned to the building (custodians, cleaning personnel, cooks, kitchen personnel, etc.) and the districtwide maintenance department personnel. Working with nonacademic personnel to help them to do their jobs better will require the same kinds of human relations skills as working with academic staff.

Maintenance of the Building and Grounds

The building and grounds require much attention to create an attractive, safe learning-living-working environment for students and staff. Many large districts have a director of maintenance and operations whose overall responsibility is to see that skilled persons are employed and deployed to respond to refurbishment and major maintenance needs of all the buildings in the district. However, it is the responsibility of the principal, working with the custodial staff, to identify major needs and to ensure that those are systematically attended to. The day-to-day custodial and light maintenance functions will, even in larger districts, fall to the building custodial staff.

Effective supervision of building maintenance programs need not require an inordinate amount of time and can be regularized through the use of a simple checklist. Such a checklist is shown in Figure 16–9.

The principal and the custodial staff should give particular attention to common internal building flaws: inadequate lighting fixtures, roof or wall leaks, dirt in the corners, broken windows, torn sashes, and so on. The entire staff, including instructional personnel, should assist in identifying maintenance needs and reporting them immediately to the office for attention. Many times, annoying maintenance defects are allowed to continue simply because a teacher or another staff member has not reported them and they have gone unnoticed by the custodial staff.

Grounds and Playgrounds

The school site needs to be attractively maintained. The high cost of land often is reflected in small school sites and inadequate play areas. This is true especially in urban areas where children are often most in need of wide open spaces in which to play and experience nature. Size of site need not deter the latter, however. With a little ingenuity, arboreta and nature walks can be constructed in the most constricted of places. Effective design will often provide adequate play space. In both instances, however, attention needs to be directed to making the available space attractive and safe.

Frequent inspections are key. Debris-strewn school sites are inexcusable, and unsafe equipment is both unconscionable and perhaps an issue for litigation in the instance of student or staff injury.

Bell[3] has discovered that three types of equipment account for about 87 percent of all student injuries: swings and swing sets, climbing bars, and slides. Children are exuberant and like to show their prowess on such things. She indicates that 75 percent of all injuries occur from falls from this sort of equipment. The answer? Close supervision and equipment that is in good repair.

Description of Service

School: _____

Name: _____

Frequency of Service

Description of Service	7:00–8:45	8:45–9:00	9:00–9:15	9:15–10:00	10:00–10:15	10:15–10:30	10:30–11:00	11:00–1:30	1:30–2:00	2:00–2:15	2:15–3:30
Unlock building and turn off alarm	▓										
Sweep all entrances and put out mats	▓										
Police entire building	▓										
Police all restrooms and flush out commodes	▓										
Drop cafeteria tables down		▓									
Dust-mop cafeteria, front and back hall			▓								
Break											
Clean glass				▓							
Set up for lunch					▓						
Repolice restrooms before lunch						▓					
Lunch											
Cafeteria Duty							▓				
Dust-mop back and front halls								▓			
Recheck restrooms and clean wash areas								▓			
Break									▓		
Clean downstairs lounge										▓	
Clean upstairs lounge										▓	
Recheck restrooms and clean wash areas										▓	▓
Clean drinking fountain in cafeteria											▓

FIGURE 16–9 Day Schedule, Head Custodian: Elementary School

Evaluating the Appearance of the Building and Site

Routine work schedules and well-understood expectations are important to the maintenance of the school plant. Time-lines and systematic planning for the completion of major maintenance and repair projects need to be supplemented with daily and weekly time schedules to ensure that routine custodial and maintenance tasks get done.

Regular evaluation of the building's appearance is important. An example of one district's evaluation survey can be seen in Figure 16–10. These survey forms are best developed in concert with the staff so that expectations are clear and standards well understood.

Principal: School: Custodian: Date:

Entrances:	S	G	A	P		Windows:	S	G	A	P
Walks:						Furniture:				
Floor mats:						Fixtures:				
Door facings:						Teacher's station:				
Glass:						**Cafetorium:**				
Transoms:						Floors:				
Door tracks:						Windows:				
Offices:						Fixtures:				
Doors:						Lights:				
Facings:						Fountains:				
Walls:						Machines:				
Floors:						Doors:				
Furniture:						Fixtures:				
Windows:						**Storerooms:**				
Fixtures:						Walls:				
Trash:						Tool racks:				
Hallways:						Supplies:				
Floors:						Equipment:				
Walls:						**Restrooms:**				
Lights:						Floors:				
Water fountains:						Walls:				
Learning Centers:						Partitions:				
Shelves:						Windows:				
Floor:						Commodes:				
Furniture:						Urinals:				
Glass:						Wash basins:				
Door:						Mirrors:				
Classrooms:						Floor drains:				
Door facings:						Ventilation:				
Walls:						Lights:				
Lights:						Furniture:				
Floors:						**Garbage Area:**				
Boards:						**Incinerator:**				

COMMENTS:

S — Superior
G — Good
A — Average
P — Poor

FIGURE 16–10   Custodian-Maintenance Survey: Building Inspection Checklist

Working with Classified Personnel

Custodians, maintenance personnel, cooks, aides, and secretaries all have important parts to play in the development of the productive learning climate. Frequently, the contributions of these people are not fully recognized. Unless attention is directed to the needs and contributions of support personnel, the risk is that, at best, a wary truce will exist between these personnel and the professional staff.

Evidence of such a condition will be found in the not-so-sly digs each will direct at the other in private meetings and in less-than-adequate services being rendered. Paper towel dispensers that always seem to be out of towels; corners of the cafeteria left unswept; inordinately long waits that occur for equipment to be delivered or repaired; and any number of other examples that any reader of this book could supply—are indicators that all is not well. In some instances, of course, this may be because of a lack of skill or a lack of clear understanding about organizational expectations. If so, that should be quickly remedied—either with "on-the-job" training or replacement.

Engaging support personnel in the same kinds of goal-setting and problem-solving activities that have been suggested for the professional staff is necessary. Administration by edict works no better with custodians and maintenance personnel than it does with the certificated staff. At the beginning of each school year, the principal needs to meet with the custodial staff to chart long-range objectives for building maintenance for the year and to work out a systematic plan for addressing these. Many of the custodial activities will be routine and daily or weekly in nature, of course. Some will not be. Also, the performance of even the routine custodial functions will be affected by such things as special events and even the time of day. Cooperative development of the work schedule is desirable and will result in the important things getting done, getting done well, and in a timely manner.

Selection and Retention of Classified Personnel

The selection, training, and appraisal of support persons is an important managerial task. Yet this has received very little attention in professional literature. Improperly trained workers or workers who are unsure of their responsibility—whether in the cafeteria, in the boiler room, or in the principal's office—are a liability. Similarly, the nonacademic staff member who does not understand or particularly like children, while perhaps not common, is also a liability that a school cannot afford.

Personnel policies for the employment, in-service growth, and retention of good nonacademic personnel should be carefully developed. Job descriptions, adequate compensation, and other benefits must reflect the school's interest in maintaining a nonacademic work force of the highest quality.

The standards of employment should not only evidence an interest in appropriate technical competence, but also a realization that most of these personnel will be working with children in some way or another. The latter simply suggests that appropriate attitudes and understandings about young people may be one of the most important employment and retention criteria. Evaluation of performance is essential.

Summary

The focus of this chapter has been financial and building management. Financial resources are never in great supply. The proper allocation of available resources requires careful planning—the kind of planning that delivers resources in a systematic way to the point of greatest need. Long-range planning and a process for involving the staff are fundamental. Important aspects of school site-based budget building and implementation have been presented in this chapter.

Properly accounting for the available funds is a responsibility of the principal. Special attention must be directed to the training of other personnel to carry out this function, with oversight and monitoring by the principal. A thorough knowledge of district policies is essential. Special attention must be directed to the management of activity funds. Regular, independent audits are recommended.

The physical environment of the school contributes mightily to the learning environment. An attractive, well-kept school building is essential. It is also important that the principal ensure that there are appropriate response mechanisms so that teachers can go about their work with the right equipment at the right time.

A good school environment also depends on many kinds of personnel. The principal's responsibility is to deploy these people in the most effective ways. To do so will require carefully developed job descriptions and the ability to help them see the importance of the job in the proper functioning of the educational institution.

Activities

1. Case Study 3 presents a budget issue of some complexity. Members of your staff in some of the departments are ready to go to war over a share of the available budget dollars. Set forth a process for resolving the issue in a manner consistent with the budget concepts presented in this chapter. Assume your district is committed to decentralized decision making.

2. Issues of school security and maintenance permeate Case Study 11. Where will you start to address these issues?

3. Some money appears to be missing from one of your school activity accounts. This situation is described in Case Study 15. Make any reasonable assumptions and begin the problem resolution process. What steps will you take to prevent this from happening again? What might you have done to have not been "blindsided"?

Endnotes

1. See Chapter 5 for a complete discussion of the GII, CII, CI, AII, and AI decision processes from the Vroom-Jago model.
2. Lloyd Choice, Principal, Kashmere High School, Houston, Texas, Independent School District.
3. Sue Oliver Bell, "Making Playgrounds Safe," *Principal* 73, no. 2 (November 1993): 18–19.

Selected Readings

Alexander, Kern, and Richard G. Salmon. *Public School Finance* (Boston: Allyn and Bacon, 1995).

Drake, Thelbert L., and William H. Roe. *School Business Management* (Boston: Allyn and Bacon, 1994).

Kell, Sue Oliver. "Making Playgrounds Safe." *Principal* 73, no. 2 (November 1993): 18–20.

Natale, Joseph. "A Design for Administering Maintenance Programs." *Planning and Changing* 14, no. 2 (Summer 1993): 83–90.

Thompson, David C., R. Craig Wood, and David S. Honeyman. *Fiscal Leadership for Schools* (New York: Longman, 1994).

Case Studies in School Leadership and Management

Problem Analysis, Decision Processing, Decision Making: Introduction to the Cases

In order to arrive at the maximum feasible decision, it is first necessary to define the problem correctly. Then, one needs to think about the decision processes that are available in order to resolve the problem. Many response patterns are open to any executive. Selecting the right one will determine whether the problem will be resolved or at least mitigated or whether even greater problems result. Anticipating the consequences of any particular process or act is more than an intellectual exercise.

A school executive's day is characterized by one encounter after another with staff members, students, parents, community members, politicians, and others—the kinds of individuals or subgroups are myriad and diverse. For the school principal, a simple walk down the hall from the office to resolve a problem in the cafeteria may result in half a dozen or more encounters with this or that teacher, custodian, parent, or child, all of whom have questions and requests and problems that the principal is asked to solve. Hurried answers are shouted over the shoulder. The principal is thrust into a maelstrom during the routine of most days. The rapidity and intensity of encounters and the life span of the problems will vary. Frequently, the time frames will be short and the databases will seem too meager.

The fact is, though, few problems have to be solved at the moment. There is almost always some time—albeit often not much—to reflect on the nature of the problem and the likely decision process that will result in a satisfactory solution. The fundamental questions to be asked are:

- Do I have at hand the information necessary to solve this problem?
- Whose support will be necessary in order to effect a long-term solution?

• How likely is it that I will get this support if I go ahead and make the decision on my own?

On the pages that follow are case studies about problems that occur in and around schools—student problems, angry clients, budget crunches, maintenance issues, staff appraisal difficulties, dilemmas about curriculum, conflicts about a multitude of issues— most not simple. Your task is one of analyzing assigned cases and "deciding how to decide." In any given case, select analytical processes that seem to you to be most appropriate. (The Maier and Vroom-Jago models may be especially helpful, but whatever approach you choose, be prepared to defend your reasoning.)

As you analyze the cases, make only those assumptions that are reasonable, given the limited number of facts that are provided. And remember, *you* are the executive who is confronted by the issue   not someone else. It is *your* problem. You don't have to solve the problem, however. Your task is to analyze the issue and set in motion a process that you believe will result in a good solution. Determine what you believe is the main problem or issue and indicate any subproblems or issues.

Case Studies: Primary Subject Matter and Decision Level

Subject Matter

Case	Curriculum	Personnel	Students	Public Relations	Finance
1	X	X			X
2	X				
3	X			X	X
4		X	X	X	
5	X		X		
6	X			X	
7		X			
8	X	X			
9		X			
10					X
11		X	X	X	
12		X		X	
13			X	X	
14	X	X		X	
15					X
16		X			
17		X		X	
18	X		X	X	
19		X			
20	X			X	
21			X		
22	X			X	

Table of Contents

Case 1: The Project Is Late

You have accepted an assignment as principal of one of the largest schools in the district. The school is widely recognized as being a trouble spot. Antagonism between teachers and administrators abounds. Even the department heads show antagonism toward the administration. They identify with the teachers. And no one, including yourself, is especially pleased with a new state mandate with regard to pay for performance. (You know it's going to be difficult to implement under any circumstance.)

This is your first principalship and you are anxious to do well. However, during your first month on the job, you have not had much success in gaining the acceptance of the eight department heads. They seem friendly in the interactions with each other but noticeably cool and suspicious toward you.

Today, you received a visit from your superintendent. One of the curriculum projects on which your group is working is six months overdue. Unless it is completed soon, outside funding ("seed money," which is desperately needed) will be in jeopardy. You were previously unaware that this problem was so severe and your boss now indicates that immediate action is required.

You know that some of the department heads are skeptical of the value of the project in question. It will require a complex organizational change. Ultimately, it will probably result in the collapsing of two departments into one budgetary unit, the reassignment of one department head, and a reduction of six teachers and one paraprofessional.

Case 2: *Your Kids Don't Read Well Enough*

You are the principal of a K–6 school. The children in grades 4 through 6 do not seem to be reading as well as might be expected.

There are a number of troubling indicators. As you review scores on the standardized reading tests used, you see that your students are, in the main, well below the norms for your school district as a whole, as well as for the nation. Various teachers have expressed concern about the reading skills of their students. The librarian has mentioned the low circulation rate of even the usually more popular trade books. Junior high school and senior high school principal colleagues have remarked to you frequently that students from your school don't do very well at their schools.

Your school has a heterogeneous student population with slightly more children from homes at the lower end of the economic continuum. Staff turnover is about average for the district.

Case 3: *Don't Mess with My Budget*

You are the principal. As you conduct a review of the school's science program, you are aware of the following:

1. Students from your unit do not do well on the ACT (American College Test) or similar tests and complain about not being able to get into prestigious colleges and universities.
2. Enrollments in advanced science classes have been dropping steadily over the past five years.
3. Many of your science teachers did not major in science; it is their second teaching field.
4. Some members of the community have been clamoring for "a better science program."
5. The superintendent of schools and the deputy in the district's division of instruction have just mounted an effort to persuade the board of education that massive additional resources need to be expended on the reading program in the middle schools.
6. Principals in your district have considerable latitude in the development and implementation of an instructional budget.
7. The amount of your instructional budget is determined by a basic allotment plus a factor, which is largely a result of the average daily attendance in the previous year.
8. There is a good bit of jealousy among the academic departments about matters of budget.

9. A change of attendance zone boundaries has recently occurred because a new free-way displaced several hundred families. The impact of this on your school is a 10 percent increase in students from homes in which English is not the primary language.

10. No overall increase in your budget for next year can be expected. Your average daily attendance is about the same from year to year.

Case 4: *Trouble Brewing in Hughes Middle School*

You are the new principal of Hughes Middle School. The school has had three different principals in the past five years. It is August 1 and school will be opening in a few weeks. You have the following facts at hand:

1. Enrollment is 1,200 students in grades 5 through 8 and the school is in an urban setting.

2. Although the total population of the school is relatively stable, there is much transience. About 35 percent of your students will "turn over" in any given year, some leaving and returning within the year, many just leaving or entering.

3. Your student population is 30 percent African American, 20 percent Hispanic, and about 10 percent Asian, mostly Vietnamese. Projections are for an increasingly declining white population. Many of the white parents in the attendance area send their children to one of two private schools, one of which is parochial.

4. A little over one-quarter of the students come from nearby public housing project.

5. About one-fourth of the students are bused in because of a special extended day program that your district maintains in a few of its middle schools.

6. The attendance area that your school serves has an adult population composed of 65 percent white, 20 percent black, and 13 percent Hispanic. Socioeconomic status (SES) indicators suggest a wide range of economic levels. Housing ranges from luxury class to substandard housing. Recently, young married couples with no children have been taking advantage of some housing bargains in one of the neighborhoods and there has been a substantial in-migration of these couples.

7. The teaching staff has a 20 percent annual turnover and is bimodal in teaching experience—that is, a large number are in their first three years of teaching and a large number have over 15 years of experience. Only a few of your teachers are in their intermediate years.

8. There doesn't seem to be a very active PTO.

9. Your predecessor left no plans for the three-day staff in-service program that is to begin each school year.

Case 5: *The Curriculum Is Not Working; Fix It*

You are the principal of a large elementary school (average daily attendance = 925). Your school district has always searched for ways to increase student learning and has frequently been on the "cutting edge" statewide in its efforts to do this. Recently, the district has adopted the whole language approach as a curricular and instructional thrust. To the surprise of everyone, including yourself, the expected increase in student learning as evidenced by the results on state and national standardized tests has not been realized in your school. In fact, scores have dropped significantly in English, reading, and social studies. Moreover, your staff turnover rate has increased greatly over what it was just two years ago.

You are puzzled. Other schools in the district have not experienced this decline and nearby districts who have a similar curriculum are successfully implementing it. You have had consultations and visits from instructional specialists from the district office and they have reported that the materials seem to be used appropriately and your teachers seem generally well qualified and satisfied with the curriculum.

You suspect that there must be at least some parts of the new curriculum that are responsible for the lack of success of your students. Also, you are not all that satisfied that some of your teachers are working hard to fully implement the program. This view is not widely shared among your immediate subordinates—department and grade-level chairs or your dean of instruction. Most of them attribute the problem to poor in-service training of the teachers, to a lack of additional resources to provide for the extra time teachers say the program requires, and to generally low morale on your staff. There is a considerable depth of feeling on the part of your staff and much potential disagreement among subordinates about the issue. Some are angry with the students for the poor test scores; others are becoming openly hostile about the "extra" time they say the program is taking; still others resent the implication that they are not doing a good job.

This morning you receive a phone call from your district superintendent. The superintendent has just reviewed the test scores for the district, school by school, and is calling to express concern. The superintendent indicated that the problem was yours to solve in any way you think best, but wants to know within the week what steps you plan to take.

You share the superintendent's concern and know that many of your people are also concerned.

Case 6: *Values Clarification Dispute*

You are the principal of a large middle school located in a large city. An aspect of the districtwide guidance program is a values clarification unit. One of your 12-year-old students, a participant in the program, requested help with his assignment from his mother. The mother is furiously angry about the program now.

The sixth-grade worksheet the student was working with read as follows:

"Your oldest sister loves and trusts her husband. You see him coming out of a restaurant with another woman. He and the woman get in a car and drive away together. What would you do?"

The mother was nonplused and decided to find out what it was that the students were being "guided" to do. She relates, "I did not go to the school as an outraged person; I just wanted to find out what was going on." She secured a copy of the guidance program in values clarification from the director of guidance and now she is really upset. She points to lessons that deal with who should be allowed to live in the case of a limited number of dialysis machines, and other lessons that ask the student to respond to such questions as "One time I cheated and it was OK; another time I cheated and it was wrong."

The mother states, "I have always trusted the school and the teachers but these are areas that they have no business being in. They attack the values the parent is trying to instill. I'm really bothered that none of the parents I talked with has any idea that this sort of thing is going on."

Asked for his opinion, the president of the Teachers' Association remarked that the class is a waste of instructional time. "It's the biggest waste of time we have in the district. Our teachers complain that they aren't provided time enough for remedial work with students who need academic help but 30 minutes or more a week is spent on Mickey Mouse activities like this. The teachers hate it and are embarrassed to have to present it."

The newspaper has picked up the story.

Case 7: Reduction in Force

You are principal of a small elementary school (primary grades only, and no kindergarten) with a faculty numbering 19. The formal education and teaching experience of your staff is quite similar, permitting you to use them interchangeably at various grade levels and in various "teaming" arrangements. During the past two years, your pupil enrollment has decreased. This has probably stabilized for the time being, but the result has been a very favorable teacher-pupil ratio. In fact, you are slightly overstaffed. Your teachers have begun to worry about possible reassignments to other schools and have expressed this concern to you. Basically, they are happy where they are.

Yesterday, you were informed by your superintendent that a request had been received by the personnel office from one of your colleagues in another primary school unit. Her school is experiencing rapid growth in the number of students and her data justify her request for at least four additonal faculty. Even with these four additional staff members, her pupil-teacher ratio will still exceed yours. There is a "budget crunch" and a districtwide hiring freeze. The superintendent indicates that your colleague's faculty needs must be met from the ranks of your teachers. You agree with the superintendent's logic.

All of your teachers are capable of handling the new assignments, and from the standpoint of present and future changes, there is no particular reason why any one more than any other should remain on your faculty. The problem is complicated even further because the school to which the reassignments will be made is in what is generally regarded in the district as a highly undesirable location.

Case 8: Which Textbook Will It Be?

You are the principal of a middle school, grades 6 through 9, and there is need to review the social studies series currently in use. You have a strong opinion that the current series does not adequately depict the contributions made by minorities and women. Because your own teaching field is social studies, you have more than a casual interest in and knowledge about the issue. The social studies department seems split on the matter. Two teachers do not want to use any text at all, several teachers are satisfied with the current text, and three others favor at least two other series. The board requires one adopted text series but does permit supplemental works when it can be shown that there is good reason to do so. It is now January; a recommendation is due in the central office one month from today.

The chairperson of the department is undecided on the matter and requests that you "do something." A review of staff evaluations reveals that one of the teachers who wants no text at all is among the top-rated teachers in the school. She is unhappy with the more conservative posture of many of her colleagues and has indicated that unless a more positive stand on the multicultural nature of society is taken by the department, she will go elsewhere. A *cause célèbre* looms.

Case 9: *That's My Parking Place!*

You have recently been appointed principal of a new school currently under construction. Your team of five department heads and two assistant principals has been selected and they are now working with you to help select staff, purchase equipment, and generally anticipate the problems that are likely to arise when the building is opened in the fall—3½ months from now.

Yesterday, you received a final set of architectural plans for the building and for the first time you examined the parking facilities that are available. There is a large lot across the road from the school intended for teaching staff, support personnel, and students. In addition, there are 12 parking spaces immediately adjacent to the school intended for visitors, disabled, and reserved parking. School-district policy requires a minimum of 3 general visitor spaces and 2 spaces for the disabled. This leaves you with only 7 spaces to allocate among yourself, 5 department heads, and 2 assistant principals. There is no way to increase the number of spaces without changing the structure of the building.

Up to now, there have been no obvious status differences among your team who has worked together extremely well in the planning phases. To be sure, there are salary differences, but experience and degree levels are the primary cause of this. One of your people has her doctorate; four others have master's degrees. Each has just recently accepted the new position and expects reserved parking privileges as a privilege of the new status.

Case 10: *The New Photocopier*

Losses in enrollments because of population shifts and an eroding tax base have resulted in deep budget cuts. You, as the principal, must trim all nonessential expenditures. You have decided to investigate whether your office needs the large, fast, highly flexible copier currently in use. It could be replaced with any of a number of cheaper machines on the market and a substantial cost savings effected. You have the specifications for both the current and the smaller machines and the salespersons have advised you of the various features of each, including fidelity of reproduction, copies per minute, number of copies collated (if at all), and other features. Other useful information is readily available from your staff as well as the business office.

It is clear that your support staff prefers the current machine, some outspokenly so. They are not as concerned as you are about costs and are well aware of the many advantages the current machine has in making their own workload easier. Moreover, if you had a smaller machine installed, there would be the need to improvise on some of the larger jobs, or, from time to time, to take work over to the district office. Some of the staff could make life more difficult for you by making up reasons to take work "downtown." It would not be possible to develop a policy to fit every contingency, so you would either be in position of constantly monitoring the reproduction tasks or of running the risk of flagrant misuse of the district's equipment, which would be charged against your operating budget, as well as a waste of time of some of your support staff.

Nevertheless, even though they will all be affected, the staff knows that a substantial amount of money is involved. Most also believe that making these kinds of decisions is what you are being paid for.

Case 11: How Safe Is the School?

You are principal of a large urban high school. Numerous break-ins and incidents of violence have characterized several of the high schools in the district. Your high school is one of these. The window breakage alone in the district required $375,000 for repairs last year. Beyond this, the costs for repainting and other building repairs exceeded national averages by far.

Teachers are complaining that they do not feel safe, and some parents complain that their children have had money extorted from them by other "students" on their way to and from school as well as on the school grounds. Also, within recent months, there was a parking lot incident in which a teacher was shot at by an unidentified youth.

The restroom walls always seem to need cleaning; spray-painted scatology abounds in the restrooms and on sidewalks. School equipment doesn't seem to last long—it breaks or it disappears.

And now, an enterprising news team from a local TV station has started a well-watched series on "How Safe Are Our Schools?"

Case 12: Mrs. Davis Is a Bad Teacher

You are principal of Ubben Elementary School, a prekindergarten through grade 5 school with a population of 725. It is nearly the end of the school day and you are reviewing your mail. A handwritten letter from a parent captures your attention. It reads as follows:

Dear Principal, Assistant Principal, and School Board:

My husband and I, as parents of a third-grader and a fourth-grader at Ubben Elementary, would like to bring to your attention some problems in Mrs. Davis's class. Our daughter Samantha is in Mrs. Davis's third grade. In the past few weeks, our conversations with Samantha have turned up some disturbing facts about Mrs Davis's interactions with her students. Among other things that Samantha reports are the following: The entire class is denied recess if any one child misbehaves. Mrs. Davis repeatedly tells her class that they are "dumb," "stupid," ignorant fools," and that their behavior is much worse "than her two-year-old."

We concede that an eight-year-old's perceptions can be very different from an adults—after all, missing recess on several occasions for something you didn't do is very upsetting for an eight-year-old. However, I have sat in on Mrs. Davis's class and have observed her behavior in the classroom. On one occasion, she and the class were returning from lunch and some of the children were talking and moving about, which I think is normal for eight-year-olds. She yelled at the children to sit down and then screamed, waving her arms. Everyone sat down. As an adult, I was frightened. Can you imagine what an eight-year-old would feel? If she demonstrated that kind of behavior while I was present, I can't imagine how she is when she is alone with the children. We also have evidence of unfair grading practices.

We are requesting that Samantha be transferred out of Mrs. Davis's class immediately. This, of course, is only a partial solution—it won't solve the problem for the rest of the class. There is a complete lack of a positive learning climate.

Verbal abuse is just as destructive as physical abuse. We have always had a high regard for the district and we are shocked that someone like Mrs. Davis could be employed. Surely others have complained.

We would like to hear from you immediately.

Sincerely,

Case 13: Ricky

You are an assistant principal of a large junior high school (2,500 students). One of your duties is to chair special education Admission, Review, and Dismissal meetings (ARDs) for students who are emotionally disturbed. Ricky, who has a long history of being disruptive in school, has once again come to your attention. He is on medication for hyperactivity, but recently it seems to have a diminishing effect. Ricky is entering adolescence and is currently being retested by his physician. His behavior has been getting progressively worse.

Ricky is now scheduled to be in a self-contained classroom all day. However, the school also houses a regular school program and most students who attend are "normal" adolescents or near adolescents. This permits Ricky and his emotionally disturbed colleagues opportunities for interaction with the rest of the student body during lunch periods, in halls and restrooms, and before and after school in schoolwide organized activities. Regardless of the situation, Ricky doesn't get along. He fights, bites, and scratches his fellow students and screams at teachers and students alike. His behavior problems show little sign of improving. The school year is about half over.

A districtwide Central Unit for the Emotionally Disturbed has just opened. You mention this possibility to Ricky's parent and indicate that you are scheduling a midterm ARD for next week. The parent becomes very upset. "You will turn Ricky into a hoodlum; he'll only become worse" is her response. She also says she wants Ricky "mainstreamed" into the regular program "as PL 94-142 requires" and threatens to file a lawsuit unless this is done. She also states that both the principal and Ricky's teacher are "against Ricky" and that no matter what happens she insists that her child be removed immediately from the current class.

Case 14: Back to the Basics

You are the principal of a large junior high school. Your school system is on a "back-to-the-basics" mode, reflecting the outspoken criticism of several board members and their constituencies. This, coupled with a new educational reform bill passed in the state legislature, is having a negative effect on your district's highly successful career education program and, to a significant degree, on the fine arts program. Your school has achieved special state recognition for its efforts and achievements in both. Nevertheless, the school board has decided that career education should be eliminated and has reduced the budget amounts to be spent districtwide in the fine arts to the barest of minimums.

You are now faced with counselors, teachers, and parents who are very concerned about the demise of the career education program. Counselors are concerned that the career counseling load will now fall on them. They say, "I don't know much about that." Parents are asking, "What courses should my youngster sign up for next year?" And the superintendent expects that even though the program is going to close, the obligation of the school is still to provide career guidance services.

Also complicating the matter is what to do about the current full-time career counselor. She relates very well to adolescents and has been able to "turn tough kids around." Parents are very supportive as well. Her teaching fields are history and Latin. Latin has not been offered in years at your school and the history department "runneth over." You would hate to lose this fine teacher. The parents are upset on several counts, not the least of which is the lack of attention to the fine arts program.

Your superintendent is waiting for your staffing plan and budget proposals for next year. These are due in two weeks.

Case 15: Where Is the Money?

You are the new principal of a middle school with an enrollment of 1,400 students. Your predecessor resigned the position six weeks ago to accept a similar position at a higher salary in a district across the state.

One of your teachers has come to see you about a problem he has just discovered. The teacher has been recently transferred to his present position to replace a teacher who suddenly resigned. The teacher who is conferring with you has been with the district 11 years but only in your school since the beginning of the semester.

He is in the process of preparing his students for a statewide industrial arts exhibition and contest to be held in the capital city, 125 miles away. He has discovered that $1,345.00 he had assumed to be in the "Ind-Art" account was never deposited. The money had been earned from several special student activities (car washes, bake sales, etc.) designed to raise sufficient funds to pay student and faculty expenses for the exhibition. Without the money, students and faculty will be unable to attend.

Case 16: *How Come I'm Not a Master Teacher?*

You are Kym Nyberg, principal of a large high school in a medium-sized school district (ADA = 12,500). You are reviewing the morning mail. Among the memos and letters is the following:

TO: Kym Nyberg
FR: Kelli Jones
SU: Career Ladder—Level III

As you know, I did not qualify for Level III on the career ladder. I was and still am deeply hurt. And in addition to being hurt, I am now very angry.

I came to this district 14 years ago. I have always been so proud of our district and considered it the best in the state. I have never felt the district was unfair to me in any way until now. In those 14 years, I have been told by evaluators that I was doing a good job and that I was a "master teacher." I have always gotten good evaluations. I was told last year by an evaluator that I qualified for Level III. I am now told I do not qualify.

As I am doing the best I can, obviously I need help to improve. In order to help me improve my teaching performance, I respectfully ask three things from you and the other administrators:

1. *A computer printout of my evaluation scores for the past five years*
2. *A list of the Level III teachers on the secondary level and permission to observe these teachers so I can determine what they are doing right and I am doing wrong*
3. *A written growth plan from my administrators to help me become a Level III teacher*

Finally, please tell me why our district chose not to abide by the state guidelines for Level III.

Case 17: Welcome: Please Change Janie's Teacher

You are the new principal of Selter Elementary School. It's the third day of school and you've had a reasonably smooth opening. Selter is a large elementary school (ADA = 790) and houses grades 1 through 5. Your predecessor retired after a 30-year career in the district and is now enjoying the fruits of a successful tenure. She is on a world-spanning vacation after which she will relocate in a small town some distance away.

You are reviewing your mail and come across a letter from the president of the PTO, who you have met but once, briefly, at a preschool opening reception. She welcomes you in her first couple of lines and then turns to another subject. The final paragraph of the letter reads:

> "Oh yes, I am not happy with Janie's class assignment. You have placed her with a Level I teacher—a Miss Burket. Lovely person, so young and pleasant. But Janie requires some special help, as I'm sure you've seen from her records. Certainly a novice is ill prepared to deal with these. I know you have a number of Level II teachers but I especially admire Dr. Norris who is a Level III "Master Teacher." Janie and I were most disappointed that she was not assigned to her class. Your predecessor had indicated that this would be done. Could you arrange for Janie to be placed with Dr. Norris, please? Thank you very much."

Case 18: We Object!

You are principal of a high school (grades 9 through 12) with an enrollment of 1,500. It is mid-November. You have been at a statewide professional meeting for the past three days and have just returned to your office. The letter below is among other first-class mail that you find in your in-box. The letter arrived on Monday; today is Thursday.

> Dear Principal:
>
> We, John and Grace Michael, request that our daughter Heather be dismissed from her fifth-period class, Health, for the remainder of the semester. We are basing our decision on the fact that materials used in the classroom and methods of teaching are in complete disharmony with the values and beliefs we have tried to implement in our home. At such a vulnerable time in their lives, it is difficult, at best, for young people to be strong in the beliefs they have been taught and then stand up against the pressure of their peers. But it's something the youth of today face on a daily basis and we parents, as a collective group, hope and pray that our youth make the right choices and develop a stronger character because of those choices.
>
> But when the adults who have a direct influence on our child, through teaching, begin to promote a value system that has been rejected in our home, just consider the impact on our child (or any other) and how it will affect the

decision-making process when that young person is once again faced with peer pressure.

During a recent conversation with Ms. Blackstone and Ms. Weaver, it was interesting to us how we were told repeatedly that teachers cannot tell students what is right and what is wrong; they must choose for themselves. Yet, in the same conversation, we were told that because many students have sex and many students drink, it is okay to teach "safe sex" and "responsible drinking." If this isn't at the very least a contradiction, then certainly you must agree that it is a compromise in values. As it has become obvious to us, it must also be obvious to you that we simply do not agree with the standards being practiced and taught. It is at this point that we have reached the conclusion that Heather should be removed from this course.

Sincerely yours,

Case 19: *Mike Is the Best You Have*

Mike Flynn is your best mathematics teacher. His students always excel and he doesn't always get the best students to begin with. His classes range from Algebra I to a special advanced placement group in concepts well beyond calculus and differential equations. Parents of all students are highly supportive of Flynn. Moreover, he is frequently used by the district as an in-service training leader.

For as long as anyone can remember, Mike has had first period as his planning period. He comes to school late every morning because of his avocation, which is raising roses and doing other kinds of hybrid gardening. "Early morning hours work best for this," he says. "Especially for watering, pruning and fertilizing."

You are Mike's new principal. Two teachers have come to you within the past few days, each complaining of the "favoritism being shown Mr. Flynn." Each has asked why they cannot leave school during their planning period to tend to their personal business. Also, each has further suggested that "first period off" privileges should be extended to everyone. "Nobody else gets to do this," they say.

Case 20: *The Restructured School*

After a two-year study, the decision has been made by the professional staff of David Woolford Middle School to implement the concept of "continuous progress" programming. Several professional task forces engaged in such activities as material selection, leveling, scoping and sequencing, and staffing patterns. The school is now characterized by flexible scheduling, teaming, independent learning contracts, a new reporting system, and other new processes. In general, staff members are at Woolford because that is where they want to be. Teachers who were not favorably disposed to the restructuring were given the option to join other more traditionally organized schools. The program at Woolford has been in operation for two years.

Almost from the start, some parents complained about the program. The complaints were manifest at first in phone calls to the principal, then in some heated discussions at PTO meetings, letters-to-the-editor of a local newspaper, a spurious mimeographed neighborhood newspaper called "The Guardian," and ultimately in the formation of a "Return to the Basics" community group.

Members of this group have now called for a public meeting about the program and you, as principal, have agreed to host the meeting. The group's position is that the program is not providing an adequate education for their children.

Specifically, the charges are:

1. The children are not learning the basic skills.
2. The children are confused by so much independence.
3. The current report card reveals only individual progress; it does not tell parents how their child compares with others in the school system or the nation. Thus, "we parents cannot set realistic goals for our children."
4. Discipline is missing; the students are running amok and not "learning respect."
5. Children need a home base—a single teacher who knows them well, not an impersonal team of teachers.
6. Students are not happy with the new program. Some say, "I can't get help from my teachers because there are too many other kids and they get help first."
7. It's a "fuzzy-headed" idea thought up by left-leaning educators. Children should not be put in charge of their own learning. That's what teachers are paid to do.

The meeting will occur three days hence.

Case 21: I Wish I Was Dead

You are principal of a prekindergarten through grade 5 elementary school with an enrollment of 530. It is ten o'clock and you have just returned from a morning tour of the building. You are reviewing mail, memos, and notes from various staff that have accumulated since late yesterday afternoon when you were attending an all-district administrators' meeting at the central office.

Among other things, there is a short note from one of your fifth-grade teachers, written the afternoon before. It reads: "I thought you ought to see this." Stapled to the note is a piece of tablet paper containing the last part of an essay by one of her students, a boy named Timmy. The assigned topic for the essay was "My Favorite Things." Timmy's essay concludes, "…but I'll never get to have these things. Sometimes I wish I was dead. Sometimes I want to kill myself."

Case 22: Get Rid of That Book!

You are principal of Selter Elementary School, which houses kindergarten through sixth grade and has an enrollment of 640. It's the end of the day and it's Friday. All of the children, your secretary, and most of your staff have left. You're looking forward to the weekend. You haven't had time to look at the day's incoming mail and that's what you do before going home. The last piece of mail is a letter from a parent:

Principal
Selter Elementary School

Dear Principal:

My son Brian came home Wednesday with a book entitled *Coming of Age* written by David Thomas. Brian got the book at the Selter school library and was reluctant to show it to me when I asked about it. Small wonder! I had heard some of the other mothers talking about this at PTO just the other night. It's disgusting. I can't express how bothered I am that such a book is being circulated to young children.

Here's some of what it contains:

- *On the second page, just after the title, there is a frontal shot of a nude baby.*
- *On page 17, there is another picture of a nude baby (the same shot that is on the title page).*
- *On page 48, human sexual intercourse is described.*
- *On page 60, there is a drawing of a baby in utero.*
- *On page 67, there is a picture of a mother breastfeeding a baby.*
- *On page 81, there is a photo of a statue of a nude woman and on the opposite page there is a similar photo of a nude man, showing genitals.*

I'm no bluenose but this book shouldn't be available to grade-school children. You ought to be aware of the popularity of this book among the children and the kind of talking that is going on. Why should such a book be on our library shelves?

I know that school-district policy places the responsibility for the selection of books for general circulation in the hands of the school librarian, but you must have the authority to override such decisions. I hope you will agree with me that this book needs to be removed from the library.

Sincerely,
Scott L. Hughes, Parent

Index

DATE

2008

GAYLORD   PRINTED IN U.S.A.